QUICKEN 6
MADE EASY

QUICKEN 6 MADE EASY

David Campbell
and
Mary Campbell

Osborne **McGraw-Hill**

Berkeley New York St. Louis San Francisco
Auckland Bogotá Hamburg London Madrid
Mexico City Milan Montreal New Delhi Panama City
Paris São Paulo Singapore Sydney
Tokyo Toronto

Osborne **McGraw-Hill**
2600 Tenth Street
Berkeley, California 94710
U.S.A.

For information on translations or book distributors outside of the U.S.A., please write to Osborne **McGraw-Hill** at the above address.

Quicken 6 Made Easy

34567890 DOC 998765432

ISBN 0-07-881890-7

Publisher
Kenna S. Wood

Acquisitions Editor
Frances Stack

Associate Editor
Jill Pisoni

Editorial Assistant
Judith Kleppe

Technical Editor
Campbell and Associates

Project Editor
Cindy Brown

Copy Editor
Paul Medoff

Proofreader
Linda Medoff

Indexer
Richard Shrout

Computer Designer
Stefany Otis

Illustrator
Marla Shelasky

Cover Designer
Compass Marketing

CONTENTS AT A GLANCE

CONTENTS

III ▬▬ Business Applications

11 ▬▬ Setting Up Quicken for Your Business 283

ACKNOWLEDGMENTS

We wish to thank the many individuals at Osborne/McGraw-Hill and Intuit for their help with this project. Special thanks are due to acquisitions editor Frances Stack, project editor Cindy Brown, associate editor Jill Pisoni, copy editor Paul Medoff, and proofreader Linda Medoff for helping us meet an impossible time schedule. Special thanks also go to Margaret Campbell for checking all the keystrokes in the exercises.

INTRODUCTION

Whether you are trying to manage your personal finances or those of your business, Quicken can end your financial hassles. The package contains all the features necessary to organize your finances, yet because they're jargon-free you can focus on your financial needs without becoming an accountant or a financial planner.

If you use the package for your personal finances you will find that you can easily determine your financial worth or create a report with the information you need for your tax forms. You can also create budget reports or a list of all your cash, check, or credit card transactions. Everything you do will be with the benefit of menus and easy-to-use quick-key combinations. You will soon wonder how you managed your finances without Quicken.

If you are trying to manage a small business *and* deal with all the financial issues, Quicken can make the task seem manageable. Whether your business is a part-time venture or employs several people, Quicken provides all the capabilities you need to look at your profit and loss picture, analyze your cash flows, or put together a budget. Quicken's ability to handle the recording of payroll information makes it easy to monitor what you owe for federal and state income tax withholding, FICA, and other payroll-related costs such as workers' compensation and federal and state unemployment taxes. Although it is not quite the same as having an accountant on your payroll, Quicken can make an otherwise unmanageable task possible.

About This Book

Quicken 6 Made Easy is designed to help you master Quicken's features so you can apply them to your financial situation. Even if you are a complete novice with the computer, you will find that you can learn from the step-by-step exercises in each chapter. As you work through the exercises you will feel as though you have a seasoned computer pro guiding you each step of the way.

This book offers more than just instruction for using Quicken's features. The exercises throughout the book are based on the authors' personal and business transactions. Although names of the banks, suppliers, and employees as well as dollar amounts have all been changed, all of what you read is based on factual illustrations much like the ones you will need to record your own transactions.

Throughout the book we have included financial tips. When we started our business 12 years ago, we had to invest a considerable amount of time in finding answers to even the simplest questions such as federal and state agency filing requirements. We have tried to include some of this information to simplify what you are facing if your business is new.

How This Book Is Organized

This book is divided into three parts to make it easy for you to focus on Quicken basics, personal applications, or business applications. Part I, Quick Start, includes the first five chapters. This section covers all the basic skills needed to use the package. You will find that the exercises within these chapters make you productive with Quicken in a short period of time.

Chapter 1 provides an overview of Quicken's features. You will see examples of reports and screens that you can use for your own applications. Chapter 2 introduces the Quicken account register, in which all Quicken information is recorded. In this chapter you will learn the skills needed to record your basic financial transactions. Chapter 3 teaches you how to print several Quicken reports. You are shown how to select the correct printer settings to print all the reports you will be preparing in the book. Chapter 4 illustrates how easy it is to balance your checkbook (the account register) with Quicken. The exercise actually takes you through the reconciliation steps. Chapter 5 concludes Part I of the book. It teaches you how to create Quicken

checks. With one set of entries on a check you can print the check and update your records.

Part II focuses on personal financial applications of Quicken. It shows you how to create accounts for checking, savings, and investments. You will learn how to determine your net worth and to find the information you need to complete your tax returns in this section. Chapter 6 shows you how to set up accounts and categories for personal finances. You will learn how to enter individual transactions as well as how to memorize them and automate their entry through transaction groups. Chapter 7 introduces the concept of budgeting with Quicken and looking at the new Quicken 6 graphs. You will learn how to enter your estimates by category and how to monitor actual amounts against budgeted amounts. Chapter 8 illustrates how Quicken can be used to help complete your personal tax return. The example used demonstrates how to record your tax-related financial transactions and how Quicken can be used to summarize your tax-related transactions for the entire year. Chapter 9 shows you how to determine what you are worth financially. You will learn how to keep records on stocks and other investments and how to revalue these holdings to market values. Chapter 10, the final chapter in Part II, provides a look at additional Quicken reports and the customizing options that you can add.

Part III covers business applications of Quicken. You will learn how to use the package to manage the finances of your business, including record keeping for payroll. Chapter 11 shows you how to create a chart of accounts for your business. You will also look at entering transactions for basic business expenses and revenues. Chapter 12 teaches you about payroll entries with Quicken. It not only prints your employees' paychecks, but can handle all your other payroll-related record keeping. You can use the features in this chapter to handle payroll. Chapter 13 teaches you how to prepare a business budget with Quicken. You can enter the same value for each month or budget a different amount for each month. The budget reports that Quicken produces can provide an early warning of potential budget trouble spots. Chapter 14 discusses the forms you will need to file for business taxes. It also covers the income statement (the profit and loss statement) that tells you whether or not your business is profitable. Chapter 15 continues with coverage of another important financial report, as you have an opportunity to prepare a balance sheet that shows your assets, liabilities, and your equity (or investment) in the business.

Conventions Used

There are step-by-step examples for you to follow throughout the book. Every entry that you need to type is shown in boldface to make these exercises easy to follow. In addition, the names of menus, windows, and reports are shown with the same capitalization followed by Quicken.

The names of keys such as F2, Enter, and Tab are shown in keycaps. In situations where two keys must be pressed at the same time, the keycaps are joined with a hyphen, as in Ctrl-Enter. If you use the keyboard rather than the mouse to make menu selections, you will find it convenient that this book highlights the letter needed to make each selection. In the Main Menu and pull-down menus, this highlighted letter alone is sufficient to make your selection. In the menu at the top of the Register Report and Write Checks screens, you will need to use the Alt key in combination with the highlighted letter to activate the menu and define your selection.

In cases where there are two ways to perform the same task, we have shown you the most efficient approach. As you learn more about the package you can feel free to use whichever approach you prefer.

Quicken can provide the help you need to organize your personal finances. The package will enable you to establish accounts for monitoring checking and savings accounts, credits cards, and investments. In this section you will learn how to record and organize your financial information with Quicken's easy-to-use features. You will also learn how to prepare reports for taxes, budgeting, and computing your net worth.

PART

1

QUICK START

CHAPTER

1

AN OVERVIEW OF QUICKEN AND YOUR COMPUTER COMPONENTS

Quicken is a powerful single-entry accounting system that allows both individuals and small businesses to track their financial resources. It is an integrated system in that it accumulates the information you enter and then provides a variety of methods to group and present that information.

Quicken is as easy to use as your current manual recording methods—but it is much faster. You will be surprised at how automatic using the package can become. It can memorize and record your regular transactions or write a check for your signature. It also organizes your information for you. This chapter's overview shows you the components of the package and examples of screens used to enter data and the output that is produced. You do not need to sit at your computer to read and understand this chapter. Later chapters, however, give step-by-step directions for using Quicken's features, and you will want to follow along.

This chapter also introduces the various components of your computer system and their relationship to Quicken. You learn how Quicken uses your computer system, disk space, memory, and the keyboard. Some of the important keys are introduced through a series of visual examples. In later chapters you use these keys to enter and review Quicken data.

Quicken Overview

Quicken can handle all aspects of your financial management. Everything from initial recording and maintenance of information through organizing and reporting is handled by the package. Quicken provides features for recording your financial transactions easily. You can have a direct entry made to a register that is an accounts journal or have Quicken write a check and record the information automatically. Once your information has been recorded, you can have it presented in a variety of standard and customized reports.

Recording Financial Transactions

If you are tired of entering financial transactions in a handwritten journal, you will appreciate the recording abilities of Quicken. Entries are always neat—even if you have corrected several errors in the recording process—and there is no need to worry about math errors, since the package does arithmetic for you.

Accounts are the major organizational units in Quicken. Each piece of information you record affects the balance in a Quicken account. You can establish checking and savings accounts for both personal and business purposes. In addition, you can establish credit card accounts, asset accounts (stocks and real estate), and liability accounts (mortgage and other payable loans). You can also transfer funds among these accounts with the Transfer feature—for example, moving funds from savings to checking account. You can store all of your account in a single file on your computer. Later, as your experience grows, you might want to create additional accounts in your Quicken file.

Quicken 6 supports specialized investment accounts to allow you to track a collection of investments. You can enter information for stocks, bonds, mutual funds, and other investments. You can use features like the one shown in Figure 1-1 for updating the market price of your investments and determining your gain or loss.

Quicken can record the details of your financial transactions, both money you earn (income) and what you spend it on (expenses). Quicken can differentiate income from a number of sources, such as salary and dividend income. It also supports entry of all types of expenses, from mortgage payments to clothing purchases. If you use Quicken to record business finances, you can keep track of freight charges, payroll costs, and so on. You can also customize the package to handle additional sources of income or expenses.

The information recorded on a financial event is called a *transaction*. Purchasing an asset such as a car, or making payment for services or goods such as groceries, is considered a transaction. In Quicken, you must record your transactions in order to have the correct balance in

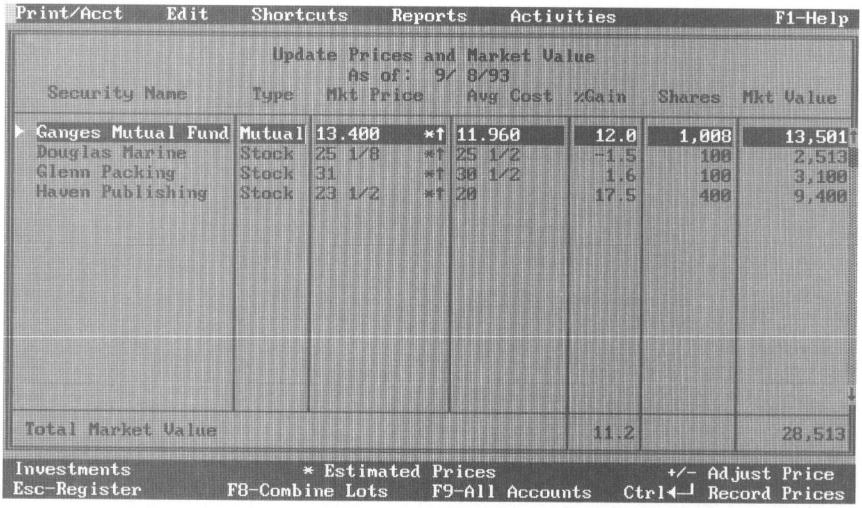

Updating the market price for your investments

Figure 1-1.

your accounts. This is accomplished by using a *register,* which is similar to a notebook or journal for record keeping. This serves the same purpose as your checkbook register, but with the power of the Quicken system you can generate powerful reports that help you manage your finances. Thus, one of the major components of the system is the register that you establish for each of your accounts (checking, savings, and other assets and liabilities). Figure 1-2 provides an example of entries in the Quicken register using Quicken 6's compressed format.

With any checking account, reconciling the balance is tedious. Quicken reduces the time needed to reconcile the difference between the bank's balance and yours. Through the reconciliation process, you can accurately maintain the balance in your checking account and avoid the embarrassment of overdrawing your account. Quicken adjusts your register for service charges and interest earned on your checking account balance.

The ability to write and print checks is another interesting Quicken feature. Quicken is capable of automating all your check writing activities. Figure 1-3 shows a check entry form on the screen. You can acquire checking supplies from Intuit (the company that developed and

Print/Acct	Edit	Shortcuts	Reports	Activities			F1-Help

Date	Num	Payee · Memo · Category	Payment	C	Deposit	Balance
1/02		Arlo, Inc.			12,500 00	16,500 00↑
1/02	101	Office All	65 00			16,435 00
1/08	102	Computer Outlet	300 00			16,135 00
1/15	103	Quick Delivery	215 00			15,920 00
1/15	104	Safety Airlines	905 00			15,015 00
1/20	105	Alltel	305 00			14,710 00
1/20	106	Postmaster	28 25			14,681 75
1/22	107	Fix-It-All	1,100 00			13,581 75
1/25	108	Laser 1	1,500 00			12,081 75
1/30	109	Quick Delivery	55 00			12,026 75
1/31	110	John Smith	1,560 13			10,466 62
1/31	111	Mary McFaul	2,284 22			8,182 40
2/01	112	Internal Revenue Service	1,379 00			6,803 40
2/28		John Smith	1,560 13			5,243 27
	1993 SPLIT	000-00-0001				
	Cat:	Payroll:Gross/B				

ANB Business	(Alt+letter accesses menu)		
Esc-Main Menu	Ctrl◄┘ Record	Ending Balance:	$30,732.70

The Quicken register window

Figure 1-2.

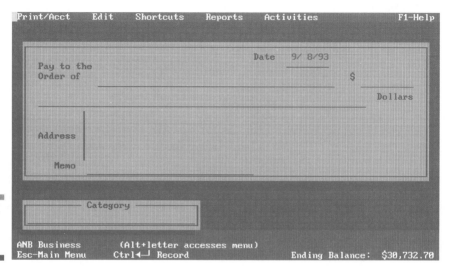

Check Writing
window
Figure 1-3.

markets Quicken) that allow you to write checks directly from the
register and print them on your printer. While this option is
particularly attractive for business activities, it can be useful for your
personal checking account as well. But even if you write your checks by
hand, you can still benefit from maintaining your transactions in
Quicken.

Reports Provided by Quicken

The value of any accounting system lies in its ability to generate useful
and informative reports that assist you in making financial decisions.
With Quicken, you can prepare personal, business, and investment
reports and preview them on the screen before printing. You can access
the detail behind a summary report while viewing the report. You can
also customize a report displayed on your screen. Figure 1-4 shows an
onscreen personal Cash Flow report.

Personal Reports

Besides providing you with a printout of your check register, Quicken
generates other reports tailored for personal financial management.
They will become valuable as the year progresses, showing how you

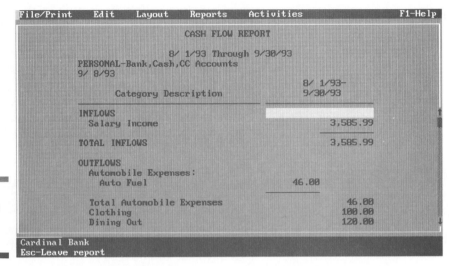

File/Print   Edit   Layout   Reports   Activities   F1-Help

```
                          CASH FLOW REPORT

                     8/ 1/93 Through 9/30/93
          PERSONAL-Bank,Cash,CC Accounts
          9/ 8/93
                                                      8/ 1/93-
                     Category Description             9/30/93
          ──────────────────────────────────────────────────────

          INFLOWS
            Salary Income                                3,585.99

          TOTAL INFLOWS                                  3,585.99

          OUTFLOWS
            Automobile Expenses:
              Auto Fuel                       46.00
                                            ────────
            Total Automobile Expenses                       46.00
            Clothing                                       100.00
            Dining Out                                     120.00
```

Cardinal Bank
Esc-Leave report

Cash Flow
Report screen
display
Figure 1-4.

have spent your money, as well as how much you have. You can create
personal reports that summarize cash inflow and outflow, monitor your
budget, summarize tax activities, and look at an overall measure of how
well you are doing.

Business Reports

Quicken handles accounting transactions for businesses as well as for
individuals. Because a small business has reporting needs that are
different from an individual's, the package provides a separate list of
standard business reports. Some of the business reports that you can
create are a profit and loss report, an analysis of cash flow, a balance
sheet, accounts payable and receivable reports, and a payroll report.
Quicken also allows you to create customized reports for either home or
business use.

Investment Reports

With Quicken's investment accounts, you can record and track all of
your investments. The five standard investment reports provide
information on portfolio value, investment performance, capital gains,
investment income, and investment transactions.

1

Creating Graphs

Reports provide a summary or detailed record of transactions. They can be shared with others wanting to look at your financial status but they do not provide a quick overview look at a financial situation. Graphs have always done a much better job at giving a picture of a situation with a quick look and now Quicken 6 provides them. You can use graphs to look at trends and other comparison information on your screen as shown in Figure 1-5, where you can see a comparison between budget and actual figures for categories over budget. Quicken 6 provides 21 different graphs in four different areas. Figure 1-6 provides another example with a Portfolio Value Trend by Security.

Financial Planners

Earlier versions of Quicken have provided a loan calculator to let you look at monthly payments under different assumptions. Quicken 6 has added four more financial planners to let you perform what-if analysis in other areas such as retirement or college planning, investments, and even refinancing a loan.

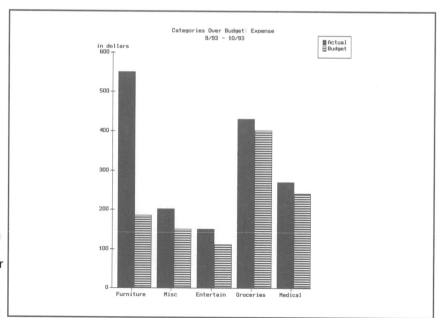

Expense
Categories Over
Budget Graph
Figure 1-5.

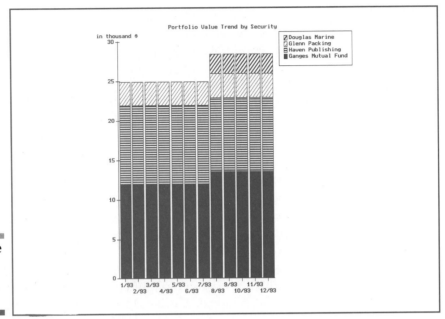

Portfolio Value
Trend by
Security
Figure 1-6.

Changing Preference Settings

Quicken provides features for customizing the package to meet your
needs. This means you can make changes to fit your exact reporting
requirements. It also means you can customize Quicken to work
properly with the computer equipment you have selected. You make
these changes by selecting Set **P**references to display the menu of
custom settings for Quicken, as shown here:

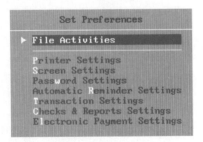

Quicken's Help Features

1

Onscreen help is only a keystroke away with Quicken. All you ever need to do is press F1 (Help). Quicken assesses the type of help you need and displays a superimposed help screen. Quicken's assessment of your situation is called *context-sensitive help*. Figure 1-7 shows the help screen that Quicken displays if you press F1 from the Main Menu. The highlighted text in Quicken 6 is called *hypertext*. This text provides access to help on the highlighted topic when selected. You can select this text by moving the cursor to it with the arrow keys and pressing Enter. In the section "The Keyboard, Mouse, and Screen Display" later in this chapter, you learn how to use a mouse to make selections.

If you are in another area of Quicken, the help presented might be very different. With the register on the screen, for example, Quicken assumes you need help with completing entries and so provides that information. You can also press Ctrl-F1 for direct access to the Help Index at any time. Quicken 6 also provides tutorials and assistant features to help you get started.

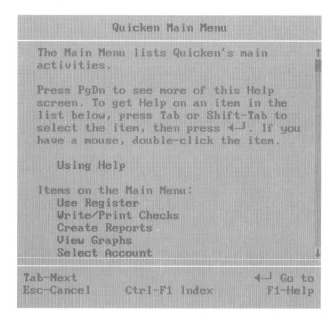

Help screen for the Main Menu

Figure 1-7.

Quicken and Your Computer System

You may have had your computer long enough to feel like a pro operating it, but if Quicken is your first computer package, read the rest of this chapter carefully. It will eliminate much of the confusion experienced by new users in attempting to figure out what is in memory, what is on disk, and exactly how their computer makes it possible for a package like Quicken to do so much work so quickly. If you are already knowledgeable about your system, you may want to skim the rest of the chapter just to see how Quicken works with the computer. It is assumed you are using an IBM PC or compatible running the DOS operating system.

Memory

There are two kinds of memory in your computer: RAM and ROM. *ROM* is read-only memory—you cannot affect its contents so it's of little concern. *RAM* is random-access memory—temporary storage inside your computer. RAM contains the program you are running (for example Quicken, 1-2-3, or dBASE) and the data you are currently working with in the program.

If you lose the power to your machine, you lose the contents of RAM. This is why permanent storage media such as disks are an essential component of your computer system. If your data is saved to disk, you can always load it into memory again if it is lost in a power failure.

The amount of RAM in your system is determined by the computer you have purchased and any additional memory you may have added to the system. Memory is measured in kilobytes (K) or megabytes (MB), with 1K representing the space required to store approximately a thousand characters of information and 1MB representing the space required to store approximately one million characters. Some systems have as little as 256K of memory, while others may have 1MB or even 6MB of memory capacity. Quicken requires a system with at least 512K in order to run the program. The amount of memory you have determines the number of transactions you can have in a Quicken account and the complexity of the reports you can generate, since Quicken uses memory for these activities.

Disk Storage

1

Disk storage on your system may consist of one or more hard disks and floppy disks in either 3 1/2-inch or 5 1/4-inch sizes. Quicken requires a hard disk, with at least 2.6MB of available space. Like RAM, disk space is measured in either K or MB.

Most hard disks provide from 20 to 120MB of storage capacity. This means you will have room for Quicken as well as other software packages such as dBASE, WordPerfect, or 1-2-3.

A letter is used to represent each drive. Typically, hard disks are called drives C and D, while floppy disk drives are designated drives A and B.

All the program files you need for Quicken are stored on your hard disk. The following illustration shows a possible configuration of the directories on a hard disk.

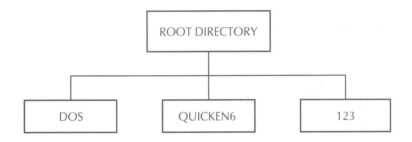

In this illustration, the root directory (main directory) would be used to contain batch files (files containing DOS instructions) on the hard disk. Separate directories are maintained for DOS and any other program. When you install Quicken on your hard disk, it creates its own directory and a batch file called Q.BAT.

The Keyboard, Mouse, and Screen Display

The screen and the keyboard or mouse serve as the central communication points between you and Quicken. Everything you want to tell the package must be entered through the keyboard or selected with a mouse. If you are using a keyboard, you are already familiar with many of the keys; they are used to enter data regardless of the type of program you are using. Function keys and key combinations have special meanings in Quicken; they are used to issue the commands. Even if you have used these keys in other programs, you will find that they provide different options in each program and thus are assigned to different tasks in Quicken.

The mouse allows you to make selections and perform tasks without using the keyboard. You will have new terms and new ways of doing things to learn as you click, double-click, and drag with a mouse to accomplish activities. You will learn about each of these new options in this section.

Quicken uses the screen to communicate information to you. Quicken supports both monochrome monitors (one color) and monitors that can display many colors. Your screen must have a graphics card to view graphs. Explanation of the screen is also covered here, since it often provides information about which keys to use for various features and commands.

Keyboard Styles

Not all keyboards are alike, although virtually all of them provide every key you need to use Quicken. However, you may have to look around to find the keys you need, especially if you are getting used to a new keyboard. On all the older model PCs and compatibles, the arrow keys move the cursor (or highlight) around on your screen. These keys are located on the *numeric keypad,* at the far right side of the keyboard. They are also used to enter numbers when the Num Lock key is depressed to activate them. With Num Lock off, the arrow keys move the cursor in the direction indicated on the key top. If these keys are not set properly for your use, just press Num Lock and they assume their other function.

On newer model keyboards, called the IBM *enhanced keyboards,* there are separate arrow keys to the left of the numeric keypad that move the cursor. This allows you to leave the number lock feature on for numeric data entry and use these arrow keys to move around on the screen.

Mouse Devices

Quicken 6 supports all Microsoft-compatible mouse devices. Quicken automatically recognizes a compatible mouse and displays a mouse pointer that looks like a small rectangle on the screen. As you roll the mouse over your desktop, the mouse pointer moves to different locations on your screen.

Your mouse device may have one, two, or three buttons on top. Button one is the leftmost button, and you will perform most tasks using it. Buttons two and three are optional and allow you to perform additional Quicken tasks.

Mouse Actions   A mouse button can be used to perform a variety of actions. You can click the button by pressing it and quickly releasing it. You can double-click a button by completing two clicks in rapid succession. You can Shift-click the mouse by pressing the Shift key while you click the button. You can hold the button down by pressing it without releasing the button. You can drag with the mouse by continuing to hold down the mouse button while rolling the mouse across the desktop. Mouse actions require you to position the mouse pointer on the desired screen element before proceeding.

Left Mouse Button Tasks   As mentioned, the left mouse button is used for most Quicken tasks. With this button, you can accomplish the following actions:

✦ Select a command from the Main Menu or pull-down menus.

✦ Accomplish the action of a function key with a click of the key representation.

✦ Finalize a record by clicking on Ctrl Record.

✦ Select a register transaction.

✦ Return to the Main Menu by clicking Esc-Main Menu.

✦ Display a Split Transaction window by clicking the Split button in the selected transaction.

✦ Display the Category and Transfer List window by clicking the Cat: button.

✦ Scroll through transactions by clicking the vertical scroll bar.

✦ Page up or page down with a click on the side of the scroll box.

Double-clicking is not used as often as the click action. You can use a double-click to select any item in a list. Using Shift-click is like pressing the plus key, as long as the Date or Number field is selected. Dragging moves you to a different location in a list as you drag the scroll box vertically. Holding down the mouse button with the mouse pointer in a list or register scrolls up or down the list or register.

Optional Right or Center Mouse Button Tasks   The right button on a two-button mouse performs the same two tasks as the center button on a three-button mouse. You can click the button instead of pressing Esc to leave the current task. You may need to click repeatedly to return to the Main Menu if you have already made several selections. A Shift-click can be used in the Date or Number field to decrease the number by 1, just as you can do by pressing the minus key.

Third Mouse Button Tasks   If you have a three-button mouse you can press its third or right button to access help. This help will be context sensitive.

Menu Selections

Quicken provides menus to simplify your feature and command selections. Quicken's Main Menu, shown here, leads to all the major tasks or activities the program performs.

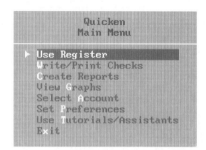

```
                    Quicken
                   Main Menu

   ► Use Register
     Write/Print Checks
     Create Reports
     View Graphs
     Select Account
     Set Preferences
     Use Tutorials/Assistants
     Exit
```

Quicken supports two menu styles. If you are a new Quicken user, when you install Quicken 6, it automatically selects its new style menus, which provide highlighted letters for each Main Menu option, as shown in the preceding illustration. The menu options that appear at the top of subsequent screens and activate pull-down menus also have highlighted letters.

The older style Main Menu has a number in front of each Main Menu selection. If you would like to change your current menu style, you can select Set **P**references, **S**creen Settings, Menu **A**ccess and then choose either Function keys or Alt-key. The techniques learned in the following sections for the use of the mouse and keyboard allow you to use either type menu.

Since there are two different menu styles as well as the ability to use either the mouse or the keyboard, there is a variety of correct options for making menu selections. Rather than listing each option in the exercises that follow, instructions are provided to select the required menu option. You can choose whichever method you prefer for making the selection.

Making Menu Selections with a Mouse

To select an activity from any menu, you first need to move the mouse pointer to the desired activity. Next, you must click the left mouse button. Subsequent menus that may be displayed support the same selection method.

You can activate pull-down menus at the top of the screen by clicking the desired option, depending on which style menus you use.

Making Menu Selections with the Keyboard

If you are using the keyboard to make menu selections, you can select any activity from the Main Menu by using the ⬆ and ⬇ keys, on the right side of your keyboard, to move your cursor to the desired activity and then pressing the Enter key. (The keys on your keyboard will display arrow symbols rather than words.) If you are using the Alt -key style menu, you can type the highlighted letter to select an option. With the older style menus, you can type the number or letter to the left of the desired menu activity. Remember that if you have the older style keyboard, the arrows are on the numeric keypad, so Num Lock has to be off in order to move the cursor.

Effects of Menu Selections

When you make a selection from the Main Menu, Quicken sometimes superimposes another menu on top of it. You make a selection from this submenu to refine the task you want to complete. Again, you can use the arrow keys, type a character, or type a number to make your selection, depending on which style menu you have.

In addition to the Main Menu selections, Quicken also provides *pull-down menus* on many of the screens. These menus are called pull-down menus since they come down from the top of the screen, as shown in Figure 1-8. The name of each menu is shown at the top of the screen. With the Alt-key style menus, a letter in each of the options is highlighted. You can press the Alt key in combination with this letter to pull down the menu. On the older style menus, you can activate the pull-down menus by pressing one of the keys labeled F1 through F10—the *function keys*. These keys are located either at the top or at the left side of your keyboard, depending on the model. You can also make selections with the Quick keys, described in the next section, without pulling down the menus. To close a menu without making a selection, press the Esc key, or if you are using a mouse, click the right mouse button (two button) or middle mouse button (three button).

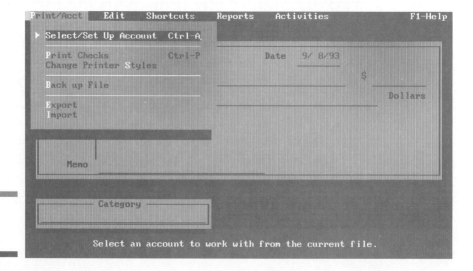

Pull-down
menu
Figure 1-8.

1

Some selections result in the appearance of a *window* on the screen. Windows differ from menus in that there are a number of pieces of information for you to complete. If you want to use the option already chosen (the *default*), there is no need to make a change. You can simply press Enter to accept that choice and move to the next *field,* where you will supply information. If you do not understand what is expected in a field, you can press F1 (Help) for an explanation. Figure 1-9 shows one of the Quicken windows. This one is for entering printer settings when you are customizing printer support.

QuickFill Saves Entry Time

No matter how proficient you are with the keyboard, the quickest way to enter data is to have Quicken do it for you. Quicken 6's new QuickFill feature is designed to do just that. If you are typing a category, security, or action, Quicken checks its list as soon as you type a character and displays the first match it finds. As you type additional letters Quicken is able to refine the match. You can press Enter to accept the entry or use Ctrl-+ to advance through other options on the list that also match. For the payee field, Quicken checks payees in memorized transactions and the last three months of transactions.

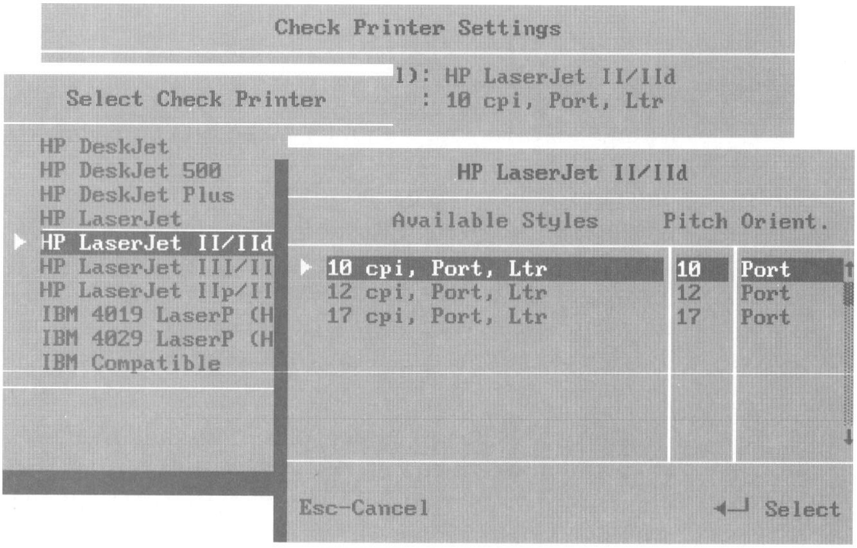

A Quicken
window
Figure 1-9.

When you accept the payee, Quicken copies the entire transaction which you can edit if you choose.

Quick Keys

Quick keys provide access to commands. You can use them throughout Quicken to speed up transaction entry in the register, check writing, and report printing. All Quick key commands are initiated by pressing the (Ctrl) key in combination with another key. When you pull down a menu, you see "Ctrl-" and a letter next to menu items that can be activated with a Quick key combination. The Quick key combinations work while the menu is pulled down, but they also work without your pulling the menu down. The more you use the Quick keys, the easier it will be to remember the combination needed for each activity.

As you work with them, you will find that a few of the combinations are assigned different tasks depending on the activity you are performing. For example, (Ctrl)-(B) searches backward when you are using Find in the register, but it creates a backup of your files when you are at the Main Menu.

As you become familiar with Quicken, you will find these keys help you reduce time spent on financial record keeping. The Quick keys are listed on the Command Card at the end of this book.

Special Keys

If you have used your computer with other programs, you will find that many of the special keys work the same in Quicken as in other programs. For example, the (Esc) key is used to cancel your most recent selection. It can be used to close any menu except the Main Menu, and it also closes most windows, returning you to the previous screen. The (Spacebar), at the bottom of the keyboard, is used when making entries to add blank spaces. The (Backspace) key deletes the last character you typed, the character to the left of the cursor. (Del) deletes the character above the cursor.

The (Shift) key is used to enter capital letters and the special symbols at the top of non-letter keys. It also provides access to the numbers on the numeric keypad when (Num Lock) is off. (Caps Lock) enters all letters in capitals if you press it once, but it does not affect the entry of special symbols, which always require the (Shift) key. To enter lowercase letters with (Caps Lock) on, hold down the (Shift) key. To turn (Caps Lock) off, just press it a second time.

The (Tab) key usually moves you from field to field. Pressing (Shift) and (Tab) together moves the cursor backward through the fields on the screen. (Ctrl)-(End) moves the cursor to the bottom of the display; (Ctrl)-(Home) moves you to the top of the display.

The (Pg Up) and (Pg Dn) keys move you up and down screens and menus.

Quicken uses the (+) and (-) keys on the numeric keypad to quickly increase and decrease numbers such as date and check number. When these keys are pressed once, the number increases or decreases by one. However, since the keys all repeat when held down, holding down either of these keys can rapidly effect a major change. The (+) and (-) keys perform their functions in appropriate fields whether (Num Lock) is on or off. You can (Shift)-click the right mouse button (two-button) or center mouse button (three-button) for the same effect.

The Command Card at the end of the book provides a concise reference to each of these keys.

The Calculator

Quicken has its own calculator, which allows you to perform basic computations on the screen. You can perform computations using the mathematical operators such as + for addition, – for subtraction, * for multiplication, and / for division. Simple calculation involving two numbers or more complex formulas is possible. The calculator displays its results on screen. However, once the numbers leave the screen, you cannot bring them back into view. As a caution, this could make error detection difficult for lengthy calculations.

A significant feature of Quicken's calculator is its ability to compute a payment amount or other figure needed in the *current transaction entry* (the one in use) and then place, or *paste,* the result onto the screen. Figure 1-10 shows the calculator being used to compute the total of nine invoices for $77.00 each. In this manner, one check could be written to cover all nine invoices. You can also compute discounts or interest on a loan. Once Quicken computes the amount, you can use the Paste feature to place the amount in the payment field.

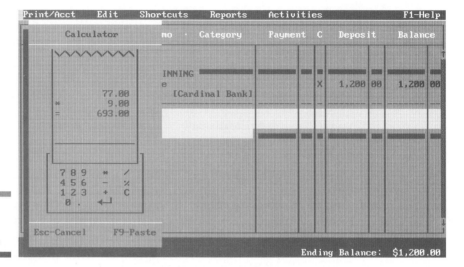

The Quicken calculator
Figure 1-10.

You activate the calculator through the menu bar at the top of the Check Register, Write Checks, or Reconciliation screen by selecting Activities, Calculator. You can also activate it by using the Quick key Ctrl-O. When the calculator is activated, Quicken automatically turns on the numeric keypad so you can use it in making your calculations.

C H A P T E R

2

MAKING REGISTER ENTRIES

If you maintain a checking account or monitor a savings account, you are already familiar with the concept of the Quicken register. The register is the backbone of the Quicken system. It allows you to maintain information on checking accounts, cash accounts, and other assets and expenses. With the register, you maintain current status information for an account so you know the precise balance. You also keep a history of all the transactions affecting the balance. The capabilities of the Quicken register extend beyond the entries normally made in a checkbook register since they allow you to easily categorize entries as you make them. This extra capability extends the usefulness of the recorded information and facilitates report creation.

In this chapter you will learn to create and maintain a single account. This account will represent a checking account balance, and the transactions will simulate transactions similar to the ones you might have in a personal account. The techniques you learn will be used repeatedly as you work with the Quicken package.

Maintaining a Register

Quicken's register works much like the manual checking account register shown in Figure 2-1. Starting with the account balance at the beginning of the period, each check written is recorded as a separate entry, including the date, amount, payee, and check number. Additional information can be added to document the reason for the check. This information can be useful in the preparation of taxes or to verify that an invoice has been paid. As each check is entered, a new balance is computed. Other bank charges such as check printing, overdraft charges, and service fees must also be subtracted from the account balance. Deposits are recorded in a similar fashion. Since interest earned on the account is often automatically credited to the account, it should be entered as it appears on the monthly bank statement. (Quicken cannot compute the interest earned on your account since there is no way for the package to know the dates checks clear at your bank, and this information is needed to compute the interest earned.)

Although it is easy to record entries in a manual check register, most individuals at least occasionally make a mistake in computing the new balance. Recording transactions in Quicken's register eliminates this problem. It also provides many other advantages such as categories for classifying each entry, automatic totaling of similar transactions within a category, easily created reports, and a Search feature for quickly locating specific entries.

		RECORD ALL CHANGES OR CREDITS THAT AFFECT YOUR ACCOUNT								
NUMBER	DATE	DESCRIPTION OF TRANSACTION	PAYMENT/DEBIT		T	FEE IF ANY (-)	DEPOSIT/CREDIT (+)		BALANCE $	
	1/1 1993	Opening Balance 1st U.S. Bank					1,200	00	1,200	00
									1,200	00
100	1/4 1993	Small City Gas & Light Gas & Electric	67	50					67	50
									1,132	50
101	1/5 1993	Small City Times Paper Bill	16	50					16	50
									1,116	00
	1/7 1993	Deposit - Salary monthly pay					700	00	700	00
									1,816	00
102	1/7 1993	Small City Market Food	22	32					22	32
									1,793	68
103	1/7 1993	Small City Apartments Rent	150	00					150	00
									1,643	00
104	1/19 1993	Small City Market Food	43	00					43	00
									1,600	00
105	1/25 1993	Small City Phone Company Phone Bill	19	75					19	75
									1,580	93
	2/10 1993	Dividend Check Dividend from ABC Co.					25	00	25	00
									1,605	93

Manual entries in a checking account register **Figure 2-1.**

Before entering any transactions in Quicken's register, you need to create a file and set up an account. This means assigning a name to the account and establishing a balance. You will also want to learn a little about Quicken's built-in categories, which allow you to categorize every transaction. You may already do this with some transactions in your check register, marking those you will need to refer back to, for instance. This activity is optional in Quicken, but using the categories will increase the usefulness of the reports you can create.

Establishing Your File and an Account

Establishing a file and an account is easy once you install Quicken and start it with the instructions in Appendix A, "Special Quicken Tasks."

The exact procedure that you follow depends on whether you have used Quicken 6 before. If this is your first use of the package and you do not have data from an earlier release, Quicken will provide an assistant to help you get started with the setup. If you have data from Quicken 5, you can use the data in Quicken 6 without conversion. Quicken will locate your old files during installation and allow you to use them without change. If you do not have Quicken 5 data but have used Quicken 6 before, you need to set up your new file and account without the assistant.

Regardless of which situation matches yours, you need to have a file for storing any data entered with Quicken. When you provide a name, Quicken adds four different filename extensions since one Quicken file actually consists of four different files on your disk. You also need to provide an account name. Quicken can store data for various account types, with as many as 255 accounts in one Quicken file. You will find all the steps you need in the sections that follow, regardless of your situation.

Using the Assistant as a New Quicken 6 User

The first time you start Quicken, you are presented with the Assistant screen shown in Figure 2-2. Quicken leads you through the process of naming a file for use, selecting a set of categories to use with your entries, and defining an account to use. Follow these steps after you see the initial screen in Figure 2-2:

1. Select option 2 to set up your own data and press (Enter).

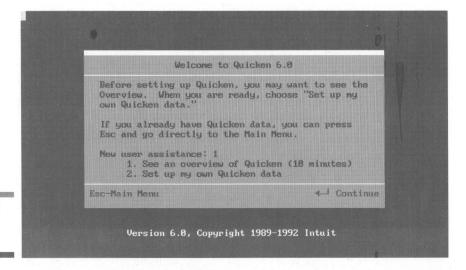

The Assistant screen
Figure 2-2.

2

2. Read the information screens that describe Quicken files and accounts, pressing Enter after each.

3. Answer the two questions that test what you remember about the information screens.

4. Press Enter to accept 1 for a bank account.

5. Press Ctrl-Backspace to delete the suggested account name from the Set Up an Account window shown in Figure 2-3.

6. Type **1st U.S. Bank** then press Enter.

7. Type **1200** and press Enter.

8. Type **1/1/93** and press Enter.

9. Review the information and press F10 after making any changes.

10. Continue pressing Enter until Quicken asks for the filename and location.

11. Type **QDATA** and press Enter.

12. Review the location where Quicken plans to store your data and press Enter when it shows the location that you want to use.

13. Select 3 to choose the Both Home and Business category from the options shown in Figure 2-4 and press Enter.

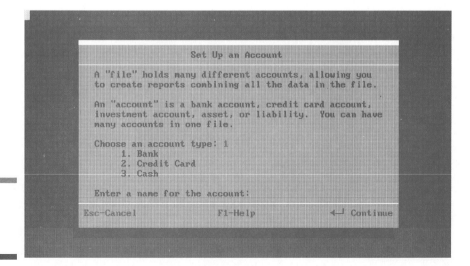

Setting up a
Quicken
account
Figure 2-3.

14. Continue pressing (Enter) until the Welcome to Quicken screen is displayed again.

15. Press (Esc) until the Main Menu is displayed.

16. Select Use **R**egister from Quicken's Main Menu to open the register for the 1st U.S. Bank account, as shown in Figure 2-5.

Converting Quicken 5 Data with Quicken 6

If you have followed the directions in Appendix A, Quicken has searched your hard disk and located your Quicken 5 files. Since they can be read directly by Quicken 6, there is no need to convert them.

If you change the name of the install directory Quicken suggests, your Quicken 5 data will not be available until you select Set **P**references from the Main Menu, select **F**ile Activities, and then set File **L**ocation to the Quicken 5 directory.

If you are using a release of Quicken prior to Quicken 5, your files must be converted before using them with Quicken 6. Contact Intuit for the required utility program.

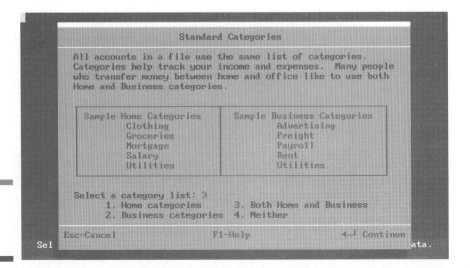

Sample
Quicken
categories
Figure 2-4.

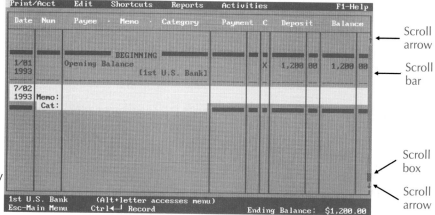

New Account
Register window
Figure 2-5.

Creating a New File

The steps in this section enable you to create a new Quicken 6 file if
you want new files later. You also learn how to change the location of
the file. Follow these steps:

1. From the Main Menu, select Set **P**references.
2. Select **F**ile Activities.
3. Select Set File **L**ocation and change the pathname if necessary.
4. Press (Enter) to finalize the entry.
5. Select **S**elect/Set Up File.
6. Select <Set Up New File>.
7. Type **QDATA** as a name for the file, which can consist of from one
    to eight characters, and then press (F10) (Continue).
8. Select Both Home and Business for the categories and press (Enter).
    Highlight the file and press (Enter). Quicken takes you to the screen
    for creating an account.
9. Press (Esc) until you are back at the Main Menu. You will follow the
    separate instructions in the next section for creating an account
    since the stand-alone procedure described can be used by itself if
    you ever need to create a new account without a file.

Creating a New Account

The account used for the examples in the next few chapters is called 1st U.S. Bank. In the unlikely event that this name happens to be the same as one of your existing accounts, you need to use another name to maintain the integrity of your existing data. Follow these steps:

1. From the Main Menu, select Select **A**ccount.
2. Select New Account and press [Enter].
3. Type **1** for the account type and press [Enter].
4. Type **1st U.S. Bank** and press [Enter].
5. Type **1200** and press [Enter].
6. Type **1/1/92** and press [F10].
7. Type **1**, press [Enter] to specify Bank Statement as the source of the 1,200 entry and press [Enter] again.
8. Press [Esc] to display the Main Menu.

Performing the Task if You Are Already Using Quicken 6

Even though you already have a file and one or more accounts set up from your earlier Quicken sessions, you will want to create a file and an account that match the ones used in the examples. You can follow the instructions in the two preceding sections for Quicken 5 users to set up a file and an account.

The Quicken Register

You can choose Use **R**egister from the Main Menu to display the register for 1st U.S. Bank. Figure 2-5 shows the top of the initial Register window. Although you have not yet recorded any transactions, Quicken has already entered the account name, the opening balance, and the opening date. Quicken has also automatically entered X in the C (cleared) field of the register, indicating that the balance has been reconciled and is correct. This field will be used in Chapter 4, "Reconciling Your Quicken Register," when you reconcile your entire account.

The area at the far right of the register window is the *scroll bar*. It has an arrow at the top and bottom and a scroll box inside it. As you enter more transactions, you can use a mouse with these screen elements to scroll through the register.

The highlighted area below the opening balance entry is where the first transaction will be entered. Remember, a transaction is just a record of a financial activity such as a deposit or withdrawal (credit or debit). The fields used are the same for all transactions (see Figure 2-5). Table 2-1 provides a detailed description of each of these fields.

As you make the entries for the first transaction, notice that Quicken moves through the fields in a specific order. After entering data in a

Field	Contents
Date	Transaction date. You can accept the current date entry or type a new date.
Num (number)	Check number for check transactions. Leave field blank by pressing Enter for noncheck transactions.
Payee	Payee's name for check transactions. For ATM transactions, deposits, service fees, and so on, a description is entered in this field.
Payment	Payment or withdrawal amount. For deposit transactions, this field is left blank. Quicken supports entries as large as $9,999,999.99.
C (cleared)	Press Enter to skip this field when entering transactions. You will use it in Chapter 4 for reconciling accounts and noting checks that have cleared the bank.
Deposit	Deposit amounts. For a payment transaction, this field is left blank. The same rules as for Payment apply.
Balance	A running total or the sum of all prior transactions. It is computed by Quicken after you complete each transaction.
Memo	Optional descriptive information documenting the transaction.
Category	Optional entry used to assign a transaction to one of Quicken's categories. Categories are used to organize similar transactions and can facilitate reporting.

Fields in Register Window
Table 2-1.

field, you press (Enter) and the cursor automatically moves to the next field in which you can enter data. Some fields, such as Date and Payee, must have an entry in all transactions, and either the Payment or Deposit field requires an entry. Other fields are optional and are used when needed. If you do not need an entry in an optional field, you just press (Enter) and the cursor moves to the next field. For example, the check number (Num) field is used only when writing checks and so would be optional.

Recording Your Transactions in the Register

The highlighting is already positioned for your first transaction entry when you open the Register window. If you have used the (↑) key to move to the opening balance entry, you need to press (Ctrl)-(End) to reposition the highlight properly. In the next sections you enter eight sample transactions representing typical personal expenses and deposits. Don't worry if you make a mistake in recording your first transaction. Just leave the mistake in the entry and focus on the steps involved. In the second transaction you will correct your errors. Follow these steps to complete the entries for the first transaction (use the (←) key, if necessary, to move the cursor to the month in the date field):

1. Type **1/4/93** and press (Enter).

Notice that "1/04" is displayed on the first line of the Date field and that the cursor automatically moves to the second line of the column the second time you press the (/) key. Also note that even though you only entered 93, Quicken displays the full year, 1993.

At this point you can see how Quicken dates are changed. Move the cursor to the Date field using (←), and press (+) or (−) to increase or decrease the current date. A light touch to the key alters the date by one day. Holding down these keys causes a rapid date change. If you use the (+) or (−) option to change the date, (Enter) or (Tab) is still required to move to the next field. If you use (+) and (−) to change the transaction date and want to return to the current system date for the next transaction, press (T) with the cursor in the Date field. (If you test this feature now, be sure to reenter the 1/4/93 date before proceeding.)

2. Type **100** and press (Enter) to place the check number in the Num field.

2

3. Type **Small City Gas & Light** and press [Enter] to complete the entry for Payee for this check.

There is a limit of 31 characters on the Payee line for each transaction. Notice that the cursor moves to the Payment field, where Quicken expects the next entry.

4. Type **67.50** and press [Enter].

Since this is a check transaction, the amount should be placed in the Payment field. Notice that when you type the decimal, Quicken automatically moves to the cents column of the Payment field.

5. Type **Gas and Electric** and press [Enter].

You are limited to 31 characters on the Memo line. Since this is your first category entry, a message displays. Press [F10] to acknowledge it.

6. Type **Utilities** in the Cat (category) field. Your screen should look like the one in Figure 2-6.

If you are going to use a category, you must enter a valid Quicken option to stay within the standard category structure. To see Quicken's Standard Categories, press [Ctrl]-[C] and use the arrow keys to review your options. Press [Esc] to return to the register.

7. Press [Enter] to complete the transaction data entry. Quicken displays the OK to Record Transaction? window to see if you are ready to record the transaction.
8. Select Record Transaction to confirm the recording of the transaction. Your screen displays a balance of 1,132.50.

You have now completed your first transaction successfully. Since everyone makes mistakes in entries, you will want to learn how to correct those errors. This is easily done with Quicken.

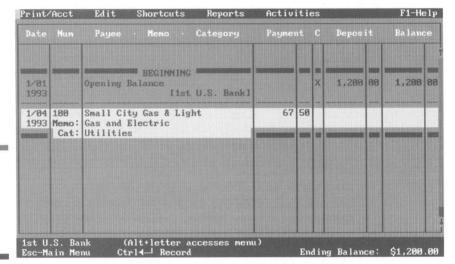

Screen before
completing
first sample
transaction
entry
Figure 2-6.

Making Revisions to the Current Transaction

One of the advantages Quicken has over manual entries is that changes can be made easily and neatly. An incorrect amount or other error can be altered as soon as you notice the mistake or later on. The procedure you use depends on whether you have already recorded the transaction. Quicken's QuickFill feature can save you time, whether you are correcting an existing transaction or entering a new transaction.

Correcting Your Example

In this section you learn how to correct mistakes in the current transaction, practicing the techniques covered briefly in Chapter 1, "An Overview of Quicken and Your Computer Components." First, make the following transaction entries:

1. Type **1/5/93** and press ⌷Enter⌷.

Notice that Quicken automatically entered the 1/4/93 date for you. It always records the date from the previous transaction unless there was

2

none, in which case it records the current date. Here, you must enter the date since you are entering several days' transactions in one session. If you enter transactions daily, you do not need to change the date between transactions since each of your entries will be for the current day.

   2. Type **110** and press Enter.

Notice that the previous check number was 100. This check number should have been recorded as 101.

   3. Press ← five times to move the cursor to the second 1 in the entry.

   4. Type **01** to change 110 to 101 and then press Enter to finalize.

This correction method employs Quicken's character replacement feature; new characters type over the old entries.

   5. Type **S** and notice that Quicken automatically fills in the same payee from the previous transaction.

This illustrates the new Quicken 6 QuickFill feature. If you press Enter, Quicken completes the current transaction with the entries from the previous transaction. Quicken uses QuickFill for Payee and Category fields as you record in the account register. Quicken checks the Category List for categories and looks at the payees in the last three months of transactions as it searches for an entry that matches what you type. Quicken uses the first match it finds and shows the date of the transaction in angle brackets as in <1/4> for a transaction recorded on 1/4/93. You can press Ctrl-+ to look through the list for additional matches. Ctrl-− moves backward through the list.

If QuickFill is not operating for you, select Set **P**references and then select **T**ransaction Settings. After moving to option 8, type **Y** to activate the QuickFill feature.

   6. Continue typing **malll City Times**, since Quicken has not provided the match that you need.

This entry contains an extra *l*. Use Ctrl-← twice to move to the *C* in "City." Then press the ← key twice to move your cursor to the third *l* and press Del to delete the character at the cursor.

7. Press (Enter) to finalize the Payee entry.

8. Type **6.50** for the payment amount.

Note that if you had intended to enter 16.50, moving to the 6 and typing a 1 would change the entry to 1.50, not the 16.50 you need. Even if you have insert mode on (a flashing cursor), you still cannot insert the 1.

9. Move the cursor one position to the left of the 6 by pressing ← five times. With insert mode off (small underscore cursor), type **1** and Quicken places the 1 in front of the 6.

10. Press (Enter) to move to the Memo field.

11. Type **Magazine subscription** and press (Enter).

If you had intended this entry to be the newspaper bill, you would need to make a change. Use ↑ to reactivate the Memo field.

12. Press (Ctrl)-(Backspace), which deletes the entire entry. Then, type **Paper bill** and press (Enter).

13. Type **M** for the category.

Quicken uses the QuickFill feature and presents the Medical category. You want to use the Miscellaneous category.

14. Press (Ctrl)-(+) and Quicken displays the Misc category designation. Press (Ctrl)-(+) again and Quicken displays the Mort Int category. Press (Ctrl)-(-) to return to the Misc category.

If you had continued to type Mi in the category field, Quicken would have presented Misc as the category, and you would have stopped typing and accepted it by pressing (Enter).

15. Press (Enter) to complete your second transaction.

16. Select Record Transaction or press (Enter) to confirm the update. Your register should look like the one in Figure 2-7.

A number of mistakes were included in this transaction, but you can see how easy it is to make corrections with Quicken.

2

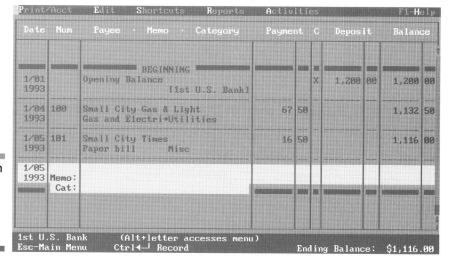

Register screen after second sample transaction
Figure 2-7.

NOTE: Pressing Ctrl-Enter completes and records a transaction.

Additional Transaction Entries

You are now somewhat familiar with recording transactions in the Quicken register. In order to test your knowledge and expand your transaction base for later, enter the following additional transactions in your register, using the same procedure as in the previous transaction entries. Remember to leave a blank space in the Num field of deposits when a check number is not provided. You can use the QuickFill when entering Payee or Category fields.

Date:	1/7/93
Payee:	Deposit-Salary
Deposit:	700.00
Memo:	Monthly pay
Category:	Salary

Date: 1/7/93
Num: 102
Payee: Small City Market
Payment: 22.32
Memo: Food
Category: Groceries

Date: 1/7/93
Num: 103
Payee: Small City Apartments
Payment: 150.00
Memo: Rent
Category: Housing

Date: 1/19/93
Num: 104
Payee: Small City Market
Payment: 43.00
Memo: Food
Category: Groceries

When entering this transaction, Quicken 6 copies the information contained in the Payment, Memo, and Cat fields when you press `Enter` after completing the Payee field. Press `Ctrl`-`Backspace` to clear the 22.32 payment amount. Type the correct payment amount and press `Ctrl`-`Enter`.

Date: 1/25/93
Num: 105
Payee: Small City Phone Company
Payment: 19.75
Memo: Phone bill
Category: Telephone

Date:	2/10/93
Payee:	Dividend check
Deposit:	25.00
Memo:	Dividends check from ABC Co.
Category:	Div Income

After typing and recording the entries for the last transaction, your screen should resemble the one in Figure 2-8. Press Ctrl-Enter to record the last transaction.

Viewing a Compressed Register

You can switch back and forth between the standard register and a *compressed register*, which lets you see three times as many transactions on your screen. For a view that shows one line for each transaction, like Figure 2-9, press Ctrl-Q or select Register View from the Activities menu. Pressing Ctrl-Q again toggles back to the original view. To change the default Quicken setting to the compressed view, choose **S**creen Setting from the Set **P**references menu, and then choose **R**egister View and option 2 Compressed to save two lines for every transaction displayed.

```
 Print/Acct     Edit     Shortcuts     Reports     Activities          F1-Help

  Date   Num      Payee  ·  Memo  ·   Category     Payment  C   Deposit     Balance

 1/07           Deposit-Salary                              |    700 00   1,816 00
 1993           Monthly pay      Salary

 1/07  102      Small City Market                22 32      |             1,793 68
 1993           Food             Groceries

 1/07  103      Small City Apartments           150 00      |             1,643 68
 1993           Rent             Housing

 1/19  104      Small City Market                43 00      |             1,600 68
 1993           Food             Groceries

 1/25  105      Small City Phone Company         19 75      |             1,580 93
 1993           Phone bill       Telephone

 2/10           Dividend check                             |     25 00   1,605 93
 1993  Memo: Dividends check from ABC Co.
        Cat: Div Income

 1st U.S. Bank       (Alt+letter accesses menu)
 Esc-Main Menu      Ctrl◄┘  Record                    Ending Balance:  $1,605.93
```

Register screen after typing and finalizing entries in last transaction
Figure 2-8.

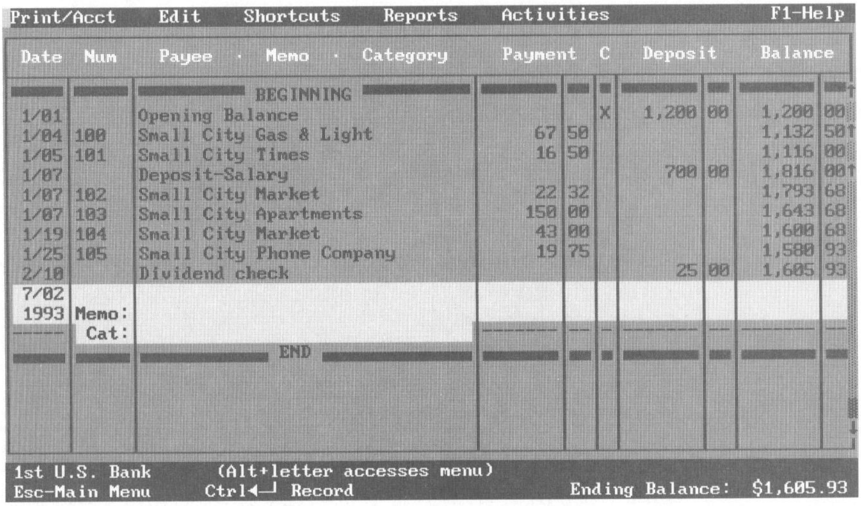

```
Print/Acct    Edit     Shortcuts    Reports    Activities              F1-Help

Date   Num      Payee   ·  Memo  ·  Category      Payment  C  Deposit    Balance

━━━━━━━━━━━━━━━━━━━━━━━━BEGINNING━━━━━━━━━━━━━━━━━━━━━━━━
1/01            Opening Balance                        X   1,200 00   1,200 00
1/04  100       Small City Gas & Light        67 50                   1,132 50↑
1/05  101       Small City Times              16 50                   1,116 00
1/07            Deposit-Salary                             700 00     1,816 00↑
1/07  102       Small City Market             22 32                   1,793 68
1/07  103       Small City Apartments        150 00                   1,643 68
1/19  104       Small City Market             43 00                   1,600 68
1/25  105       Small City Phone Company      19 75                   1,580 93
2/10            Dividend check                              25 00     1,605 93
7/02
1993  Memo:
      Cat:
━━━━━━━━━━━━━━━━━━━━━━━━━━END━━━━━━━━━━━━━━━━━━━━━━━━━━━


1st U.S. Bank        (Alt+letter accesses menu)
Esc-Main Menu        Ctrl◄┘  Record              Ending Balance:  $1,605.93
```

Compressed register shows one line for each transaction.
Figure 2-9.

Ending a Quicken Session and Beginning a New One

You do not need to finish all your work with Quicken in one session. You can end a Quicken session after entering one transaction or continue and enter transactions representing up to several months of financial activity, but you should always use the orderly approach provided here and never turn your system off without first exiting from Quicken.

Ending a Quicken session requires that you go to the Main Menu. You can use Esc when the register is active to return to the Main Menu. Select E**x**it to end your session. All of the data in your Quicken files will be saved for subsequent sessions.

To reenter Quicken, use the instructions provided earlier in this chapter to boot your system (if necessary); then, type **Q** and press Enter to access the Quicken package. You always enter the Main Menu when you first load the package. Selecting Use **R**egister takes you back to the register to record additional transactions. Quicken always brings the last account you worked with to the screen.

NOTE: Quicken automatically enters the current date in the Date field for the first transaction in a session.

2

Remember that for purposes of the examples, you will specify dates that are unlikely to agree with the current date. This approach allows you to create reports identical to the ones that will be presented later. If you are now reentering Quicken, use 2/10/93 as the date.

Reviewing Register Entries

Reviewing transaction entries in the Quicken register is as easy as, and more versatile than, flipping through the pages of a manual register. You can scroll through the register to see all the recorded transactions or use the Find feature to search for a specific transaction. You can also focus on transactions for a specific time period with the Go to Date feature.

Scrolling Through the Register

You can put some of the keys introduced in Chapter 1 to work in the Quicken register. You can probably guess the effects some of the keys will have from their names. The ⬆ and ⬇ keys move the highlighting up or down a transaction. Quicken scrolls information off the screen to show additional transactions not formerly in view. Once a transaction is highlighted, the ➡ and ⬅ keys move across the current transaction. The (Pg Up) and (Pg Dn) keys move up and down one screen at a time.

The functions of some keys vary between releases of Quicken; some key functions are not as obvious as those just discussed. The following examples show how the keys work in Quicken 6.

The (Home) key moves the cursor to the beginning of the current field in a transaction. When (Home) is pressed twice, the cursor moves to the beginning of the current transaction. If you press (Home) three times or press (Ctrl)-(Home), Quicken moves the cursor to the top of the register.

The [End] key moves the cursor to the end of the current field. If you press [End] twice, Quicken moves the cursor to the last field in the current transaction. If you press [Ctrl]-[End], Quicken moves the cursor to the bottom of the register.

Pressing [Ctrl]-[Pg Up] moves the highlight to the beginning of the current month. Pressing it a second time moves the highlight to the beginning of the previous month. Pressing [Ctrl]-[Pg Dn] moves the highlight to the first transaction in the next month. You can use the mouse rather than the keyboard to scroll in the register. The following mouse actions will help you locate the place you want to be quickly:

- ✦ Click the vertical scroll bar arrows to scroll to the next or previous transaction.

- ✦ Hold the mouse button down on the scroll bar to move quickly through the transactions.

- ✦ Click above or below the scroll box to move up or down one page of transactions.

- ✦ Drag the scroll box up or down in the scroll bar to move to a different location.

As you enter more transactions, the value of knowing quick ways to move between transactions will become more apparent.

Using the Find Feature

Quicken's Find feature allows you to locate a specific transaction easily. You can find a transaction by entering a minimal amount of information from the transaction on a special Find window. Activate the Find window with the Quick key [Ctrl]-[F] or press [Alt]-[E] to activate the Edit menu and then select Find. The Edit menu displays all the Quick key sequences such as [Ctrl]-[F] for Find.

Quicken can look for an exact match entry in any field with a forward or backward search. You can also use Quicken's wildcard feature to locate a transaction with only part of the information from a field. After looking at the examples in the next two sections, you can refer to the rules for finding entries in Table 2-2.

Entry	Quicken Finds
electric	electric, Electric, ELECTRIC, electric power, Electric Company, Consumer Power Electric, new electric
=Electric	Electric, ELECTRIC, electric
~electric	groceries, gas—anything but electric
e..c	electric, eccentric
s?n	sun, sin, son—any single letter between an *s* and an *n*
..	ice, fire, and anything else except blanks
~..	all transactions with a blank in that field

Locating
Transactions
Table 2-2.

Finding Matching Entries

To look for a transaction that exactly matches data, all you need to do is fill in some data in the window. Quicken will search for entries in the Num, Payee, Memo, Category, Payment, C, or Deposit field. You do not need to worry about capitalization of your data entry since Quicken is not case sensitive. When you enter the data for your first Find operation, the fields will be blank. For subsequent Find operations you can edit the data in the window, type over what's there, or clear the entire window by pressing Ctrl-D and begin again with blank fields. For example, to locate a specific check number in the 1st U.S. Bank register developed earlier, complete the following steps:

1. Press Ctrl-Home.

This ensures that you start at the beginning of the register so you can conduct a complete forward search through the data. (Quicken also supports a backward search to allow you to locate entries above the currently highlighted transaction.)

2. Press Alt-E to open the Edit menu.
3. Select **F**ind.
4. Move the cursor to the Num field by pressing the ← key five times and type **103**.
5. Press Ctrl-N to find the next matching transaction. Quicken closes the Find window and highlights the transaction.

Quicken started the search with the current transaction and proceeded toward the bottom of the register attempting to find matching transactions, in this case the one with 103 in the Num field. You could have entered data in other fields in the Find window if you wanted to specify multiple criteria for locating transactions. You might make entries for the Date, Payee, and Memo fields all in one Find window. Quicken finds only transactions that match all of your entries.

The more transactions in the register, the more useful Quicken's Find capability becomes. For instance, you might want to find all the transactions involving a specific payee or all the transactions on a certain date. Visually scanning through hundreds of transactions could take a long time and you could still miss a matching transaction. Quicken makes no mistakes and finds the matching transactions quickly.

You can also speed up the search process by bypassing the Edit menu and using the Quick keys for your Find selections. Let's perform a second Find operation, one that begins the search with the current transaction and searches back toward the first entry in the register. To use the Quick keys to do this, follow these steps:

1. Press Ctrl-F to open the Find window. (This approach replaces opening the Edit menu and selecting Find.)
2. Type **100**, and then press Del until the digits from the previous Num entry have been removed.
3. Press Ctrl-B to search backward through the entries and highlight the transaction for check number 100.

If you were performing a search in which several transactions might match your entry, you could continue to search with repeated presses of Ctrl-N (forward) or Ctrl-B (backward) after completing the entries in the Find window.

Key Word Search

You can enter a less than exact match and still locate the desired transactions if you search the Payee, Category, or Memo field. Quicken will locate any entry that contains the text you type. To look for an exact match, you must precede your entry with an = (equal sign), or change Set **P**references, **T**ransaction Setting, and Exact matches on find and filter to Y. Try this for a quick look at the Key Word Search feature:

2

1. Press Ctrl-F to open the Find window.
2. Press Ctrl-D to clear all the entries from this window.
3. Type **Small** in the Payee field.
4. Press Ctrl-N to search from the current location toward the end of the document. Quicken highlights the next entry for "Small City Times."

If you continue to press Ctrl-N, Quicken moves through the transaction list, highlighting each entry containing "Small". After you have found all matching transactions, pressing Ctrl-N again causes Quicken to display a message indicating there are no more matching transactions.

Searching for Multiple Entries

You can use multiple key word search entries in a Find window or combine the Key Word Search feature with exact match entries. As an example, follow these steps to look for transactions with "Market" in the Payee field, a payment of 22.32, and "Groceries" for the category entry:

1. Press Ctrl-Home to move to the beginning of the register.
2. Press Ctrl-F to open the Find window.
3. Press Ctrl-Backspace to clear the Payee field.
4. Type **Market** in the Payee field and press Enter.
5. Type **22.32** in the Payment field and press Enter two times.
6. Type **Groceries** in the Category field. Your Find entries should look like this:

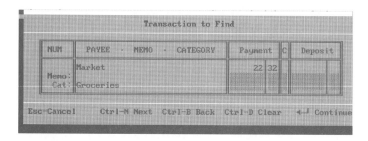

7. Press Ctrl-N.

Your transaction for Small City Market should be highlighted. Press
Ctrl-N again to repeat the forward search. Quicken displays the message
indicating that there are no further matches.

8. Press Esc to end the search.

Using the Go to Date Feature

You may sometimes want to find one or more transactions for a given
date. The Go to Date feature allows you to locate the first transaction
entry for a specified date. You can use either the Edit menu or Ctrl-G to
begin a date search. If you use Alt-E to open the Edit menu, you then
select **G**o to Date.

When the window opens, fill in the date that you are searching for. A
date search works a little differently than Find since you do not have to
be concerned with whether the date is before or after the current
transaction. The following steps illustrate a date search:

1. Press Ctrl-Home. Then select Ctrl-G to open the Go to Date window.
2. Type **1/7/93**, as shown here:

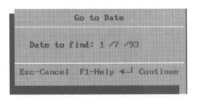

and press Enter. Quicken goes to the first transaction for the date
you entered.

You could now examine all the remaining transactions for the date by
pressing ↓.

Revising Transactions

You have already learned how to make revisions to transactions in the
check register as you are recording a transaction, but sometimes you

2

may need to make changes to previously recorded transactions. It is important to note that although Quicken allows you to modify previously recorded transactions, you cannot change the balance amount without entering another transaction. This protects you from unauthorized changes in the register account balances. By forcing you to enter another transaction, Quicken is able to maintain a log of any change to an account balance.

You may also find it necessary to void a previously written check, deposit, or any other adjustment to an account. Voiding removes the effect of the original transaction from the account balance, although it maintains the history of the original transaction and shows it as voided. To remove all trace of the original transaction, you must use Quicken's Delete Transaction command. You can use either Quick keys or selections from Quicken's Edit menu to void and delete transactions. To reinstate voided transactions, you delete the word "VOID" and the X in the C column (which was entered automatically) and press Ctrl-Enter to finalize the change.

Changing a Previous Transaction

The following steps must be used when changing a previously recorded transaction:

1. Move to the desired transaction.
2. Then use the same techniques discussed in the "Making Revisions to the Current Transaction" section of this chapter.

Quicken does not allow you to change the balance amount directly. You need to enter another transaction to make an adjustment. Another option is to void the original transaction and enter a new transaction.

Voiding a Transaction

When you void a transaction, you undo the financial effect of the transaction. Using the Void operation creates an automatic audit trail (or record) of all transactions against an account, including those that have already been voided. Let's try the Void option with check number 100; follow these steps:

1. Move the highlighting to check number 100.
2. Press [Ctrl]-[V] and select Void Transaction to void the current transaction.

Another option is pressing [Alt]-[E] and selecting **V**oid Transaction from the Edit menu. With either approach, the word "VOID" is now entered in front of the payee name, as shown in Figure 2-10.

3. Press [Esc] to return to the Main Menu. Quicken displays the Leaving Transaction window.
4. Press [Enter] to select item 1, record changes, and leave.

If after voiding a transaction you want to continue to work in the check register, you can move to the category field by using [Tab], [Enter], or the arrow keys. Press [Enter] one more time to select item 1, Record transaction, from the OK to Record Transaction? window. If you change your mind and do not want to void the transaction, you can highlight item 2, Do not record, before pressing [Enter].

Print/Acct	Edit	Shortcuts	Reports	Activities			F1-Help
Date	Num	Payee · Memo · Category	Payment	C	Deposit	Balance	

		BEGINNING				
1/01 1993		Opening Balance [1st U.S. Bank]		X	1,200 00	1,200 00
1/04 1993	100 Memo: Cat:	VOID:Small City Gas & Light Gas and Electric Utilities		X		1,132 50
1/05 1993	101	Small City Times Paper bill Misc	16 50			1,116 00
1/07 1993		Deposit-Salary Monthly pay Salary			700 00	1,816 00
1/07 1993	102	Small City Market Food Groceries	22 32			1,793 68

1st U.S. Bank	(Alt+letter accesses menu)		
Esc-Main Menu	Ctrl◄┘ Record	Ending Balance:	$1,605.93

Voided
transaction
Figure 2-10.

2

Deleting a Transaction

You can delete a transaction with [Ctrl]-[D] or by opening the Edit menu with [Alt]-[E] and selecting **D**elete transaction. Try this now by deleting the voided transaction for check number 100.

1. If you are at the Main Menu, open the Register window again by selecting Use **R**egister and pressing [Enter].
2. Move the highlighting to the voided transaction for check number 100.
3. Press [Ctrl]-[D] to delete the transaction. Quicken displays the OK to Delete Transaction? window.
4. Press [Enter] to confirm the deletion.

Reinstating a Transaction

There is no "undo" key to eliminate the effect of a delete; you must reenter the transaction. For practice, reinstate the transaction for check number 100 with these steps:

1. Press [Ctrl]-[End] to move to the end of the register.
2. Type **1/4/93** and press [Enter] to set the date to 1/4/1993.
3. Type **100** and press [Enter] to supply the check number in the Num field.
4. Type **Small City Gas & Light** and press [Enter] to complete the entry for the payee for this check.
5. Type **67.50** and press [Enter].
6. Type **Gas and Electric** and press [Enter].
7. Type **Utilities** and press [Enter] to complete the transaction.
8. Press [Enter] when the OK to Record Transaction? window displays. The transaction is reentered into the register.

You can see from this example that you expended a considerable amount of effort to rerecord this transaction. Avoid unnecessary work by confirming the void or deletion before you complete it.

CHAPTER

3

QUICKEN REPORTS

In Chapter 2, "Making Register Entries," you discovered how easy it is to enter transactions in the Quicken system. In this chapter you find out about another major benefit—the ability to generate reports. These reports present your data in an organized format that allows you to analyze the data. With Quicken 6, a Report menu allows you to customize a report while viewing it and to zoom in for a closeup look at details. You can use Quicken to produce a quick printout of the register or create reports that analyze and summarize data. Some of these reports, such as the Cash Flow report and the Itemized Categories report, would require a significant amount of work if they were compiled manually. This chapter focuses on these basic types of reports and some customizing options. More complex report types are covered in later chapters.

Before looking at the various reports, let's look first at how Quicken works with printers. Although Quicken supports most popular printers without any special effort on your part, you should know a few of the essentials of printers. This chapter teaches you how to change the basic print settings if Quicken does not create acceptable output with the current configuration. You can define three different printers or predefine three different options for one printer.

Default Printer Settings

Quicken is preset to interface with most of the popular printers including IBM compatibles; Hewlett-Packard LaserJets, DeskJet, and ThinkJet; IBM ProPrinter and 4216; Epson; NEC 3530 and 8023A; and Okidata 83, 92, 182, 192, 292, and 320. Default parameters set the number of characters per inch, the paper type, and the standard port on your machine for connecting the first printer. If you have one of the printers listed here or own a model that mimics one of them, you will be able to print your Quicken reports without making any changes. If you are using a serial printer, a laser printer producing less than acceptable results, or want to use settings different than the default, consult "Changing the Printer Settings" at the end of this chapter. If not, Quicken will probably interface with your printer and you will not need to make any changes to the Quicken printer settings.

Printing the Check Register

Although it is convenient to enter transactions on the screen, a printout of your entries is often easier to review and much more portable than a computer screen. Try printing the register first without changing the print settings. If your output is very different from the sample shown in this chapter, try customizing your print settings and then print the register again. You will find instructions for making these changes at the end of this chapter. To print your register, follow these steps:

1. Select Use **R**egister from Quicken's Main Menu.

Your latest register transactions should appear on the screen.

2. Select **P**rint/Acct from the menu title at the top of the screen. The menu shown in Figure 3-1 is displayed.
3. Select **P**rint Register.

Alternatively, pressing (Ctrl)-(P) opens the Print Register window directly, without first going through the Print/Acct menu. Figure 3-2 shows the Print Register window. Depending on your installation selections, your screen may show different printer options.

4. Type **1/1/93** and press (Enter).

This entry selects the first transaction to be printed by date.

5. Type **1/31/93** and press (Enter).

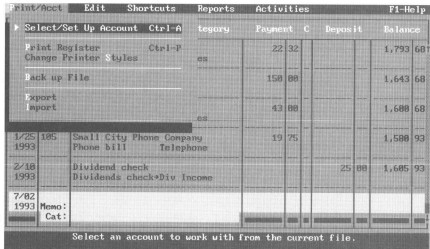

Print/Acct menu

Figure 3-1.

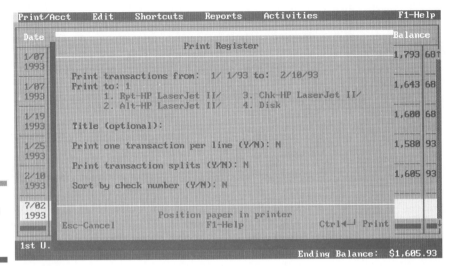

This entry establishes the last transaction to be printed. The dates
supplied in steps 4 and 5 are inclusive; that is, Quicken will print all
register transactions with dates from 1/1/93 through 1/31/93.

6. Select 1, for Report Printer, and press (Enter) to tell Quicken where to
   print the output from the print operation.

This is the default option—the selection Quicken makes unless you
designate another option. You have the ability to print to three
different printers: (1) a report printer, (2) an alternate report printer (a
second printer or a different print option for the first printer, such as
landscape or compressed), or (3) a check printer. Quicken allows you to
select different print options for different types of output. Thus, for a
quick draft of a report you might select the alternate printer, a
high-speed device of marginal quality, and later choose a report printer
to print the final copy on a laser printer. You will learn how to select
these printing options in the "Changing the Printer Settings" section
later in the chapter.

Selecting option 4, Disk, creates an ASCII text file for exporting
Quicken data to other computer programs. You would use the Disk
option if you wanted to use the data from the register in your word
processor or some other program that can read ASCII text files.

7. Type **January Transactions** and press (Enter).

This customizes the title of the check register. If you do not make an entry in this field, Quicken uses the default option Check Register for the report heading. You can use up to 36 characters to customize your heading.

8. Press (Enter).

This selects Quicken's default option to allow three lines for each transaction Quicken prints. If you want to have more transactions printed on each page, type **Y** and press (Enter). This option prints the document using only one line per transaction by abbreviating the information printed.

9. Press (Enter).

You can ignore the prompt about transaction splits. This type of transaction is introduced in Chapter 6, "Expanding the Scope of Financial Entries." For now, leave the default setting as N. This is another default option. Quicken prints the register in order by date and then by check number. If you wanted to first sort by check number and then by date, you would type **Y** and press (Enter). If you are writing checks from two different checkbooks, changing this option can affect the order in which transactions are listed.

10. Press (Ctrl)-(Enter).

Once you have completed the Print Register window, Quicken is ready to print the check register for the period you defined. Make sure your printer is turned on and ready to print before completing this entry.

Your printed register should look like the sample transactions shown in Figure 3-3. Notice that the date at the top-left corner of your report is the current date, regardless of the month for which you are printing transactions.

Printing the Cash Flow Report

The Cash Flow report generated by Quicken compares the money you have received during a specified time period with the money you have

```
                         January Transactions
1st U.S. Bank                                              Page 1
6/30/93


Date   Num        Transaction       Payment  C  Deposit    Balance
-----  -----  --------------------  ---------  -  ----------  ---------
1/01          Opening Balance                 X  1,200.00  1,200.00
1993 memo:
        cat: [1st U.S. Bank]


1/04   100    Small City Gas & Light    67.50              1,132.50
1993 memo: Gas and Electric
        cat: Utilities


1/05   101    Small City Times          16.50              1,116.00
1993 memo: Paper bill
        cat: Misc


1/07          Deposit-Salary                        700.00  1,816.00
1993 memo: Monthly pay
        cat: Salary


1/07   102    Small City Market         22.32              1,793.68
1993 memo: Food
        cat: Groceries


1/07   103    Small City Apartments    150.00              1,643.68
1993 memo: Rent
        cat: Housing


1/19   104    Small City Market         43.00              1,600.68
1993 memo: Food
        cat: Groceries


1/25   105    Small City Phone Company 19.75              1,580.93
1993 memo: Phone bill
        cat: Telephone
```

1st U.S. Bank
checking
account
register
printout
Figure 3-3.

spent. Quicken provides this information for each category used in the
register. In addition, the Cash Flow report will combine transactions
from your Bank, Cash, and Credit Card accounts. (Cash and Credit
Card accounts are discussed in Chapter 6.) Preparing the Cash Flow
report for the transactions you recorded in the 1st U.S. Bank account in
Chapter 2, "Making Register Entries," involves the following steps from
the Main Menu:

3

1. Select **C**reate Reports.

You can also access the Reports menu directly from the register by selecting the menu title **R**eports. You will see a pull-down menu offering options for standard personal, business, and investments reports as well as custom reports.

2. Select **P**ersonal Reports from the Reports menu.

Quicken then allows you to define the type of report you want from the pull-down menu added to the screen.

3. Select **C**ash Flow. You will see the Cash Flow Report window, as shown here:

```
                          Cash Flow Report

     Report title (optional):

     Report on months from:   1/93 through:   7/93

 Esc-Cancel          F7-Layout  F8-Options  F9-Filter        ←┘ Continue
```

4. **Cash Flow Report** - and your name, and then press [Enter].

If you press [Enter] without making an entry, Quicken uses the default title for the report. With this report, the default title is "Cash Flow Report." If you choose to personalize the report, you can use up to 39 characters for a report title.

5. Press [+] or [−] or one of the other keys discussed in Chapter 2, "Making Register Entries," to change your beginning report date to 1/93, and press [Enter].

Quicken automatically places the beginning of the current year's date in this space. You need to decide whether to press [+] or [−], depending on the current date in your system.

6. Press either [+] or [−] to change your report ending date to 1/93.

It is important to note that Quicken is designed to generate reports for an entire month. In this example, Quicken prepares the Cash Flow report for transactions recorded for the month of January 1993. If you want to prepare a report for less than a full month, you need to modify the Quicken settings in order to override the default period of one month. You learn how to make this modification in Chapter 6, "Expanding the Scope of Financial Entries."

7. Press (Enter), and the Cash Flow report appears on your screen.

Notice that the entire report does not appear on your screen.

8. Press ↓ to bring the rest of the report to the screen.

Notice the Cash Flow report has inflows and outflows listed by category.

9. Move the highlight to the outflow for groceries.

10. Press (Ctrl)-(Z) to use Quicken 6's Zoom feature, which lets you look at the transactions that make up the 65.32 shown for groceries. The screen in Figure 3-4 shows the grocery transactions displayed with the Zoom feature.

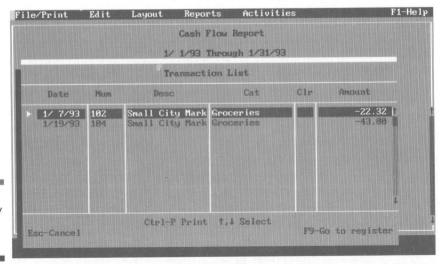

Using Quicken's new Zoom feature

Figure 3-4.

11. Press [Esc] to return to the report.

You can continue to examine the details for any of the entries and then print the report when you are finished.

12. Select the **F**ile/Print menu and then select **P**rint Report.

This brings the Print Report window to your screen. You need to select the type of printer you are using. The default option is the standard report printer.

3

NOTE: [Ctrl]-[P] is the Quick key for printing without menu selections.

13. Press [Enter] to select the Report Printer default option. The report shown in Figure 3-5 is printed.

```
                       Cash Flow Report - Mary Campbell
                          1/ 1/93 Through 1/31/93
 1st U.S. Bank                                              Page 1
 6/30/93
                                              1/ 1/93-
                        Category Description   1/31/93
                        --------------------- ----------
                        INFLOWS
                           Salary Income         700.00
                                              ----------
                        TOTAL INFLOWS            700.00

                        OUTFLOWS
                           Groceries              65.32
                           Housing               150.00
                           Miscellaneous          16.50
                           Telephone Expense      19.75
                           Water, Gas, Electric   67.50
                                              ----------
                        TOTAL OUTFLOWS           319.07
                                              ----------
                        OVERALL TOTAL            380.93
                                              ==========
```

Standard Cash
Flow report
Figure 3-5.

You have the option of having Quicken send the Cash Flow report to (1) the report printer, (2) an alternate report printer, (3) a check printer, (4) a disk, as an ASCII file, or (5) a disk, as a 1-2-3 file. If you need to customize any of the printer settings, press F9 (Set Up Printer) before accepting any of the options. This lets you specify a custom report printer or alternate report printer and then select this new option from the menu. Use ↓ or ↑ to select the printer options listed.

14. To leave the report, press Esc until you get to the Main Menu.

Redoing the Last Report

Quicken remembers the last report that you defined and lets you redo it easily, whether you have zoomed in to focus on detail or added transactions. The following steps demonstrate how you can view the Cash Flow report from the Main Menu with Quicken 6's new Redo Last Report feature:

1. Select **C**reate Reports.
2. Select **R**edo Last Report.

Presto!—the Cash Flow report reappears on your screen.

Printing the Itemized Categories Report

The Itemized Categories report lists and summarizes all the transactions for each category used in the register during a specific time period. Although here you will be using this report to work only with the information in the 1st U.S. Bank checking account, the report is much more sophisticated than it may appear. It summarizes information from your Bank, Cash, and Credit Card accounts and, unlike the Cash Flow report, also incorporates category information from Other Asset and Other Liability accounts, which you will establish in Chapter 6, "Expanding the Scope of Financial Entries."

You can print your Itemized Categories report by following these steps (starting from the Main Menu):

1. Select **C**reate Reports.
2. Select **P**ersonal Reports.

3. Select **I**temized Categories.
4. If the title field of the Itemized Categories Report window is blank, press (Enter). If not, press (Ctrl)-(Backspace) until the existing title is erased, and then press (Enter).

This action selects the Quicken default title of "Itemized Category Report." You could also personalize the report title by typing **Itemized Category Report** - and your name and pressing (Enter).

3

5. Type **1/93** and press (Enter).

Quicken automatically places in this window either the current year's beginning date or the date of the last report you created. You could also change the date with the special date change keys, such as (+) and (-).

6. Type **1/93**.

This tells Quicken to create a report of itemized categories through the end of January.

7. Press (Enter).

This brings the Itemized Categories report to the screen. You can scroll down the report by using (↓).

8. Press (Ctrl)-(P).

This opens the Print Report window on your screen.

9. Press (Enter) to print the Itemized Categories report.

You have the same options here that you had with the Cash Flow report. By pressing (Enter), you select the Report printer option. Once again, you could have selected printing to an alternate report printer or a check printer, or creating an ASCII file or a 1-2-3 file. Pressing (Enter) prints the Itemized Categories report. Note that the report is two pages long. If your printer has the compressed print capacity, you may want to print your reports in that mode to capture more of the report on each page. The top of page 1 of the Itemized Categories report is shown in Figure 3-6.

```
                         ITEMIZED CATEGORY REPORT
                          1/ 1/93 Through 1/31/93
        1st U.S. Bank                                          Page 1
        6/30/93

         Date   Num      Description      Memo     Category   Clr  Amount
         ----  ------  ----------------  --------  ---------  -  --------

                INCOME/EXPENSE
                  INCOME
                    Salary Income
                    -------------
          1/ 7        Deposit-Salary   Monthly pay  Salary       700.00
                                                                --------
                      Total Salary Income                        700.00
                                                                --------
                  TOTAL INCOME                                   700.00


                  EXPENSES
                    Groceries
                    ---------
          1/ 7 102    Small City Market   Food      Groceries    -22.32
          1/19 104    Small City Market   Food      Groceries    -43.00
                                                                --------
                      Total Groceries                            -65.32
```

Itemized
Categories
report
Figure 3-6.

10. To leave the report, press [Esc] until you are in the Main Menu.

Format Options with the Cash Flow and Itemized Categories Reports

When printing both the Cash Flow and Itemized Categories reports, you have several customization options. These are not like the custom reports discussed in later chapters, since you can make only limited modifications. In most situations these options will meet your needs, but remember that you can access help on each of the options once you open the Customizing window. Just as in other areas of Quicken, you get help by pressing [F1].

Although the customizing options for the reports require a little time to learn, the end result can be a dramatic difference in the appearance and content of the reports. Since the customization options for the Cash

Flow and Itemized Categories reports are similar, the important options are covered together. You can use them to change the labeling information on the report as well as the basic organization of the entries.

Changing the Column Headings

3

Quicken allows you to change the column headings on both the Itemized Categories and Cash Flow reports. You can print a report for the standard monthly time period or change it to one week, two weeks, half a month, a quarter, half a year, or one year. You make this change from the Create Summary Report window, shown in Figure 3-7. Figure 3-8 shows a report created with time periods used as the column headings.

Follow these steps to create a Cash Flow report showing weekly time periods (starting from the Main Menu):

1. Select **C**reate Report.
2. Select **P**ersonal Reports.
3. Select **C**ash Flow.

Create Summary Report window to customize a Cash Flow report
Figure 3-7.

```
Print/Acct    Edit    Shortcuts    Reports    Activities         F1-Help
                     Create Summary Report                              e
                                                                       681
    Report title (optional): Cash Flow - Dave Campbell
                                                                       --
    Restrict to transactions from:  1/ 1/93 through:  1/31/93         68
                                                                       --
    Row headings (down the left side): 1
         1. Category          3. Payee                                 68
         2. Class             4. Account
                                                                       --
    Column headings (across the top): 1                               93
         1. Don't Subtotal    5. Month          9. Category
         2. Week              6. Quarter       10. Class               --
         3. Two Weeks         7. Six Months    11. Payee               93
         4. Half Month        8. Year          12. Account
                                                                       --
    Use Current/All/Selected accounts (C/A/S): S

  Esc-Cancel            F8-Options  F9-Filter              ← Continue
 1
                                              Ending Balance:  $1,605.93
```

```
                      Cash Flow - Dave Campbell
                      1/ 1/93 Through 1/31/93
1st U.S.Bank                                              Page 1
7/ 2/93
                                      1/01-     1/16-   OVERALL
                Category Description    1/15      1/31    TOTAL
          ---------------------- --------- --------- ---------

          INFLOWS
            Salary Income          700.00      0.00   700.00
                                 --------- --------- ---------

          TOTAL INFLOWS            700.00      0.00   700.00


          OUTFLOWS
            Groceries               22.32     43.00    65.32
            Housing                150.00      0.00   150.00
            Miscellaneous           16.50      0.00    16.50
            Telephone Expense        0.00     19.75    19.75
            Water, Gas, Electric    67.50      0.00    67.50
                                 --------- --------- ---------

          TOTAL OUTFLOWS           256.32     62.75   319.07


                                 --------- --------- ---------
          OVERALL TOTAL           443.68    -62.75   380.93
                                 ========= ========= =========
```

Weekly report
for cash flow
Figure 3-8.

4. Type **Cash Flow** - and your name and press (Enter).

5. Type **1/93** and press (Enter).

You can just press (Enter) if you used this same time period for your last report.

6. Type **1/93** again.

Pressing (Enter) creates the report without customizing.

7. Press (F7) (Layout) to open the Create Summary Report window.

Quicken responds to your request by displaying the Create Summary Report window shown in Figure 3-7. Notice that the heading and the dates from the previous screen are still displayed. You can make further changes if needed or press (Enter) four times to move to the Column Headings field.

3

8. Select Half Month.

In addition to the time period, you can include either the payee or the category if you wish (but not both).

9. Type **A** to select **A**ll accounts for the last option in the window.
10. Press (Enter) to continue.

Quicken displays the completed report on the screen. Figure 3-8 shows the result of the preceding steps.

Changing the Row Headings

The Create Summary Report window shown in Figure 3-7 also allows you to change the row headings shown in a Cash Flow or Itemized Categories report. Instead of categories as row headings, as in Figure 3-8, one of your options is to change the screen to show the payee in this location. Figure 3-9 shows the report created after changing the Row Headings field to option 3, Payee, and the column heading back to the default, 1.

You can make your changes from the menu at the top of the report. To change the row headings, you would select **L**ayout, select **R**ow Heading, and then select **P**ayee. Changing the column headings requires you to select **L**ayout, Column **H**eadings, and **O**ne Column.

```
                            Cash Flow - Dave Campbell
                            1/ 1/93 Through 1/31/93
         1st U.S. Bank                                           Page 1
         6/30/93

                                                    1/ 1/93-
                                Payee                1/31/93
                         --------------------------  -----------
                         Deposit-Salary                 700.00
                         Small City Apartments         -150.00
                         Small City Gas & Light         -67.50
                         Small City Market              -65.32
                         Small City Phone Company       -19.75
                         Small City Times               -16.50
                                                     -----------
                         OVERALL TOTAL                  380.93
                                                     ===========
```

Using payee
names as row
headings
Figure 3-9.

Changing the Report Options

You can also access a second set of options from the Create Summary Report window by pressing F8 (Options) to display the Report Options window for the Cash Flow report. The options allow you to select report organization and determine how transfers are handled. The Report Options window for the Itemized Categories report has a few more items at the bottom than the Cash Flow report, as shown in Figure 3-10.

The Report Organization field allows you to change from the default organization of separate totals for income and expenses to one that shows the cash flow basis.

The Transfers field allows you to define how you want your reports to handle transfers between accounts. For example, when Quicken transfers cash from your check register to your savings register, do you want these transfers included or excluded from the individual reports? Transfers will be covered in more detail in Chapter 10, "Creating Custom Reports."

The extra items at the bottom of the Report Options window for the Itemized Categories report allow you to specify that any combination

Report Options window for Itemized Categories report
Figure 3-10.

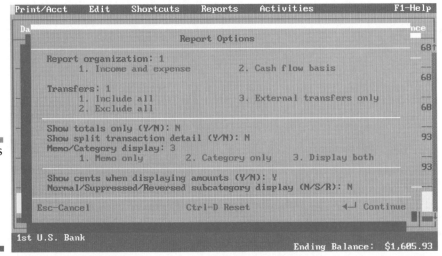

of totals, memos, and categories, or any one of these alone, is shown on the report. Notice that you have the option of showing cents and subcategories in the report form. The default setting for cents is Y. For subcategories, the default setting is N for Normal, which causes subcategories to display.

3

Filtering Reports

Filters allow you to select the data to be shown on a report. You will want to read the overview that follows and then do the exercise at the end for practice with filters. You can choose to show a specific payee, memo field matches, or category matches. This allows you to create a report for all entries relating to utilities or groceries, for example. You can use a standard report form to display a report for a specific payee, such as Small City Times, or you can enter **Small** to locate records that contain "Small". You open the Filter Report menus from the report menus by pressing the F9 key.

If you want to customize Quicken to find only records that exactly match your entries, you can select Set **P**references and then select **T**ransaction Settings. You need to set option 7, Exact matches on finds and filters, to Y.

The Filter Report option (on the Create Summary Report menu) for the Itemized Categories Report window is shown in Figure 3-11. The window currently shows "Small" in the Payee field. Processing this request will create a report of all the records with a Payee entry beginning with "Small". This item allows you to modify the printed report further by limiting the report to transactions meeting the following criteria: payee, memo, category, and class.

The Filter Transactions window provides many additional options. You can designate whether to include transactions below, equal to, or above a designated amount. To do this, move to the item Below/Equal /Above by pressing Enter or Tab, typing **B**, **E**, or **A**, and pressing Enter again. Next, you would enter the amount to be used in the comparison and press Enter.

The next field on the Filter Transactions window allows you to limit printing to payments, deposits, unprinted checks, or all if you enter a **P**, a **D**, a **U**, or an **A** in this field.

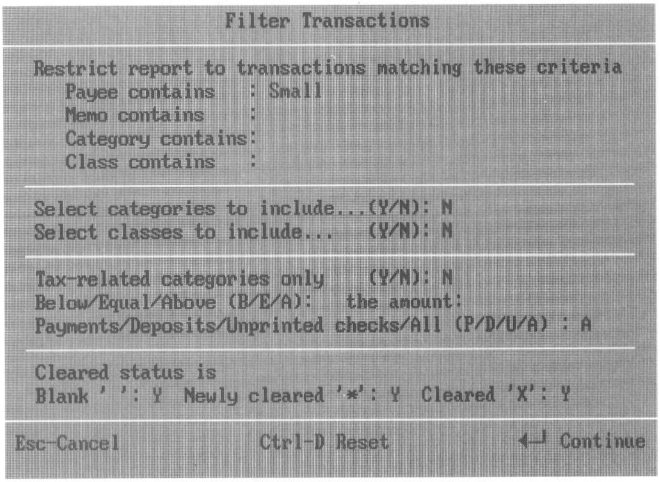

```
                        Filter Transactions

        Restrict report to transactions matching these criteria
             Payee contains    : Small
             Memo contains     :
             Category contains :
             Class contains    :

        Select categories to include...(Y/N): N
        Select classes to include...    (Y/N): N

        Tax-related categories only     (Y/N): N
        Below/Equal/Above (B/E/A):   the amount:
        Payments/Deposits/Unprinted checks/All (P/D/U/A) : A

        Cleared status is
        Blank ' ': Y  Newly cleared '*': Y  Cleared 'X': Y

   Esc-Cancel             Ctrl-D Reset            ←┘ Continue
```

Filter
Transactions
window for
Itemized
Categories
report
Figure 3-11.

Try Quicken's Filter feature now to create a Cash Flow report for all the transactions that begin with "Small" in the Payee field. From the Main Menu, complete the following steps:

1. Select **C**reate Reports.
2. Select **P**ersonal Reports.
3. Select **C**ash Flow.
4. Type a new title and press (Enter) or press (Enter) without an entry to accept the current title.
5. Check the From and Through dates and type **1/93** if either date does not contain this entry.
6. Press (F9) to activate the Filter window.
7. Type **Small** and press (Ctrl)-(Enter) to return to the Cash Flow Report window.
8. Press (Enter) until the report is created.

Since it shows categories for the row headings, you cannot tell if the correct information is displayed, but you can make a customization to have Quicken list the payee names. With Quicken 6 you can use the menu at the top of the report to make your changes.

9. Select the **L**ayout menu option and then select **R**ow Headings.

10. Select Payee and press (Enter).

11. Press (Esc) until you are back at the Main Menu.

Working with Category Totals

You can create an Itemized Categories report that only shows the totals. To create a total report for January transactions, follow these steps (starting from the Main Menu):

1. Select **C**reate Reports.

2. Select **P**ersonal Reports.

3. Select **I**temized Categories.

4. Press (Enter) to accept the default title.

5. Type **1/93** and press (Enter) for the date if the field does not already contain 1/93. Type **1/93** for the Through date, if it contains a different entry.

6. Press (F7) to open the Create Transaction Report window.

7. Press (F8) to open the Report Options window.

8. Press (Enter) or (Tab) to move to Show totals only and type **Y**.

9. Press (Ctrl)-(Enter) to return to the Create Transaction Report window.

10. Press (Ctrl)-(Enter) again to create the report.

Wide Reports

Some of the Quicken reports contain too much information to fit across one screen. You encountered a wide-screen report in this chapter when you prepared the Itemized Categories report. Although you cannot see the entire report on the screen at once, you can use the arrow keys to navigate around the screen and change the portion of the report that you are viewing.

Quicken automatically prints wide reports on multiple pages. You can tape the sheets together, or if your printer permits, you can use special features such as landscape printing (with the paper turned sideways) on a laser printer, or compressed characters on laser or dot-matrix printers. You will learn how to make these changes to the print settings momentarily. For now, all you need to know is how Quicken handles a report that is too wide for the screen and how you navigate to look at the different parts of the screen.

You can tell when you are viewing a wide report by the border framing that Quicken uses. When a complete report is shown, all the edges are framed. When only a partial report is displayed, the edges where there is additional information do not have a frame. When you initially view a wide report, there is no frame on the right edge. You will notice the arrows displayed in the lower-right corner of the screen, indicating the report extension.

Moving Around the Screen

You can move around the report by using the arrow keys. In addition, you may want to move quickly around the report by using several other Quicken keystrokes.

✦ Press [Tab] to move one field to the right.

✦ Press [Shift]-[Tab] to move one field to the left.

✦ Press [Pg Up] to move up one screen.

✦ Press [Pg Dn] to move down one screen

✦ Press [Home] twice to move to the upper-left corner of the report.

✦ Press [End] twice to move to the lower-right corner of the report.

✦ Remember you can also use the scroll bars at the side and bottom of a report if you are using a mouse.

Full- and Half-Column Options

The Itemized Categories report allows you to view the Payee, Memo, and Category fields at full or half width. Figure 3-12 shows the report at the default half-column width setting. This allows the report to print across 80 columns and to display on the screen. To expand the columns to full width select **L**ayout, then Full Column **W**idth. Once the columns are shown at full width, selecting **L**ayout followed by Half Column **W**idth returns the columns to half width. This kind of key is called a *toggle*.

```
File/Print    Edit    Layout    Reports    Activities              F1-Help

                        Itemized Category Report
                        1/ 1/93 Through 1/31/93
    1st U.S. Bank
    7/ 2/93

    Date    Num    Description         Memo        Category    Clr Amount

            INCOME/EXPENSE
             INCOME
              Salary Income

    1/ 7        Deposit-Salary      Monthly pay   Salary          700.00

           Total Salary Income                                    700.00

        TOTAL INCOME                                              700.00

    1st U.S. Bank
    Esc-Leave report
```

Using the default half-column width display for the Itemized Category report **Figure 3-12.**

Printing Wide Reports

Quicken normally prints wide reports by printing in vertical strips, which you can then tape together. You do not have to modify your printing instructions in order to print wide reports.

If your printer supports compressed or landscape printing, you can capture more of a report on a page by using one of these features. Landscape mode prints 104 characters across an 11- by 8 1/2-inch page and compressed print prints 132 characters on an 8 1/2- by 11-inch page (at 10 characters per inch). You can use the Set **P**references option in the Main Menu, or, when the report is displayed on the screen, go to the Print Report window by selecting **F**ile/Print, selecting **P**rint Report, pressing F9 (Set Up Printer), selecting Settings for Printing Reports, and choosing a style with more characters per inch (cpi) or Landscape printing.

Changing the Printer Settings

Unless you want to use a special feature or the current settings are not working properly, you can skip this section. If you choose to go through this section, be sure to have your printer manual handy to check the specific features offered by your printer.

Quicken allows you to set printer parameters for up to three printers or to set up one printer to interface with Quicken in three different modes: the report printer, an alternate report printer, and a check writing printer. The procedure is identical for modifying any of these options once you choose the one you want to change.

As discussed earlier, during installation you can select from many popular printers. The preset parameters for a printer are for pitch, paper size, and the parallel printer port 1.

You can change the printer settings by selecting Set **P**references from Quicken's Main Menu and then selecting **P**rinter Settings to alter the print settings. Another way to accomplish the same task is to select **F**ile/Print, and then **P**rint Report to open the Print Report window when a Quicken report is displayed on your screen, and then press [F9] (Set Up Printer). The menus and screens presented will be identical either way. The following example was developed by changing the settings once the report was displayed on the screen.

Once you have a Quicken report displayed, follow these steps to change the print settings:

1. Select **F**ile/Print and then **P**rint Report to open the Print Report window.

Quicken displays the Print Report window shown here:

```
                        Print Report

   Print to: 1
         1. Rpt-HP LaserJet II╱   4. Disk (ASCII file)
         2. Alt-HP LaserJet II╱   5. Disk (1-2-3 file)
         3. Chk-HP LaserJet II╱

                   Position paper in printer
   Esc-Cancel        F9-Set Up Printer              ◄┘ Print
```

If you want to print with one of the default settings, choose option 1 or 2.

2. Press [F9] (Set Up Printer).

From this step on, you will not be able to make the same entries shown in the example. Since each printer is different, you will want to

3

configure Quicken to work with your printer rather than the printer used here. Quicken displays a list of the three printer settings that can be changed: Printing Checks, Printing Reports, and Alternate Printing Reports.

3. Select settings for Printing Reports.

Quicken displays a list of printers and their available styles. You can move in this list with the arrow keys to locate the style you want or press Esc and select another printer from the list, as shown in Figure 3-13. If you select a style with more characters per inch or landscape mode (or both), Quicken alters the report display to correspond to your selection.

4. If you want to change the style, move the cursor to the desired option and press Enter. Quicken displays a screen like the one in Figure 3-14. The default is to print to LPT1, which is the standard port on your machine for connecting the first printer. If you are setting up a second printer, you need to know whether it is attached to LPT2 or some other port. Other settings let you set the lines per page, characters per line, print pitch, and a pause between

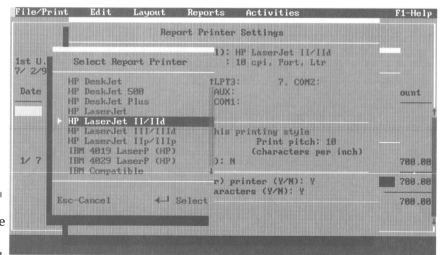

Selecting a
printer and style
Figure 3-13.

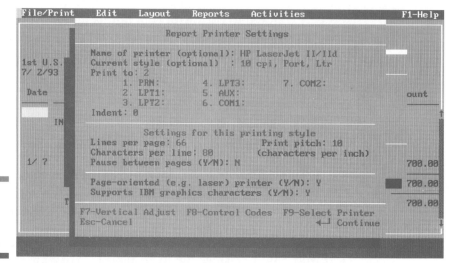

Choosing
specific print
settings
Figure 3-14.

pages. Table 3-1 lists some hints for altering these settings,
although your printer manual will be your specific reference source.

Problem	Solution
Output too wide for a page	Use compressed or landscape mode
No form feed at the end of the report	Change the print control codes
Partial blank page left in printer	Check the page length
Unreadable output	Wrong printer is selected
Strange characters print	Printer cable is loose or incorrect printer type selected
Unable to access font cartridges	Set control codes for desired print options

Printing
Problems and
Possible
Solutions
Table 3-1.

NOTE: If you wanted to change the printer rather than the style, you would press Esc, select a new printer, select a style, and press Enter.

3

5. Press F8 (Control Codes) to display the control codes that are transmitted to your printer every time you print.

Figure 3-15 provides an example of printer control codes generated by Quicken for the HP LaserJet II. You can change these codes to use different fonts, line widths, and so on. Knowing which codes to use is a bit tricky unless you are familiar with your printer manual. Each manufacturer uses different codes to represent the various print features. For now, press Enter to move through them without making changes or press Esc. Quicken takes you back to the Report Printer Settings window.

6. Press Ctrl-Enter to view the Print Report window.
7. Type the number of the printer you wish to use and press Enter.

HP LaserJet II control codes generated by Quicken
Figure 3-15.

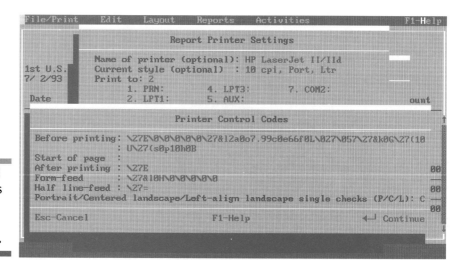

CHAPTER

4

RECONCILING YOUR QUICKEN REGISTER

Reconciling your account is the process of comparing your entries with those of the bank. This allows you to determine whether differences between the bank's record of your balance and your record are due to errors or timing differences. Timing differences occur because your balance is accurate up to the present date but the bank records were compiled at an earlier date before transactions you have recorded cleared the bank. These timing differences must be reconciled to ensure there is no discrepancy caused by an error. If you are serious about monitoring your financial activities, a monthly reconciliation of your checking accounts, both personal and business, should be considered a necessary step in your financial record keeping.

In addition to timing differences, there may be transactions not recorded in your register or errors in the amount entries. With manual check registers, there can also be addition and subtraction errors when checks and deposits are recorded. This is one type of error you do not need to worry about with Quicken since its calculations are always perfect if you record the amount correctly.

Another cause of differences is transactions the bank has recorded on your bank statement that you haven't entered in your register. For example, you may have automatic monthly withdrawals for house or automobile payments or savings transfers to another bank account or mutual fund. In addition, you may have a bank service charge for maintaining your checking account or printing checks, or you may have earned interest. These differences are addressed in more detail throughout this chapter.

In this chapter you will look at how reconciliation works and walk through a reconciliation exercise. The last part of the chapter deals with problems that can occur and the methods for getting your account to agree with your bank's records. This part of the chapter does not require entries, since it is designed to show potential problems rather than additional corrections to your entries.

Quicken's Reconciliation Process

Quicken reduces the frustration of the monthly reconciliation process by providing a systematic approach to reconciling your checking accounts. Since there are more steps in this process than in the exercises you have completed so far, looking at some overview information first will help you place each of the steps in perspective to the overall objective of the process.

A Few Key Points

There are three points to remember when using the Quicken reconciliation system. First, Quicken reconciles only one checking account at a time, so you have to reconcile each of your personal and business accounts separately.

Second, you should make it a habit to reconcile your checking accounts on a monthly basis. You can easily monitor your checking balances once you begin a monthly routine of reconciling your accounts, but attempting to reconcile six months of statements at one sitting is a frustrating experience, even with Quicken.

Third, before beginning the formal Quicken reconciliation process, visually examine your bank statement and look for any unusual entries, such as check numbers that are out of the range of numbers you expected to find on the statement. (If you find checks 501 and 502 clearing, while all the rest of the checks are numbered in the 900s, you might find the bank has charged another customer's checks against your account.) This examination provides an indication of what to look for during the reconciliation process.

4

An Overview of the Process

When you begin reconciliation, Quicken asks for information from your current bank statement, such as the opening and ending dollar balances, service charges, and any interest earned on your account. (Quicken also records these transactions in the check register and marks them as cleared since the bank has already processed these items.)

Once you have entered this preparatory information, Quicken presents a summary screen for marking cleared items. All the transactions you recorded in the 1st U.S. Bank account, as well as the service charge and interest-earned transactions, are shown on this screen.

Quicken maintains a running total of your balance as you proceed through the reconciliation process. Each debit or credit is applied to the opening balance total as it is marked cleared. You can determine the difference between the cleared balance amount and the bank statement balance at any time. Your end objective is a difference of zero.

The first step is to check the amounts of your Quicken entries against the bank statement. Where there are discrepancies, you can switch to your Quicken register and check the entries. You may find incorrect amounts recorded in the Quicken register or by your bank. You may also find that you forgot to record a check or a deposit. You can create or change register entries from the Register window.

Once you have finished with the entry, you put an asterisk (*) in the C column to mark the transaction as cleared. After resolving any differences between your balance and the bank's, you can print the reconciliation reports. The asterisks are used in the cleared column until Quicken confirms an entry. Then Quicken automatically replaces them with an X, which you will see as this lesson proceeds.

Preparing the Printer for Reconciliation

Before you begin reconciliation, you should check your printer settings. This is important because at the end of the reconciliation process, you are given an opportunity to print reconciliation reports. You can't change printer settings after Quicken presents you with the Print Reconciliation Report window; it's too late. If you attempt to make a change by pressing (Esc), you are returned to the Main Menu and have to start over. However, you will not need to complete the detailed reconciliation procedure again.

Use Set Preferences in the Main Menu to check your printer settings now. When you return to the Main Menu, you will be ready to start the reconciliation example.

A Sample Reconciliation

From reading about the objectives of the reconciliation process, you should understand its concept. Actually doing a reconciliation will fit the pieces together. The following exercise uses a sample bank statement and the entries you made to your register in Chapter 2, "Making Register Entries." These steps assume you are starting from the Main Menu:

1. Select Use Register.

You should be in the 1st U.S. Bank register with the entries created in Chapter 2.

2. Select Activities.

Quicken displays the pull-down Activities menu shown here:

3. Select Reconcile to enter Quicken's reconciliation system and press F10 if this is your first reconciliation.

You see the Reconcile Register with Bank Statement window, shown in Figure 4-1. Figure 4-2 is a copy of your first bank statement from 1st U.S. Bank; you will use it to respond to Quicken's prompts for information.

The first time you reconcile an account, Quicken automatically enters the opening balance shown in the register. Since you are reconciling

Reconcile
Register with
Bank Statement
window
Figure 4-1.

1st U.S. Bank				DATE 2/5/93
P.O. Box 123				PAGE 1 OF 1
Small City, USA				

John D. Quick
P.O. Box ABC
Small City, USA

DATE	DESCRIPTION	AMOUNT	BALANCE
1-1	Deposit	1,200.00	1,200.00
1-6	100 check	77.50-	1,122.50
1-7	Deposit	700.00	1,822.50
1-11	101 check	16.50-	1,806.00
1-12	103 check	150.00-	1,656.00
1-20	102 check	22.32-	1,633.68
2-1	Loan payment deduction	225.00-	1,408.68
2-1	Service charge	11.50-	1,397.18
2-1	Interest	1.03	1,398.21

Date	Check	No.	Amount
1-6	#	100	77.50-
1-11	#	101	16.50-
1-20	#	102	22.32-
1-12	#	103	150.00-

Bank statement
for 1st U.S.
Bank account
Figure 4-2.

STATEMENT

your account with the first monthly bank statement, this should be the balance on your screen.

4. Type **1398.21** and press (Enter) to complete the Bank Statement Ending Balance field.
5. Type **1/1/93** and press (Enter).
6. Type **2/1/93** and press (Enter).
7. Type **11.50** and press (Enter) to complete the Service Charge field.

You must enter all the service and similar charges in a lump sum. In this case, the bank has a monthly service charge and a check printing charge that total 11.50 (3.50 + 8.00). Although it is easy enough to add these two simple numbers in your head, if you need to compute a more complex addition, you can always call up the Calculator with (Ctrl)-(O). You would type the first number you want to add, press (+), then type the next number, and so on. You can transfer the total into a numeric field on the screen with (F9) (Paste).

8. Type **Bank Chrg** and press (Enter).

Entering a category is optional; however, to take full advantage of Quicken's reporting features, you should use a category for all transactions.

9. Type **2/1/93** as a date for the bank charge and press (Enter).
10. Type **1.03** and press (Enter) to complete the Interest Earned field.
11. Type **Int Inc** and press (Enter).
12. Type **2/1/93** and press (Enter).

The screen in Figure 4-3 appears. This is a summary screen where you will mark cleared items. It also shows totals at the bottom. You will find all your register entries and the new service charge and interest transactions in this window. If you press the (↓), you will see that the new transactions are marked as cleared with an asterisk in the C column. Also note that the cleared balance shown is your opening balance of 1200.00 modified by the two new transactions. Quicken also monitors the difference between this cleared total and the bank statement balance.

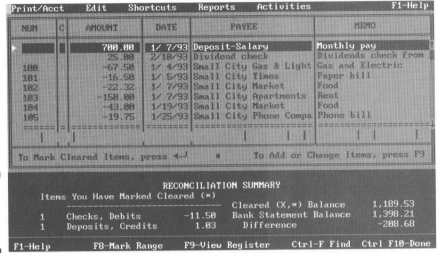

13. The cursor in the left margin points to the 1/7/93 deposit. Press
    ⟨Enter⟩ after verifying this is the amount shown on your bank
    statement.

Note that Quicken enters an * in the C column on this screen and also
in the C field of your check register.

14. Press ⟨↓⟩, and the arrow cursor points to the entry for check
    number 100. Since the bank statement entry and the summary
    entry do not agree, press ⟨F9⟩ (View Register).

You see the screen shown in Figure 4-4. The transaction for check
number 100 is highlighted in the 1st U.S. Bank register. If you looked at
your canceled check for this transaction, you would see that it was for
77.50 and that it cleared the bank for that amount. Since the register
entry is wrong, you must make a correction.

15. Press ⟨Shift⟩-⟨Tab⟩, type **77.50**, and press ⟨Enter⟩.

Because you pressed ⟨F9⟩ in the previous step, your cursor was in the C
column. Pressing ⟨Shift⟩-⟨Tab⟩ lines your cursor up with the beginning of
the payment field and allows you to enter the new figure.

```
Print/Acct    Edit     Shortcuts     Reports     Activities            F1-Help
 Date  Num    Payee  ·  Memo  ·  Category    Payment  C  Deposit    Balance
 1/04 100   Small City Gas & Light            67 50               1,132 50
 1993 Memo: Gas and Electric
      Cat: Utilities
 1/05 101   Small City Times                  16 50               1,116 00
 1993       Paper bill         Misc
 1/07       Deposit-Salary                          *    700 00   1,816 00
 1993       Monthly pay        Salary
 1/07 102   Small City Market                 22 32               1,793 68
 1993       Food               Groceries

                       RECONCILIATION SUMMARY
           Items You Have Marked Cleared (*)
                                        Cleared (X,*) Balance     1,889.53
        1    Checks, Debits     -11.50  Bank Statement Balance    1,398.21
        2    Deposits, Credits  701.03  Difference                 491.32
 Esc-Main Menu      F8-Mark Range       F9-View as List        Ctrl F10-Done
```

Check Register
window
Figure 4-4.

16. The cursor is now in the blank C column; type * and press (Enter).

17. Press (F9) (View as List) and select option 1 when you see the Leaving Transaction window.

Quicken enters the changes and returns to the Uncleared Transaction List window. Notice that you have corrected the amount to 77.50 and that Quicken indicates that the account has been reconciled by the * in the C column.

18. Press (F8) (Mark Range), and the Mark Range of Check Numbers as Cleared window appears.

This Quicken feature allows you to simultaneously mark a series of checks as having cleared the bank during the reconciling period, provided that the checks are consecutive. Before typing the range of checks to be cleared, remember to compare the amounts shown in the uncleared transaction list with the bank statement amounts. Marking a range of check numbers only works when the amounts are the same.

19. Type **101** and press (Enter).

20. Type **103** and press (Enter).

Your screen shows that 101 through 103 have had an asterisk added to the cleared column. Notice that your Difference amount is 225.00. When you check the bank statement, you might remember that this difference corresponds to the amount of the automatic deduction for an automobile loan you have with 1st U.S. Bank. Since this amount is not shown on your list of uncleared items, the transaction is not yet recorded in your register.

21. Press [F9] (View Register).
22. Press [Ctrl]-[End] to move to the end of the register, and then press [Home] twice to move to the first field.
23. Type **2/1/93** in the date column and press [Enter] twice.

You enter the date 2/1/93 in the date column so the transaction will be recorded on the same date that the bank deducted the amount from your account. You can record the date as the current date if you wish. Press [Enter] twice to move to the Payee field; since this is an automatic deduction, you don't use a check number.

24. Type **Automatic Loan Payment** in the Payee field and press [Enter].
25. Type **225** in the Payment field and press [Enter].
26. Type ***** in the C field and press [Enter].
27. Press [Enter] again to move the cursor to the Memo field.
28. Type **Auto payment** and press [Enter].
29. Press [Ctrl]-[C]. Press [↓] until the subcategory for Auto Loan is highlighted and press [Enter]. This step demonstrates how you can enter a category from Quicken's category list without typing a category name.
30. Press [Ctrl]-[Enter] to record the transaction.

The transaction is inserted in the correct date location in the register and the Difference field indicates that you have balanced your checking account for this month by showing an amount of 0.00. Figure 4-5 shows the transaction for the automatic loan payment and a difference of 0.00; you can complete the reconciliation from this screen or press [F9] (View as List) and return to the List of Uncleared Items screen and end the reconciliation process.

```
 Print/Acct     Edit      Shortcuts      Reports     Activities            F1-Help

  Date  Num     Payee  ·  Memo  ·  Category      Payment   C   Deposit    Balance

  1/25  105   Small City Phone Company          19 75              1,570 93↑
  1993        Phone bill          Telephone

  2/01        Automatic Loan Payment           225 00 *           1,345 93
  1993        Auto payment        Auto:Loan

  2/10        Dividend check                              25 00    1,370 93
  1993        Dividends check→Div Income

  2/01
  1993  Memo:
        Cat:

                          RECONCILIATION SUMMARY
          Items You Have Marked Cleared (*)
          ------------------------------------ Cleared (X,*) Balance    1,398.21
              6    Checks, Debits     -502.82   Bank Statement Balance   1,398.21
              2    Deposits, Credits   701.03   Difference                  0.00

 Esc-Main Menu        F8-Mark Range       F9-View as List        Ctrl F10-Done
```

Additional entries in the Check Register window
Figure 4-5.

4

31. Press [Ctrl]-[F10], and the Congratulations! Your Account Balances window appears.

32. Type **Y** and press [Enter]; the Print Reconciliation Report window, shown in Figure 4-6, appears. If you have not turned your printer on, you should do so now.

You must complete this window to print the reconciliation reports. As explained in the section preceding step 1, it is too late to change your printer settings at this point.

33. Select the desired printer and press [Enter].

34. Type **2/11/93** and press [Enter].

This changes the reconciliation date to conform to the example date.

35. Press [Enter] to accept the default heading for the report.

36. Type **F** and press [Enter] to select Full Report.

You have now completed your reconciliation process, and Quicken is printing your reconciliation reports.

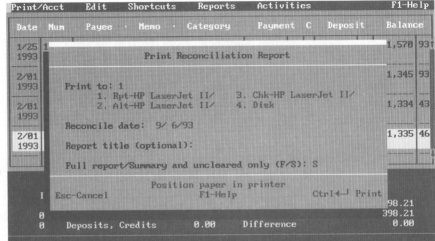

37. When printing stops, press Esc to close the Print Reconciliation
    Report window.

NOTE: If the automobile referred to in the reports is used for
business, the interest on loan payments for it is tax deductible
(with certain limitations).

Quicken's Reconciliation Reports

Since you selected Quicken's Full Report option, you have received four
reconciliation reports entitled "RECONCILIATION SUMMARY,"
"CLEARED TRANSACTION DETAIL," "UNCLEARED TRANSACTION
DETAIL UP TO 2/11/93," and "UNCLEARED TRANSACTION DETAIL
AFTER 2/11/93." Three of these reports are shown in Figures 4-7
through 4-9. (Note that spacing in these figures may differ from what
appears on your screen because adjustments were made to fit all of the
onscreen material onto these pages.)

The first page of the Reconciliation Summary report, shown in Figure
4-7, shows the beginning balance of 1,200.00 and summarizes the
activity the bank reported for your account during the reconciliation

```
                                Reconciliation Report
1st U.S. Bank                                                        Page 1
7/1/93
                                RECONCILIATION SUMMARY



        BANK STATEMENT -- CLEARED TRANSACTIONS:


                Previous Balance:                                  1,200.00
                                                               --------------
                    Checks and Payments:        6 Items           -502.82
                    Deposits and Other Credits: 2 Items            701.03
                                                               --------------
                Ending Balance of Bank Statement:                 1,398.21
        YOUR RECORDS -- UNCLEARED TRANSACTIONS:

                Cleared Balance:                                  1,398.21
                                                               -------------
                    Checks and Payments:        2 Items            -62.75
                    Deposits and Other Credits: 1 Item             25.00
                                                               -------------
                Register Balance as of  2/11/93:                 1,360.46
                                                               -------------

                    Checks and Payments:        0 Items             0.00
                    Deposits and Other Credits: 0 Items             0.00
                                                               -------------

                Register Ending Balance:                         1,360.46
```

Reconciliation Summary Report Figure 4-7.

period in the section labeled "BANK STATEMENT -- CLEARED TRANSACTIONS:". The first part of the section headed "YOUR RECORDS -- UNCLEARED TRANSACTIONS:" summarizes the difference between your register balance at the date of the reconciliation, 2/11/93, and the bank's balance. In this case, there are two checks that have been written and one deposit made to your account that were not shown on the bank statement. The report shows any checks and

```
1st U.S. Bank              Reconciliation Report              Page 2
9/6/93
                          CLEARED TRANSACTION DETAIL


 Date    Num      Payee            Memo            Category   Clr   Amount
-------  -----  ----------------  ----------------  ----------  ----  -----------


Cleared Checks and Payments

1/ 4/93 100    Small City Gas & Gas and Electri Utilities   X    -77.50
1/ 5/93 101    Small City Times Paper bill       Misc        X    -16.50
1/ 7/93 102    Small City Marke Food             Groceries   X    -22.32
1/ 7/93 103    Small City Apart Rent             Housing     X   -150.00
2/ 1/93        Automatic Loan P Auto payment     Auto:Loan   X   -225.00
2/ 1/93        Service Charge                    Bank Chrg   X    -11.50
                                                             ----------
Total Cleared Checks and Payments                 6 Items    -502.82



Cleared Deposits and Other Credits

1/ 7/93        Deposit-Salary   Monthly pay      Salary      X    700.00
2/ 1/93        Interest Earned                   Int Inc     X      1.03
                                                             ----------
Total Cleared Deposits and Other Credits          2 Items    701.03

                                                             ===========
Total Cleared Transactions                        8 Items    198.21
```

Cleared
Transaction
Detail report
Figure 4-8.

deposits recorded since the reconciliation date. In your sample
reconciliation, no transactions were entered after 2/11/93, so the
register balance at that date is also the register ending balance.

The CLEARED TRANSACTION DETAIL report, shown in Figure 4-8,
provides a detailed list with sections called "Cleared Checks and
Payments" and "Cleared Deposits and Other Credits"—the items they
contain were part of the reconciliation process. Notice that this report
provides detail for the CLEARED TRANSACTIONS section of the
RECONCILIATION SUMMARY report.

The UNCLEARED TRANSACTION DETAIL UP TO 2/11/93 report,
shown in Figure 4-9, in sections headed "Uncleared Checks and

```
1st U.S. Bank               Reconciliation Report          Page 2
9/6/93              UNCLEARED TRANSACTION DETAIL UP TO 2/11/93

Date    Num      Payee          Memo        Category   Clr   Amount
------- -----  --------------- ------------ ------------ ---- -----------
Uncleared Checks and Payments

1/19/93  104   Small City Marke Food         Groceries        -43.00
1/25/93  105   Small City Phone Phone bill   Telephone        -19.75
                                                           ---------
Total Uncleared Checks and Payments          2 Items         -62.75

Uncleared Deposits and Other Credits
2/10/93        Dividend check   Dividends check Div Income     25.00
                                                           ---------
Total Uncleared Deposits and Other Credits   1 Item           25.00
                                                           ===========
Total Uncleared Transactions                 3 Items         -37.75
```

Uncleared
Transaction
Detail Up to
2/11/93 report
Figure 4-9.

4

Payments" and "Uncleared Deposits and Other Credits," provides the
details of uncleared transactions included in your register up to the date
of the reconciliation. This report provides detail for the UNCLEARED
TRANSACTIONS section of the RECONCILIATION SUMMARY report.

The UNCLEARED TRANSACTION DETAIL AFTER 2/11/93 report (not
shown) provides detail for those transactions that are recorded in the
check register after the date of the reconciliation report. In this
illustration there were no transactions recorded; this is shown in the
final section of the RECONCILIATION SUMMARY report.

These four reports are all printed automatically when you select
Quicken's Full Report option. If you had selected Quicken's Summary
option, which is the default option, you would have received only the
RECONCILIATION SUMMARY report and the UNCLEARED
TRANSACTION DETAIL UP TO 2/11/93 report.

Additional Reconciliation Issues and Features

The reconciliation procedures shown earlier provide a foundation for
using Quicken to reconcile your accounts. However, there are some

additional issues covered in this section that may prove useful in balancing your accounts in the future.

Updating Your Opening Balance

The importance of maintaining a regular reconciliation schedule has already been noted, and you should balance your checking account before you begin to use Quicken to record your transactions. However, there may be times when the opening balance Quicken enters in the Reconcile Register with Bank Statement window differs from the opening balance shown in the check register.

This can happen in three different situations. First, when you reconcile in Quicken the first time, there may be a discrepancy due to timing differences. Second, there may be a difference if you start Quicken at a point other than the beginning of the year and then try to add transactions from earlier in the year. Third, balances may differ if you use the reconciliation feature *after* recording Quicken transactions for several periods.

First-Time Reconciliations

If you open a new account and begin to use Quicken immediately, there will not be a discrepancy, but a discrepancy will occur if you do not enter the first transaction or two in Quicken. For example, suppose you opened an account on 12/31/92 for 1300.00 and immediately wrote a check for a 1992 expenditure of 100.00. Then you decided to start your Quicken register on 1/1/93, when the balance in your manual register was 1200.00. The bank statement would show the opening balance at 1300.00. In order to reconcile the difference between the bank statement and the Quicken Register balance on 1/1/93, you can do one of two things.

The first alternative is to open the check register by using F9 (View Register) while in the reconciliation procedures. Enter the 100.00 check, correct the opening balance to reflect the beginning bank balance of 1300.00, and proceed with the reconciliation process.

A second option is to have Quicken enter an adjustment in the reconciliation to correct for the difference between the check register's and the bank statement's beginning balances. When Quicken enters the opening balance as 1200.00 and you change it to agree with the bank statement's 1300.00, Quicken displays a Create Opening Balance Adjustment window, shown in Figure 4-10, which provides a written description of the nature of the problem and offers to make an adjustment.

At this point, you will have a –100.00 balance in the Opening Bal Difference field. Note that your Difference field is –208.68 at this point. If you press (Esc) and proceed through the reconciliation process described in the "A Sample Reconciliation" section of this chapter, you will have a difference balance of 0.00, but still have the Opening Bal Difference.

Instead of pressing (Esc), you can have Quicken make a correction by following these steps:

1. Type **Y** and press (Enter) twice.

Quicken then reconciles the balances by making an adjustment to the check register for the 100.00 transaction. The Problem: Check Register Does Not Balance with Bank Statement window appears.

2. If you want to search for the problem on your own, press (Esc) followed by (F9) (View as List) to return to the list of transactions and the Reconciliation Summary.

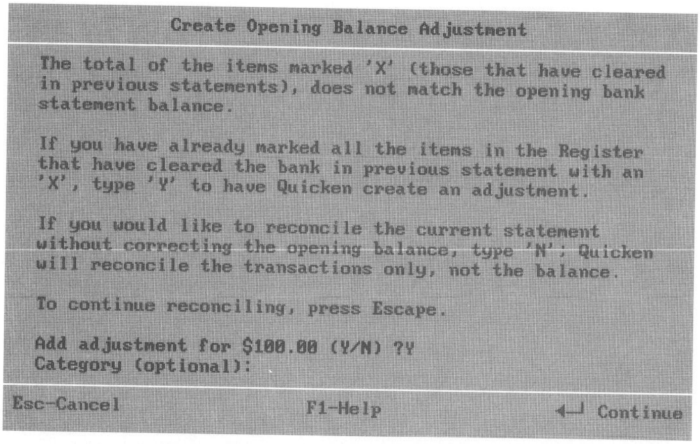

4

Create Opening Balance Adjustment window
Figure 4-10.

```
            Create Opening Balance Adjustment

  The total of the items marked 'X' (those that have cleared
  in previous statements), does not match the opening bank
  statement balance.

  If you have already marked all the items in the Register
  that have cleared the bank in previous statement with an
  'X', type 'Y' to have Quicken create an adjustment.

  If you would like to reconcile the current statement
  without correcting the opening balance, type 'N'; Quicken
  will reconcile the transactions only, not the balance.

  To continue reconciling, press Escape.

  Add adjustment for $100.00 (Y/N) ?Y
  Category (optional):

  Esc-Cancel              F1-Help             ←┘ Continue
```

If you want Quicken to make an adjustment for you, press (Enter) instead, and the Adding Balance Adjustment Entry window appears. Then type **Y** and press (Enter) twice. The Register Adjusted to Agree with Statement window appears after Quicken makes an adjustment for the difference.

Then type **Y** and press (Enter). Quicken brings the Print Reconciliation Report window to the screen. You can now complete the reconciliation report printing process. Note that if you select N in any of these windows, you will be returned to the reconciliation process.

Adding Previous Transactions to Quicken

You most likely purchased Quicken at a point other than the beginning of your personal or business financial reporting year. In this case, you probably started recording your transactions when you purchased Quicken and entered your checking account balance at that time as your opening balance. This discussion assumes that you have been preparing reconciliations using Quicken and now want to go back and record all your previous transactions for the current year in Quicken. Obviously, your bank balance and Quicken balance will not agree after the transactions have been added.

Follow these steps:

1. Since you are going to be adding to your Quicken register, be sure to have the latest printout of your Quicken register. If not, print your check register now, before you enter any additional transactions. This gives you a record of your transactions to date, which is important should you later need to reconstruct them.

2. Go to your Quicken Register window and change the date and balance columns to correspond to the bank statement that you used at the beginning of the year.

NOTE: The importance of saving your earlier bank statements is apparent. Old statements are not only important for the reconstruction of your Quicken system, but also in the event you are audited by the Internal Revenue Service. It only takes one IRS audit to realize the importance of maintaining a complete and accurate history of your financial transactions.

3. Using your manual records and the past bank statements, enter the previous transactions in your Quicken register. Remember to enter bank service charges and automatic payment deductions if you have not been doing so prior to using Quicken.

4. When you have completed the updating process, compare your ending check register balance with the printed copy you made in step 1. This is important because if they do not balance, you have made an error in entering your transactions. If this is the case, determine whether the difference is an opening account balance difference or an error. (Your options for fixing any discrepancies between opening balances were described earlier in this chapter in the section "First-Time Reconciliations.")

5. The next time you reconcile your Quicken account (assuming you have reconciled the account before), type the opening balance on the latest bank statement over that provided by Quicken in the Reconcile Register with Bank Statement window.

6. Before completing the new reconciliation, go to the check register and type **X** to indicate the cleared transactions in the C column for all transactions that have cleared in previous months.

7. Reconcile the current month's transaction. (Go to the section "A Sample Reconciliation" if you need help.)

First-Time Reconciliation for Existing Users

Although you may have been using Quicken for some time, you may not have used the Reconciliation feature before. The recommended process is as follows:

1. Begin with the first bank statement, and start reconciling each of the past bank statements as if you were reconciling your account upon receipt of each of the statements.

2. Follow this process for each subsequent statement until you have caught up to the current bank statement.

Correcting Errors

Hopefully, there will not be many times when you need Quicken to correct errors during the reconciliation process. However, there may be times when you can't find the amount displayed in the Difference field on your reconciliation screen, and rather than searching further for your error, you want to have Quicken make an adjustment to balance your register with your bank statement.

This situation could have occurred in the 1st U.S. Bank reconciling process described in the section "Quicken's Reconciliation Process." Recall that you made an adjustment of 10.00 to check number 100 in order to correct for your recording error, but if you had been careless in the reconciliation process you might have missed the error when comparing your bank statement with your check register. In this case, your Uncleared Transaction List window would show a $10.00 difference after clearing all items. If you search for the difference and still can't find the amount, you can follow these steps to have Quicken make the adjustment.

CAUTION: This process could have a serious impact on your future reports and check register; don't take this approach to the reconciliation difference lightly.

1. Press Ctrl-F10 and the Problem: Check Register Does Not Balance with Bank Statement window will appear. This time Quicken informs you that there's a $10.00 difference.

At this point you can still return to the register and check for the difference by pressing the Esc key.

2. Press Enter, and the Adding Balance Adjustment Entry window appears.
3. Type Y and press Enter.

You have told Quicken that you do not want to search any longer for the difference and you want an adjustment to be made. The adjustment will be dated the current date and will be recorded as "Balance Adjustment." If you had typed N, Quicken would have returned you to the reconciliation screen and you would have continued to search for the difference.

4. Press (Enter) again and the Register Adjusted to Agree with Statement window appears telling you that *'s have been changed to X's.

This indicates that Quicken has made a check register entry for the difference and that you are going to accept the Balance Adjustment description in the Payee row of the register. (You can always make a correction later if you find the error.) Otherwise, you could have used another description such as misc. or expense/income.

5. Type **Y** and press (Enter); a Print Reconciliation Report window, like the one displayed in Figure 4-6, appears. Now you can complete the window as described in the "A Sample Reconciliation" section of this chapter.

4

CHAPTER

5 WRITING AND PRINTING CHECKS

In addition to recording the checks you write in Quicken's register, you can also enter check writing information on your screen and have Quicken print the check. Although this requires you to order special preprinted checks that conform to Quicken's check layout, it means that you can enter a transaction once—on the check writing screen—and Quicken will print your check and record the register entry.

You can order Quicken checks in five different styles (both tractorfeed and laser options are available) to meet varying needs. Regardless of the style, there is no problem with acceptance by banks, credit unions, or savings and loans since they have the required account numbers and check numbers preprinted on the checks.

You can create standard 8 1/2- by 3 1/2-inch checks, a voucher-style check that has a 3 1/2-inch tear-off stub, and wallet-style checks in the 2 5/6- by 6-inch size with a tear-off stub added. You can order all these for traditional printers or order the regular or voucher checks for laser printers directly from Intuit.

You can generate an order form from Quicken's check writing screen. If you want to print out the order form, you can choose **W**rite/Print Checks from the Main Menu. Then select **A**ctivities, and then Order **S**upplies. If you select a printer number and press (Enter), the order form prints and you can return to the Main Menu by pressing (Esc) when the printing completes. You will see from the form that Quicken also sells window envelopes to fit the checks and can add a company logo to your checks.

Even if you are not certain whether you want to order check stock, you can still try the exercises in this chapter. You may be so pleased with the ease of entry and the professional appearance of the checks that you will decide to order checks to start entering your own transactions. You will definitely not want to print your own checks without the special check stock since banks will not cancel payments on checks without a preprinted account number.

You can also enter transactions in Quicken for transmission to the CheckFree payment processing service via a modem. Your Quicken register entries will be updated after transmission and the CheckFree Processing Center will handle the payment for you. This chapter provides some information on this service since you might want to consider it as a next step in the total automation of your financial transactions.

Writing Checks

Writing checks in Quicken is as easy as writing a check in your regular checkbook. Although there are a few more fields on a Quicken check, most of these are optional and are designed to provide better record keeping for your expense transactions. All you really need to do is fill in the blanks on a Quicken check form.

Entering the Basic Information

To activate the check writing features, you can select **W**rite/Print Checks from the Main Menu. The exercise presented here is designed to be entered after the reconciliation example in Chapter 4, "Reconciling Your Quicken Register," but it can actually be entered at any time. If you are already in the register, there is no need to return to the Main Menu first; all you need to do is select **A**ctivities and select **W**rite Checks from the pull-down menu.

Figure 5-1 shows a blank Quicken check form on the screen. The only field that has been completed is the Date field; by default, the current date is placed on the first check. On checks after the first, the date matches the last check written. For this exercise, you change the dates on all the checks written to match the dates on the sample transactions.

You should already be familiar with most of the fields on the check writing form from the entries you made in Quicken's register. However, the Address field was not part of the register entries. It is added to the check for use with window envelopes; when the checks are printed, all you have to do is insert them in envelopes and mail them.

As many as three monetary amounts may appear in the bottom-right corner of the screen. The Checks to Print field holds the total dollar

5

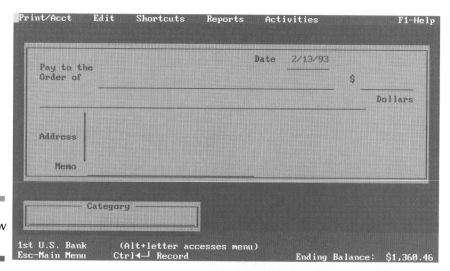

Blank check
writing window
Figure 5-1.

amount of all the checks written but not yet printed. This will not show until you fill in the first check and record the transaction.

Current Balance is a field that changes from 0.00 only if you write checks with dates after the current date, called *postdated checks*. Postdated checks do not affect the current balance but alter the ending balance. They are written to record future payments. If you are reading this chapter before February 1993, all of your transactions will be postdated, since the dates on the checks are in that month. Ending Balance is the balance in the account after all of the checks written have been deducted.

You can use Tab or Enter to move from field to field on the check form. If you want to move back to a previous field, you can use Shift-Tab. When you are finished entering the check information and are ready to record it, you can press Ctrl-Enter to automatically record the transaction. Another possibility is to press Enter with the cursor at the end of the last field category. With the latter approach, Quicken prompts you to confirm that you want to record the transaction. If you use this approach, type **1** and press Enter; the check is recorded for later printing.

Follow these instructions to enter the information for your first check:

1. Type **2/13/93** and press Enter.

You can also use + or - to change the date.

2. Type **South Haven Print Supply** and press Enter.
3. Type **58.75** and press Enter.

Amounts as large as $9,999,999.99 are supported by the package. Notice that when you complete the amount entry, Quicken spells out the amount on the next line and positions you in the Address field. Although this entire field is optional, if you are mailing the check, entering the address here allows you to use a window envelope.

4. Type a quotation mark (") to automatically copy the payee name down to this line.
5. Type **919 Superior Avenue** and press Enter.

6. Type **South Haven, MI 49090** and press [Enter] until the cursor is in the Memo field.

7. Type **Printing Brochure - PTA Dinner** and then press [Tab] or [Enter].

8. Press [Ctrl]-[C].

This is a quick way to bring up the category list to select an appropriate category.

9. Move the cursor to the Charity field since you are donating the cost of this printing job by paying the bill for the Parent Teacher Association. Press [Enter] to add the entry to the Category field.

Remember, you can also use Quicken 6's QuickFill feature by typing **C** and pressing [Ctrl]-[+] until the Charity category appears on your screen. With either approach, your screen looks like the one in Figure 5-2.

10. Press [Ctrl]-[Enter] to complete and record the transaction.

You can enter as many checks as you want in one session. Use the preceding procedure to enter another transaction. Check each field

5

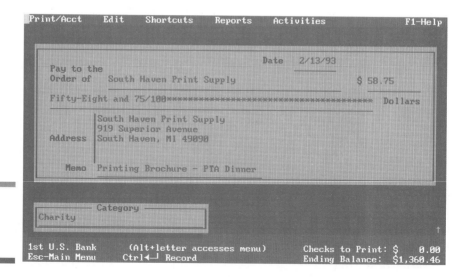

Entering the first check transaction
Figure 5-2.

before you press [Tab] or [Enter], but don't worry if you make a mistake or two; you learn how to make corrections in the next section. Enter this check now:

Date:	2/13/93
Payee:	Holland Lumber
Payment:	120.00
Address:	Holland Lumber
	2314 E. 8th Street
	Holland, MI 49094
Memo:	Deck repair
Category:	Home Rpair

Remember, you could use [Ctrl]-[C] to select Home Rpair from the category list.

Press [Ctrl]-[Enter] when you are through to record the transaction. Although Quicken moves you to the next check, you can press [Pg Up] to see the check, as shown in Figure 5-3.

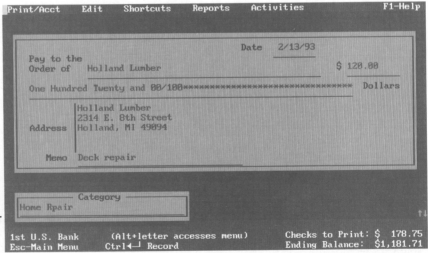

Entering a
check for
Holland Lumber
Figure 5-3.

Reviewing and Making Corrections

Corrections can be made to a check before or after completing the transaction. Although it is easiest to make them before completion, the most important thing is catching the error before printing the check. To prevent problems, you will always want to review your transactions before printing.

Now let's enter one more transaction exactly as shown in Figure 5-4, including the spelling error in the Memo field. Then you will take a look at making the required corrections. Press (Pg Dn) to move to a new check form if you are still looking at the check for Holland Lumber, and make the following entries without recording the transaction. (Do not correct the misspelling.)

Date:	2/13/93
Payee:	Fennville Library
Payment:	10.00
Address:	Fennville Library
	110 Main Street
	Fennville, MI 49459
Memo:	Building func contribution
Category:	Charity

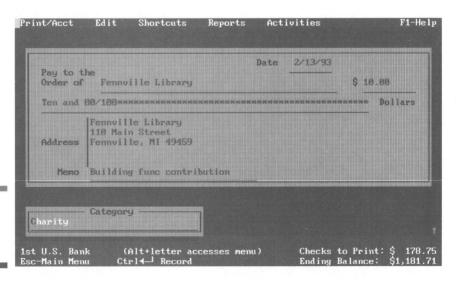

Entering a check with errors

Figure 5-4.

One mistake in the entries in Figure 5-4 is obvious. The word "fund" in the Memo field is spelled wrong. Suppose you were planning to be a little more generous with the contribution; the amount you intended to enter was 100.00. Quicken has already generated the words for the amount entry, but it changes the words if you change the amount. All you need to do is move back to the fields and make corrections, since the transaction has not been recorded yet. Follow these instructions:

1. Press (Tab) three times to move to the Amount field.

Although (Tab) normally takes you to the next field, pressing it at the last field takes you to the first field on the screen. Another approach is to press (Shift)-(Tab). Each time you press it, the cursor moves back one field. This works, but it needs to be pressed a few more times than (Tab) because of the cursor location and the destination field.

2. Use (→) to position the cursor immediately after the 1 in the Amount field.
3. Press (Ins) to turn on insert mode, and type another **0**.

The amount now reads "100.00."

4. Press (Ins) to turn insert mode off.
5. Press (Tab) six times to move to the Memo field.
6. Press (Ctrl)-(→) twice to move to the *c* in "contribution." Press (←) twice. Type **d** to replace the *c* in "func." The correct check will be for $100.00 with a Memo field entry of "Building fund contribution."
7. Press (Ctrl)-(Enter) to record the transaction.

You can browse through the other transactions by using (Pg Up) and (Pg Dn) to move from check to check. Pressing (Home) repeatedly takes you to the first check and pressing (End) repeatedly takes you to the last check, which is a blank check form for the next transaction. Make any changes you want, but record them with (Ctrl)-(Enter) before using (Pg Up) or (Pg Dn) to move to a new check. Quicken updates the balances if you change an Amount field.

To delete an entire transaction, you can use (Ctrl)-(D) and confirm the delete. Since the checks have not been printed, there is no problem in deleting an incorrect transaction. After printing, you must void the entry in the register rather than deleting the check, since you will need a record of the disposition of each check number.

If you are curious about how these entries look in the register, you can select **A**ctivities. Press `Enter` to select the register. `Ctrl`-`R` is the shortcut for these actions. You see the checks you have written in the register with ***** in the Num field. Figure 5-5 shows several entries made from the check writing screen.

Postdating Checks

Postdated checks are written for future payments. The date on a postdated check is after the current one; if you enter a check on September 10 for a December 24 payment, the check is postdated. Postdated entries are allowed to permit you to schedule future expenses and write the check entry while you are thinking of it. It is not necessary to print postdated checks when you print checks. Quicken displays both a current and an ending balance for your account.

Depending on when you are entering the February 1993 checks in these examples, Quicken may be classifying the entries as postdated. The only difference is you have the option to print only checks before a certain date when postdated checks are recorded.

5

Print/Acct	Edit	Shortcuts	Reports	Activities			F1-Help
Date · Num	Payee · Memo · Category			Payment	C	Deposit	Balance
2/01 1993	Service Charge Bank Chrg			11 50	X		1,334 43↑
2/01 1993	Interest Earned Int Inc				X	1 03	1,335 46
2/10 1993	Dividend check Dividends check→Div Income					25 00	1,360 46
2/13 1993	***** South Haven Print Supply Printing Brochu→Charity			58 75			1,301 71
2/13 1993	***** Holland Lumber Deck repair Home Rpair			120 00			1,181 71
2/13 1993	***** Fennville Library Memo: Building fund contribution Cat: Charity			100 00			1,081 71
1st U.S. Bank	(Alt+letter accesses menu)						
Esc-Main Menu	Ctrl↵ Record					Ending Balance:	$1,081.71

Check transactions in the register with asterisks for check numbers

Figure 5-5.

Complete these entries to write a check for an upcoming birthday by entering the following after returning to the check writing window:

Date:	3/8/93
Payee:	Keith Campbell
Payment:	25.00
Memo:	Birthday gift
Category:	Gifts

Note that the Address field was deliberately left blank since this is a personal check that will not be mailed. What makes this check different than all the others is that while the current date is supposedly 2/13/93, the check is written for 3/8/93 (later than the current date). Press Ctrl-Enter to finalize.

Now that you have written a few checks, you should try printing a few. You can use plain paper even if you have check stock, since these are just practice examples.

Putting Earlier Tactics to Work

Even though you are working with the check writing screen, many of Quicken's special features that you learned to use in earlier chapters still work. You can use the Calculator if you need to total a few invoices or perform another computation for the check amount. All you have to do is move to the Amount field and press Ctrl-O to activate the Calculator. Once you have completed your computations, use F9 (Paste) to place the result in the Amount field.

The Find and Go to Date options also work. You can use shortcut keys to invoke these features or the pull-down Edit menu (see Chapter 2, "Making Register Entries").

Printing Checks

Printing checks is easy. The only difficult part of the process is lining the paper up in your printer, but after the first few times even this will seem easy, as Quicken has built some helps into the system for you.

You can print some or all of your checks immediately after writing them, or you can defer the printing process to a later session. Some users wait until a check is due to print it and others elect to print all their checks immediately after they are written.

Check Stock Options

Quicken checks come in three sizes—regular checks, wallet checks, and voucher checks. Figure 5-6 provides a sample wallet check. The voucher design is shown in Figure 5-7. All styles are personalized and can be printed with a logo. The account number, financial institution number, and check number are printed on each check. Special numbers have been added to the edges of the checks for tractor-feed printers to assist in the alignment process.

Printing a Sample to Line Up Checks

Although you are ready to print the checks you created in the last exercise, if you have never lined up checks in the printer before you will want to walk through the steps required. This will ensure perfect alignment of the preprinted check forms with the information you plan to print. The procedure is different for tractor-feed printers and laser printers. The laser printer is actually the easier of the two since all you really need to do is insert the checks into the paper tray.

5

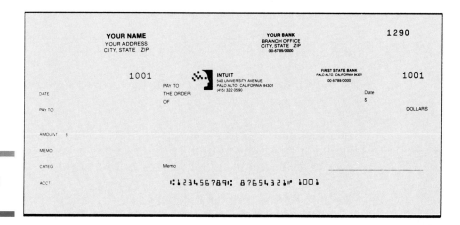

A sample
wallet check
Figure 5-6.

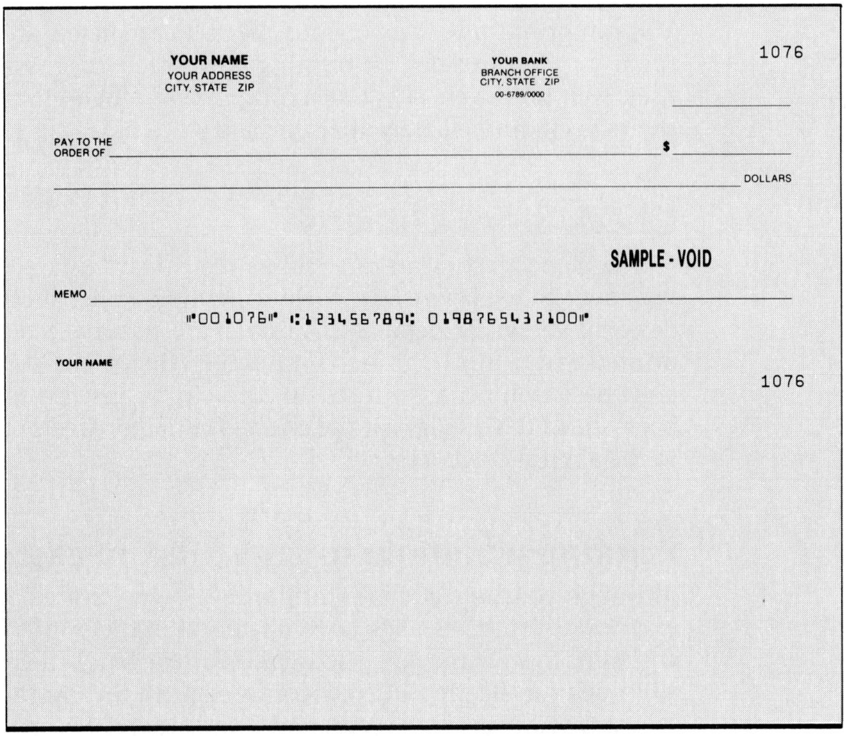

YOUR NAME
YOUR ADDRESS
CITY, STATE ZIP

YOUR BANK
BRANCH OFFICE
CITY, STATE ZIP
00-6789/0000

1076

PAY TO THE
ORDER OF _____ $ _____

_____ DOLLARS

SAMPLE - VOID

MEMO _____

⑈⑈OO1O76⑈⑈ ⑈1234567890⑈ O198765432100⑈⑈

YOUR NAME

1076

A sample
voucher check
Figure 5-7.

Tractor-Feed Printers

Quicken comes with some sample checks for practicing check printing on a tractor-feed printer. Naturally, you will only be interested in this option if you have a tractor-feed printer.

To print a sample check with a tractor-feed printer, follow these instructions from the Write/Print Checks menu:

1. Insert the sample checks in the tractor-feed as you do with any printer paper.

You can purchase Forms Leader pages from Intuit that assure proper alignment of the checks in the printer. This way you won't waste a check at the beginning of each check writing session.

2. Turn on your printer and make sure that it is on line and ready to begin printing.

3. Select **P**rint/Acct, and then select **P**rint Checks.

Another option is to press Ctrl-P rather than opening the Acct/Print menu. The Print Checks window appears.

4. Type the number of the printer you will be using and press Enter.

This is likely to be **3** for the check printer. The next two selections let you control how many checks will be printed.

5. Press Enter to accept the defaults of ALL and checks dated through the current date.

6. Press F9 (Print Sample); then, after reading Quicken's sample check note, press Enter.

Quicken prints your sample check. Check the vertical alignment by observing whether the "XXX" for date and amount, the word "Payee" for "Pay to the Order of," and the phrase "This is a void check" for the memo are printed just above the lines on the sample check.

NOTE: Do not move the check up or down after printing; Quicken does this automatically.

7. Press Enter if the sample check has aligned properly. If not, continue with the remaining steps.

8. (You will use this step only if your sample check did not align properly.) Look at the pointer line printed on your sample check. The arrow at each end points to a number on your tractor-feed sheet; this is your printer *position number*.

NOTE: If your pointer line is not on one continuous line, you must check your printer settings to see that the pitch is 10 and that the indent value is 0. You cannot at this time continue with the following steps to achieve the correct results. Note the correct alignment position and consult Table 5-1, "Correcting Printer Errors."

5

Print Problem	Correct Solution
Print lines are too close	Printer is probably set for eight lines to the inch—change to six
Print lines wrap and the date and amount are too far to the right	Too large a pitch is selected—change to 10 pitch
Print does not extend across the check—the date and amount print too far to the left	Too small a pitch size is selected (perhaps compressed print)—change to 10 pitch and turn off compressed print if necessary
Print does not align with lines on check	Checks not aligned properly in printer—reposition following instructions in this chapter
Print seems to be the correct size but is too far to the right or left	Reposition checks from right to left
Printout shows the printer control codes	Printer control codes must be preceded with a backslash (\\)
Printer is spewing paper or producing illegible print	The wrong printer has probably been selected—check selection in the printer list
Printer does not print	Printer is probably not turned on, not on line, or not chosen in the printer list; or the cable may be loose
Print looks correct but is indented	Change indent setting to 0 in Print Settings window

Correcting
Printer Errors
Table 5-1.

Press (Esc) to leave the print process for now.

9. Type the position line number and press (Enter).

Quicken automatically causes a form feed and prints another sample check. This time your check should be properly aligned; if you need to fine-tune the alignment, use the knob on your printer to manually adjust the alignment.

10. Make any horizontal adjustments that may be necessary by moving the paper clamps.

Once you have aligned your checks properly, you should examine the location of the checks in your printer; notice where your position numbers line up with a part of your printer, such as the edge of the sprocket cover.

11. Press (Enter) in the Position Number field when your sample check is properly aligned.

You are now ready to print your checks.

5

Laser Printers

Quicken's laser-printer checks come either one or three to a page and, as mentioned, are the easiest of the checks to print. When using these forms, all you need to do is insert the forms into your printer the same way you insert regular paper (face up, with the top of the paper positioned toward the printer, and so on). If you tear the tractor-feed strips off the sample checks that come with Quicken, you can use them with your laser printer. You can also use regular printer paper. You can purchase Laser Form Leaders from Intuit to allow you to use check stock that is less than a full sheet in length.

The key point to remember with laser printers is to check the printer settings before printing your checks. This can be accomplished from Quicken's Write/Print Checks menu:

1. Select **P**rint/Acct.
2. Select Change Printer **S**tyles.
3. Select Settings for Printing **C**hecks.
4. Press (Esc) to access the Select Check Printer window, and then use (↑) or (↓) to place the arrow next to your type of printer and press (Enter).
5. Select a style and press (Enter).
6. Press (Enter) or (Tab) eight times to arrive at "Page-oriented," type **Y**, and press (Enter) (if the setting is already set for Y you can just press (Enter)).

7. Press Ctrl-Enter to close the Check Printer Settings window.

8. Press Ctrl-P to open the Print Checks window.

Place a sheet of plain paper in your printer.

9. Press F9 (Print Sample).

Hold the sample up to the light with a sheet of check stock to check alignment.

10. Press Ctrl-Enter.

11. If the sample printed OK, complete the Enter Check Numer window. If you are not pleased with the alignment, press F7 (Vertical Adjust) and type the number of 1/12th inch adjustments needed.

This number is entered in Partial Page Adj when you are using a partial page, and Full Page Adj when you are using a page with three checks. You will need to specify an H or L, for higher or lower, next to the type of page adjustment that you want. After making this adjustment, press Enter to print the checks. Quicken prompts you to see if the checks have printed OK. If you respond with No, the Print Checks window appears again for reprinting. Review Table 5-1 if you are still having problems.

Selecting Checks to Print

When you are ready to print checks, you need to tell Quicken the printer you want to use, the check style you have selected, the checks to print, and the first check number. The instructions that follow assume that you have already checked the alignment for your check stock and that you are beginning from the Main Menu.

1. Select **W**rite/Print Checks.

2. Select **P**rint/Acct and then select **P**rint Checks.

Another option is to press Ctrl-P rather than opening the Acct/Print menu. The Print Checks window appears.

3. Type the number of the printer you will be using and press Enter.

This will probably be **3** for the check printer.

4. Type **S** to print selected checks. Typing **A** causes Quicken to print all the checks.

5. Press (Enter) or (Tab) and then type the number that corresponds to the check style you wish to use, and then press (Enter).

Since you have already printed samples, there is no need to print additional ones now. In subsequent sessions you might want to use (F9) (Print Sample) to print a sample before proceeding.

6. Press (Ctrl)-(Enter) and the Select Checks to Print window appears, as in Figure 5-8. Checks that will be printed show "Print" in the far-right column. You can mark additional checks for printing by highlighting the entry and pressing (Spacebar). This allows you to select specific checks.

If any checks are marked for printing that you do not want to print, you can press (Spacebar) with the cursor pointing at the check to turn off the print command for that check. (Spacebar) toggles the print designation on and off.

7. Press (Enter) and type **1001** to enter the beginning check number in the Enter Check Number window.

```
                         Select Checks to Print

     Date           Payee              Memo              Amount
  ► 2/13/93 South Haven Print Sup Printing Brochure - P      58.75   Print
    2/13/93 Holland Lumber         Deck Repair              120.00   Print
    2/13/93 Fennville Library      Building fund contrib    100.00   Print
    3/ 8/93 Keith Campbell         Birthday gift             25.00   Print




          Spacebar-Select/Deselect    F9-Select All ↑,↓ Select
  Esc-Cancel                          F1-Help              ◄┘ Continue
```

Selecting the checks to print
Figure 5-8.

Your entry should match the one shown here:

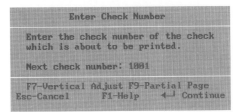

```
             Enter Check Number

    Enter the check number of the check
    which is about to be printed.

    Next check number: 1001

    F7-Vertical Adjust F9-Partial Page
    Esc-Cancel       F1-Help    ←┘ Continue
```

You must always make this check number agree with the number of the first check you place in the printer. You should double-check this entry since Quicken will use it to complete the register entry for the check transaction. As it prints a check, it replaces the asterisks in the register with the actual check number. You can use ⊕ and ⊖ to change the check number. You can also select F9 (Partial Page) or F7 (Vertical Adjust) to tell Quicken where to start printing laser checks and if you want to adjust the printing alignment.

8. Press Enter to print your checks.
9. Quicken 6 responds with a Did Checks Print OK? window.

Review the checks printed and check for errors in printing. If you used preprinted check forms, your checks might look something like the ones in Figure 5-9.

If there are no errors, press Enter to close the check printing windows and to return to the Write Checks screen. Press Ctrl-R to look at the register entries with the check numbers inserted. If there are problems with the checks, follow the directions in the next section.

Correcting Mistakes

Quicken allows you to reprint checks that have been printed incorrectly. Since you are using prenumbered checks, new numbers will have to be assigned to the reprinted checks as Quicken prints them. First, make sure before starting again that you correct any feed problems with the printer.

If you find yourself frequently correcting printer jams and having to reprint checks, you may want to print checks in smaller batches or set your printer to wait after each page.

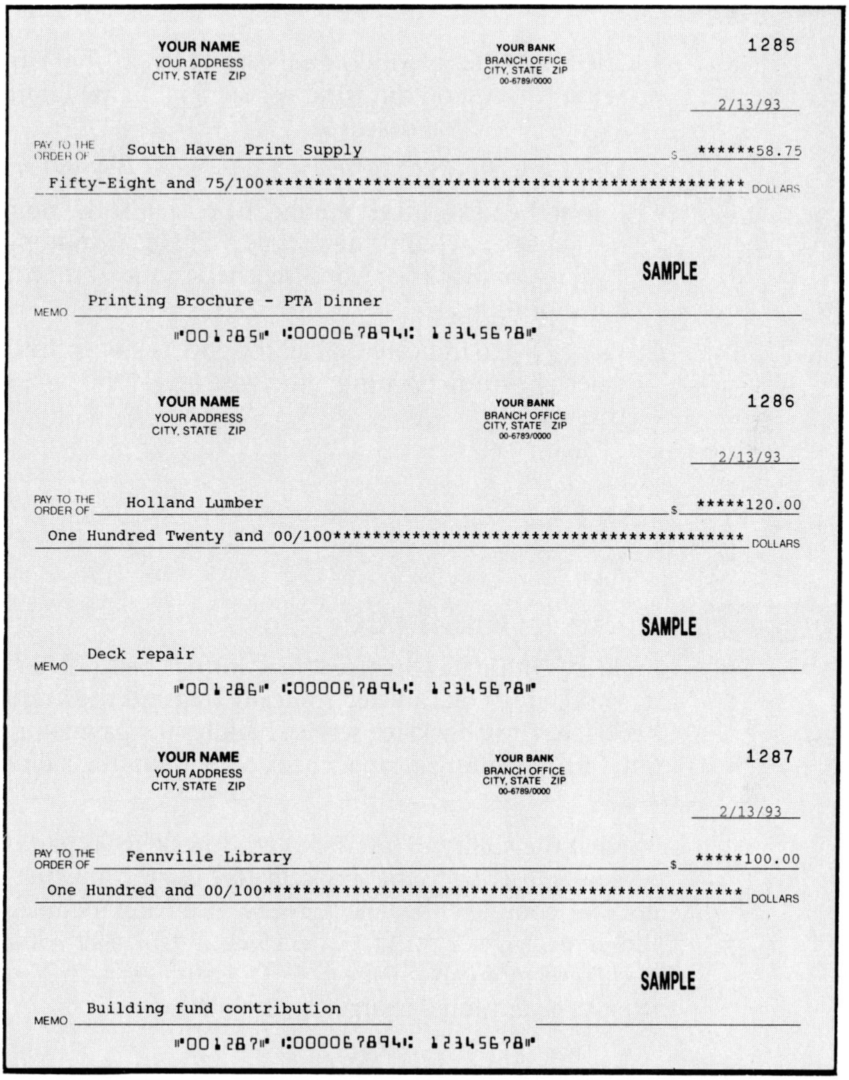

YOUR NAME
YOUR ADDRESS
CITY, STATE   ZIP

YOUR BANK
BRANCH OFFICE
CITY, STATE   ZIP
00-6789/0000

1285

2/13/93

PAY TO THE
ORDER OF   South Haven Print Supply $ ******58.75

Fifty-Eight and 75/100*** DOLLARS

SAMPLE

MEMO   Printing Brochure - PTA Dinner

⑈⑈0012850 ⑈000067894⑈ 123456780⑈

YOUR NAME
YOUR ADDRESS
CITY, STATE   ZIP

YOUR BANK
BRANCH OFFICE
CITY, STATE   ZIP
00-6789/0000

1286

2/13/93

PAY TO THE
ORDER OF   Holland Lumber $ *****120.00

One Hundred Twenty and 00/100** DOLLARS

SAMPLE

MEMO   Deck repair

⑈⑈0012860 ⑈000067894⑈ 123456780⑈

YOUR NAME
YOUR ADDRESS
CITY, STATE   ZIP

YOUR BANK
BRANCH OFFICE
CITY, STATE   ZIP
00-6789/0000

1287

2/13/93

PAY TO THE
ORDER OF   Fennville Library $ *****100.00

One Hundred and 00/100*** DOLLARS

SAMPLE

MEMO   Building fund contribution

⑈⑈0012870 ⑈000067894⑈ 123456780⑈

Standard check
sample printout
Figure 5-9.

Complete the following steps to restart and finish your printing batch:

1. If you did not press (Enter) when you finished printing checks,
   Quicken is still waiting for you to identify the first incorrectly
   printed check and reprint the desired checks (for checks that did
   not print or that printed incorrectly). Type the check number of
   the first check you want to reprint and press (Enter).

2. The Print Checks window appears. Press Ctrl-Enter to open the Select Checks to Print window. The highlighted transaction will be on the check you designed.

3. Select the checks to be reprinted by using Spacebar and press Enter.

4. Check the next Check Number field against the number of the next check in your printer. Type a change if appropriate. Press Enter to confirm the beginning check number for this batch and begin printing.

5. Press Enter to indicate that all the checks have printed correctly when they stop printing; otherwise repeat the steps described in this section.

Using CheckFree

CheckFree eliminates the need for printing checks. After entering data into Quicken 6, you can electronically transmit the information to CheckFree. The CheckFree service handles the payments for you by printing and mailing a paper check or by initiating a direct electronic transfer.

Although the ability to interface with CheckFree is part of Quicken 6, you must subscribe to the service before using it the first time. To subscribe, complete the CheckFree Service Form included in the Quicken package or contact CheckFree at (614) 899-7500. Currently, CheckFree's monthly charge of $9.00 entitles you to 20 transactions without an additional charge.

Setting Up Quicken to Interface with CheckFree

To use CheckFree with Quicken, you must change your settings and set up the bank account specified on the CheckFree Service Form. Then, set up your modem so that you can use Quicken's electronic payment capability. You must also compile an electronic payee list and write electronic checks.

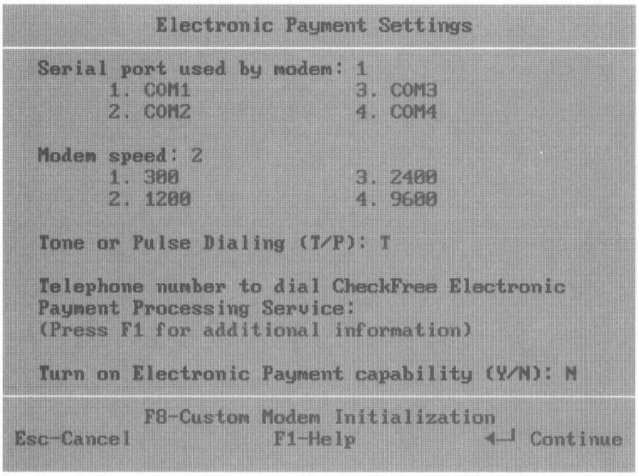

```
                    Electronic Payment Settings
        Serial port used by modem: 1
                   1. COM1                3. COM3
                   2. COM2                4. COM4

        Modem speed: 2
                   1. 300                 3. 2400
                   2. 1200                4. 9600

        Tone or Pulse Dialing (T/P): T

        Telephone number to dial CheckFree Electronic
        Payment Processing Service:
        (Press F1 for additional information)

        Turn on Electronic Payment capability (Y/N): N

                    F8-Custom Modem Initialization
        Esc-Cancel              F1-Help            ←┘ Continue
```

Electronic
Payment
Settings window
Figure 5-10.

5

Completing Modem Settings

To set up your modem to establish a link between your computer and your bank via the telephone line, select Set **P**references from the Main Menu. Next, choose E**l**ectronic Payment Settings, followed by **M**odem Settings. The Electronic Payment Settings window shown in Figure 5-10 is displayed. You can accept the defaults for the modem speed and the computer port to which the modem is attached or change them to conform to your needs.

You must enter the phone number supplied by CheckFree for transmission. Next, turn on the electronic payment feature by typing a **Y** in the last field on the screen. When entering the phone number, type a comma if your phone system requires a pause. Rather than return to the Main Menu, you can edit the settings for the current account to use it with CheckFree, as discussed next.

Completing Account Settings

You can change your account settings for any bank account for use with CheckFree provided you supply the bank information to CheckFree on their service form. To change an account for use with CheckFree, choose **A**ccount Settings from the menu after selecting Set **P**references and E**l**ectronic Payment Settings. Quicken presents a window with your current account listed, like the one shown here:

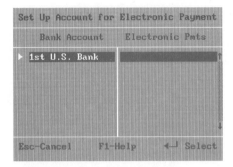

Highlight the name of the account you wish to enable electronic transmissions for and press Enter. Respond with a **Y** on the next screen to enable payments, and then complete the form shown in Figure 5-11 for your account. CheckFree supplies you with the number for the last field on this form. After returning to the Main Menu, you are ready to enter electronic payees or either check or register transactions and transmit them.

Writing Electronic Checks

The procedure for writing electronic checks is almost identical to the format for creating checks that you print, covered earlier in this chapter. Your check displays Electronic Payment if you have electronic payments set for the current account, although you can toggle to a paper check with F9 any time you need to. Quicken automatically

Electronic
Payment
Account
Settings form
Figure 5-11.

```
                 Electronic Payment Account Settings
   Your First Name:            MI:    Last:

   Street Address     |                              |


   City:                         State:    Zip:

   Home Phone:

   Social Security Number:
   (Press F1 if you have multiple CheckFree accounts)

   CheckFree Personal Identification Number:

 Esc-Cancel                  F1-Help              ↵ Continue
```

postdates the payment date by five working days to allow for transmission of the payment to the payee. The Pay To field must contain the name of an electronic payee. If your entry does not match an existing payee, Quicken allows you to add it. Once you are finished with your entries, press ⌈Ctrl⌉-⌈Enter⌉.

Quicken lists your electronic checks in the register. The check numbers will consist of a number of > symbols before transmission and E_PMT after transmission. You can enter these electronic payments directly in the register rather than through the Write Checks screen if you prefer.

Transmitting Electronic Payments

Electronic payments are transmitted through the Write/Print Checks screen or the register. Select Print/Acct, then Transmit Payments to display the Transmit Payments window. You can preview your transmission with ⌈F9⌉ (Print Sample) or press ⌈Enter⌉ to start the transmission process.

5

P A R T

2

HOME
APPLICATIONS

CHAPTER

6

EXPANDING THE SCOPE OF FINANCIAL ENTRIES

The purpose of the last five chapters was to quickly get you started using Quicken's features. The basics you learned in those chapters will help you better manage your checking account transactions. For some individuals this will be sufficient. Others will want to increase their knowledge of Quicken to take full advantage of its capabilities. Even if you think you learned all the tasks you need in the first few chapters, read the first two sections in this chapter. These sections will teach you about Quicken files and setting up an account separate from the one you used for the practice exercises. Then, if you feel you know enough to meet your needs, stop reading at the end of the section titled "Quicken Files" and enter some of your own transactions.

Even personal finances can be too complex to be handled with a single account. In one household, there may be transactions for both individual and joint checking accounts, credit card accounts, and savings accounts. Quicken allows you to set up these different accounts within one Quicken file, which enables you to include information from multiple accounts in reports.

Accounts alone are not always enough to organize transactions logically. You may find you need to change the categories to assign to your transactions; you may even want to establish main categories with subcategories beneath them. You used categories earlier to identify transactions as utilities expense or salary income. Using subcategories, you might create several groupings under the utilities expense for electricity, gas, and water.

Classes are another way of organizing your transactions to provide a different perspective from categories. You might think of classes as answering the "who," "what," "when," or "where" of a transaction. For example, you could assign a transaction to the clothing category and then set up and assign it to a class for the family member purchasing the clothing.

In this chapter you will also learn how to assign transactions to more than one account—for example, how to transfer funds between accounts.

All of these features are presented here using the assumption that you are recording transactions for your personal finances. If you are interested in using Quicken to record both personal and business transactions, read the chapters in this section first. When you get to Chapter 11, "Setting Up Quicken for Your Business," you learn how to set up Quicken for your business. You can then select a category structure and create accounts that will allow you to manage both business and personal transactions.

The material in these chapters builds on the procedures you have already mastered. You should feel free to adapt the entries provided to match your actual financial transactions. For example, you may want to change the dollar amount of transactions, the categories to which they are assigned, and the transaction dates shown.

Again, be aware of the dates for the transaction entries in these chapters. As you know, the date of the transaction entry, relative to the current date, determines whether a transaction is postdated. The current date triggers the reminder to process groups of transactions you want to enter on a certain date. Using your current date for transaction entries will cause this not to occur. Also, creating reports that match the examples in this book will be difficult unless you use the dates presented for the transaction. The varied dates used permit the creation of more illustrative reports.

6

Quicken Files

When you first started working in Chapter 2, "Making Register Entries," you created a file called QDATA. Although you only entered one filename, Quicken created four files on your disk to manage your accounts and the information within them. Since all the files have the same filename but different filename extensions, this book will refer to them collectively as a file. When you copy a Quicken data file, all four of these files must be copied.

You worked with only one account in QDATA, but you can use multiple accounts within a file. You might use one account for a savings account and a different one for checking. You can also have accounts for credit cards, cash, assets, and liabilities, although most individuals do not have financial situations that warrant more than a few accounts.

You could continue to enter the transactions from this chapter in the 1st U.S. Bank account in the QDATA file, or you could set up a new account in the QDATA file. However, if you adapted the chapter entries to meet your own financial situation, your new data would be intermingled with the practice transactions from the last few chapters. To avoid this, you will need to establish a file for the practice transactions. In this section, you will learn how to set up new transactions that are stored separately from the existing entries. You will also learn how to create a backup copy of a file to safeguard the data you enter.

Adding a New File

You already have the QDATA file for all the transactions entered in the first section of this book. Now you will set up a new file and create accounts within it. Later, if you wish, you can delete the QDATA file to free the space it occupies on your disk.

The file will be called PERSONAL and will initially contain a checking account called Cardinal Bank. This account is similar to the 1st U.S. Bank checking account you created in QDATA. Since it is in a new file, a different name is used. Other appropriate names might be BUSINESS CHECKING and JOINT CHECKING, depending on the type of account. Naturally, if you have more than one account at Cardinal Bank, they can not all be named Cardinal Bank. In the section "Creating a New Savings Account" later in this chapter, you will add the account Cardinal Saving to the PERSONAL file.

From the Main Menu, follow these steps to set up the new file and to add the first account to it:

1. Select Set Preferences.
2. Select File Activities.
3. Select Select/Set Up File.

Quicken displays the window shown in Figure 6-1. Notice the entry for the existing file, QDATA.

4. Move the cursor to <Set Up New File> and press (Enter).

Quicken presents a window for entering the filename and the file location categories you wish to use.

5. Type **PERSONAL** as the name for the file and press (Enter).
6. Check the directory shown on the line "Location for data files" and make changes to reference a valid directory if a change is required.
7. Press (Enter) to complete the creation of the new file.

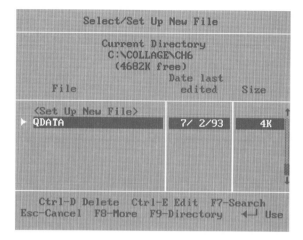

Setting up a
new file
Figure 6-1.

8. Type **1** and press Enter. This will restrict your categories to Home categories when Quicken presents the Default Categories window.

Quicken creates four files for each filename by adding four different filename extensions to the name you provide. This means you must provide a valid filename of no more than eight characters. Do not include spaces or special symbols in your entries for filenames.

Quicken displays the window for selecting or creating files with the PERSONAL file added, as shown in Figure 6-2.

9. Move the cursor to "PERSONAL."
10. Press Enter and Quicken displays the Set Up New Account window shown in Figure 6-3.
11. Type **1** to choose Bank account for the account type and press Enter.
12. Type **Cardinal Bank** and press Enter.

The Starting Balance and Decription Window displays.

13. Type **2500** for the balance and press Enter.
14. Type **7/13/93** and press Enter.

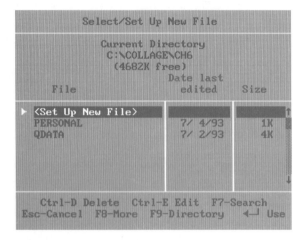

Window
showing
the new
PERSONAL file
Figure 6-2.

15. Type **Personal Checking** and press Ctrl-Enter.

16. Type **1**, press Enter to specify the Bank Statement as the source for
the 2500 entry, and press Enter again to continue.

```
                      Set Up New Account

 Account Type:

        1. Bank Account      Use for checking, savings,
                             or money market accounts.
        2. Credit Card       Use to track credit card
                             transactions.
        3. Cash Account      Use for cash expenditures or
                             petty cash.
        4. Other Asset       Track what you own, such as
                             your house, capital equipment,
                             or accounts receivables.
        5. Other Liability   What you owe, such as
                             mortgages or bank loans.
        6. Investment Acct   Use for stocks, bonds, or
                             mutual funds.

 Name for this account:

 Esc-Cancel              F1-Help            ◄┘ Continue
```

The Set Up
New Account
window
Figure 6-3.

Quicken returns you to the window for selecting an account.

17. Highlight Cardinal Bank and press Enter.

Changing the Active File

The result of the last exercise was the creation of a second file. You can work in either file at any time and select any account within a file. To change from the current file, PERSONAL, to QDATA, follow these steps:

1. Press Esc to return to the Main Menu, and then select Set Preferences.
2. Select File Activities.
3. Select Select/Set Up File.
4. Move the cursor to QDATA in the list and press Enter.
5. Move the cursor to 1st U.S. Bank in the account list and press Enter.
6. Press Esc to return to the Main Menu.

The QDATA file is now active. The register and check writing screen show the 1st U.S. Bank account as active. Change the file back to PERSONAL and activate the account for Cardinal Bank by following the same steps.

Backing Up a File

You will want to create backup copies of the data managed by the Quicken system on a regular basis. This allows you to recover all your entries in the event of a disk failure since you will be able to use your copy to restore all the entries. You need a blank formatted disk to record the backup information the first time. Subsequent backups can be made on this disk without reformatting it. You can create a formatted disk without exiting Quicken.

Formatting a Disk

To format the disk from within Quicken, first open the register from the Main Menu, and then follow these steps:

1. Select Activities and then select Use DOS.

6

The DOS prompt displays on your screen; you can enter DOS commands as if Quicken were not in memory.

2. Type **FORMAT A:** and press (Enter).

The system will ask you to insert a new disk for drive A and press (Enter) when ready.

3. Place a blank disk in drive A, close the drive, and press (Enter) in response to the DOS prompt to insert a disk.

The system will format the disk and ask you if you want to format another disk.

4. Type **N** and press (Enter).
5. Type **EXIT** and press (Enter) to return to Quicken.

The disk you just formatted will be used to store a backup copy of the current files. You can also exit Quicken, format the disk, and start Quicken again.

Creating Backup Files

Quicken has a Backup and Restore feature that allows you to safeguard the investment you have made in entering your data. You can back up all your account files from the **P**rint/Acct menu on the register screen. To back up selected files, select the **B**ack Up File option found in the File Activities item in the Set **P**references selections. Follow these steps to back up the current file:

1. Press (Esc) to return to the Main Menu and select Set **P**references.
2. Select **F**ile Activities.
3. Select **B**ack Up File.
4. Place your blank, formatted disk in drive A, type **A** as the drive, and then press (Enter).
5. Select PERSONAL and press (Enter).
6. Press (Enter) to acknowledge the completion of the backup when Quicken displays the successful backup message.
7. Press (Esc) three times to return to the Main Menu.

With backups, if you ever lose your hard disk, you can re-create your data directory and then use the Restore option to copy your backup files to the directory. You can also copy Quicken data files from one floppy drive to another as a quick means of backup if you do not have a hard disk.

8. Select Use **R**egister to open the register screen, as shown in Figure 6-4.

Customizing Categories

When you set up the new PERSONAL file, you selected Home categories as the standard categories option. This selection provides access to the more than 40 category choices displayed in Table 6-1. You can see that some categories are listed as expenses and others as income; some of them even have subcategories. Any subcategories that you create later will also be shown in this column. The last column in the table shows which categories are tax related.

6

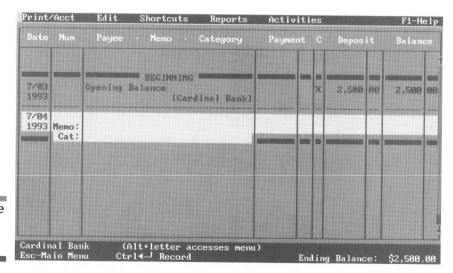

Register for the
new account
Figure 6-4.

Category	Type	Tax Related
Bonus	Income	Yes
Canada Pen	Income	Yes
Div Income	Income	Yes
Gift Received	Income	Yes
Int Inc	Income	Yes
Invest Inc	Income	Yes
Old Age Pension	Income	Yes
Other Inc	Income	Yes
Salary	Income	Yes
Auto	Expense	No
Fuel	Subcategory	No
Loan	Subcategory	No
Service	Subcategory	No
Bank Chrg	Expense	No
Charity	Expense	Yes
Childcare	Expense	Yes/No depending on income bracket
Christmas	Expense	No
Clothing	Expense	No
Dining	Expense	No
Dues	Expense	No
Education	Expense	No
Entertain	Expense	No
Gifts	Expense	No
Groceries	Expense	No
Home Rpair	Expense	No
Household	Expense	No
Housing	Expense	No
Insurance	Expense	No

Standard
Personal
Categories
Table 6-1.

Category	Type	Tax Related
Int Exp	Expense	Yes
Invest Exp	Expense	Yes
Medical	Expense	Yes
Misc	Expense	No
Mort Int	Expense	Yes
Other Exp	Expense	Yes
Recreation	Expense	No
RRSP	Expense	No
Subscriptions	Expense	No
Supplies	Expense	Yes
Tax	Expense	Yes
Fed	Subcategory	Yes
FICA	Subcategory	Yes
Other	Subcategory	Yes
Prop	Subcategory	Yes
State	Subcategory	Yes
Telephone	Expense	No
UIC (Unemploy Ins)	Expense	Yes
Utilities	Expense	No
Gas & Electric	Subcategory	No
Water	Subcategory	No

Standard
Personal
Categories
(*continued*)
Table 6-1.

6

Editing the Existing Category List

You can change the name of any existing category, change its classification as income, expense, or subcategory, or change its tax-related status. To modify a category, follow these steps:

1. Press (Ctrl)-(C) from the register to display the category list.
2. Move the arrow cursor to the category you want to change.

3. Press ⌃Ctrl⌄-⌃E⌄ to edit the information for the category.

4. Change the entries you wish to alter.

5. Press ⌃Ctrl⌄-⌃Enter⌄ to complete the changes.

If you change the name of the category, Quicken will automatically change it in any transactions that have already been assigned to that category.

Adding Categories

You can also add your own categories to provide additional options specific to your needs. For example, if you have just set up housekeeping, buying furniture might be a major budget category. Since you would otherwise have to lump these purchases with others in the Household category, you might want to add Furniture as a category option. Typing **Furniture** in the category field when you enter your first furniture transaction automatically makes it a category option. When Quicken does not find the category in the existing list, it displays a window asking if you want to select a category or add the category to the list. You would choose Add to Category List.

However, if you have a number of categories to add, it is simpler to add them before starting to enter data. To use this approach for adding the Furniture category, follow these steps:

1. Press ⌃Ctrl⌄-⌃C⌄ from the register.

2. Press ⌃Home⌄ to move to the top of the category list.

<New Category> will appear as the top entry in the list.

3. Press ⌃Enter⌄.

Quicken will allow you to enter a new category by using the window shown here, which contains entries for a new Furniture category that you could add to your Category list:

```
                        Set Up Category

    Name:

    Income, Expense or Subcategory (I/E/S): E

    Description (optional):
    Tax-related (Y/N): N
    Tax Schedule
     <No Schedule Selected>

    Esc-Cancel        F9-Tax Schedules        ←┘ Setup
```

4. Type **Furniture** and press Enter.
5. Type **E** and press Enter.
6. Type **Household Furniture** and press Enter.
7. Type **N** and press Enter to complete the entry.

6

Categories will be added as transactions are entered for the remaining examples in this chapter. You should feel free to customize the categories as you enter them.

NOTE: Available RAM will limit the number of categories you can create in each category list. If you have a 512K system with barely enough memory to run Quicken, you may have a limit of 150 categories, whereas a 640K system may support 1000 categories. You are also limited to 15 characters for each category entry.

Requiring Categories in All Transactions

Another customization option Quicken offers is a reminder to place a category entry in a transaction before it is recorded. If you attempt to record a transaction without a category, Quicken will not complete the transaction until you confirm that you want to enter it without a category.

To require the entry of categories, choose Set **P**references from the Main Menu and then select **T**ransaction Settings. Press Enter until item 5 is active, and type **Y**. Press Ctrl-Enter to finalize the settings change.

The next time you attempt to record a transaction without a category, Quicken will stop to confirm your choice before saving.

Using Subcategories

Now that you have set up your file and new account and have customized your categories, you are ready to enter some transactions. Since you are already proficient at basic transaction entry from earlier chapters, you will want to look at some additional ways of modifying accounts as you make entries.

One option is to create categories that are subcategories of an existing category. For instance, rather than continuing to allocate all your utility bills to the Utilities category, you could create more specific subcategories under Utilities that let you allocate expenses to electricity, water, or gas. You could add the subcategories just as you added the new category for furniture, but you can also create them when you are entering transactions and realize that the existing categories do not provide the breakdown you would like.

Entering a New Subcategory

When you enter both a category and a subcategory for a transaction, you type the category name, followed by a colon (:) and then the subcategory name. It is important that the category be specified first and the subcategory second.

You will enter utility bills as the first entries in the new account. Follow these steps to complete the entries for the gas and electric bills, creating a subcategory under Utilities for each:

1. With the next blank transaction in the register highlighted, type **7/25/93** as the date for the first transaction and press (Enter). Type **101** and press (Enter).

2. Type **Consumer Power** and press (Enter). Type **35.45** for the payment amount and press (Enter). Type **Electric Bill** and press (Enter). Type **Utilities:Electric** and press (Enter) again.

Quicken prompts you with the Category Not Found window and allows you to add the category or select one from the category list. Notice that only the Electric entry is highlighted in the Category field since Utilities is already in the category list.

3. Type **1** to select Add to Category List. Quicken displays the Set Up Category window for you to define the category.
4. Press (Enter) to accept S for the subcategory.
5. Type **Electric Utilities** and press (Enter).

Although this description is optional, it is a good idea to enter one so your reports will be informative. Your screen now looks like this:

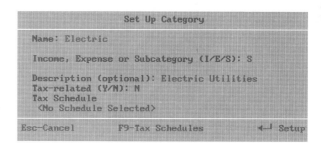

6. Press (Enter) to select N (for No) for Tax-related. Then press (Enter) to complete the transaction.
7. Press (Ctrl)-(Enter) to record the transaction entry.

Quicken displays a message indicating that this is your first subcategory.

Completing the Utility Subcategories

To create a subcategory for the gas bill, enter the following information in each of the fields shown.

Date:	7/25/93
Num:	102
Payee:	West Michigan Gas
Payment:	17.85
Memo:	Gas Bill

6

Don't record the transaction. With the cursor in the category field, follow these steps:

1. Press Ctrl-C to display the Category Transfer List window.
2. Use the ↓ to move to Utilities Gas & Electric.
3. Press Ctrl-E to edit the current category.
4. Change the name on the Edit Category screen to Gas and press Enter twice.
5. Change the description to Gas Utilities and press Ctrl-Enter.
6. Press Enter to use the category.
7. Press Ctrl-Enter to finalize the transaction entry.

You still need to enter the telephone bill, but since Quicken already defines Telephone as a Home category, you cannot consider Telephone as a subcategory of Utilities. However, you could edit the Telephone category and change it from an expense to a subcategory. For now, add it as a separate category, and put the following entries in the transaction fields.

Date:	7/30/93
Num:	103
Payee:	Alltel
Payment:	86.00
Memo:	Telephone Bill
Category:	Telephone

Splitting Transactions

Split transactions are transactions that affect more than one category. You can decide how the transaction affects each of the categories involved. If you split an expense transaction, you are saying that portions of the transaction should be considered as expenses in two different categories. For example, a check written at a supermarket may cover more than just groceries. You might purchase a $25.00 plant as a gift at the same time you purchase your groceries. Recording the entire amount of the check as groceries would not accurately reflect the purpose of the check. Quicken allows you to record the $25.00 amount as a gift purchase and the remainder for groceries. In fact, after allocating the $25.00 to gifts, it even tells you the remaining balance that needs to be allocated to other categories. You could also enter a transaction in which you cashed a check and use the split transaction capability to account for your spending. With Quicken, you can even split transactions by entering percentages rather than actual dollar amounts. As an example of splitting transactions, enter the following transaction for check number 100.

Date:	7/20/93
Num:	100
Payee:	Cash
Payment:	100.00
Memo:	Groceries & Misc

6

Don't record the transaction. With the cursor in the Category field, follow these steps:

1. Press Ctrl-S (or select **Edit** and then select **S**plit Transaction).
2. Type **Groceries**, the name of the first category you want to use.

You can stop typing as soon as QuickFill provides a match.

3. Press Enter and then type **Grocery & Market** and press Enter again.
4. Type **75%** and press Enter. Quicken records 75 percent of the total entered, or 75.00.
5. Type **Misc** as the next category and press Enter.
6. Type **Drug & Hardware Store** and press Enter.

Quicken displays 25.00 as the amount for the second category, as shown in Figure 6-5.

7. Press Ctrl-Enter to accept the amount entry.

The first category entered for the split transaction appears in the register as the category. The word "SPLIT" also appears under the check number.

8. Press Ctrl-Enter to record the transaction.

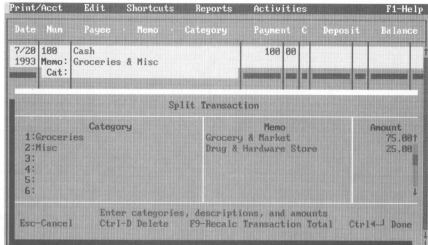

Splitting the
cash transaction
Figure 6-5.

There are many other times when you might elect to use split
transactions. Assigning part of a mortgage payment to interest and the
balance to principal is a good example. Credit card purchases can also
be handled in this fashion if you elect not to set up a special credit card
account. Normally, the split transaction approach is a better alternative
if you pay your bill in full each month.

Notice that up to the point when you enter the category, there is no
difference between a split transaction entry and any other entry in the
register. Complete the following entries to add another split transaction
for a credit card payment:

1. Type **8/3/93** as the date and press (Enter).
2. Type **105** as the check number and press (Enter).
3. Type **Easy Credit Card** for the Payee entry and press (Enter).
4. Type **450.00** and press (Enter) to complete the payment amount
   entry.
5. Type **July 25th Statement** for the Memo field and press (Enter).
6. Select **E**dit and then select **S**plit Transaction, or press (Ctrl)-(S).

Quicken displays the Split Transaction screen with up to six category fields displayed. You can assign as many as 30 split categories.

7. Press Ctrl-C with the cursor in the first Category field.

8. Select Clothing and press Enter twice.

9. Type **Blue Blouse** in the Description field and press Enter.

10. Type **50** and press Enter.

Quicken allocates the first $50.00 of credit card expense to Clothing and shows the $400.00 balance below this entry.

11. Complete the remaining entries shown in Figure 6-6 to detail how the credit card expenses were distributed.

When you press Ctrl-Enter for final processing, you will see the Number field for this transaction contains the word "SPLIT" under the check number, and "Clothing" is displayed in the Category field.

12. Press Ctrl-Enter to record the transaction.

6

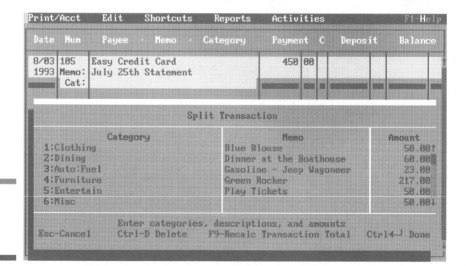

Splitting the credit card transaction
Figure 6-6.

Using Multiple Accounts

Quicken makes it easy to create multiple accounts. Since here all the accounts will be created in the same file, you can choose to have separate reports for each account or one report that shows them all. You will have an account register for each account that you create.

Types of Accounts

Savings accounts, investment accounts, cash accounts, and credit card accounts are all possible additional accounts. Savings accounts and investment accounts should definitely be kept separate from your checking account since you will want to monitor both the growth and balance in these accounts.

The need for cash and credit card accounts varies by individual. If you pay the majority of your expenses in cash and need a detailed record of your expenditures, a cash account is a good idea. With credit cards, if your purchases are at a reasonable level and you pay the balance in full each month, the extra time required to maintain a separate account may not be warranted. In the initial example in this chapter, neither cash nor credit card accounts are used. If you decide you need them, you can use the same procedures to create them that you used to create the savings account. The section "Using a Separate Credit Card Account" near the end of the chapter provides additional information about maintaining a separate credit card account.

Creating a New Savings Account

If you want to transfer funds from your checking account to a savings account, you must have a savings account set up. Follow these steps to create the new account:

1. Select **P**rint/Acct and then select Select/Set Up **A**ccount.
2. Select <New Account> and press (Enter).
3. Type **1** for Bank Account type and press (Enter).
4. Type **Cardinal Saving** for the account name and press (Enter).
5. Type **500.00** for the balance and press (Enter).
6. Type **7/15/93** as the date and press (Enter).

7. Type **Savings account** for the description and press Enter.

8. Type **1** as the source of the starting balance and press Enter twice.

Quicken will open the Select Account to Use window.

9. Select Cardinal Bank and press Enter.

Transferring Funds to a Different Account

It is easy to transfer funds from one account to another as long as both accounts are established. You might transfer a fixed amount to savings each month to cover long-range savings plans or to cover large, fixed expenses that are due annually or semi-annually. Follow these steps to make a transfer from the checking account to the savings account:

1. Complete these entries for the transaction fields down to Category:

6

Date:	8/5/93
Payee:	Cardinal Saving
Payment:	200.00
Memo:	Transfer to savings

2. Press Ctrl-C with Category highlighted. Press End to move to the end of the list, select [Cardinal Saving] from the Category and Transfer list, and press Enter.

3. Press Ctrl-Enter to confirm the transaction.

You will notice brackets around the account name in the Category field of the register. Although not visible on screen, Quicken automatically creates the parallel transaction in the other account. It will also delete both transactions as soon as you specify that one is no longer needed.

Memorized Transactions

Many of your financial transactions are likely to repeat. You pay your rent or mortgage payments each month. Likewise, utility bills and credit card payments are paid at about the same time each month. Cash inflows in the form of paychecks are also regularly scheduled. Other payments such as groceries also repeat but probably not on the same dates each month.

Quicken can *memorize* transactions that are entered from the register or check writing screen. Once memorized, these transactions can be used to generate similar transactions. Amounts and dates may change, and you can edit these fields without having to reenter the payee, memo, and category information.

Memorizing a Register Entry

Any transaction in the register can be memorized. Memorized transactions can be recalled for later use, printed, changed, and deleted. To try this, you will need to add a few more transactions to the account register to complete the entries for August. Add these transactions to your register:

Date:	8/1/93
Payee:	Payroll deposit
Deposit	1585.99
Memo:	August 1 paycheck
Category:	Salary

Date:	8/2/93
Num:	104
Payee:	Great Lakes Savings & Loan
Payment:	350.00
Memo:	August Payment
Category:	Mort Pay

NOTE: Mort Pay is a new category you should add since you do not have the information required to split the transaction between the existing interest and principal categories in the Home category list. Use Entire Mortgage Payment as the description when you add the category.

Date: 8/4/93
Num: 106
Payee: Maureks
Payment: 60.00
Memo: Groceries
Category: Groceries

Date: 8/6/93
Num: 107
Payee: Orthodontics, Inc.
Payment: 100.00
Memo: Monthly Orthodontics Payment
Category: Medical

Date: 8/15/93
Num: 108
Payee: Meijer
Payment: 65.00
Memo: Groceries
Category: Groceries

You now have transactions representing an entire month entered in the checking account. You can elect to have Quicken memorize as many as you think will repeat every month. To memorize the transaction for Consumer Power, follow these steps:

1. Highlight the Consumer Power transaction in the register.
2. Select **S**hortcuts, then **M**emorize Transaction (or press Ctrl-M to select **M**emorize Transaction without opening the menu).

Quicken will highlight the transaction and prompt you for a response.

3. Press Enter to confirm and memorize the transaction. You can also memorize transactions that have not been recorded in the register,

but you will have to press Ctrl-Enter after memorizing them to update the register.

Using the same procedure, memorize all the remaining transactions except the transactions written to Maureks and Meijer and the one for Cash.

Quicken will memorize split transactions in the same way as any other transactions. You should carefully review the split transactions for information that changes each month. For example, the entry for the credit card payment is likely to be split across several categories if you are entering the detail in the check register rather than in a separate credit card account. You will want to edit both the categories into which the main transaction is split and the amounts.

You can use Ctrl-T to display the memorized transactions; your list should match Figure 6-7. If you want to print the list once it is displayed, press Ctrl-P, type a number to select your printer, and press Enter to print. To remove the list from the screen, press Esc. To enter a new transaction, select <New Transaction>.

Using Memorized Transactions

To recall a memorized transaction and place it in the register, move to the next blank transaction form (unless you want the recalled transaction to replace a transaction already on the screen). Press Ctrl-T

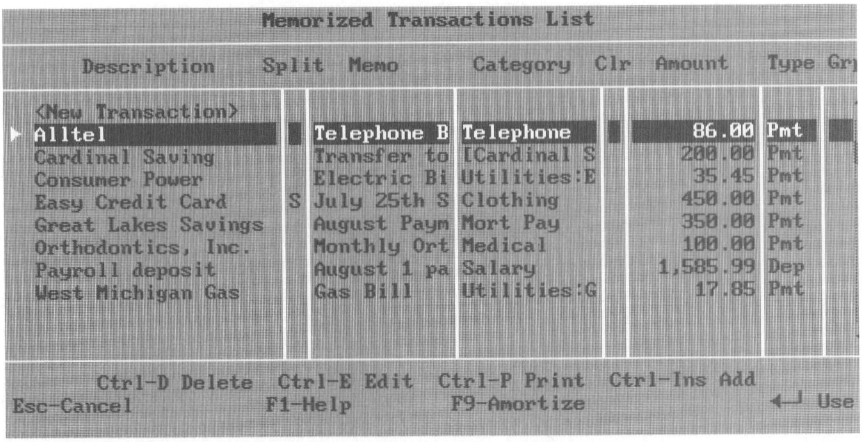

```
                    Memorized Transactions List

       Description      Split  Memo        Category   Clr  Amount   Type Gr

     <New Transaction>
   ▶ Alltel                    Telephone B Telephone          86.00 Pmt
     Cardinal Saving           Transfer to [Cardinal S       200.00 Pmt
     Consumer Power            Electric Bi Utilities:E         35.45 Pmt
     Easy Credit Card       S  July 25th S Clothing           450.00 Pmt
     Great Lakes Savings       August Paym Mort Pay           350.00 Pmt
     Orthodontics, Inc.        Monthly Ort Medical            100.00 Pmt
     Payroll deposit           August 1 pa Salary           1,585.99 Dep
     West Michigan Gas         Gas Bill    Utilities:G         17.85 Pmt


         Ctrl-D Delete   Ctrl-E Edit   Ctrl-P Print  Ctrl-Ins Add
    Esc-Cancel           F1-Help        F9-Amortize              ↵ Use
```

List of
memorized
transactions
Figure 6-7.

to recall the Memorized Transactions List window. Use the arrow keys to select the transaction you want to add to the register and then press [Enter]. If you type the first few letters of the Payee field before pressing [Ctrl]-[T], Quicken will take you to the correct area of the transaction list since transactions are displayed in alphabetical order by payee. The selected transaction appears in the register with the date of the last transaction you entered, not that of the date that was stored when you memorized the transaction. You can edit the transaction in the register and press [Ctrl]-[Enter] when you are ready to record the entry.

Changing and Deleting Memorized Transactions

Quicken allows you to change a memorized transaction in the Memorized Transactions list by pressing [Ctrl]-[T] to activate the list, and then pressing [Ctrl]-[E] to edit the highlighted transaction.

To delete a memorized transaction, you must first activate the transaction list by pressing [Ctrl]-[T] or by selecting **S**hortcuts and then selecting **R**ecall Transaction. Select the transaction you want to delete and press [Ctrl]-[D]. A warning message will appear asking you to confirm the deletion. When you press [Enter], the transaction is no longer memorized.

6

Memorizing a Check

The procedure for memorizing transactions while writing checks is identical to the one used for memorizing register transactions except that you must be in the check writing window. Memorized check and register transactions for the same account will appear in the same Memorized Transactions list and can be edited, deleted, or recalled from either the check writing or register window.

Working with Transaction Groups

Although recalling a memorized transaction works well for reentering a single transaction, for several transactions that all occur at the same time it is more efficient to define a *transaction group*. When you are ready to pay these transactions, you can have Quicken record the entire group for you automatically, after you make any changes in amounts or other information. You can even have Quicken remind you when it is time to record these transactions again.

Defining a Transaction Group

Quicken allows you to set up as many as 12 transaction groups. Defining a group is easy, but it requires several steps after all the transactions that will be placed in the group are recorded. You will need to select a number for the group you want to define. Next you will describe the group. Last, you will need to assign specific memorized transactions to the group. Although expense transactions are frequently used to create groups, you could also include an entry for a direct deposit payroll check that is deposited at the same time each month.

For your first transaction group, which you will title Utilities, you will group the telephone, gas, and electricity transactions that occur near the end of each month. Follow these steps to create the transaction group from the Cardinal Bank account register:

1. Select **S**hortcuts and then select Transaction **G**roups, or press Ctrl-J.

Quicken displays the window shown in Figure 6-8.

2. Highlight 1, since this is the first unused transaction group, and press Enter.

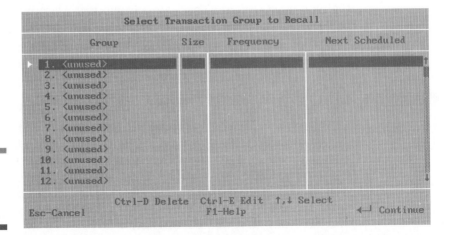

Setting up a
transaction
group
Figure 6-8.

Quicken displays a window to allow you to define the group. Figure 6-9 shows this screen with the entries you will make in the next step.

3. Type **Utilities** as the name for the group and press [Enter] twice.

Even though the group is named Utilities, the transaction for the telephone expense will be included since it is paid at the same time as the utility bills each month. If you wanted, you could use another name such as Month-end Bills and also include the payment to Easy Credit Card. You should look at your transactions for a month or two to decide how to best define your transaction groups. You can specify which account to load for this file if you are using Quicken 6.

4. Type **6** to select Monthly as the frequency for the reminder and press [Enter]. When you don't want to be reminded, you can choose None.

5. Type **8/25/93** as the next scheduled date for the reminder and press [Enter].

6

Quicken will remind you three days in advance of this date. In the next section you will learn how to adjust this setting. Next, Quicken displays a window that allows you to assign transactions to Group 1. Only memorized transactions are present on this list. The transactions are

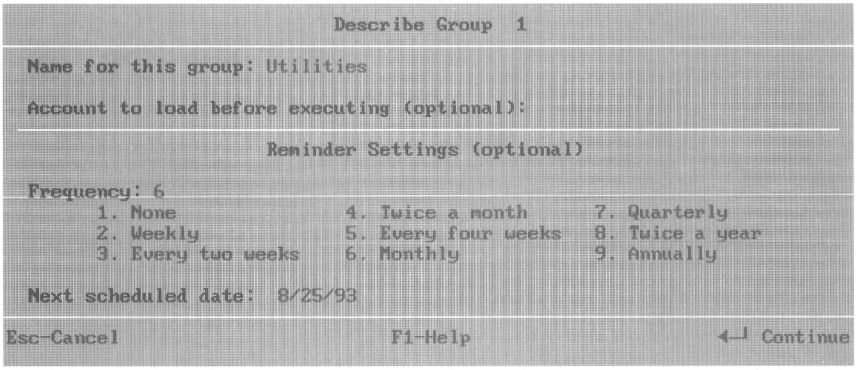

Defining the
memorized
transactions in
a group
Figure 6-9.

```
                          Describe Group  1

   Name for this group: Utilities

   Account to load before executing (optional):

                     Reminder Settings (optional)

   Frequency: 6
          1. None              4. Twice a month      7. Quarterly
          2. Weekly            5. Every four weeks    8. Twice a year
          3. Every two weeks   6. Monthly             9. Annually

   Next scheduled date:  8/25/93

   Esc-Cancel                      F1-Help                    ◄┘ Continue
```

listed in alphabetical order by payee to make it easy to locate the desired transactions.

6. Highlight Alltel and press [Spacebar] to mark the transaction.

Note the 1 in the Group column indicating that the transaction is now a part of Group 1.

7. Move the cursor to Consumer Power and press [Spacebar].
8. Move the cursor to West Michigan Gas and press [Spacebar].

Quicken marks this transaction as part of the group.

9. Press [Enter] to indicate you are finished selecting transactions.

You may want to define other transaction groups to include your payroll deposit, mortgage payment, and anything else you pay at the beginning of the month. You do not need to define additional groups to complete the remaining exercises in this section.

If you want to create a transaction group that is executable at the Write Checks screen, you need to include information to complete a check form. You can identify these transactions in the Assign Transactions window with a Chk entry in the Type field instead of a Pmt entry, which indicates an account register transaction.

Changing a Transaction Group

You can add to a transaction group at any time by selecting Transaction Groups after selecting Shortcuts. As you proceed through the normal definition procedure, you can select additional transactions for inclusion in the group.

To change the description or frequency of the reminder, use the same procedure as before, but make the changes on the windows presented.

To delete a transaction group, select Shortcuts and then select Transaction Groups. Select the group you want to delete and press [Ctrl]-[D]. Quicken eliminates the group but does not delete the memorized transactions that are part of it. It also does not affect any transactions recorded in the register by using the transaction group.

If you want to alter a transaction that is part of the transaction group, you will need to alter the recorded, memorized transaction. This means you will have to bring up the recorded transaction on the Write Checks screen or in the register, depending on the type of transaction you have. Then, you will need to rememorize the transaction. Follow the procedures in "Changing and Deleting Memorized Transactions" earlier in this chapter.

Having Quicken Remind You to Record Transactions

Quicken will remind you to enter upcoming transaction groups. This reminder will either occur at the DOS prompt when you boot your system or at the Main Menu when you first load Quicken. Hard disk users who have the default setting for Billminder still set to Yes will see a message at the DOS prompt reminding them to pay postdated checks or record transaction groups. If you do not have a hard disk or if you have turned Billminder off, the prompt will not appear until you start Quicken.

Recording a Transaction Group

Once you have defined a transaction group you do not need to wait for a reminder when you want to record the group in your register or check writing window. Since you can memorize entries for either the register or the check writing window, you must have the appropriate group defined for your current needs. A group type called CHK is created in the check writing window and can be recorded in the account register or the check writing window. Payment (Pmt) groups are recorded in the account register and can be used only to record account register entries. To execute a transaction group from the account register, complete the following steps:

1. Once you are in the register with the next blank transaction, select Shortcuts, and then select Transaction Groups.

Quicken will display a list of files.

2. Select the Utilities group by moving the arrow cursor to it and
   pressing (Enter).

Quicken will display the date of the next scheduled entry of the
Utilities group, as shown here:

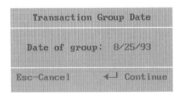

3. Press (Enter) to confirm that this date is valid and to enter the group
   of transactions in the account register.

Quicken indicates when the transactions have been entered to allow
you to make modifications if needed. The window displayed is shown
here:

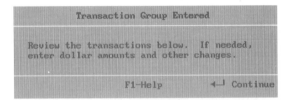

After pressing (Enter) to return to the register, you modify the utilities
transaction group entries just recorded and add the last transaction for
Meijer to complete the August transactions for your account register.
(Press (Ctrl)-(Enter) to record each transaction after the modifications have
been made.) Enter these transactions now:

Num: 109
Payee: Alltel
Payment: 23.00

Num: 110
Payee: Consumer Power
Payment: 30.75

Num: 111
Payee: West Michigan Gas
Payment: 19.25

Record the final transaction for the month of August as follows:

Date: 8/27/93
Num: 112
Payee: Meijer
Payment: 93.20
Memo: Food
Category: Groceries

Notice that Quicken's Quick Fill feature completed the entire transaction for you when you typed **Meijer**. You only needed to change the memo and payment amount.

Using Classes

You have used categories as one way of distinguishing transactions entered in Quicken. Since categories are either income, expense, or a subcategory, these groupings generally define the transaction to which they are assigned. Also, the status of a category as tax related or not affects the transactions to which it is assigned. Specific category names and descriptions provide more specific information about the transactions to which they are assigned. They explain what kind of income or expense a specific transaction represents. You can tell at a glance which costs are for utilities and which are for entertainment. In summary reports, you might see totals of all the transactions contained in a category.

Classes allow you to "slice the transaction pie" in a different way. Classes recategorize to show where, to whom, or for what time period the transactions apply. It is important not to think of classes as a replacement for categories; they do not affect category assignments. Classes provide a different view or perspective of your data.

For example, you might use classes if you have both a year-round home and a vacation cottage. One set of utility expenses is for the year-round residence and another is for the vacation cottage utility expenses. If you define and then assign classes to the transactions, they will still have categories representing utility expenses, but you will also have class assignments that let you know how much you have spent for utilities in each of your houses.

Since the expenses for a number of family members can be maintained in one checking account, you might want to use classes for those expenses that you would like to review by family member. You can use this approach for clothing expenses and automobile expenses if your family members drive separate cars. Another method for automobile expenses is to assign classes for each of the vehicles you own. You can then look at what you have spent on a specific vehicle at the end of the year and make an informed decision regarding replacement or continued maintenance.

Quicken does not provide a standard list of classes. As with categories, you can set up what you need before you start making entries, or you can add the classes you need as you enter transactions. Once you have assigned a class to a transaction, you enter it in the Category field by placing it after your category name (if one exists) and any subcategories. You always type a slash (/) before entering the class name, as in Utilities: Electric/Cottage.

To create a class before entering a transaction, you can use Ctrl-L to open the Class List window, as shown in Figure 6-10. You would select <New Class> and press Enter to create a new entry. Quicken displays the Set Up Class window shown here,

```
                    Set Up Class

    Name:

    Description (optional):

    Esc-Cancel              F1-Help              ←┘ Setup
```

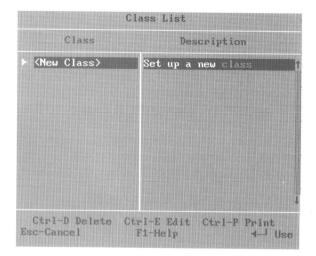

The Class List
window
Figure 6-10.

where you can enter the name and description of a class. Each new class is added to the Class List window. To create a class as you enter a transaction, simply type the category and any subcategories, followed by a slash and the class name you want to use, and press Enter. The following is an example of a class entry for "Jim" that could be used if you wanted to separately categorize personal expenses for each individual in the household:

If Jim were not an existing class, the Class list would appear for your selection and you could create it. You will find more detailed examples of class entries in later chapters.

Using a Separate Credit Card Account

If you charge a large number of your purchases and do not pay your credit card bill in full each month, a separate account for each of your credit cards is the best approach. It will enable you to better monitor

6

your individual payments throughout the year. Also, your reports will show the full detail for all credit card transactions, just as your checking account register shows the details of each check written.

You will need to set up accounts for each card by using the procedure followed when you created the account for Cardinal Saving earlier in the chapter. You can enter transactions throughout the month as you charge items to each of your credit card accounts, or you can wait until you receive the statements at the end of the month. Figure 6-11 shows how your credit card account appears on the screen. You record transaction information in the same fashion as you record checkbook entries designating the "Payee", "Memo", and "Category" fields for each transaction. The "Charge" field is used to record transaction amounts and the "Payment" entry is recorded as part of the reconciliation process. You should use a reconciliation procedure similar to the one you used for your checking account to verify that the charges are correct. To reconcile your credit card account and pay your bill, select Reconcile/Pay Credit Card from the Activities menu of the credit card register.

You can use Quicken's Transfer features to transfer funds between your checking account and credit card. If you have overdraft protection, you

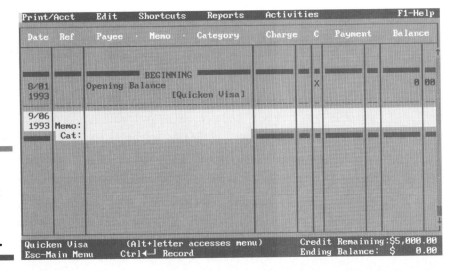

Example of how a credit card account appears on the screen

Figure 6-11.

can also create a transaction to record the overdraft charges to your credit card and checking accounts.

A new feature added to Quicken 6 lets Quicken record all credit card transactions for you. Intellicharge is your own Quicken Visa card which provides this new option. You can receive your Intellicharge transactions on diskette or modem each month. With this feature you select Get IntelliCharge data from the Activities menu and your data is read into your credit card account. Even the categories are completed for you as the data is recorded. You can reconcile your account and decide on the payment amount.

Important Customizing Options as You Set Up Your Accounts

6

Quicken provides a number of options for customizing the package to meet your needs. These include the addition of passwords for accessing accounts, options already discussed such as requiring category entries, and other options that affect the display of information on your screen and in reports. Once you know how to access these settings, you will find that most are self-explanatory. All of the changes are made by selecting Set Preferences from the Main Menu.

Adding Passwords

To add passwords, select Password Settings from the Set Preferences menu. Quicken presents the following menu:

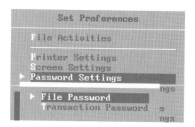

This menu allows you to decide if you want to password protect a file by using a main password, or only existing transactions by using a transaction password. Although you can add protection with a password at both levels, you will need to select each individually.

If you select File Password, Quicken asks you to enter a password. Once you press (Enter), the password will be added to the active file, and anyone wishing to work with that file must supply it. The transaction password is used to prevent changes to existing transactions prior to a specified date, without the password. If you choose Transaction Password, you will be presented with a window that requires you to enter both a password and a date.

If you want to change a password or remove it in a subsequent session, you must be able to provide the existing password. Quicken will then provide a Change Password window for the entry of the old and new passwords. After completing the entries and pressing (Enter), the new password will be in effect. The window is shown here:

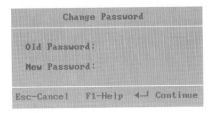

Changing Other Settings

The screen presented when Set Preferences is selected is shown here:

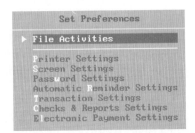

The following is a summary of what each option accomplishes. You have used the File Activities option for tasks such as creating a file or backup. The Printer Settings option allows you to change the style for the existing printer or choose another printer. The Screen Settings option allows you to change screen colors and menu display options. You looked at adding passwords in this chapter with Password Settings. The Automatic Reminder Settings option allows you to set the number of days' notice that you want for postdated checks, transaction groups, and investments. The Transaction Settings option affects confirmation of entries, categories, dates, and filters. The Checks and Reports Settings option affects the numbering of checks and the printing of checks and reports. The Electronic Payment Settings option affects the account used for electronic payments and the modem settings.

6

CHAPTER

7

QUICKEN AS A BUDGETING TOOL

The popular conception of a budget is that it is a constraint on your spending. But that is not what budgets are designed to be. Instead, a budget is a financial plan that shows your projected income and expenses to allow you to plan your expenses within the limits of your income. Although a budget may sometimes necessitate a temporary denial, this denial will supply the funds for expenses you have given greater priority.

Given the same income, five families would prepare five

different budget plans. One family might budget to save enough for a down payment on a new house. Another family might construct its budget to afford a new car. A third family might enjoy eating out and traveling and budget accordingly. Within the constraints of your income, the choice is yours.

If a budget is meant to facilitate getting what you want, why do so many people procrastinate in putting together a budget? It may be because budgeting takes time or that it forces decisions, or perhaps it is simply that most people are not sure where to begin. The one thing that is certain is that budgeting is an important component of every successful financial plan. You should create a budget even if you have already successfully built a financial nest-egg. It will allow you to protect your investment and ensure that your spending meets both your short- and long-range goals.

Quicken is ideally suited for maintaining your budget information. The program guides you through the budget development process and requires only simple entries to record budgeted amounts in the categories you specify. After an initial modest investment of time, Quicken generates reports for use in monitoring your progress toward your financial goal, and you do not need to wait until the end of the budget period to record your progress. You can enter your expenses daily and check the status of your actual and budgeted amounts at any time you wish.

In this chapter you will prepare budget entries for several months. Transaction groups from Chapter 6, "Expanding the Scope of Financial Entries," will be used to expedite the entry process while providing a sufficient number of transactions to get a sense of what Quicken can do. After making your entries, you will see how Quicken's standard reports can help you keep expenses in line with your budget and take a quick look at the insight graphs can provide.

Quicken's Budgeting Process

Quicken allows you to enter projected income and expense levels for any category. You can enter the same projection for each month of the year or change the amount allocated by month. Quicken matches your planned expenses with the actual expense entries and displays the results in a budget report. There is one entry point for budget information, but Quicken will combine actual entries from all of your bank, cash, and credit card accounts in the current file. Although Quicken can take much of the work out of entering and managing your budget, it cannot prepare a budget without your projections. If you have never prepared a budget before, you should take a look at a few budget planning considerations, shown in the special "Budget Planning" section of this chapter. Once you have put together a plan, it is time to record your decisions in Quicken.

You can enter Quicken's budgeting process by selecting the Activities pull-down menu in the account register or the Write/Print Checks options. The process described in the following section assumes you are in the account register for Cardinal Bank that you prepared in Chapter 6. Quicken's budgeting process will be presented in three stages: specifying budget amounts, making modifications, and printing the report.

Specifying Budget Amounts

In this section, you enter budget amounts for the transaction categories you entered in the Cardinal Bank account register. Later, when you create your own budget, you will need to expand the budget entries to include all the categories of income and expense you want to monitor. In earlier releases of Quicken, you made these entries after requesting a budget report, but with Quicken 5 and 6, there is a special activity for setting up a budget.

7

There are a few points to consider before you complete the budget entries. First, Quicken includes categories and subcategories in budget reports if Quicken finds actual or budgeted amounts in the categories or subcategories.

Second, it doesn't matter what period of time you define as the reporting period. (You can also customize the report for other time periods than on a monthly reporting basis—for instance, yours could be every quarter or half year.)

Third, all the categories you have available in your category list are shown in the Budget window. This includes Quicken's predefined personal category list as well as any new categories you have added.

Budget Planning

The budgeting process must begin before you start making budget entries in Quicken. You must start with an analysis of expected income. If your income flow is irregular, estimate on the low side. Remember to use only the net amount received from each income source. Also, do not include projected salary increases until they are confirmed.

The next step is analyzing projected expenses. The first item considered must be debt repayment and other essentials such as medical insurance premiums. In addition to monthly items such as mortgage and car loan payments, consider irregular expenses that are paid only once or twice a year. Tuition, property tax, insurance premiums, children's and personal allowances, and church pledges are examples. Project expenses such as medical, pharmacy, and dental bills for one year. Compute the required yearly expenses and save toward these major expenses so the entire amount does not need to come from a single month's check.

The next type of expense you should plan into your budget is savings. If you wait until you cover food, entertainment, and all the other day-to-day expenses, it is easy to find that there is nothing left to save. You should plan to write yourself a check for at least five percent of your net pay for savings when you pay your other bills.

The last type of expense you must budget for is the day-to-day expenses such as food, personal care, home repairs, gasoline, car maintenance, furniture, recreation, and gifts.

Naturally, if your totals for expenses exceed income projections, you must reassess before entering projected amounts in Quicken.

During the first few months of budgeting, err on the side of too much detail. At the end of the month you will need to know exactly how your money was spent. You can make realistic adjustments between expense categories to ensure that your budget stays in balance.

Finally, with Quicken 6, you can assign budget amounts to subcategories as well as categories.

To set up the budget, follow these steps from the Register window:

1. Select **A**ctivities and then select Set up **B**udgets.

Quicken opens the Budget window, shown in Figure 7-1. Notice that the window is arranged in rows and columns. Normally, you would enter realistic amounts that matched your budget plan. In this exercise, you enter budget amounts provided for you. You also learn to use some of the pull-down menu options to help you complete your entries.

2. Press ⊡ until the highlight is on the Salary Income category in the Jan column.

3. The regular cursor should be blinking within the highlight. Type **1585.99** and press (Enter).

Quicken rounds your entry to 1586 and displays it in the Salary Income and Budget Inflow categories at the bottom of your screen.

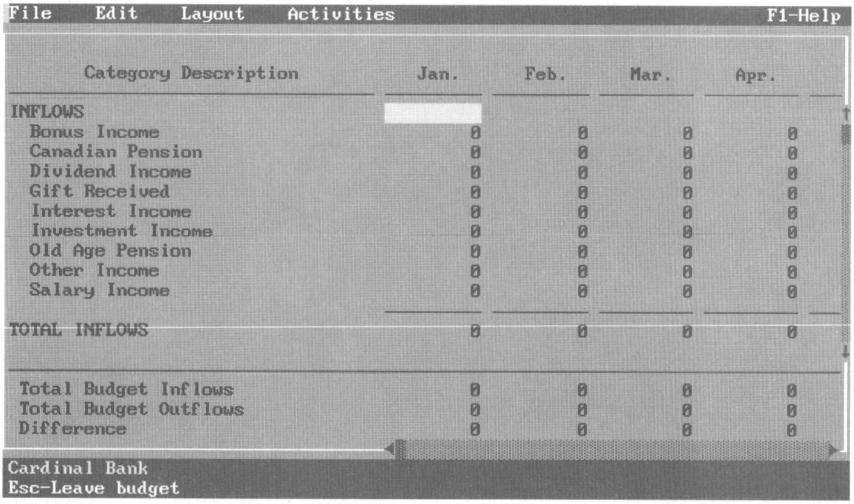

7

Quicken's Budget window
Figure 7-1.

4. Press ⬆ to move back to the Salary Income entry for January. Select **E**dit and then select **F**ill Right to copy the salary across, as shown in Figure 7-2.

It is necessary to move back up to the entry because you finalized the salary entry by pressing Enter, and Quicken moved the highlight down to the next row. You can use **E**dit **F**ill Right immediately after typing an entry without having to move up if you type the entry and do not finalize it with Enter.

5. Using ⬇ to scroll down the list, move the highlight to the January entry for the Electric Utilities subcategory under Water, Gas, Electrics.

Notice as you move down that the bottom part of the screen shows a constant summary of budget inflows and outflows, with the scrolling occurring above this area.

6. Type **25**, but do *not* press Enter.
7. Select **E**dit, and then select **F**ill Right to copy the 25 across for all the months.

Quicken's Budget window after **E**dit **F**ill Right is used for salary
Figure 7-2.

File Edit Layout Activities				F1-Help
Category Description	Jan.	Feb.	Mar.	Apr.
INFLOWS				
Bonus Income	0	0	0	0
Canadian Pension	0	0	0	0
Dividend Income	0	0	0	0
Gift Received	0	0	0	0
Interest Income	0	0	0	0
Investment Income	0	0	0	0
Old Age Pension	0	0	0	0
Other Income	0	0	0	0
Salary Income	1,586	1,586	1,586	1,586
TOTAL INFLOWS	1,586	1,586	1,586	1,586
Total Budget Inflows	1,586	1,586	1,586	1,586
Total Budget Outflows	0	0	0	0
Difference	1,586	1,586	1,586	1,586

Cardinal Bank
Esc-Leave budget

8. Move to the Electric Utilities entry for October (use Ctrl-→), type **30**, and press Enter to replace the 25.

Notice that Quicken changed the dollar amount for only one month. If you wanted to change November and December as well, you would need to use **Edit Fill** Right again.

9. Press ↑, select **Edit**, and then select **Fill** Right.

Notice that this time, all the values for subsequent months have changed to 30. You might make this type of change because new power rates are expected or because you have installed a number of new outside lights.

10. Using the following information, move to the January column and complete the Budget Amount column for the categories. Remember, the process involves using ↑ or ↓ to move the arrow cursor to a specific category, typing the budget amount shown in the list, and pressing Enter.

Category Description	Budget Amount
Auto Fuel	30
Clothing	70
Dining Out	55
Entertainment	55
Entire Mortgage Payment	350
Groceries	200
Household Furniture	0
Medical & Dental	120
Miscellaneous	75
Telephone Expense	30
Gas (subcategory under Water, Gas, and Electric)	20

11. To enter a budgeted amount of 200 as a transfer to the Cardinal Saving account each month, select **Edit** and then select Budget Transfers.

7

Quicken adds the transfer accounts to the categories shown. Budget Transfers is a toggle type selection that allows you to turn these categories on and off each time you select it.

12. Move to the To Cardinal Saving January entry in the Outflow section, type **200**, select **E**dit, and then select Fill **R**ight to copy 200 across for all the months.

In the early stages, it generally takes several months to develop sound estimates for all your expenditure categories. For example, this illustration shows a desired transfer to savings of $200.00 per month. If there are any excess cash inflows at the end of the month, you transfer the excess to savings. On the other hand, if there is an excess of outflow over inflow, you need a transfer from savings. Once you have established your spending patterns and monitored your inflows and outflows, you may find that there are months of excess inflows during parts of the year and excess outflows during others, such as during the holiday season. You can use budgeting to plan for these seasonal needs and anticipate the transfer of funds between savings and checking accounts.

13. Select **E**dit and then select Budget **T**ransfers to toggle the transfer categories off again.

14. Press (Home) twice and then use **E**dit Fill **C**olumn to copy the values across from January to all the other months, as shown in Figure 7-3. Notice that this changes the figure for Electric Utilities in Oct-Dec back to 25. When you use Fill **C**olumn, you cannot selectively copy across, you need to customize after using this selection.

15. For the household furniture transaction, enter **185.00** for the month of October and **250.00** for December. These amounts match your Chapter 6 entries and supply the budget figures for October and December in this chapter's example.

Creating a Budget Report

Now that you have your initial budget entries complete, you will want to prepare a monthly budget summary to compare budget and actual amounts. To create a budget report like the one shown in Figure 7-4, follow these steps:

1. Select **A**ctivities and then select **R**egister.
2. Select **R**eports from the Register menu.
3. Select **P**ersonal and then select Monthly **B**udget.
4. Press (Enter) to accept a default title; type **8/93** and press (Enter).
5. Type **8/93** and press (F8).
6. Press (Enter) twice, type **N**, and press (Ctrl)-(Enter) twice.
7. Press (Ctrl)-(P) to open the Print Report window, select your printer, and press (Enter) to print the report.

If your printer has compressed-print capabilities, you may wish to use that setting when printing reports. That way you will capture more of your report on a page. Some reports will be printed across two pages unless you use the compressed-print feature.

Modifying the Budget Report

You will notice when you print the budget report that it is dated for the one-month period you defined at the opening budget screen prompt. Also notice that Quicken automatically combines all the bank, cash,

7

File Edit Layout Activities				F1-Help
Category Description	Jan.	Feb.	Mar.	Apr.
Total Automobile Expenses	30	30	30	30
Bank Charge	0	0	0	0
Charitable Donations	0	0	0	0
Childcare Expense	0	0	0	0
Christmas Expenses	0	0	0	0
Clothing	70	70	70	70
Dining Out	55	55	55	55
Dues	0	0	0	0
Education	0	0	0	0
Entertainment	55	55	55	55
Entire Mortgage Payment	350	350	350	350
Gift Expenses	0	0	0	0
Groceries	200	200	200	200
Total Budget Inflows	1,586	1,586	1,586	1,586
Total Budget Outflows	1,030	1,030	1,030	1,030
Difference	556	556	556	556
Cardinal Bank				

Some of the budget outflows after **E**dit Fill **C**olumn is used **Figure 7-3.**

```
                    MONTHLY BUDGET REPORT
                    8/ 1/93 Through 8/31/93
        PERSONAL-Bank,Cash,CC Accounts                    Page 1
        8/23/93
                                     8/ 1/93    -    8/31/93
            Category Description     Actual    Budget    Diff
        -------------------------- ----------------------------

            INFLOWS
              Salary Income          1,586     1,586       -0
                                   --------- --------- ---------

            TOTAL INFLOWS            1,586     1,586       -0


            OUTFLOWS
              Automobile Expenses:
                Auto Fuel               23        30       -7
                                   --------- --------- ---------

                Total Automobile Expenses  23     30       -7
              Clothing                  50        70      -20
              Dining Out                60        55        5
              Entertainment             50        55       -5
              Entire Mortgage Payment  350       350        0
              Groceries                218       200       18
              Household Furniture      217         0      217
              Medical & Dental         100       120      -20
              Miscellaneous             50        75      -25
              Telephone Expense         23        30       -7
              Water, Gas, Electric:
                Electric Utilities      31        25        6
                Gas Utilities           19        20       -1
                                   --------- --------- ---------

                Total Water, Gas, Electric  50    45        5
                                   --------- --------- ---------

            TOTAL OUTFLOWS           1,191     1,030      161


                                   --------- --------- ---------
            OVERALL TOTAL             395       556     -161
                                   ========= ========= =========
```

Monthly Budget
report for all
accounts
Figure 7-4.

and credit card accounts in the actual and budgeted figures of the
Monthly Budget report. This means that as you scroll down the report,
you don't see the $200 transfer to Cardinal Saving. Quicken views all of

your accounts as a single unit for budget report purposes and considers the transfer to have a net effect of zero since it is within the system. Thus, the $200 is not shown on the report. You will see how you can change this shortly since a transfer of $200 to savings can be a significant event from a budgeting perspective and, consequently, something that you might want to show on a report.

You can see in Figure 7-4 that you were over your budget for the period by $161, represented by a negative value for the overall total difference. When Quicken compares your budgeted versus actual expenditures for each category, if your actual expenditures exceed the budgeted amount, a *positive* number is shown in the Diff column of the report. If the actual expenditure is less than the budgeted amount, a *negative* number appears in that column. In reading the report, you can quickly see whether you met your budget objectives. As already noted, the actual outflows exceed the budgeted outflows (1191 – 1030 = 161).

On closer examination, you can see there was the unexpected expenditure for furniture during the month that was not budgeted. All your budgeted categories appear with the amount you were over or under budget in each. This category-by-category breakdown is the heart of budget analysis and pinpoints areas for further scrutiny.

You may want to modify the report you just printed to cover only the current account, Cardinal Bank. This change will allow you to see the transfer to the savings account as part of your report for the month. This can be accomplished by following these steps:

1. Press Esc until you see the Monthly Budget Report box again.
2. To customize your report, press F7. The Create Budget Report window will open.
3. Press Enter three times, type **5**, and press Enter again. This tells Quicken you want a monthly report prepared.
4. Type **C** and press Enter. The modified report appears. Notice that only the current account was used in preparing this report, and the transfer to savings shows in the outflow section.
5. Press Ctrl-P and the Print Report window will open. Select your printer and press Enter.

Your new budget report for the file PERSONAL and the account
Cardinal Bank, shown in Figure 7-5, is displayed on the screen and then

```
                         Monthly Budget Report
                         8/ 1/93 Through 8/31/93
        PERSONAL-Cardinal Bank                            Page 1
        8/23/93
                                        8/ 1/93    -    8/31/93
                Category Description    Actual   Budget    Diff
        --------------------------------- --------------------------

            INFLOWS
              Salary Income             1,586    1,586      -0
                                       --------- --------- ---------
            TOTAL INFLOWS               1,586    1,586      -0


            OUTFLOWS
              Automobile Expenses:
                Auto Fuel                 23       30        -7
                                       --------- --------- ---------
                Total Automobile Expenses 23       30        -7
              Clothing                    50       70       -20
              Dining Out                  60       55         5
              Entertainment               50       55        -5
              Entire Mortgage Payment    350      350         0
              Groceries                  218      200        18
              Household Furniture        217        0       217
              Medical & Dental           100      120       -20
              Miscellaneous               50       75       -25
              Telephone Expense           23       30        -7
              Water, Gas, Electric:
                Electric Utilities        31       25         6
                Gas Utilities            19        20        -1
                                       --------- --------- ---------
                Total Water, Gas, Electric 50       45         5
              TO Cardinal Saving         200      200         0
                                       --------- --------- ---------
            TOTAL OUTFLOWS             1,391    1,230       161


                                       --------- --------- ---------
            OVERALL TOTAL               195      356      -161
                                       ========= ========= =========
```

Monthly Budget report for Cardinal Bank account
Figure 7-5.

printed. Notice that the transfer to Cardinal Saving is shown in your report, but your results haven't changed. The upper-left corner of your report shows that the report is for the Cardinal Bank account only. Reexamine Figure 7-4 and notice that the report included the bank, cash, and credit card accounts. Unless you have chosen otherwise, Quicken lists these three account types, even though such accounts have not been established.

Tying the Budget Report to Other Quicken Reports

You have now completed the basic steps in preparing your budget report. Now let's see how the report relates to the reports prepared in Chapter 3, "Quicken Reports." Figures 7-6 and 7-7 present a Cash Flow report and a portion of an Itemized Categories report for the budget period for the Cardinal Bank account. Since the example is based on only one month, the Cash Flow report (shown in Figure 7-6) and the Actual column in the Monthly Budget report (in Figure 7-5) contain the same inflows and outflows. Normally, the budget summary would cover information for a longer period of time (such as a quarter or year) and you would prepare a Cash Flow report for each of the months included in the budget report. You should think through your reporting requirements instead of just printing all the reports.

You may be wondering why the Cash Flow report shows a positive $194.79 net cash inflow, while the budget report indicates that you were over budget by $161. This occurs because the Cash Flow report looks only at actual cash inflows and outflows. On the other hand, the budget examines what you want to spend and what you actually spent. Looking at the budget column of Figure 7-5, you can see that there would have been an additional $356.00 to transfer to savings if you had met your budget objectives.

Figure 7-7 provides selected detailed category information for the budget period. Notice that the Easy Credit Card Split Transaction window provides detail for each of the categories used when recording the credit card payment. Also notice that the Groceries category is printed by check number and provides detail for the groceries amount on the Monthly Budget and Cash Flow reports. When looking at extended budget and cash flow reporting, the details provided from the

7

```
                    Cash Flow Report
                8/ 1/93 Through 8/31/93
PERSONAL-Cardinal Bank                          Page 1
8/24/93
                                           8/ 1/93-
        Category Description                8/31/93
-------------------------------- --------------------
        INFLOWS
        Salary Income                      1,585.99
                                           ----------
        TOTAL INFLOWS                      1,585.99

        OUTFLOWS
          Automobile Expenses:
            Auto Fuel                23.00
                                     ----------
            Total Automobile Expenses          23.00
          Clothing                             50.00
          Dining Out                           60.00
          Entertainment                        50.00
          Entire Mortgage Payment             350.00
          Groceries                           218.20
          Household Furniture                 217.00
          Medical & Dental                    100.00
          Miscellaneous                        50.00
          Telephone Expense                    23.00
          Water, Gas, Electric:
            Electric Utilities      30.75
            Gas Utilities           19.25
                                     ----------
            Total Water, Gas, Electric         50.00
          TO Cardinal Saving                  200.00
                                           ----------
        TOTAL OUTFLOWS                      1,391.20

                                           ----------
        OVERALL TOTAL                         194.79
                                           ==========
```

Cash Flow
report for
budget period
Figure 7-6.

```
          EXPENSES
            Automobile Expenses:
            -------------------

            Auto Fuel
            ---------
8/ 3 105  S Easy Credit Card  Gasoline - Jee Auto:Fuel -23.00

            Total Auto Fuel                        -23.00
                                                 ---------
          Total Automobile Expenses                -23.00
                                                 ---------
            Clothing
            --------
  8/ 3 105  S Easy Credit Card   Blue Blouse   Clothing -50.00
                                                 ---------
            Total Clothing                         -50.00

            Dining Out
            ----------
8/ 3 105  S Easy Credit Card    Dinner at the  Dining  -60.00
                                                 ---------
            Total Dining Out                       -60.00

            Entertainment
            -------------
8/ 3 105  S Easy Credit Card  Play Tickets  Entertain -50.00
                                                 ---------
            Total Entertainment                    -50.00

            Entire Mortgage Payment
            -----------------------
8/ 2 104 Great Lakes Savings August Payment Mort Pay -350.00
                                                 ---------
            Total Entire Mortgage Payment         -350.00

            Groceries
            ---------
8/ 4 106    Maureks         Groceries      Groceries -60.00
8/15 108    Meijer          Groceries      Groceries -65.00

8/27 112    Meijer          Food           Groceries -93.20
                                                 ---------
            Total Groceries                       -218.20
```

Partial Itemized
Categories
report for
budget period
Figure 7-7.

7

Itemized Categories report can provide useful insights into your spending patterns by showing where you spent and the frequency of expenditures by category. This information can help in analyzing the changes you might want to make in your spending patterns. (Please note that some of the lines in Figure 7-7 might look slightly different from what appears on your screen. Some adjustments had to be made to fit the material on screen onto the page.)

Budget Report Extension

The reports prepared so far in this chapter give you an overview of the budgeting process by looking at expenditures for one month. You would extend your examination over a longer period to tell if the over-budget situation in August was unusual or part of a trend that should be remedied.

To do this, you will need to add transactions for other months. Fortunately, the transaction groups discussed in Chapter 6, "Expanding the Scope of Financial Entries," can be used to make the task easy. As you add more information to the reports, you will learn how to create wide reports with Quicken.

Additional Transactions

In order to provide a more realistic budget situation, you will extend the actual budget amounts for several months by creating new register transactions. This will also give you an opportunity to practice techniques such as recalling memorized transactions and making changes to split transactions. Remember, you will be using the transactions recorded in Chapter 6. Figure 7-8 presents the check register entries you will make to expand your database for this chapter. Recording the first transaction in the Cardinal Bank account register involves these steps:

1. Press Ctrl-T to display the list of memorized transactions.

You were instructed to memorize most of the transactions in Chapter 6. If you did not, memorize all the transactions from Chapter 6 now, except for the grocery payments to Maureks and Meijer.

```
                              Check Register
        Cardinal Bank                                          Page 1
        10/31/93


        Date   Num      Transaction              Payment  C  Deposit   Balance
        -----  ----   -------------------------  -------- --  -------- --------

        9/ 1          Cardinal Saving             194.79             2,260.70
        1993 memo: Transfer to savings
             cat: [Cardinal Saving]


        9/ 2          Payroll deposit                      1,585.99  3,846.69
        1993 memo: September 1 paycheck
             cat: Salary


        9/ 2 113    Great Lakes Savings & Loan  350.00              3,496.69
        1993 memo: September Payment
             cat: Mort Pay


        9/ 2 114    Easy Credit Card             233.00             3,263.69
        1993 SPLIT August 25th Statement
                     Clothing           50.00
                        Red Blouse
                     Dining             60.00
                       Dinner at the Boathouse
                     Auto:Fuel          23.00
                       Gasoline - Jeep Wagoneer
                     Entertain          50.00
                        Play Tickets
                     Misc               50.00
        9/ 3 115    Maureks                       85.00             3,178.69
        1993 memo: Food
             cat: Groceries


        9/ 8          Cardinal Saving             200.00            2,978.69
        1993 memo: Transfer to savings
             cat: [Cardinal Saving]


        9/ 8 116    Orthodontics, Inc.           170.00             2,808.69
        1993 memo: Monthly Orthodontics Payment
             cat: Medical
```

Additional
account register
entries
Figure 7-8.

7

```
    Date  Num      Transaction            Payment  C  Deposit        Balance
    ----- ----  --------------------------  --------- -- --------     --------
    9/20  117   Maureks                      95.00                    2,713.69
    1993 memo: Food
           cat: Groceries

    9/25  118   Alltel                       29.00                    2,684.69
    1993 memo: Telephone Bill
           cat: Telephone

    9/25  119   Consumer Power               43.56                    2,641.13
    1993 memo: Electric Bill
           cat: Utilities:Electric

    9/25  120   West Michigan Gas            19.29                    2,621.84
    1993 memo: Gas Bill
           cat: Utilities:Gas

    10/1        Cardinal Saving             166.35                    2,455.49
    1993 memo: Transfer to savings
           cat: [Cardinal Saving]

    10/2        Payroll deposit                        1,585.99       4,041.48
    1993 memo: October 1 paycheck
           cat: Salary

    10/2  121   Great Lakes Savings & Loan  350.00                    3,691.48
    1993 memo: October Payment
           cat: Mort Pay

    10/4  122   Easy Credit Card            957.00                    2,734.48
    1993 SPLIT September 25th Statement
                    Clothing                 75.00
                      White Dress
                    Dining                   45.00
                      Dinner at the Boathouse
                    Auto:Fuel                37.00
                      Gasoline - Jeep Wagoneer
                    Furniture               550.00
                      Table and chairs
                    Entertain               100.00
                      Play Tickets
                    Misc                    150.00
```

Additional account register entries (*continued*)
Figure 7-8.

```
   Date  Num      Transaction      Payment  C  Deposit    Balance
   ----- ----  -------------------  -------- --  --------  --------

   10/ 5 123    Maureks             115.00              2,619.48
   1993 memo: Food
         cat: Groceries

   10/ 5        Cardinal Saving     200.00              2,419.48
   1993 memo: Transfer to savings
         cat: [Cardinal Saving]

   10/ 8 124    Orthodontics, Inc.  100.00              2,319.48
   1993 memo: Monthly Orthodontics Payment
         cat: Medical

   10/19 125    Maureks             135.00              2,184.48
   1993 memo: Food
         cat: Groceries

   10/25 126    Alltel               27.50              2,156.98
   1993 memo: Telephone Bill
         cat: Telephone

   10/25 127    Consumer Power       37.34              2,119.64
   1993 memo: Electric Bill
         cat: Utilities:Electric

   10/25 128    West Michigan Gas    16.55              2,103.09
   1993 memo: Gas Bill
         cat: Utilities:Gas
```

Additional account register entries (*continued*)
Figure 7-8.

2. Move the arrow cursor to the transaction you want to recall, Cardinal Saving, and press Enter.

3. Make any changes in the transaction. In this case, change the date to 9/1 and the amount to 194.79, and press Ctrl-Enter.

As explained earlier, excess cash in any month should be transferred to savings. This helps prevent impulsive buying if you are saving for larger outflows in later months of the year. But remember that when you plan an actual budget, you can build in varying monthly savings rather than use the approach of setting a minimum amount and transferring any excess of inflow or outflow at the beginning of each month.

4. Complete the example by entering all the information in your register exactly as shown in Figure 7-8.

In looking at the transactions shown in Figure 7-8, notice that you will primarily be recalling memorized transactions, transaction groups, and split transactions throughout the recording process. The only transactions that are not memorized are the grocery checks; for those you can utilize Quicken 6's QuickFill feature to minimize typing.

You use the Split Transaction windows to enter the Easy Credit Card transactions for check numbers 114 and 122 respectively. Notice that the Furniture category is not used in check 114 but is part of the credit card transaction for check 122. All the information you need to record these two transactions is included in Figure 7-8.

5. After entering the last transaction in Figure 7-8, select **R**eports, and the Reports menu will open.

6. Select **P**ersonal and then select Monthly **B**udget Report.

7. Press Enter to accept Quicken's default report title.

8. Type **8/93** and press Enter.

9. Type **10/93** and press F7, and the Create Budget Report window will appear.

10. Press Enter, three times.

11. Type **5** to select month for column headings and press Enter.

12. Type **C** and press Enter, and the Monthly Budget report appears.

Wide-Screen Reports

The Monthly Budget report you just generated is spread across more than one screen and may be difficult to comprehend until you realize how it is structured. In this section, you will explore the wide-screen report and become more familiar with Quicken results.

The steps listed here will help you become familiar with the Monthly Budget report generated from the additional data that you entered:

1. Use Tab, Shift-Tab, Pg Up, Pg Dn, Home, and End to become familiar with the appearance of the wide report for the budget.

Notice how easy it is to move around the report. Also notice that the File/Print option at the top accesses the Print features. [Home] always returns you to the left side and then the top of the wide-screen report as you press it repeatedly. [End] always takes you to the right side and then the bottom of the report. [Tab] moves you right, and [Shift]-[Tab] moves you left one screen. [Pg Up] moves you up one screen, while [Pg Dn] moves you down one screen.

You can move across the report an entire screen at once in two different ways. If you have the older type Quicken menus with numbered selections and function keys, you can press [Tab] to move one screen to the right and [Shift]-[Tab] to move one screen to the left. With the newer style Quicken menu, you press [Ctrl]-[←] and [Ctrl]-[→] to take the same action. When the Quicken 6 menus are installed, [Tab] and [Shift]-[Tab] move only one column at a time.

2. If you have the compressed print option, it is recommended that you use that setting to produce wide reports. This printer option significantly increases the amount of information you can print on a page.

When you print wide-screen reports, Quicken numbers the pages of the report so you can more easily follow on hard copy.

Report Discussion   The steps for preparing and printing the report will become familiar with a little practice. The real issue is how to use the information. Let's look at the report and discuss some of the findings.

1. Press [End] twice. Quicken takes you to the lower-right side of the quarterly report. This shows that for the quarter you spent $1,041 more than you had budgeted.
2. Using [↑], move up the report one line at a time until the title "Entire Mortgage Payment" is in the upper-left corner of the screen.

You now have the quarterly outflow information on the screen for the three months of data you prepared earlier.

Notice that a part of the explanation for the actual outflows exceeding the inflows is due to $361 being transferred to savings. Most of us would not view that as poor results. On the other hand, you can see that you have spent $582 more on furniture than you had budgeted. This may be because sale prices justified deviating from the budget. But it could also be compulsive buying that can't be afforded over the long run. If you find yourself over budget, the special section entitled "Dealing with an Over-Budget Situation" provides some suggestions for improving the situation.

Figure 7-9 shows the budget summary for the period 8/1/93 through 10/31/93. It was produced by requesting a Monthly Budget report using Six Months for the column headings. The **L**ayout **H**ide **C**ents option in the Report window was used to toggle off the display of cents. Remember that the information Quicken uses in the Budget column came from the budgeted amounts you established earlier in this chapter. The information in the Actual column is summarized from the account register entries recorded in your Cardinal Bank checking account. You could also request a Cash Flow report by month for the budget period and examine the monthly outflow patterns. You might want to print out itemized category information for some categories during the period for more detailed analysis of expenditures.

Graph Options   Quicken 6's new graph capabilities provide other budget monitoring tools. Quicken provides different graph options under the View **G**raphs selection on the Main Menu. Both the Income and Expense selection and Budget and the Actual Selections choice that appear on the next menu will provide tools for monitoring your budget.

One interest you may have is taking a look at the composition of your expenditures. This helps you to identify areas of major costs and lets you take a look to see if any of them can be reduced. To display a graph showing expense composition on your screen follow these steps:

1. From the Main Menu select View **G**raphs to see this menu:

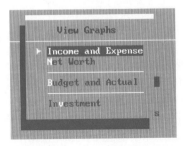

```
                         Monthly Budget Report
                       8/ 1/93 Through 10/31/93
PERSONAL-Cardinal Bank                                  Page 1
10/31/93
                                  8/ 1/93    -    10/31/93
                Category Description  Actual   Budget    Diff
------------------------------------  -------------------------
        INFLOWS
          Salary Income               4,758    4,758      -0
                                      ---------- ---------- --------
        TOTAL INFLOWS                 4,758    4,758       0
        OUTFLOWS
          Automobile Expenses:
            Auto Fuel                   83       90       -7
                                      ---------- ---------- --------
            Total Automobile Expenses  83       90       -7
          Clothing                     175      210      -35
          Dining Out                   165      165        0
          Entertainment                200      165       35
          Entire Mortgage Payment    1,050    1,050        0
          Groceries                    648      600       48
          Household Furniture          767      185      582
          Medical & Dental             370      360       10
          Miscellaneous                250      225       25
          Telephone Expense            80       90      -10
          Water, Gas, Electric:
            Electric Utilities         112       75       37
            Gas Utilities              55       60       -5
                                      ---------- ---------- --------
            Total Water, Gas, Electric 167      135       32
          TO Cardinal Saving           961      600      361
                                      ---------- ---------- --------
        TOTAL OUTFLOWS               4,916    3,875    1,041

                                      ---------- ---------- --------
        OVERALL TOTAL                 -158      883   -1,041
                                      ========== ========== ========
```

Three-month
budget report
Figure 7-9.

Dealing with an Over-Budget Situation

Expenses cannot continue to outpace income indefinitely. The extent of the budget overage and the availability of financial reserves to cover it dictate the seriousness of the problem and how quickly and drastically cuts must be made to reverse the situation. Although the causes of an over-budget situation are numerous, the following strategies can help correct the problem:

♦ If existing debt is the problem, consider a consolidation loan—especially if the interest rate is lower than existing installment interest charges. Then, don't use your credit until the consolidated loan is paid in full.

♦ If day-to-day variable expenses are causing the overrun, begin keeping detailed records of all cash expenditures. Look closely at what you are spending for eating out, entertainment, and various impulse purchases such as clothing, gifts, and other nonessential items.

♦ Locate warehouse, discount, thrift, and used clothing stores in your area and shop for items you *need* at these locations. Garage sales, flea markets, and the classified ads can sometimes provide what you need at a fraction of the retail cost.

♦ Be certain that you are allocating each family member an allowance for discretionary spending and that each is adhering to the total.

♦ If you cannot find a way to lower expenses any further, consider a free-lance or part-time job until your financial situation improves. Many creative people supplement their regular income with a small-business venture.

♦ Plan ahead for major expenses by splitting the cost of car insurance, property taxes, and so on over 12 months and transferring each month's portion to savings until it is time to pay the bill. If you have saved for it, you can then transfer the amount saved to the checking account the month of the anticipated expenditure.

2. Select **I**ncome and Expense.

3. Select **E**xpense Composition.

4. Type **7/93** and press Enter.

5. Type **9/93** and press Enter.

6. If you haven't created a graph before, Quicken will prompt you to establish default graph settings. Press Enter to accept the default graphics driver and Ctrl-Enter to accept the default text and graph size.

Quicken displays the graph shown in Figure 7-10.

7. Press Esc until the Main Menu is displayed.

NOTE: Quicken does not support printing of the graphs that you create. To print a Quicken graph you could capture the screen that displays it with a screen capture utility such as INSET or COLLAGE and then print it from the utility program that captured the screen for you.

7

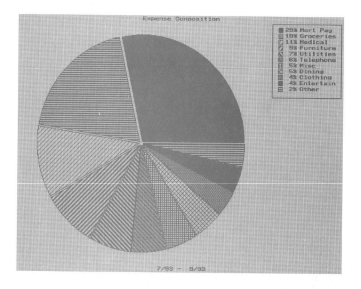

Expense
Composition
graph
Figure 7-10.

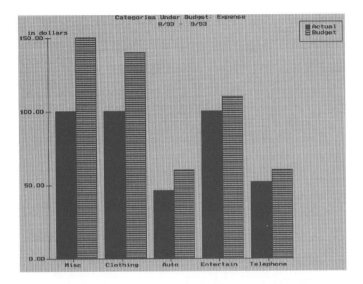

Expense
Categories
Under Budget
graph
Figure 7-11.

Quicken allows you to focus in on the detail for budget categories with a graph as well. You might want to look at categories that were either under or over budget. To see a bar chart that displays the actual versus budget for categories under budget follow these steps:

1. Select View **G**raphs from the Main Menu.
2. Select **B**udget and Actual.
3. Select Categories **U**nder Budget.
4. Type **8/93** and press Enter.
5. Type **9/93** and press Enter.
6. Type **E** and press Enter.

The graph shown in Figure 7-11 displays on your screen.

7. Press Esc until the Main Menu displays.

You should feel free to experiment with the other graph types. None of your selections will affect register entries, so you do not have to worry about making mistakes.

CHAPTER

8

USING QUICKEN TO ORGANIZE TAX INFORMATION

Quicken's contribution to your financial planning and monitoring goes beyond recording transactions. You have already used Quicken to handle your budget entries and reports. Quicken can also help you with your tax preparation. Although using the package probably won't make tax preparation fun, it can reduce the tax-time crunch by organizing your tax information throughout the year. If you plan your categories and classes correctly and you faithfully complete all your entries, the hard part is done. You will then be able to use Quicken's summaries to provide the entries for specific lines on tax forms.

In this chapter, you will see how Quicken can help you at tax time. After looking at a few ideas for organizing needed tax information, you will modify the account register prepared in Chapters 6 and 7 to better show your tax-related information. You will prepare tax summary information from the Standard Reports option of the package. You will also look at Quicken's features that allow you to assign categories to lines within tax schedules. This allows Quicken to better organize your tax information.

NOTE: You must remember that Quicken reports will not be considered sufficient documentation of tax-deductible expenses. See the special section "Essential Tax Documentation" for a list of some of the forms you might need to substantiate expense claims to the IRS in an audit.

Quicken Tax Overview

This chapter focuses on how Quicken can help you prepare your tax returns. You can use Quicken's categories and classes to categorize data for your taxes. Categories are defined as tax related or not and can be assigned to tax schedules. You can change the tax-related status and tax schedule assignment of any of the existing categories by editing the current category in the category list with Ctrl-E. You can also define a tax-related status for any new category as you enter it.

Quicken can be used to collect information for specific line items on tax forms such as Form 1040, Schedule A (itemized deductions), Schedule B (dividends and interest), and Schedule E (royalties and rents). Figures 8-1 and 8-2 show two of these forms. Defining and using classes for your transactions will allow you to collect additional details from your financial transactions. Assigning tax schedules and lines to categories allows Quicken to accumulate the information that you need for a particular line on a tax form.

Form **1040** Department of the Treasury—Internal Revenue Service
U.S. Individual Income Tax Return 1991 (L)

For the year Jan.–Dec. 31, 1991, or other tax year beginning _____ , 1991, ending _____ , 19 __ | OMB No. 1545-0074

Label (See instructions on page 11.) Use the IRS label. Otherwise, please print or type.

LABEL HERE

Your first name and initial | Last name | Your social security number

If a joint return, spouse's first name and initial | Last name | Spouse's social security number

Home address (number and street). (If you have a P.O. box, see page 11.) | Apt. no.

City, town or post office, state, and ZIP code. (If you have a foreign address, see page 11.)

For Privacy Act and Paperwork Reduction Act Notice, see instructions.

Presidential Election Campaign (See page 11.)

Do you want $1 to go to this fund? . . . . | Yes | No
If joint return, does your spouse want $1 to go to this fund? | Yes | No

Note: Checking "Yes" will not change your tax or reduce your refund.

Filing Status

Check only one box.

1 ☐ Single
2 ☐ Married filing joint return (even if only one had income)
3 ☐ Married filing separate return. Enter spouse's social security no. above and full name here. ▶ _____
4 ☐ Head of household (with qualifying person). (See page 12.) If the qualifying person is a child but not your dependent, enter this child's name here. ▶ _____
5 ☐ Qualifying widow(er) with dependent child (year spouse died ▶ 19 __). (See page 12.)

Exemptions (See page 12.)

6a ☐ **Yourself.** If your parent (or someone else) can claim you as a dependent on his or her tax return, do not check box 6a. But be sure to check the box on line 33b on page 2.

b ☐ **Spouse** . . . .

c **Dependents:**

(1) Name (first, initial, and last name)	(2) Check if under age 1	(3) If age 1 or older, dependent's social security number	(4) Dependent's relationship to you	(5) No. of months lived in your home in 1991
		:		
		:		
		:		
		:		
		:		

If more than six dependents, see page 13.

No. of boxes checked on 6a and 6b
No. of your children on 6c who:
• lived with you
• didn't live with you due to divorce or separation (see page 14)
No. of other dependents on 6c

d If your child didn't live with you but is claimed as your dependent under a pre-1985 agreement, check here ▶ ☐

e Total number of exemptions claimed . . . .

Add numbers entered on lines above ▶

Income

Attach Copy B of your Forms W-2, W-2G, and 1099-R here.

If you did not get a W-2, see page 10.

Attach check or money order on top of any Forms W-2, W-2G, or 1099-R.

7 Wages, salaries, tips, etc. *(attach Form(s) W-2)* . . . . . | 7
8a Taxable interest income *(also attach Schedule B if over $400)* . . . | 8a
b Tax-exempt interest income (see page 16). DON'T include on line 8a | 8b |
9 Dividend income *(also attach Schedule B if over $400)* . . . | 9
10 Taxable refunds of state and local income taxes, if any, from worksheet on page 16 . | 10
11 Alimony received . . . . | 11
12 Business income or (loss) *(attach Schedule C)* . . . . . | 12
13 Capital gain or (loss) *(attach Schedule D)* . . . . . | 13
14 Capital gain distributions not reported on line 13 (see page 17) . . | 14
15 Other gains or (losses) *(attach Form 4797)* . . . . . | 15
16a Total IRA distributions | 16a | 16b Taxable amount (see page 17) | 16b
17a Total pensions and annuities | 17a | 17b Taxable amount (see page 17) | 17b
18 Rents, royalties, partnerships, estates, trusts, etc. *(attach Schedule E)* . | 18
19 Farm income or (loss) *(attach Schedule F)* . . . . . | 19
20 Unemployment compensation (insurance) (see page 18) . . . | 20
21a Social security benefits. | 21a | 21b Taxable amount (see page 18) | 21b
22 Other income (list type and amount—see page 19) . . . . | 22
23 Add the amounts shown in the far right column for lines 7 through 22. This is your **total income** ▶ | 23

Adjustments to Income (See page 19.)

24a Your IRA deduction, from applicable worksheet on page 20 or 21 | 24a
b Spouse's IRA deduction, from applicable worksheet on page 20 or 21 | 24b
25 One-half of self-employment tax (see page 21) . . . | 25
26 Self-employed health insurance deduction, from worksheet on page 22 . | 26
27 Keogh retirement plan and self-employed SEP deduction | 27
28 Penalty on early withdrawal of savings . . . . | 28
29 Alimony paid. Recipient's SSN ▶ | 29
30 Add lines 24a through 29. These are your **total adjustments** . . . ▶ | 30

Adjusted Gross Income

31 Subtract line 30 from line 23. This is your **adjusted gross income.** If this amount is less than $21,250 and a child lived with you, see page 45 to find out if you can claim the "Earned Income Credit" on line 56. . . . . ▶ | 31

Cat. No. 12600W

8

Federal Form 1040

Figure 8-1.

SCHEDULES A&B (Form 1040) Department of the Treasury (L) Internal Revenue Service	Schedule A—Itemized Deductions (Schedule B is on back) ► Attach to Form 1040. ► See Instructions for Schedules A and B (Form 1040).	OMB No. 1545-0074 19**91** Attachment Sequence No. **07**

Name(s) shown on Form 1040 | Your social security number

Medical **and** **Dental** **Expenses**		**Caution:** *Do not include expenses reimbursed or paid by others.*	
	1	Medical and dental expenses. (See page 38.)	1
	2	Enter amount from Form 1040, line 32 | **2** |	
	3	Multiply line 2 above by 7.5% (.075)	3
	4	Subtract line 3 from line 1. Enter the result. If less than zero, enter -0- . . . ►	4
Taxes You **Paid** (See page 38.)	5	State and local income taxes	5
	6	Real estate taxes	6
	7	Other taxes. (List—include personal property taxes.) ►	7
	8	Add lines 5 through 7. Enter the total . . . . ►	8
Interest **You Paid** (See page 39.)	9a	Home mortgage interest and points reported to you on Form 1098	9a
	b	Home mortgage interest not reported to you on Form 1098. (If paid to an individual, show that person's name and address.) ►	
Note: Personal interest is no longer deductible.			9b
	10	Points not reported to you on Form 1098. (See instructions for special rules.)	10
	11	Investment interest (attach Form 4952 if required). (See page 40.)	11
	12	Add lines 9a through 11. Enter the total . . . . ►	12
Gifts to **Charity** (See page 40.)		**Caution:** *If you made a charitable contribution and received a benefit in return, see page 40.*	
	13	Contributions by cash or check	13
	14	Other than cash or check. (You **MUST** attach Form 8283 if over $500.)	14
	15	Carryover from prior year	15
	16	Add lines 13 through 15. Enter the total . . . . ►	16
Casualty and **Theft Losses**	17	Casualty or theft loss(es) (attach Form 4684). (See page 40.) . . . . . ►	17
Moving **Expenses**	18	Moving expenses (attach Form 3903 or 3903F). (See page 41.) . . . . . ►	18
Job Expenses **and Most Other** **Miscellaneous** **Deductions** (See page 41 for expenses to deduct here.)	19	Unreimbursed employee expenses—job travel, union dues, job education, etc. (You **MUST** attach Form 2106 if required. See instructions.) ►	19
	20	Other expenses (investment, tax preparation, safe deposit box, etc.). List type and amount ►................	20
	21	Add lines 19 and 20	21
	22	Enter amount from Form 1040, line 32 | **22** |	
	23	Multiply line 22 above by 2% (.02)	23
	24	Subtract line 23 from line 21. Enter the result. If less than zero, enter -0- . . . ►	24
Other **Miscellaneous** **Deductions**	25	Other (from list on page 41 of instructions). List type and amount ►................	
			25
Total **Itemized** **Deductions**	26	• If the amount on Form 1040, line 32, is $100,000 or less ($50,000 or less if married filing separately), add lines 4, 8, 12, 16, 17, 18, 24, and 25. Enter the total here. . . . . }►	26
		• If the amount on Form 1040, line 32, is more than $100,000 (more than $50,000 if married filing separately), see page 42 for the amount to enter.	
		Caution: *Be sure to enter on Form 1040, line 34, the **LARGER** of the amount on line 26 above or your standard deduction.*	

For Paperwork Reduction Act Notice, see Form 1040 instructions. | Cat. No. 12614K | Schedule A (Form 1040) 1991

Schedule A for
itemized
deductions
Figure 8-2.

Essential Tax Documentation

The entries in your Quicken register will not convince the IRS that you incurred expenses as indicated. You need documentation of each expense to substantiate your deductions in the event of an audit. Although you may be able to convince the IRS to accept estimates for some categories based on other evidence, the following are some ideas of the optimal proof you will want to be able to present:

Expense Claimed	Proof
Dependents other than minor children	Receipts for individuals' support. Records of the individuals' income and support from others
Interest	Creditor statements of interest paid
Investments	Purchase receipts and brokerage firms' confirmation receipts
Medical and dental care	Canceled check with receipt indicating individual treated
Medical insurance	Pay stubs showing deductions or other paid receipts
Moving expenses	Itemized receipts and proof of employment for 12 months in previous job
Pharmacy/drugs	Itemized receipts and canceled checks
Real estate taxes	Receipt for taxes paid. Settlement papers for real estate transactions in the current year
Unreimbursed business expenses	Itemized receipts, canceled checks, and mileage logs

8

In fact, once you become familiar with Quicken, you can use the package to accumulate the exact information you need to prepare your taxes. For example, you may decide to tag specific tax information by setting up classes for categories that are tax related and specific to a particular tax form. At the end of the year, you can have Quicken print the transactions that you need for a particular line. In your own Quicken system, you may want to identify the specific forms associated with these items. For example, "Tax Fed/1040" indicates a class for transactions affecting Form 1040. Another approach is to create a class that represents a line item on a specific form. For example, "Mort Int/A--9A" is more specific. The class entry "A--9A" indicates Schedule A, line 9A—mortgage interest paid to financial institutions. You could then have Quicken generate the tax-related information by tax form or line item and use these totals to complete your taxes.

In this chapter, tax-related categories for federal income tax withholding and state income tax withholding are created. A category for local income tax withholding will also be established. You will split entries for mortgage payments into mortgage interest and payments against the principal. Also, you will modify some of the transactions from earlier chapters to provide the additional tax information that you'll need here.

In later chapters, you will combine Quicken's personal tax-related reports with the business reports. In these, you will have a powerful tax-monitoring and planning tool.

Planning to Use Quicken for Taxes

There is no one correct way to record tax information in Quicken. The best method is to tailor your transaction entries to the information that will be required on your tax forms. This is a good approach even if you have an accountant prepare your return. Remember, if you organize your tax information, your accountant will not have to—and you will pay less for tax preparation as a result.

Start the planning process with the forms you filed last year. This may be just the Form 1040 that everyone files or it may include a number of schedules. Although the forms change a little from year to year and your need to file a certain form can be a one-time occurrence, last year's forms make a good starting place. Form 1040, partially shown in Figure 8-1, is the basic tax form used by individuals. Schedule A, shown in Figure 8-2, is used for itemized deductions.

You can choose from three different methods to have Quicken accumulate information for the various tax forms and schedules that you will need to prepare at the end of the year. The first method is to use category assignments to identify tax-related information and to produce a tax summary at the end of the year that contains all of the tax-related category entries. This is the simplest method, but it provides the least detail.

With Quicken 5 and 6, you have the option of assigning each category and subcategory to a tax schedule. You can even assign the category or subcategory to a particular line on this schedule. To make this assignment, you display the category list with Ctrl-C from the Register window, highlight the category for which you want to make a tax schedule assignment, and press Ctrl-E to edit the category. When the Edit Category window appears, you can press F9 (Tax Schedules) to select a tax schedule. After you select a schedule, a second list displays to allow you to select a line entry on the selected schedule. The lines are given names rather than numbers to make your selection easier. If you use these methods, you can produce a tax schedule report that lists all tax-related entries by line within schedules.

The third option for categorizing tax data is to use a class assignment. Class assignments provide a way to further organize categories and subcategories. You can assign multiple classes to your existing categories and subcategories. You make these assignments as you enter transactions by typing a / followed by the class name after a category or subcategory. Although this is more work than using Quicken's tax schedule assignments, it does offer the potential of providing the greatest level of detail within your existing category structure.

If you have unreimbursed business expenses that exceed a certain percentage of your income, you might want to set up a class for Form 2106, which is used exclusively for these expenses, or set up a category for these expenses and assign this category to tax schedule 2106 with Quicken's Tax Schedule feature. If you own and manage rental properties, you must use Schedule E to monitor income and expenses for these properties. With Quicken, you can classify the income and expense transactions for Schedule E.

With Form 2106 expenses, you will not know until the end of the year if you have enough expenses to deduct them. With the class code approach, you would use a class called 2106 for transactions of unreimbursed business expenses and check the total at year-end. Travel and entertainment expenses, meals, and professional association dues and subscriptions would all be assigned this class code to ensure that you collect them all. If you use the tax schedule assignment method, you would need to set up a new category for unreimbursed business expenses and assign this category to tax schedule Form 2106.

Another thing to watch for is the timing of expense recognition. *Expense recognition* determines which tax year expenses at the beginning or end of the year will affect. This is a particular problem for items that are charged since the IRS recognizes an expense as occurring the day you charge it rather than the day you pay for it. Unreimbursed air travel charged in December 1992 and paid by check in January 1993 is counted in 1992 totals since you incur the liability for payment the day you charge the tickets. A separate Quicken account for credit purchases makes these necessary year-end adjustments easier than when you just keep track of credit card payments from your checkbook.

If you decide to use classes rather than tax schedule assignments to categorize tax information, you might decide your class codes should indicate more than the number of the tax form where the information is used. As you look at the forms shown in Figures 8-1 and 8-2, you will find that each of the lines where information can be entered is numbered. For example, line 7 of your 1040 is "Wages, salaries, tips, etc.," which you could probably fill in with the total from the Salary category—if you have only one source of income.

But when you set up Quicken categories for income from several sources, you might want to assign a class called "1040--7" to each income transaction, so you could display a total of all the entries for this class. Likewise, you can set up classes for other line items such as "A--6" for real estate tax or "A--13" for cash contributions. You could also set up "1040--21a" for Social Security benefits and "1040--9" for dividend income, but if you do decide to use classes, there is no need to establish a class for every line on every form—only for those lines that you are likely to use.

REMEMBER: When creating a class you must enter the category, a slash (/), and then the class.

Classes are almost a requirement for rental property management since the same types of expenses and incomes will repeat for each property. You might use the street address or apartment number to distinguish the transactions generated by different properties. You can use the Split Transaction feature if one transaction covers expenses or income for more than one property.

Most of your entries will focus on the current tax year, but there is also longer-term tax-related information that is sometimes needed. When you sell assets such as a house or stock holdings, information must be accumulated over the time you own the asset. Maintaining information on these assets in separate accounts is the best approach to use. Separate accounts can make it much easier to calculate the profit on the sale of the asset. For example, if you purchased a house for $100,000 and sold it five years later for $150,000, it might seem as though the profit is $50,000. However, if you have accurately recorded improvements such as a new deck and a fireplace, these amounts can be added to the cost of the asset since they are items that added value. When the $35,000 cost of these improvements is added to the price of the house, the profit is $15,000 for tax purposes. Take a look at the sample transaction in the next section and the tax reports before making your final decisions about classes and categories for your tax information. Depending on the complexity of your tax situation, simple category assignments might be sufficient.

8

Recording Detailed Tax Information

In Chapter 7, "Quicken as a Budgeting Tool," you recorded detailed transaction information in the account register for your Cardinal Bank checking account. Scroll through those transactions and notice how the monthly paycheck and mortgage payment transactions were treated.

For the paycheck, you entered the amount of the check, net of deductions for items such as FICA, federal withholding, medical, and state withholding. For the monthly mortgage payment, you established a tax-related category called Mort Pay and used that for the entire payment. However, Quicken can provide much better tax-related information in both these areas. You will want to make the suggested changes if you want Quicken to accumulate tax schedule information for you. The following sections will show you how.

Gross Earnings and Salary Deductions

Highlight the first payroll transaction you recorded in your Cardinal Bank personal account register in Chapter 6, "Expanding the Scope of Financial Entries." The amount of the net deposit was $1585.99—you didn't record any of the tax-related information for deductions. The entry you made then was adequate for maintaining a correct check register. It is also adequate for budgeting purposes since you only need to match cash inflows and outflows, and the net amount of the payroll check represents the inflow for the period. However, for tax purposes, more information is needed. By completing the following entry, you will be able to monitor the amounts on your pay stub. You will also be able to verify the accuracy of your Form W2 at the end of the year.

To expand the payroll transaction, you need some additional information. The gross earnings for the pay period were $2000.00. The deductions withheld for FICA taxes were $124.00, medical insurance was $42.01, federal taxes were $130.00, state taxes were $80.00, and local taxes were $10.00.

The following steps illustrate how you can use Quicken's Split Transaction feature to capture all the information related to the tax aspects of your paycheck and still show the net deposit of $1585.99 to the checking account.

1. With the first payroll entry highlighted, press Ctrl-S, and the Split Transaction window appears on your screen.
2. Press Enter to leave Salary as the category.
3. Type **Gross Wages Earned** in the Memo field and press Enter.
4. Type **2000.00** in the Amount field and press Enter.

These modifications set your Salary category as your gross earnings for the period. Each time you record your paycheck this way, Quicken accumulates your year-to-date gross earnings. After recording this portion of the transaction, you are left with –414.01 in the Amount field. This is Quicken's way of telling you there is currently a negative difference between the amount of the net deposit and the gross wages recorded. This difference equals the amount of withholding from your paycheck that will be recorded in the remaining steps.

5. Type **Tax:FICA** and press (Enter).
6. Type **FICA Withholding** and press (Enter).
7. Type **–124.00** and press (Enter).

Once again, Quicken records the information in the Split Transaction window and leaves a balance of –290.01 in the Amount field for row 3. This category is predefined as tax related in Quicken, even though FICA withholding is not ordinarily tax deductible on your Form 1040. This is because you should monitor this amount if you change jobs during the year. Since there is a limit on the amount of earnings taxed for FICA, switching jobs can cause you to pay more than you owe; the second employer will not know what was withheld by the first. You can include excess FICA payments on your Form 1040 with other withholding amounts (on line 58). If you earn less than the upper limit, this category will not be used in your tax preparation process.

8

8. Type **Tax:MCARE** and press (Enter).
9. Select Add to Category List.
10. Press (Enter) to accept S for subcategory.
11. Type **Medicare Withholding** and press (Enter).
12. Type **Y** for tax related and press (Ctrl)-(Enter).
13. Press (Enter) and then type **Medicare Withholding** and press (Enter).
14. Type **–29.00** and press (Enter).
15. Type **Medical** and press (Enter).
16. Type **Health Ins** and press (Enter).
17. Type **–42.01** and press (Enter).
18. Type **Tax:Fed** and press (Enter).

19. Type **Federal Income Tax** and press (Enter).
20. Type **–130.00** and press (Enter) to record the amount.
21. Type **Tax:State** and press (Enter).
22. Type **State Income Tax** and press (Enter).
23. Type **–80.00** and press (Enter).
24. Type **Tax:Local** and press (Enter).

Quicken will prompt you by stating that this is not a predefined category. Tell Quicken to enter the category with the following steps:

25. Type **1** in response to the Category Not Found window prompt.
26. Type **S** and press (Enter).
27. Type **Local Tax Withholding** and press (Enter).
28. Type **Y** and press (Enter) to identify this as a tax-related category in response to the Set Up Category window.
29. Press (Enter) when the Set Up Category window closes.
30. Type **Local Income Tax**, and press (Enter).

You see the screen shown in Figure 8-3. Notice that there is no balance left to explain in the Split Transaction screen.

Split Transaction window after recording withholding and other deductions
Figure 8-3.

Print/Acct	Edit	Shortcuts	Reports	Activities			F1-Help
Date	Num	Payee · Memo ·	Category	Payment	C	Deposit	Balance
8/01		Payroll deposit				1,585 99	3,846 69↑
1993	SPLIT	August 1 paycheck					
	Cat:	Salary					
8/02	104	Great Lakes Savings & Loan		350 00			3,496 69

Split Transaction

Category	Memo	Amount
3:Tax:MCARE	Medicare Withholding	-29.00↑–
4:Medical	Health Ins	-42.01
5:Tax:Fed	Federal Income Tax	-130.00
6:Tax:State	State Income Tax	-80.00
7:Tax:Local	Local Income Tax	-9.00
8:		↓

Enter categories, descriptions, and amounts

Esc-Cancel   Ctrl-D Delete   F9-Recalc Transaction Total   Ctrl↵ Done

31. Press [Ctrl]-[Enter] and Quicken returns you to the Register window.

Since you memorized this transaction in Chapter 6, be sure to rememorize it after this change by pressing [Ctrl]-[M]. You are asked whether you want to memorize the amounts or the percentages. Using this approach requires you to delete the memorized payroll transaction without the split. You can also edit the memorized transaction to make the change.

32. Type **A** and press [Enter] to memorize the amounts.
33. Press [Ctrl]-[Enter] again to tell Quicken to accept the changed transaction.

After you complete this process, all the information in the Split Transaction window is recorded in your accounts. Your reports will show gross earnings for tax purposes at $2000.00, with tax-related deductions for FICA, medical, and federal, state, and local taxes.

Mortgage Principal and Interest

The mortgage payment transaction recorded in Chapter 6 was fine for recording changes to your checking account balance or monitoring budgeted expenses. However, it didn't capture the tax-related aspects of the transaction. Although you identified the transaction as tax related, the mortgage principal and interest were not isolated. You would not be able to tell how much to list on your tax return as interest expense. But perhaps your bank will provide you a statement with this information at the end of the year. In some cases, the bank even divides your previous month's payment among principal, interest, and escrow on the current month's bill. However, if you purchased from a private individual, you will not receive this information, although you can have Quicken calculate it for you since accurate records are necessary to take the mortage interest expense as a tax deduction. Quicken will continue to assist you by organizing it in the recording process.

On your screen, highlight the first Great Lakes Savings & Loan mortgage payment of $350.00 on 8/2/93 that you made in Chapter 6. Using Quicken's Split Transaction feature again, you will modify the record of this transaction to distribute the payment between principal and interest. The steps outlined here assume that you know which

8

payment number you are making and that you pay your insurance and taxes directly to the insurer and local taxing unit with checks recorded separately in your register. If the financial institution has established an escrow account for these payments, you could easily add that amount to this transaction. Quicken has predefined a tax-related category called Escrow.

The following procedures illustrate how Quicken can be used to create a loan amortization schedule and track your mortgage principal and interest payments:

1. With the first mortgage payment entry highlighted on the screen, select **A**ctivities, select **F**inancial Planning, and then select **L**oan Calculator.

2. Type **39999** for the principal and press (Enter).

3. Type **9.519** for the annual interest rate and press (Enter).

4. Type **25** for the total years and press (Enter).

5. Type **12** for the periods per year and press (Enter).

6. Press (F9) (View Payment Schedule) to view the schedule.

Figure 8-4 shows the top part of this schedule. You can print it out for future reference with (Ctrl)-(P). Since you are about to make your 53rd

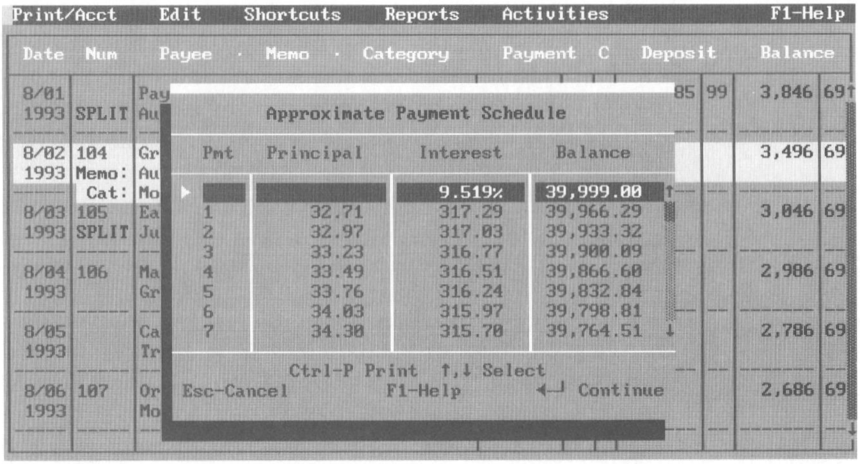

Payment schedule created with Loan Calculator
Figure 8-4.

payment, you would look down the schedule for payment 53 to get the numbers that you need.

7. Press Esc twice to return to the register.
8. Make certain your Great Lakes Savings and Loan transaction for August is highlighted.
9. Press Ctrl-S and the Split Transaction window appears.
10. Type **Mort Prin** and press Enter.

If you do not have this category on your list, add it to your list following the process described in the section "Adding a Category" in Chapter 6. When setting up the category, it is not tax-related.

11. Type **Principal Payment** and press Enter for the memo.
12. Type **49.33** and press Enter to record the portion of the transaction related to principal.
13. Type **Mort Int** and press Enter.
14. Type **Interest Portion of Payment** and press Enter.
15. The amount shown in the last column, 300.67, is correct. You see the screen shown in Figure 8-5.

8

Split Transaction window after distributing principal and interest
Figure 8-5.

16. Press Ctrl-Enter and Quicken returns you to the highlighted transaction for the mortgage payment in your register.

17. Press Ctrl-Enter to record the new split transaction information.

After recording these two transactions, you can see the expanded benefits of the information when it is organized by Quicken. Once again, you want to rememorize this transaction for monthly recording purposes. The next section takes a look at the tax information you have now entered into your Quicken system.

Printing Quicken's Tax Reports

The summary tax information generated by Quicken can be used to provide detailed information for preparing your taxes. In this section you will examine the reports generated using the information from the Cardinal Bank account register for the first month (8/1/93 through 8/31/93). The following steps generate Quicken's Tax Summary report:

1. From the account register, select **R**eports, select **P**ersonal Reports, and select **T**ax Summary. Quicken's Tax Summary Report window will appear on your screen.

2. Type **Tax Summary Report** and press Enter.

3. Press F7 and the Create Transaction Report window appears.

This step is performed so you can have Quicken print the reports for the current account and specified time period only. If you had proceeded through the previous window, reports would have been automatically prepared for all the accounts in the account group. (You will remember this step from previous chapters.)

4. Press Enter, type **8/1/93**, and press Enter again.

5. Type **8/31/93** and press Enter.

6. Press Enter to accept "Subtotal by Category."

7. Type **C** to select the current account and press Enter.

The Tax Summary report will appear on your screen. You can use F9 to change from full-width to half-width reports. You can also use the arrow keys to move through the report (the directions in which the report extends are shown in the lower-right corner of the screen).

8. Select **F**ile/Print and the **P**rint Report window will appear on the screen.

9. Choose your printer option and press Enter. Quicken will print the tax summary by category, as shown in Figure 8-6.

8

```
                        Tax Summary Report
                     8/1/93 Through 8/31/93
   PERSONAL-Cardinal Bank                        Page 1
   8/25/93


   Date Num      Description       Memo         Category    Clr   Amount
   ---- ----  ----------------  ------------  ------------  ---   -------

         INCOME/EXPENSE
            INCOME
               Salary Income
               -------------
   8/ 1        S Payroll deposit   Gross Wages    Salary     2,000.00
                                   Earned                   ----------
                  Total Salary Income                        2,000.00
                                                            ----------
            TOTAL INCOME                                     2,000.00


            EXPENSES
               Medical & Dental
               ----------------
   8/ 1        S Payroll deposit   Health Ins    Medical       -42.01
   8/ 6 107    Orthodontics, Inc.  Monthly       Medical
                                   Orthodontics  Payment      -100.00
                                                            ----------
                  Total Medical & Dental                      -142.01

               Mortgage Interest Exp
               ---------------------
   8/ 2 104 S Great Lakes Savings
               & Loan              Interest      Mort Int     -300.67
                                   Portion of Payment        ----------
                  Total Mortgage Interest Exp                 -300.67
```

Partial Tax Summary report for the Cardinal Bank checking account using full-width printing
Figure 8-6.

Tax Summary Report

The report in Figure 8-6 is a full-width version of the report, with complete information for all transaction fields. If you printed the same version of the report without the wide-print option, the result would be a narrower report. Although the same information is included on both reports, the full-width version presents the detail with fewer abbreviations. The additional space between fields also makes it easier to understand. This format would be preferable for presentation to tax consultants and preparers.

Quicken prints the complete detail for each of the tax-related categories as the default report. This format allows you to use the totals generated at the end of the tax year for entry on your tax returns. The totals generated in Figure 8-6 would be used on the following lines of your personal income tax form for 1991:

Income/Expense Category	Tax Return Location
Total Salary Income	Form 1040 line 7
Total Federal Tax Withholding	Form 1040 line 54
Total Medical & Dental	Schedule A line 1
Total Mortgage Interest Exp	Schedule A line 9a
Total State Tax Withholding	Schedule A line 5
Total Local Income Tax	Schedule A line 5

This also provides an excellent summary and could prove useful in the event of an IRS tax audit inquiry.

As you will see in Chapter 10, "Creating Custom Reports," all Quicken reports can be customized in many different report formats (months, quarters, half years, and so on). One variation discussed in the previous chapter compared reports prepared for a separate account, Cardinal Bank, and one prepared for all accounts. The report for all accounts used the bank checking accounts, cash, and credit card accounts from the PERSONAL file. Here, while Figure 8-6 was prepared for a single account, Cardinal Bank, Figure 8-7 illustrates a Tax Summary report including all accounts in the PERSONAL file. Note that the second

```
                        Tax Summary Report
                      8/1/93 Through 8/31/93
PERSONAL-All Accounts                                    Page 1
9/12/93


Date   Acct    Num     Description        Memo       Category   Clr  Amount
------ ------- ---  ------------------- ---------- ----------- --- -------


          INCOME/EXPENSE
             INCOME
                Salary Income
                -------------
8/ 1 Cardinal  S Payroll deposit      Gross Wages  Salary    2,000.00
                                                             ---------
                  Total Salary Income                        2,000.00
                                                             ---------
               TOTAL INCOME                                  2,000.00

             EXPENSES
                Medical & Dental
                ----------------
8/ 1 Cardinal   S Payroll deposit      Health Ins  Medical      42.01
8/ 6 Cardinal 107 Orthodontics, In     Monthly Ort Medical    -100.00
                                                             ---------
                  Total Medical & Dental                      -142.01

                Mortgage Interest Exp
                ---------------------
8/ 2 Cardinal 104 S Great Lakes Savi   Interest Po Mort Int  -300.67
                                                             ---------
                  Total Mortgage Interest Exp                 -300.67

                Taxes:
                ------


                Federal Tax
                -----------
8/ 1 Cardinal   S Payroll deposit      Federal Inc Tax:Fed   -130.00
                                                             ---------
                    Total Federal Tax                         -130.00

                Local Tax Withholding
                ---------------------
8/ 1 Cardinal   S Payroll deposit      Local Incom Tax:Local   -9.00
                                                             ---------
                    Total Local Tax Withholding                -9.00
```

Tax Summary
report for
PERSONAL file
accounts
Figure 8-7.

8

```
     Date    Acct     Num   Description    Memo        Category      Clr Amount
     ------  -------  ------ ------------   ----------  ------------- --- -------

                     Medicare Withholding
                     --------------------
     8/ 1 Cardinal    S Payroll deposit   Medicare Wi  Tax:MCARE         -29.00
                                                                       ---------
                        Total Medicare Withholding                      -29.00

                     Social Security Tax
                     -------------------
     8/ 1 Cardinal    S Payroll deposit   FICA Withho  Tax:FICA         -124.00
                                                                       ---------
                        Total Social Security Tax                      -124.00

                     State Tax
                     ---------
     8/ 1 Cardinal    S Payroll deposit   State Incom  Tax:State         -80.00
                                                                       ---------
                        Total State Tax                                 -80.00
                                                                       ---------
                        Total Taxes                                    -372.00
                                                                       ---------
                     TOTAL EXPENSES                                    -814.68

                                                                       ---------
                  TOTAL INCOME/EXPENSE                                 1,185.32
                                                                       =========
```

Tax Summary report for PERSONAL file accounts *(continued)*
Figure 8-7.

column from the left (Acct) shows the source of the tax-related transaction. In this report, all the sources were from the Cardinal Bank account, but you can see how, in a more complex situation, this would be useful in tracking the source of a tax-related transaction. For year-end tax purposes, a report of all accounts provides an overview by category that integrates the various accounts. For your tax-reporting needs, you should select the report format best suited to your tax preparation and planning needs.

Another example of modifying Quicken's report features is shown in Figure 8-8. In this case, Quicken was instructed to print only the

```
                          TAX SUMMARY REPORT
                        1/1/93 Through 12/31/93
PERSONAL-All Accounts                                          Page 1
8/26/93


Date Acct  Num     Description      Memo       Category   Clr  Amount
---- ---- ----  ----------------- ----------- ------------ --- -------

          INCOME/EXPENSE
            EXPENSES
              Medical & Dental
              ----------------
  8/ 1 Cardinal      S Payroll deposit  Health Ins  Medical    -42.01
  8/ 6 Cardinal 107    Orthodontics, In Monthly Ort Medical   -100.00
  9/ 8 Cardinal 116    Orthodontics, In Monthly Ort Medical   -170.00
 10/ 8 Cardinal 124    Orthodontics, In Monthly Ort Medical   -100.00
                                                              -------
            Total Medical & Dental                            -412.01
                                                              -------
          TOTAL EXPENSES                                      -412.01


                                                              -------
          TOTAL INCOME/EXPENSE                                -412.01
                                                              =======
```

A sample Tax Summary report filtered for a specific category **Figure 8-8.**

8

Medical category. Although this information was included in the report shown in Figure 8-6, you can see the benefits of a filtered report as you increase the number of transactions recorded by Quicken and want details on particular items during the year-end tax planning and reporting process. Quicken's procedures for generating this type of report will be covered in Chapter 10, "Creating Custom Reports."

The final point to note on all Quicken reports is that the date of report preparation is displayed in the upper-left corner of the report. When using Quicken reports, always note the report preparation date to ensure you are using the most recent report when making your financial decisions.

Tax Schedule Report

If you choose to assign categories to tax schedules and lines, you will want to create a Tax Schedule report. This report will provide useful information only if you have edited your categories and assigned them to the schedules and forms where you want the income and expenses that they represent to appear. Figure 8-9 shows a section of a Tax Schedule report that displays the Schedule A medical expenses. Although these expenses are the same as the ones you saw in Figure 8-8, where a filter was used for a Tax Summary report, the filtered tax summary approach requires you to request many individual reports, whereas the Tax Schedule report organizes all your tax information on one easy-to-use report.

To produce the Tax Schedule report, you first assign medical expenses to Schedule A and select the "Medicine and drugs" line. You then select **R**eports from the Register window, select **P**ersonal Reports, and then select **T**ax Schedule. If you press (Ctrl)-(Enter), you can accept the default title and time period for the report.

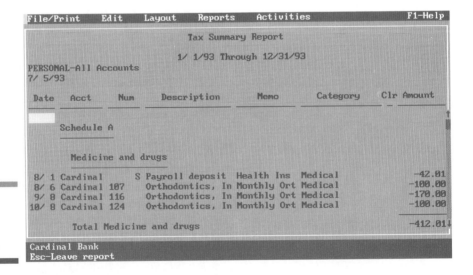

Schedule A medical expenses

Figure 8-9.

CHAPTER

DETERMINING YOUR NET WORTH

In previous chapters, you used Quicken as a tool for financial planning and monitoring. Many of the activities were simply repetitive steps; you applied the same techniques repeatedly to record transactions. These activities were procedural—they did not require analysis before entry and each transaction followed exactly the same steps.

Although these activities are an important part of managing your finances, they do not provide the total picture.

Basic Concepts of Financial Management

You probably have financial goals you would like to meet, such as buying a new car, purchasing a house, or retiring at age 60. Whatever your goals may be, you will need a certain level of financial resources to meet them. You might attempt to accumulate the necessary resources through savings or the acquisition of investments such as stocks or bonds. In this chapter, you learn to measure how successful you have been in your financial management activities.

One important measure of your financial status is your net worth. *Net worth* measures the difference between your total assets and your total liabilities at a given time. By looking at your net financial position at two points in time, you can tell how well you have managed your resources and obligations. The process of preparing a statement of net worth will differ from the procedural activities of earlier chapters. To estimate your net worth, you will need to make judgments estimating the worth of items purchased earlier. Some investments, such as stocks, have a clearly defined market value since they are publicly traded. Other investments, such as land or real estate, require a more subjective evaluation.

You have to look at more than the assets you own to determine your net worth. Although you may live in a $300,000 house, in all likelihood the bank owns more of it than you do. For net worth purposes, you have to determine what your remaining financial obligation is on the house. If you still have a mortgage of $270,000, your net worth in the property is $30,000. The following equation might give you a better perspective of your financial condition:

Financial Resources – Financial Obligations = Net Worth

As you can see, net worth describes your financial position after considering all your financial holdings and deducting all your financial obligations. In accounting terms, your financial resources are things of value that you hold (*assets*). Your assets may include checking, savings, and money market accounts. These are examples of *liquid assets*—they can be readily converted into cash. Stocks, bonds, real estate holdings, and retirement funds (Individual Retirement Accounts—IRAs—and Keogh plans) are other examples of investments you might hold. These assets are not as liquid as the previous group since converting them to cash depends on the market at the time you attempt to sell them. Your residence, vacation property, antiques, and other items of this nature would be classified as *personal assets*. These assets are the least liquid since antique and real estate values can decline, and it may take considerable time to convert these assets to cash.

The other part of the net worth equation is your financial obligations. Financial obligations include credit card balances and other shorter-term loans such as those for automobiles. In addition, you must consider longer-term loans for the purchase of a residence, vacation property, or land.

Net worth is the measure most people focus on when monitoring the success of their financial planning activities. The key point to remember is that net worth increases when your financial resources increase—through savings, compounding, and appreciation, and when you reduce the amount of your financial obligations. Take a look at the "Effects of Compounding Interest" table on the following page to see the effect of compounding on an investment and the rapid rate at which even a small investment can grow. Shown are the results of investing $100 a month at the rates specified.

Remember that financial obligations are not necessarily a sign of poor financial management. If you can borrow money and invest it so that it returns more than you are paying to use it, you have *leveraged* your resources. Of course, there is more risk in this avenue of financial planning. Don't take on more risk than you can handle—either financially or emotionally.

After completing this chapter, you will be able to begin monitoring your financial condition. In accounting terms, you can look at the bottom line. The *bottom line* in personal financial management is your net worth if you value your assets realistically. How you manage your financial assets and related obligations to increase your personal wealth will determine your net worth.

If you set an annual goal of increasing your net worth by a certain percentage, you can use Quicken to assist in recording your financial activities and monitoring your success in meeting your goal. For

Effects of Compounding Interest on $100 Invested Monthly for 20 Years

Worth at the End Of	6% Return	8% Return	10% Return
1 year	$ 1,234	$ 1,245	$ 1,257
2 years	$ 2,543	$ 2,593	$ 2,645
3 years	$ 3,934	$ 4,054	$ 4,178
4 years	$ 5,410	$ 5,635	$ 5,872
5 years	$ 6,977	$ 7,348	$ 7,744
10 years	$16,388	$18,295	$20,484
15 years	$29,082	$34,604	$41,447
20 years	$46,204	$58,902	$75,937

example, if you started using Quicken in January and record your assets and obligations throughout the year, you could contrast your financial condition at the beginning and end of the year and compare the results of your financial management with your goals. As a result of this comparison, you might decide to change your strategy in some areas of your financial plan. For instance, you might decide to switch from directly managing your portfolio of stocks to using a mutual fund with its professional managers, or you might decide to shift some assets from real estate to liquid assets that can be converted to cash more quickly.

Establishing Accounts for This Chapter

In earlier chapters, you used bank accounts in a file called PERSONAL to record all your transactions. In this chapter, you learn about Quicken's other account types. These accounts are ideally suited for recording information on assets you own, debts you have incurred, and investments. You establish a file called INVEST for the examples in this chapter. This will make it easier to obtain the same reporting results shown in this chapter even if you did not complete the examples in earlier chapters. This new file will be established for illustration purposes only. In fact, for your own financial planning, you will probably record all your activities in a single file. That way, Quicken will have access to all your personal information when preparing your reports and assessing your net worth.

Adding a New File

You have already used the following process in the "Adding a New File" section of Chapter 6, "Expanding the Scope of Financial Entries." In the new file, INVEST, you establish six new accounts to use throughout this chapter. From the Main Menu, follow these steps to set up the new file:

1. Select Set Preferences.
2. Select File Activities.
3. Select Select/Set Up File.

Your screen will have account groups for QDATA and PERSONAL.

4. Select <Set Up New File> and press Enter.
5. Type **INVEST** as the name of the file and press Enter.

Quicken creates four files from each filename. This means you must provide a valid filename of no more than eight characters. Do not include spaces or special symbols in your entries for account names.

6. Check the location for your data files and make changes to reference a valid file or directory if a change is required. Press Enter.
7. Type **1** to restrict your categories to home categories and press Enter.

Quicken displays the screen for selecting or creating files, but this time it also shows INVEST.

8. Select INVEST and press Enter.

Quicken presents a Set Up New Account window, shown in Figure 9-1.

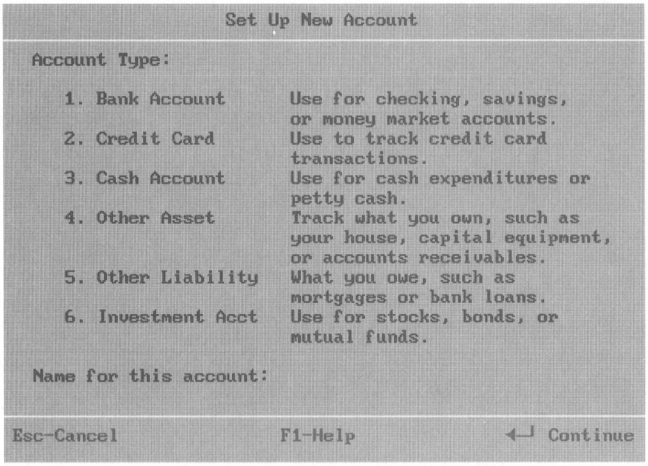

```
                    Set Up New Account

   Account Type:

         1. Bank Account       Use for checking, savings,
                               or money market accounts.
         2. Credit Card        Use to track credit card
                               transactions.
         3. Cash Account       Use for cash expenditures or
                               petty cash.
         4. Other Asset        Track what you own, such as
                               your house, capital equipment,
                               or accounts receivables.
         5. Other Liability    What you owe, such as
                               mortgages or bank loans.
         6. Investment Acct    Use for stocks, bonds, or
                               mutual funds.

   Name for this account:

   Esc-Cancel              F1-Help            ←┘ Continue
```

Set Up New
Account
window
Figure 9-1.

9. Type **6** and press Enter to establish the account type as an Investment account.

10. Type **Investments** and press Enter.

Quicken may display a warning message to inform you of the advanced nature of Investments accounts. Press Enter to exit this warning. Because Investment accounts are always established with a zero balance, you will not be asked to supply a beginning balance or date as you are when you create other account types. For all the other accounts,

11. Press Enter to accept N for the next entry since the account will be used to record information on multiple investments. When you wish to establish an account for a single mutual fund, you type a **Y**.

12. Type **Personal Investments** and press Enter.

Quicken then returns you to the Select Account to Use window. Your first account should conform to the Investments account shown at the bottom of the screen in Figure 9-2.

13. Establish the five remaining accounts as shown in Figure 9-2. Be sure to enter the correct account type, 1, 4, or 5, and balance. Use 8/1/93 as the date when entering your beginning balance for each

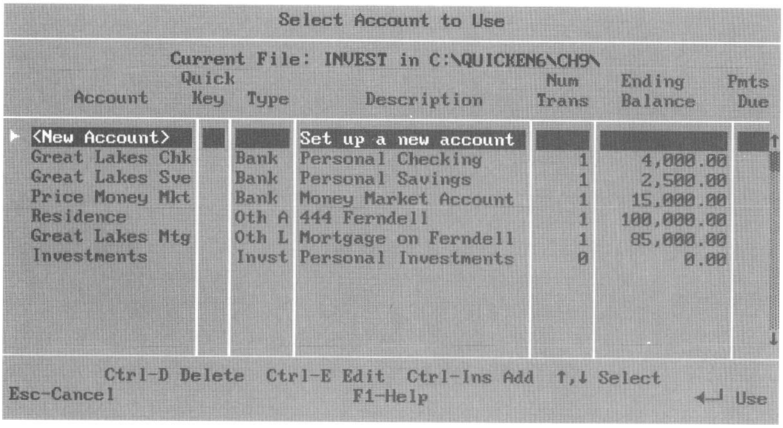

```
                          Select Account to Use

                 Current File: INVEST in C:\QUICKEN6\CH9\
                      Quick                            Num    Ending      Pmts
          Account      Key   Type      Description    Trans   Balance     Due

    ► <New Account>                Set up a new account                         ↑
      Great Lakes Chk       Bank   Personal Checking      1     4,000.00
      Great Lakes Sve       Bank   Personal Savings       1     2,500.00
      Price Money Mkt       Bank   Money Market Account   1    15,000.00
      Residence             Oth A  444 Ferndell           1   100,000.00
      Great Lakes Mtg       Oth L  Mortgage on Ferndell   1    85,000.00
      Investments           Invst  Personal Investments   0         0.00
                                                                              ↓

          Ctrl-D Delete   Ctrl-E Edit   Ctrl-Ins Add   ↑,↓ Select
    Esc-Cancel                         F1-Help                        ←┘ Use
```

Select Account
to Use window
for the INVEST
file
Figure 9-2.

9

account. When setting up the bank accounts, confirm that your Source Starting Balance is the Bank Statement when completing the Source of Starting Balance window.

The new accounts you established in this chapter are used to separately maintain records for different assets and liabilities. A little background on when to use each account type will be helpful in making selections when you start recording your own information. The three new account types and some suggested uses for each follow.

✦ *Investment accounts* are tailored to investments with fluctuating prices, such as stocks, mutual funds, bonds, or Individual Retirement Accounts (IRAs). You can establish an Investment account for each of your investment holdings or establish one account to parallel your transactions with a brokerage firm. In addition to special fields such as shares and investment accounts, these accounts can track a cash balance in an account.

✦ *Other Asset accounts* are appropriate for investments with a stable price, such as a CD or Treasury bill. They are also the most appropriate selection when there is no share price—for example, a real estate holding.

✦ *Other Liability accounts* are used to record your debts. A mortgage on a property and a car loan are examples of obligations that decrease your net worth and should be recorded in an Other Liability account.

Establishing the Initial Balance in Your Investments Account

Investment accounts are always established with an initial balance of zero. To transfer existing holdings to an Investment account, you will want to transfer the shares in at cost. You can establish a complete list of securities before beginning or add the information for each security as you enter the information to establish its cost. To activate the Investments account and record the securities, follow these steps:

1. Press Esc to return to the Main Menu, choose Select Account, and press Enter.
2. Select Investments and press Enter.

Quicken displays a first-time setup message telling you to use ShrsIn to establish the cost basis for each security.

3. Press Enter to proceed to the Investment register.

Notice that the fields differ from the bank account registers you have used previously since they are tailored to investments with a share price.

4. Type **10/10/88** as the purchase date and press Enter.

You can type an action from those listed in Table 9-1 or use Ctrl-L to highlight the action code in Quicken's list.

5. Press Ctrl-L.

The arrow cursor is on Add/Remove shares.

6. Press Enter to select it and display the two action codes shown in Figure 9-3.
7. Press Enter to select ShrsIn and move to the Security field.
8. Type **Haven Publishing** and press Enter.

Action Group	Action	Description
Add/Remove shares	ShrsIn	Used to transfer shares into an investment account.
	ShrsOut	Used to transfer shares out of an account.
Buy shares	Buy	Used to buy a security with cash in the Investment account.
	BuyX	Used to buy a security with cash from another account.
Capital gains distr	CGLong	Used to record cash received from long-term capital gains distribution.
	CGLongX	Used to transfer cash received from long-term capital gains distribution to another account.
	CGShort	Used to record cash received from short-term capital gains distribution.
	CGShortX	Used to transfer cash received from short-term capital gains distribution to another account.
Dividend	Div	Used to record cash dividends in the Investment account.
	DivX	Used to transfer cash dividends to another account.
Interest	IntInc	Used to record interest income in the investment account.
	MargInt	Used to pay margin loan from cash account.
Other transactions	MiscExp	Used to pay miscellaneous expense from cash.
	MiscInc	Used to record cash received from miscellaneous income sources.
	Reminder	Used with Billminder feature to notify of pending event.
	RtrnCap	Used to recognize cash from return of capital.

9

Investment
Actions
Table 9-1.

Action Group	Action	Description
	StkSplit	Used to change number of shares from a stock split.
Reinvest	ReinvDiv	Used to reinvest dividends in additional shares.
	ReinvInt	Used to reinvest interest in additional shares.
	ReinvLg	Used to reinvest long-term capital gains distribution.
	ReinvSh	Used to reinvest short-term capital gains distribution
Sell shares	Sell	Used when you sell a security and leave the proceeds in the Investment account.
	SellX	Used to transfer the proceeds of a sale to another account.
Transfer cash	XIn	Used to transfer cash into the Investment account.
	XOut	Used to transfer cash out of the Investment account.

Investment
Actions
(*continued*)
Table 9-1.

Quicken displays a message informing you that the security is not in the Security list.

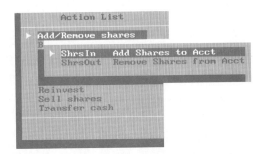

Action list for
investments
Figure 9-3.

9. Press [Enter] to select Add to Security List. A Set Up Security screen appears.
10. Type **HPB** for the symbol and press [Enter].
11. Press [Ctrl]-[L] to see a list of security types, and then select Stock and press [Enter].
12. Press [Ctrl]-[L] to see a list of optional investment goals, and then select Growth and press [Enter].

Your screen looks like this:

```
                    Set Up Security

    Name: Haven Publishing
    Symbol (optional): HPB

    Type: Stock          Goal (optional): Growth

              Ctrl L-List Types, Investment Goals
    Esc-Cancel               F1-Help              ↵ Continue
```

Alternatively, you can use [Ctrl]-[Y] at any time from the Investments register to update the entire security list at once.

13. Press [Enter], and then type **20** for the per share cost and press [Enter] again.
14. Type **500** for the number of shares.
15. Press [Enter] twice to accept the price computation and move to the Memo field.
16. Type **Initial Cost** in the Memo field and press [Ctrl]-[Enter].

Repeat the process for Ganges Mutual Fund and Glenn Packing, using the entries shown in Figure 9-4. When required to set up the new securities, repeat steps 10, 11, and 12 with the following information:

	Ganges Mutual Fund	**Glenn Packing**
Symbol	GMF	GPK
Type	Mutual fund	Stock
Goal	Growth	Income

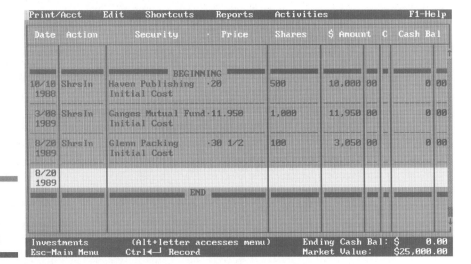

Initial
Investment
transactions
Figure 9-4.

Although you now have your stock holdings entered at cost, you still
have an additional step since you want to establish a current market
value for your holdings.

Revaluing Your Assets to Market Value

An important point to note when using Quicken is that in order to
determine your net worth, you must assign values to your investments,
liabilities, and other assets. This means that you need to exercise some
judgment in evaluating asset worth. Don't be intimidated; it's not as
complex as it might seem. The easiest assets to evaluate are your
checking, savings, and money market accounts. In these cases, you
know what your cash balance is in each of the accounts, so you can
easily determine the value at a specific time. After you complete your
monthly reconciliation, you have the current value of your accounts at
a given time. If you own stocks and bonds, you can generally determine
the valuation at a given time by looking in the financial section of your
local newspaper. If you own stock in a closely held corporation, you
will have to use other sources for valuation—for example, recent sales
of similar companies in your industry or area. In the case of land, you
might ask a realtor familiar with the local area the approximate value of

your lot or other property holdings, or once again you might be able to use recent sale prices of similar properties in your area.

Your residence presents similar problems. You know what you paid for the property, and with Quicken you can accumulate the additional cost incurred in improving it. The question is what value to place on the property when you prepare your Net Worth report. Once again, watch what properties in your area are selling for, and consider how your house compared in price with neighboring properties when you bought it. This will provide a basis for comparison in the future. However, remember that improvements you made to your house may increase the value of your home relative to others in the area. For example, adding a new bath and renovating the kitchen may significantly enhance the value of your home over time, but adding a swimming pool in a cold climate may not help the value at all.

The amount you owe or the associated liability on your home should be easy to track. You receive annual statements from the financial institutions you have borrowed money from for your residence and any home improvements. These statements indicate the remaining financial obligation you have on the house and should be used for net worth valuation purposes.

9

Remember to use prudent judgment in determining values for some of your assets when preparing your Net Worth report. A conservative but not very useful approach would be to say that any values you cannot determine from external sources should be valued at what you paid for the asset. Accountants call this *historical cost*. For your own planning and monitoring, this is not a realistic approach to determining your net worth. Attempt to determine fair value, or what you think your home could be sold for today, by taking into consideration current national and local economic conditions, and use reasonable values. Those familiar with the local market will certainly have some knowledge of the value of homes in your area. Remember that over-inflating the value of your properties does not help in accurately assessing your net worth.

The following steps allow you to enter the current value of your stocks:

1. From the Investment register, press Ctrl-U to activate the Update Prices and Market Value window.

Your next step is to establish the date for which you want to make the estimated market values as 7/31/93. You can change the date displayed to the next day with Ctrl-→, to the previous day with Ctrl-←, to the previous month with Ctrl-Pg Up, and to the next month with Ctrl-Pg Dn.

2. Press the appropriate combination of keys to make the date at the top of your screen read 7/31/93.

You can enter new market prices for any of the investments or use the + and − keys to change them by 1/8 in either direction.

3. With the arrow cursor on Ganges Mutual Fund, type **13.210** and press Enter.

4. With the arrow cursor on Glenn Packing, press Ctrl-Backspace to change the market price to 30, and then press Enter.

5. With the arrow cursor on Haven Publishing, type **22** and press Enter.

The screen in Figure 9-5 shows the updated prices. Notice that Quicken computes a new market value as well as a percentage gain.

Your First Net Worth Report

In completing the steps in the previous section, you recorded balances in all the accounts in your INVESTMENTS file. At this point, you can determine your net worth. Remember, your net worth is determined by the following formula:

Financial Resources − Financial Obligations = Net Worth

The following procedure prints your first net worth statement:

1. Press Esc to return to the Investments account register, select Alt-**R**eports, and select **P**ersonal Reports followed by **N**et Worth.

The Net Worth Report window appears.

2. Press Enter.
3. Type **8/1/93** and press Enter.

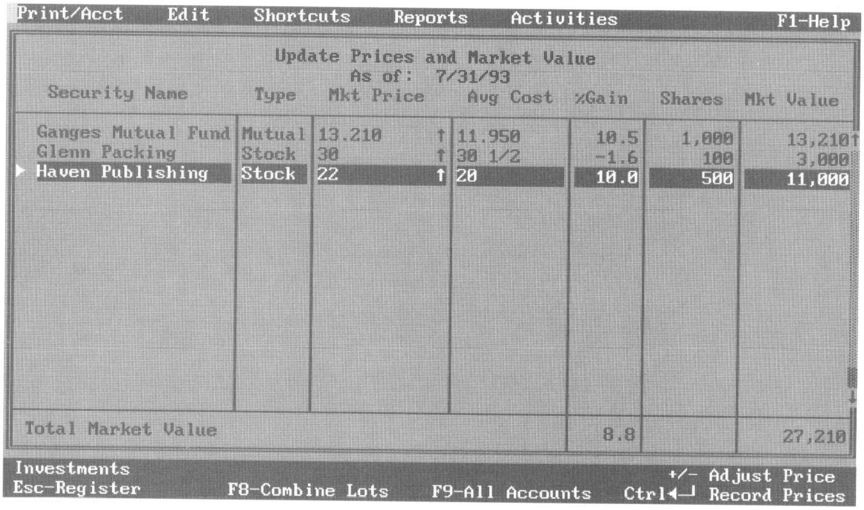

```
Print/Acct    Edit     Shortcuts    Reports    Activities         F1-Help
                      Update Prices and Market Value
                            As of:   7/31/93
        Security Name        Type   Mkt Price   Avg Cost   %Gain   Shares   Mkt Value

        Ganges Mutual Fund  Mutual  13.210    ↑ 11.950     10.5    1,000    13,210↑
        Glenn Packing       Stock   30        ↑ 30 1/2     -1.6      100     3,000
      ▶ Haven Publishing    Stock   22        ↑ 20         10.0      500    11,000




        Total Market Value                                 8.8             27,210

    Investments                                            +/- Adjust Price
    Esc-Register         F8-Combine Lots     F9-All Accounts  Ctrl◄┘ Record Prices
```

Updated prices
in the
Investment
register
Figure 9-5.

9

The Net Worth Report appears on your screen.

4. Press Ctrl-P and the Print Report window appears.
5. Complete the window prompts. When you press Enter to leave the window, your printer prints the report shown in Figure 9-6. (Again, spacing may differ because of adjustments made to fit the material onto these pages.)

Notice that the Net Worth report is presented for a specific date, in this example 8/1/93. The report presents your assets and liabilities at this date and gives you a base point against which to make future comparisons. As you can see, your net worth at 8/1/93 is $63,710.00. At the end of this chapter, you prepare another Net Worth report and compare how your net worth has changed.

Impact of Investments and Mortgage Payments on Net Worth

In this section, you will record various transactions in the file to demonstrate the effect of certain types of transactions on your net worth. You will see how Quicken can monitor your mortgage balance

```
                        NET WORTH REPORT
                         As of 8/ 1/93
INVEST-All Accounts                                       Page 1
7/ 5/93
                                             8/ 1/93
                         Acct                Balance
----------------------------------- -------------

ASSETS
  Cash and Bank Accounts
    Great Lakes Chk                         4,000.00
    Great Lakes Sve                         2,500.00
    Price Money Mkt                        15,000.00
                                         ------------
  Total Cash and Bank Accounts             21,500.00

  Other Assets
    Residence                             100,000.00
                                         ------------
  Total Other Assets                      100,000.00

  Investments
    Investments                            27,210.00
                                         ------------
  Total Investments                        27,210.00

                                         ------------
TOTAL ASSETS                              148,710.00

LIABILITIES
  Other Liabilities
    Great Lakes Mtg                         85,000.00
                                         ------------
  Total Other Liabilities                   85,000.00

                                         ------------
TOTAL LIABILITIES                           85,000.00

                                         ------------
TOTAL NET WORTH                             63,710.00
                                         ============
```

Net Worth
report for 8/1/93
Figure 9-6.

as part of your monthly record keeping in your checking account. You will also see how you can record a transaction only once and trace the financial impact on both checking and investment account registers.

Additional Stock Transactions

When you printed your Net Worth report, you were in the Investments account. You will now record the acquisition of some additional stock, dividends, dividends reinvested, and the sale of stock. The following steps demonstrate the ease of recording the transaction with Quicken 6's Investment accounts.

1. You are currently in the Investments account. Press the Esc key until you are in Quicken's Main Menu.
2. Select Use **R**egister and press Ctrl-End to move to the last entry.
3. Type **8/2/93**, in the Date field and press Enter.
4. Press Ctrl-L, select Buy shares, and press Enter.
5. Select BuyX to buy securities with money from another account and press Enter.

An extra line is added to the register entry to allow for the entry of an account field and the computation of a transfer amount.

6. Type **Douglas Marine** and press Enter.

Since this security is not in the security list, it must be added.

7. Press Enter to accept Add to Security List.
8. Type **DGM** and press Enter.
9. Press Ctrl-L, select Stock, and press Enter.
10. Press Ctrl-L, select Growth, and press Enter.
11. Press Enter to finalize the Security list entries.
12. Type **25** and press Enter.
13. Type **100** and press Enter twice.
14. Type **Buy 100 Douglas Marine** and press Enter.
15. Type **50** for the commission and press Enter.

9

The transfer amount is automatically computed as the price of the stock plus the commission.

16. Press `Ctrl`-`C`, select Price Money Mkt, and press `Enter`.
17. Press `Ctrl`-`Enter` to finalize the entry.

The next transactions record dividends and transfer them to another account or reinvest them in shares of the stock. Rather than transferring funds in and out for each transaction, you can choose to leave a cash balance in your brokerage account. Quicken allows you to mirror almost any investment situation. To record the dividend transaction, follow these steps:

1. Type **8/10/93** and press `Enter`.
2. Press `Ctrl`-`L`, select Dividend, and press `Enter`.
3. Select DivX and press `Enter`.
4. Type **Haven Publishing** and press `Enter`.
5. Type **200** in the $ Amount field and press `Enter`.
6. Type **Div @ .40 per share** and press `Enter`.
7. Press `Ctrl`-`C`, select Great Lakes Sve, and press `Enter`.
8. Press `Ctrl`-`Enter` to finalize the transaction.

The next transaction also recognizes a dividend distribution. These dividends are reinvested in shares purchased at the current market price. Follow these steps to record the transaction:

1. Type **8/15/93** and press `Enter`.
2. Press `Ctrl`-`L`, select Reinvest, and press `Enter`.
3. Select ReinvDiv and press `Enter`.
4. Type **Ganges Mutual Fund** and press `Enter`.

If you had typed **G**, Quicken would have completed the name for you using the new QuickFill feature. You have seen QuickFill at work from other entries you made in earlier chapters. Quicken tries to match the characters that you type for the payee, category, security, and action fields to entries in existing lists. If you wanted to use the Glenn Packing security, you would have pressed [Ctrl]-[+] when Ganges Mutual Fund appeared and Quicken would have displayed that security in the field.

5. Type **13.2785** and press [Enter] twice to move to the $ Amount field.

Quicken supplies the number of shares if you enter the price and the amount of the dividend that you are reinvesting.

6. Type **100.00** and press [Enter].
7. Type **Dividend Reinvestment** and press [Ctrl]-[Enter].

To record the sale of stock with the transfer of proceeds to another account, follow these steps:

1. Type **8/25/93** and press [Enter].
2. Press [Ctrl]-[L], select Sell shares, and then press [Enter].
3. Select SellX to sell the stock and transfer the cash to another account, and press [Enter].
4. Type **H** and press [Enter].

Notice that Quicken completes the rest of the typing for you. If you have several securities with names that start with *H*, you can use the [Ctrl]-[+] or [Ctrl]-[−] keypress combinations to select the security you desire in response to Quicken's QuickFill selection.

5. Type **23 1/4** and press [Enter].
6. Type **100** and press [Enter] twice.
7. Type **Sell 100 Haven Publishing** and press [Enter].
8. Type **25** for the commission and press [Enter].
9. Press [Ctrl]-[C], select Price Money Mkt, and press [Enter].
10. Press [Ctrl]-[Enter].

Your register entries will look like the ones in Figure 9-7.

```
 Print/Acct    Edit     Shortcuts    Reports    Activities              F1-Help

  Date  Action        Security      ·   Price    Shares    $ Amount  C  Cash Bal

  8/20  ShrsIn    Glenn Packing    ·30 1/2      100        3,050 00           0 00↑
  1989            Initial Cost

  8/02  BuyX      Douglas Marine    ·25         100        2,550 00           0 00
  1993            Buy 100 Douglas Marine

  8/10  DivX      Haven Publishing  ·                        200 00           0 00
  1993            Div @ .40 per share

  8/15  ReinvDiv  Ganges Mutual Fund·13.2785   7.531         100 00           0 00
  1993            Dividend Reinvestment

  8/25  SellX     Haven Publishing  ·23 1/4     100        2,300 00           0 00
  1993            Sell 100 Haven Publishing

  9/06
  1993
                          ═════════ END ═════════

  Investments        (Alt+letter accesses menu)    Ending Cash Bal: $      0.00
  Esc-Main Menu       Ctrl◄┘  Record               Market Value:      $28,178.50
```

Investment
account register
after August
transactions
Figure 9-7.

Mortgage Payment Transaction

You recorded mortgage payments in earlier chapters, but here you will
see how you can monitor your principal balance when you make your
payment. In this example, you make your monthly payment from your
checking account and monitor the impact of the payment on your
principal balance in the Great Lakes Mtg liability account. The
following steps record this transaction from the Main Menu:

1. Enter the Great Lakes Chk register and move the cursor to the Date
    field in the highlighted new transaction form. Type **8/5/93** and
    press (Enter).

2. Type **100** in the Num field and press (Enter).

3. Type **Great Lakes Bank** in the Payee field and press (Enter).

4. Type **875.00** in the Payment field.

5. Press (Enter) twice to place your cursor in the Category field.

6. Press (Ctrl)-(S), and the Split Transaction window appears on the
    screen. When you finish completing this window, your screen will
    look like the one in Figure 9-8.

7. Press (Ctrl)-(C), and the Category and Transfer List window appears.
    Select the Great Lakes Mtg account and press (Enter).

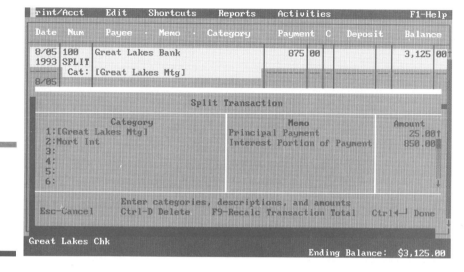

Split Transaction window in checking account **Figure 9-8.**

8. Press (Enter), type **Principal Payment**, press (Enter), type **25.00** in the Amount field, and press (Enter) again.

You have recorded the first part of the transaction shown in Figure 9-8.

9. Type **Mort Int** and press (Enter). Type **Interest Portion of Payment** and press (Enter). Press (Ctrl)-(Enter).

This step returns you to the account register.

10. Press (Ctrl)-(Enter) again and the transaction is recorded in the register.

As you can see, the balance in the account has been reduced by the amount of the payment. At the same time, Quicken has recorded the transaction in your Great Lakes Mtg account and reduced the obligation by the $25.00 principal portion of the payment.

How Transactions Affect Your Net Worth

Let's take a look at the effect of the previous transactions on net worth. If you compare the report in Figure 9-9 to the previous Net Worth report, you'll see that your net worth would have increased by $68.50 compared to the initial net worth shown in Figure 9-6. This difference

```
                          NET WORTH REPORT
                           As of 8/31/93
      INVEST-All Accounts                                  Page 1
      9/ 6/93
                                               8/31/93
                           Acct                Balance
      ----------------------------------- -----------
         ASSETS
           Cash and Bank Accounts
             Great Lakes Chk                  3,125.00
             Great Lakes Sve                  2,700.00
             Price Money Mkt                 14,750.00
                                           ------------
           Total Cash and Bank Accounts      20,575.00

           Other Assets
             Residence                      100,000.00
                                           ------------
           Total Other Assets              100,000.00

           Investments
             Investments                     28,178.50
                                           ------------
           Total Investments                 28,178.50

                                           ------------
         TOTAL ASSETS                       148,753.50

         LIABILITIES
           Other Liabilities
             Great Lakes Mtg                 84,975.00
                                           ------------
           Total Other Liabilities           84,975.00

                                           ------------
         TOTAL LIABILITIES                   84,975.00

                                           ------------
         TOTAL NET WORTH                     63,778.50
                                           ============
```

Net Worth report after stock is acquired and mortgage payment is made **Figure 9-9.**

is the net effect of the transactions you recorded during the month of August in your investment, cash, and bank accounts.

You can see from this that your net worth can grow if you either increase the value of your financial resources or decrease the amount of your obligations. In the following section, you will see how increases in the value of your investments are recorded and the effect they have on your net worth.

Recording Appreciation in Your Investment Holdings

In this section, you record the increased appreciation in your investments and residence occurring since the Net Worth report prepared on 8/1/93. Although the amounts may seem high, remember that this is an example. Also, remember that what you make in the stock market and housing market this year could be lost next year.

Appreciated Investments

Quicken permits you to record increases and decreases in the value of your holdings. As noted in the net worth formula, changes in the value of your holdings have the potential to significantly affect your net worth over a period of years. Remember the effect of compounding on your investments. The following steps illustrate the changes of your investments for the month of August:

1. Choose Select Account from the Main Menu to open the Investments account register from your INVEST file.
2. Press Ctrl-U to access the Update Prices and Market Value screen.

Notice that the market value for Ganges Mutual Fund is marked with an asterisk and has been updated since your initial adjustments on July 31, 1993. The asterisk indicates that Quicken has estimated the market value. This estimate is based on the value you entered for the dividend reinvestment transaction on 8/15.

3. Press Ctrl-→ or Ctrl-← until the date at the top reads 8/25/93.

Notice the asterisks next to the prices. An asterisk tells you that Quicken is using an estimated value for the investment. For example, Quicken valued the Glenn Packing shares at $30 per share. Since there were no shares of this stock bought or sold during August, Quicken will use the 7/31/93 price shown in Figure 9-5 until you revalue the stock. Notice that the Ganges Mutual Fund is shown at its actual value on 8/15/93 since you recorded the dividend reinvestment transaction in your account on that date. The point to note is that Quicken automatically updates your market valuation each time you provide new price information when preparing account transactions throughout the year.

4. Press Ctrl-→ until the date at the top reads 8/31/93.

5. Enter the new market prices for the stocks, as shown in Figure 9-10. Press Enter after recording each new price.

6. Press Ctrl-Enter to record the changes, and then press Esc to return to the Main Menu.

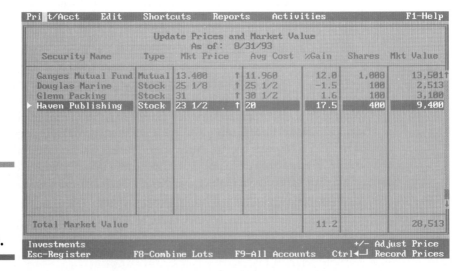

Updated register after recording revaluations

Figure 9-10.

Appreciated Residence

As your home increases in value, you will want to record this change in Quicken since it will affect your net worth. In this example, as a result of recent sales in your neighborhood, you feel $105,000 would be a conservative estimate of the market value of your home. The following steps illustrate the procedure for valuing your home at $105,000:

1. From the Select Account to Use window select the Residence account and press (Enter).

Quicken opens the Register window for this account and places the highlighting in the next blank transaction.

2. Select the **A**ctivities ((Alt)-(A)) pull-down menu.
3. Select **U**pdate Account Balance.
4. Type **105000** and press (Enter).
5. Press (Enter) to move to the Date field in the Update Account Balance window.
6. Type **8/31/93** and press (Ctrl)-(Enter).

Your screen should look like the one in Figure 9-11.

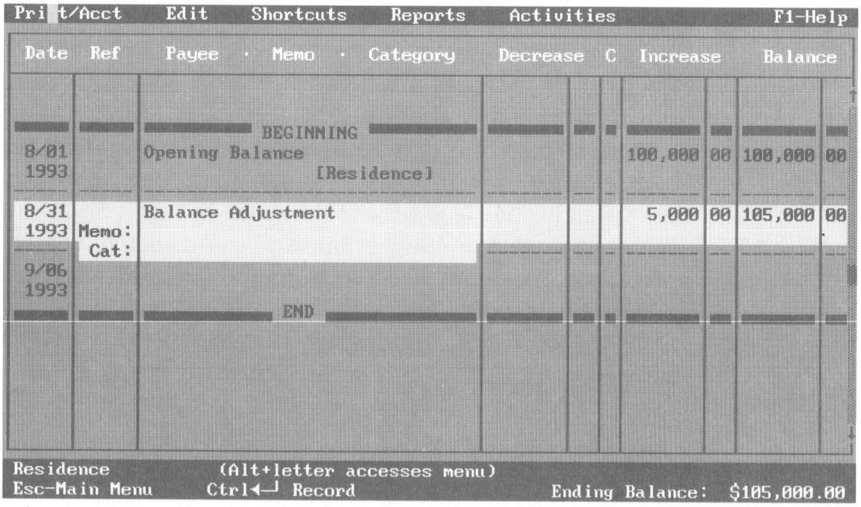

9

Residence register after adjustment is revalued
Figure 9-11.

Ending Net Worth Determination

Having prepared the adjustments to the various accounts in the INVEST file, you are now prepared to print your Net Worth report for the end of the period.

1. From the Main Menu, select **C**reate Reports, **P**ersonal Reports, and **N**et Worth. The Net Worth Report window appears.

2. Press (Enter), type **8/31/93**, and press (Enter).

The Net Worth report appears on your screen.

3. Press (Ctrl)-(P), and the Print Report window appears.

4. Complete the appropriate selections in the window. When you press (Ctrl)-(Enter) to leave the window, your printer prints the report, as shown in Figure 9-12.

An examination of Figures 9-6 and 9-12 reveals that your net worth increased by almost $6000 during the time period. What were the reasons for these changes? For the most part, the increased values of your investments and residence explain the greater net worth.

The importance of monitoring your net worth has been stressed throughout this chapter. The focus of this book is the use of Quicken to assist in your financial planning and monitoring activities. Once you have a good picture of your net worth from the Quicken reports, you can focus on additional planning. You might want to set your net worth goal for a future point or make plans to protect your existing holdings. If you have not taken any actions regarding estate planning, this is another area that must be addressed. Making a will is a most important part of this process and should not be delayed. Although the complexities of planning for the transfer of your estate are significant, the special "The Need for a Will" section at the end of this chapter highlights some problems that can be encountered when estate planning is not combined with financial planning activities. You may also be surprised to learn that a lawyer's fee for a simple will can be as little as $50. Another option is writing a will with one of the new software packages specifically designed for that purpose.

```
                       NET WORTH REPORT
                       As of 8/31/93
        INVEST-All Accounts                               Page 1
        9/ 6/93

                                             8/31/93
                             Acct            Balance
        ----------------------------------- ------------

        ASSETS
           Cash and Bank Accounts
              Great Lakes Chk                  3,125.00
              Great Lakes Sve                  2,700.00
              Price Money Mkt                 14,750.00
                                            ------------
           Total Cash and Bank Accounts      20,575.00

           Other Assets
              Residence                      105,000.00
                                            ------------
           Total Other Assets               105,000.00

           Investments
              Investments                     28,513.42
                                            ------------
           Total Investments                 28,513.42


        TOTAL ASSETS                         154,088.42

        LIABILITIES
           Other Liabilities
              Great Lakes Mtg                 84,975.00
                                            ------------
           Total Other Liabilities           84,975.00


        TOTAL LIABILITIES                     84,975.00


        TOTAL NET WORTH                       69,113.42
                                            ============
```

Net Worth report for 8/31/93 after all transactions affecting the INVEST files are recorded **Figure 9-12.**

9

Quicken's Investment Reports

Quicken provides five investment reports that provide information on your investments from different perspectives. You can look at detailed investment transactions with these reports or assess your gain or loss in investment value over a period of time. The many options available provide different variations on each of the basic reports.

Portfolio Value Report

A Portfolio Value report values all the investments in your portfolio at a given date based on price information stored in the system. The Portfolio Value report displays the number of shares, the current price, the cost basis of the shares, the gain or loss, and the current value of the shares. Follow these steps to create the report from the Investments account:

1. From the Main Menu select **C**reate Reports.
2. Select **I**nvestment Reports.
3. Choose Portfolio **V**alue.
4. Press (Enter) to accept the default report title.
5. Type **8/31/93** for the report date and press (Enter).
6. Press (F8) (Options), type **N**, and press (Enter).
7. Press (Enter) twice to accept the default entries of Don't Subtotal and Current.

The report displays on your screen (a printed copy of the report is shown in Figure 9-13).

Investment Performance Report

The Investment Performance report lets you look at the gain or loss between two points in time. The Investment Performance report indicates your return and projects an average annual return based on results of the period selected. Follow these steps to create such a report:

1. Press (Esc) until the Investment Reports menu displays, and then select Investment **P**erformance.

```
                         PORTFOLIO VALUE REPORT
                            As of 8/31/93
     INVEST-Investments                                        Page 1
     9/ 6/93


           Security        Shares  Curr Price  Cost Basis  Gain/Loss  Balance
     ----------------      --------  ----------  -----------  ---------  -------
     Douglas Marine        100.00   25 1/8       2,550         -38       2,513
     Ganges Mutual Fund  1,007.53   13.400      12,050       1,451      13,501
     Glenn Packing         100.00   31           3,050          50       3,100
     Haven Publishing      400.00   23 1/2       8,000       1,400       9,400
                                                 -------     -------     -------
     Total Investments                          25,650       2,863      28,513
                                                 ======      ======      ======
```

Portfolio Value
report

Figure 9-13.

2. Press (Enter) to accept the default report title.
3. Type **8/1/93** and press (Enter); then type **8/31/93** and press (Enter).
4. Press (Enter) to accept the default of Don't Subtotal.
5. Type **Y** for Show cash flow detail.
6. Press (F8) (Options), type **N**, and press (Enter).
7. Press (Ctrl)-(Enter) to accept the Current account default and display the report on the screen.

A printed copy of the report showing an annualized return of 64.5 percent is shown in Figure 9-14.

Capital Gains Report

The Capital Gains report is useful for tax purposes since it shows the gain or loss on sales of investments. One example of a Capital Gains report that you can create allows you to look at the difference between short- and long-term capital gains. Follow these steps to create the report:

1. Press (Esc) until the Investment Reports menu displays.
2. Select **C**apital Gains.
3. Press (Enter) to accept the default.

```
                    INVESTMENT PERFORMANCE REPORT
                        8/ 1/93 Through 8/31/93
          INVEST-Investments                                    Page 1
          9/ 6/93

                                                            Avg. Annual
           Date  Action  Description  Investments  Returns  Tot. Return
           ----  ------  -----------  -----------  -------  -----------


                  8/ 1/93 -  8/31/93
                  -------------------


           7/31          Beg Mkt Value      27,210
           8/ 2 BuyX     100 Douglas Marine  2,550
           8/10 DivX     Haven Publishing                 200
           8/25 SellX    100 Haven Publishing           2,300
           8/31          End Mkt Value                  28,513
                                             ------      ------  -----------
                 TOTAL  8/ 1/93 -  8/31/93  29,760      31,013       64.5%
```

Investment
Performance
report
Figure 9-14.

4. Type **8/1/93** and press (Enter).
5. Type **8/31/93** and press (Enter).
6. Press (F8) (Options), type   , and press (Enter).
7. Press (Ctrl)-(Enter) to display the Capital Gains report.

Figure 9-15 shows a printout of this report.

Investment Income Report

The Investment Income report shows the total income or expense from your investments. Dividends and both realized and unrealized gains and losses can be shown on this report. Follow these steps to create the report:

1. Press (Esc) until the Investment Reports menu displays.
2. Select Investment Income.
3. Press (Enter) to accept the default.
4. Type **8/1/93** and press (Enter).

```
                        CAPITAL GAINS REPORT
                      8/ 1/93 Through 8/31/93
        INVEST-Investments                                      Page 1
        9/ 6/93


         Security  Shares  Bought  Sold  Sales Price  Cost Basis  Gain/Loss
         --------  ------  ------  ----  -----------  ----------  ---------
                   LONG TERM


        Haven Publish 100 10/10/88 8/25/92    2,300       2,000        300

                                           -----------  ----------  ---------
                   TOTAL LONG TERM             2,300       2,000        300
                                           ===========  ==========  =========
```

Capital Gains
report
Figure 9-15.

9

5. Type **8/31/93** and press [Enter].

6. Press [F8] (Options), press [Enter] three times, type **N**, and press [Enter].

7. Press [Ctrl]-[Enter] to display the report on your screen.

Your report will match the printout shown in Figure 9-16.

```
                        INVESTMENT INCOME REPORT
                        8/ 1/93 Through 8/31/93
          INVEST-Investments                                  Page 1
          8/25/93
                                              8/ 1/93-
                      Category Description      8/31/93
                      ----------------------  ----------
                      INCOME/EXPENSE
                        INCOME
                          Dividend                  300
                          Realized Gain/Loss        300
                                                ----------
                        TOTAL INCOME               600


                                                ----------
                      TOTAL INCOME/EXPENSE         600
                                                ==========
```

Investment
Income report
Figure 9-16.

Investment Transactions Report

The Investment Transactions report is the most detailed of the five, and reports on all investment transactions during the selected period. Follow these steps to create the report:

1. Press (Esc) until the Investment Reports menu displays.
2. Select Investment **T**ransactions.
3. Press (Enter) to accept the default.
4. Type **8/1/93** and press (Enter).
5. Type **8/31/93** and press (Enter).
6. Press (F8) (Options) to activate the report options.

The Need for a Will

A will is important to ensure that your heirs benefit from the net worth that you have accumulated and to make sure your wishes control the distribution of your assets at your death. Without a will, the laws of your state and the rulings of a probate court would decide what happens to your assets and award the custody of your minor children. The following may also occur

◆ A probate court may appoint an administrator for your estate.

◆ State laws may distribute your assets differently than you might wish.

◆ Fees for probate lawyers will consume from 5 to 25 percent of your estate. The smaller your estate, the higher the percentage will be for the probate lawyer.

◆ If your estate is large enough to be affected by federal estate taxes ($600,000 or more), not focusing on a will and neglecting other estate planning tasks can increase the tax obligations on your estate.

7. Press Enter twice.
8. Type **Y** to include unrealized gains, and press Enter.
9. Type **N** to display only whole dollars in the report, and press Enter.
10. Press Ctrl-Enter to display the report on your screen.

Your report will match the printout shown in Figure 9-17.

```
                          INVESTMENT TRANSACTIONS REPORT
                             8/ 1/93 Through 8/31/93
        INVEST-Investments                                              Page 1
        9/6/93

                                                              Invest.   Cash +
        Date Action Secur      Categ     Price   Shares Commssn Cash Value Invest.
        ---- ------ -----      ------    ------  ------ ------- ---- ------ -------

            BALANCE 7/31/93                                    0 27,210 27,210
        8/ 2 UnrlzGn Douglas Marin Unrealized G 25.                     -50     -50

        8/ 2 BuyX     Douglas Marin          25.    100    50 -2,550 2,550
                                   [Price Money                 2,550          2,550

        8/10 DivX    Haven Publish Dividend                      200            200
                                   [Great Lakes                 -200           -200

        8/15 UnrlzGn Ganges Mutual Unrealized G 13.2785                  69      69

        8/15 ReinvDi Ganges Mutual        13.2785 7.531        -100    100
                                   Dividend                     100            100

        8/25 UnrlzGn Haven Publish Unrealized G 23 1/4                  300     300

        8/25 SellX    Haven Publish        23 1/4   100    25  2,000 -2,000
                                   [Price Money                -2,300         -2,300
                                   Realized Gain/Loss            300            300

        8/31 UnrlzGn Haven Publish Unrealized G 23 1/2                  100     100
        8/31 UnrlzGn Ganges Mutual Unrealized G 13.400                  122     122
        8/31 UnrlzGn Glenn Packing Unrealized G 31.                     100     100
        8/31 UnrlzGn Douglas Marin Unrealized G 25 1/8                   13      13
                                                              ------ ------
            TOTAL 8/ 1/93 - 8/31/93                           0  1,303  1,303

            BALANCE 8/31/93                                    0 28,513 28,513
```

Investment
Transactions
report including
unrealized
gains/losses
Figure 9-17.

9

Using Quicken 6's Financial Planning Tools

Quicken 6 has a number of new financial planning tools. These tools are designed to perform calculations that can help you with planning and decision making regarding financial goals. You used the financial tool that calculated the split between mortgage principal reductions and interest in Chapter 8. In this section you will see how the Retirement Planning, College Planning, Investment Planning, and the Refinance Calculator are similar, as they provide the information you need to make a good decision and allow you to look at different scenarios.

NOTE: All of the financial planning calculators require you to make assumptions about interest rates, yields, and so on. You should continue to monitor your assumptions over time and make corrections as the economy or other situations change.

Using the Refinance Calculator

As interest rates fall, you can use the Refinance Calculator to assess whether to approach your financial institution about refinancing your loan. You can use the information from the Loan Calculator example in Chapter 8 for an example of an actual loan. In the Chapter 8 example, you had a $40,000 loan at 9.519 percent interest for 25 years with payments of $350 a month. If you were reconsidering refinancing after 36 months, you could print out the payment schedule to see that you still had a balance of $38,642.29. You can follow these steps to plug this information into the Refinance Calculator to see how much a lower interest rate will reduce your payments and how long it will take to recover the cost of refinancing:

1. Select Activities and then Financial Planning and press Enter.
2. Select Refinance Calculator and the Refinance Calculator, shown in Figure 9-18, appears.
3. Type **350.00** and press Enter twice.

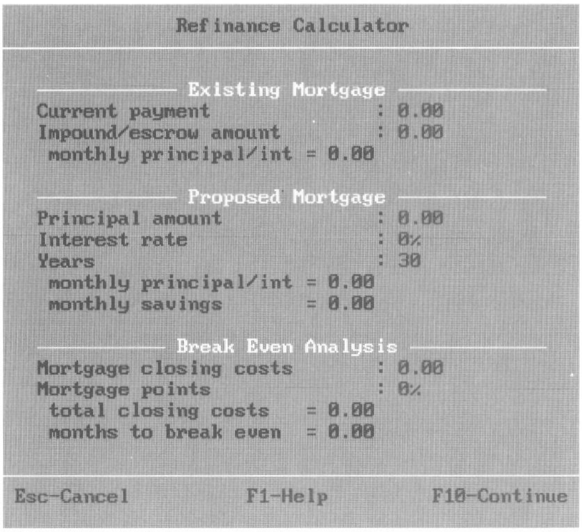

```
                    Refinance Calculator


                  ─── Existing Mortgage ───
     Current payment              : 0.00
     Impound/escrow amount        : 0.00
      monthly principal/int = 0.00

                  ─── Proposed Mortgage ───
     Principal amount             : 0.00
     Interest rate                : 0%
     Years                        : 30
      monthly principal/int = 0.00
      monthly savings       = 0.00

                  ─── Break Even Analysis ───
     Mortgage closing costs       : 0.00
     Mortgage points              : 0%
      total closing costs   = 0.00
      months to break even  = 0.00

     Esc-Cancel          F1-Help          F10-Continue
```

The Refinance
Calculator
Figure 9-18.

9

In Chapter 8, the illustration did not provide for an escrow account (insurance, property taxes, etc.) held by the mortgage company. If escrow had been included, you would have entered the monthly escrow account as well. You can obtain your escrow information from the monthly statement that your mortgage company provides.

4. Type **38642.29** and press (Enter).

This is the principal for the remaining mortgage after 36 $350 payments are applied.

5. Type **8.375** and press (Enter).

This is the interest rate quoted by your financial institution.

6. Type **22** and press (Enter).

This number assumes that you want the house paid off within the 25-year goal for the original mortgage. You can negotiate a 15-year or a 30-year loan if you prefer and change the assumption accordingly.

7. Type **900** and press (Enter).

Even when you refinance with your existing loan holder, you can expect to pay closing costs for the new loan. You lender has provided an estimate of $900.

8. Type *.25* and press (Enter), and your screen displays the Refinance Calculator shown in Figure 9-19.

The .25 represents the 1/4 point that your lender will charge to give you the 8.375 percent interest rate on the 22-year loan.

You can see that if you refinance your home under these conditions, your monthly payments will be reduced to $320.85 (principal and interest) saving you $29.15 a month. Since you must pay out $900 in closing costs plus 1/4 point, the last line on the screen tells you that you must stay in the home another 34.18 months before your monthly savings will offset the closing costs and points. You can shop around for better terms with other institutions and use the Refinance Calculator to pick the best deal.

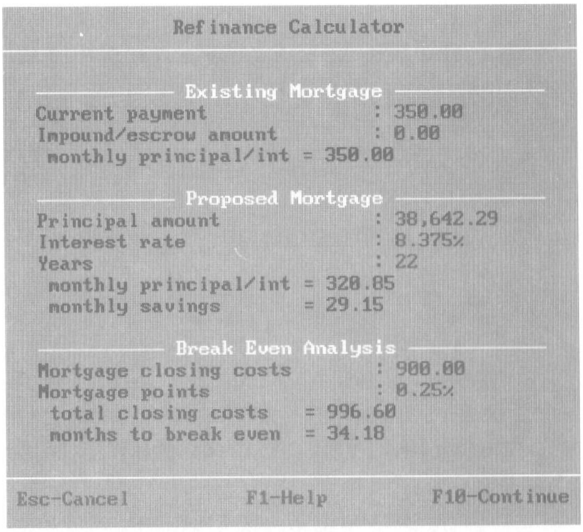

Sample figures entered into the Refinance Calculator
Figure 9-19.

```
                   Refinance Calculator


                        Existing Mortgage
        Current payment                    : 350.00
        Impound/escrow amount              : 0.00
         monthly principal/int = 350.00

                        Proposed Mortgage
        Principal amount                   : 38,642.29
        Interest rate                      : 8.375%
        Years                              : 22
          monthly principal/int = 320.85
          monthly savings       = 29.15

                        Break Even Analysis
        Mortgage closing costs             : 900.00
        Mortgage points                    : 0.25%
          total closing costs   = 996.60
          months to break even  = 34.18


        Esc-Cancel          F1-Help          F10-Continue
```

Investment Planning

Early in this chapter you saw a table illustrating the effects of investing $100 a month for 20 years. You can use the Investment Planner in Quicken 6 to see how future value information is generated. The Investment Planner is so flexible that it also allows you to calculate other things such as present value.

In order to complete the entries in the Investment Planning window, shown in Figure 9-20, you must tell Quicken that the present value is zero, since you are starting with no money in the account. The other entries are the $100 monthly payment, a period of 20 years, or 240 months, and the annual expected yield of 8 percent. The expected yield is an educated guess on your part. Quicken displays a future value of $58,902.04, which confirms the value shown in the table earlier in this chapter. Notice that Quicken also tells you that in today's dollars that is the equivalent of $26,501.62 with an expected inflation rate of 4 percent over the 20-year period. This highlights the effect that inflation has on your future purchasing power.

Although it was not used in the example, you can also have Quicken adjust your payments in Figure 9-20 for inflation. You must use the Inflate Payments Monthly option. If you want to have an inflation adjusted value of $58,902 at the end of 20 years, you would enter a **Y** for this option and then press (F9). Quicken provides a payment schedule that is adjusted for the 4 percent inflation rate. Your first payment would still be $100, but your last payment would be $221.51. Your account would have $81,126.62 to maintain your 8 percent yield and adjust for inflation.

You can see how easy it is to enter a few numbers and get some help from Quicken on your investment decisions. There are many changes that you can make as you select weekly, monthly, quarterly, or annual payment periods by pressing the (F7) key. You can adjust annual yield and inflation expectations. If you move the checkmark with (F8), you can also make present-value computations. For example, if you expect an 8 percent return and wanted to know how much money you need to deposit today to have $58.902 in the future, you can move the checkmark to Present Value. Given a 20-year time period and no new annual payments during the time period, Quicken will compute a $12,637.32 deposit that you might want to make with a finance or insurance company.

9

```
                        Investment Planning

            Present Value               :  0.00
            Additions each Month        :  100.00
            Number of Months            :  240
            Annual Yield                :  8%

          √ Future Value                = 58,902.04
              (in today's dollars)      : 26,501.62

            Expected Inflation          :  4%
            Inflate Payments Monthly (Y/N)  :  N

        F7-Change Periods                   F8-Select Calculation
        Esc-Cancel            F1-Help       F9-Show Payments
```

Investment
Planner shows
return for
investment
example
Figure 9-20.

Retirement Planning

Quicken can also be used to help project your expected income flows
from your various retirement investments (e.g., SEP-IRA, Keogh,
Individual IRA, 401k, or just your retirement savings account). Figure
9-21 shows the Quicken screen that appears when you select the
Retirement Planner by pressing Alt-A, typing an **F** and **R**, when you are
in your account register.

To complete the screen you need to provide your best estimates for
some of the information. You should review this information at least
annually to see if modifications are needed and what the impact of
changes are on your expected retirement income. Let's take a look at
the type of information you need to provide

Present Savings   Enter the current balance in your investment
account. For example, if your IRA has a balance at the beginning of the
year of $30,000, you would enter that balance here.

Tax Sheltered   Indicate whether the current account is tax sheltered
or not. Most retirement investments are tax sheltered; however,
personal savings (CDs, mutual fund accounts, etc.) that you plan to use
to supplement your retirement plans are taxable.

Annual Yield   Enter your estimate of expected annual return on this
investment. 8% displays as the default yield. You might use past returns
on this investment as a guide, however, you can not rely solely on this

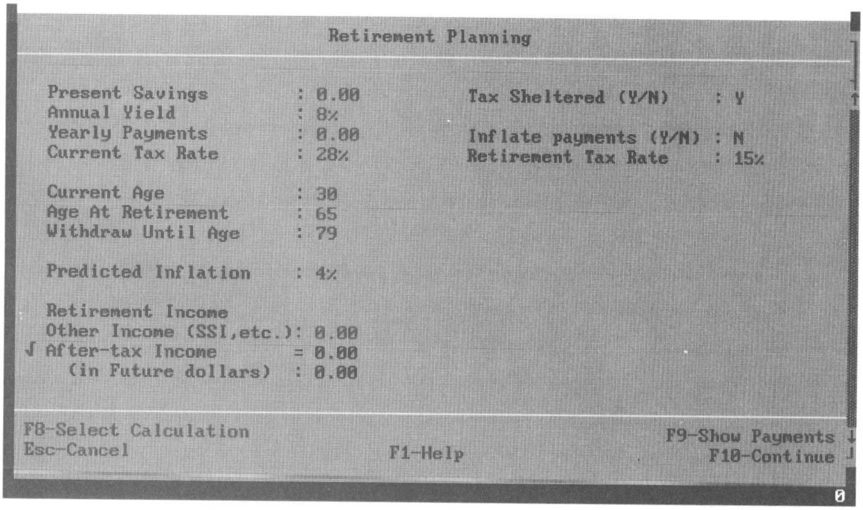

```
                              Retirement Planning

        Present Savings       : 0.00          Tax Sheltered (Y/N)   : Y
        Annual Yield          : 8%
        Yearly Payments       : 0.00          Inflate payments (Y/N) : N
        Current Tax Rate      : 28%           Retirement Tax Rate    : 15%

        Current Age           : 30
        Age At Retirement     : 65
        Withdraw Until Age    : 79

        Predicted Inflation   : 4%

        Retirement Income
        Other Income (SSI,etc.): 0.00
      √ After-tax Income       = 0.00
          (in Future dollars)  : 0.00

     F8-Select Calculation                                F9-Show Payments
     Esc-Cancel                        F1-Help            F10-Continue
                                                                          0
```

Retirement
Planning
window
Figure 9-21.

9

source. A word of caution would be to use a conservative, but realistic, estimate of your expected annual yield.

Yearly Payments   Enter your best guess of the future annual contributions that will be made to this investment. Remember to include employer matching contributions in addition to your own contributions to the account.

Inflate payments   Indicate whether Quicken should adjust your yearly payment schedule to show how much additional money you need to contribute to this investment to protect your investment against inflation. The default setting is for no inflation adjustment to your yearly payments.

Tax rates   Enter your current tax rate and your expected retirement tax rate or accept the defaults.

Age information   Change Quicken's default ages to match your situation. If you are 48, want to retire at age 62, and want to have income provided from this investment until age 80, just enter that information on your screen.

Predicted Inflation Accept Quicken's default annual rate of 4% or modify it to see what the potential impact of various rates will be.

When you enter the above information, Quicken provides you with retirement planning information in the Retirement Income section of Figure 9-21. The "After Tax Income" amount shows what your expected future income in today's dollars will be. If Quicken shows that this investment will provide $10,000, that is the equivalent to spending in today's dollars. That is, Quicken has taken your future payments and adjusted them for inflation. The "in Future dollars" row shows you what your annual payments will be in actual dollars at the time of receipt.

Quicken also allows you to enter expected payments from Social Security or other sources in order to give you a better picture of your future retirement income. By pressing the F9 key you can ask Quicken to print out your payment schedule for the retirement. This process provides valuable planning information for your future retirement. As a result of this type of exercise you might decide that you need to increase your retirement investment contribution in the future, or that you are on track for future financial security. The important point is that this type of review should be an annual planning assessment. With the ease of use and the importance of protecting your retirement quality of living, this Quicken feature can be a valuable tool.

College Planning calculator
Figure 9-22.

```
                        College Planning

   Current Tuition (annual)           : 15,000.00
   Years Until Enrollment             : 18
   Number of years enrolled           : 5
   Present Savings                    : 0.00
   Annual Yield                       : 8%

 J Yearly Payments                    = 4,977.73
   Expected Inflation                 : 6%
   Inflate Payments Yearly (Y/N)      : N

   All calculations assume saving until student
     graduates.

   F8-Select Calculation            F9-Show Payments
   Esc-Cancel          F1-Help        F10-Continue
```

College Planning

The final Quicken financial planning tool is the College Planning calculator shown in Figure 9-22. The assumptions for this college-planning scenario are

✦ Your child will attend a nationally known private university with a current tuition of $15,000 a year

✦ It will be 18 years before your child enrolls in this university

✦ Your child will pursue a major that requires 5 years of study to complete the degree requirements

✦ Your annual yield will be 8 percent over the period

✦ Predicted inflation for tuition is 6 percent

Figure 9-22 shows that you would need to make annual payments of $4977.73 from 1993 to 2015 (note the calculations are based on your continuing payments during the five years your child is in school). By pressing F9 you can see that tuition will rise to $42,815 for your child's freshman year assuming a 6 percent annual increase. If you change the assumptions to have your child complete a major in an area requiring only four years of study, your annual payments would decrease to $4,086.16.

9

CHAPTER

10

CREATING CUSTOM REPORTS

Periodically you will want to step back from the detail in your Quicken register and look at the reports and graphs the package can create. The reports can be viewed onscreen or printed to share with others. Although graphs cannot be printed with Quicken they allow you to analyze your data in just a few minutes.

Quicken can prepare both standard and custom reports. Standard reports have a predefined format most Quicken users will find acceptable for their personal, business, and investment reporting needs. However, as you become more familiar with Quicken, you may want to customize your reports to meet your unique needs. Custom reports allow you to alter the report format to meet your specific requirements. A new option added to Quicken 6 is the Redo Last Report feature. You can use this feature to recapture the last report you prepared during your current Quicken session from the Main Menu, from the **R**eports pull-down menu in your register, or by pressing Ctrl-Z at any time.

Quicken supports creating seven different standard reports for personal use: Cash Flow, Monthly Budget, Itemized Categories, Tax Summary, Net Worth, Missing Check, and Tax Schedule. You can create any one of these reports by selecting **P**ersonal Reports from the Reports menu, as shown:

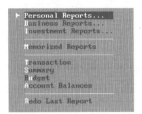

You have seen several examples of standard reports in earlier chapters. Quicken 6 allows you to customize any of the standard reports while creating them or after the reports are displayed on your screen. The preceding Reports menu shows that Quicken has the ability to access reports that you have memorized (more on memorized reports at the end of this chapter).

Quicken also provides four custom report types in the Reports menu: Transaction, Summary, Budget, and Account Balances. Selecting any of these items causes a custom Create Report window to be displayed on the screen, which allows you to create many different report frameworks. Although the exact contents of the window depend on the type of report you are creating, each of the custom windows allows you to enter information such as the accounts you want to use, directions for totaling and subtotaling the report, the type of cleared status for included transactions, and specific transactions you wish to include. Some of these options are specified with direct entries in the Report window and others require the use of F8 (Options) for additional report options or F9 (Filter) to filter records that will be included.

You already saw a custom option in Chapter 7, "Quicken as a Budgeting Tool," when you selected the current account item to customize the Monthly Budget report for Cardinal Bank, shown in Figure 7-5. In this chapter, you look at additional custom reporting options and report filtering features as you build three new custom reports. After looking at the exercises in this chapter, you will be able to create your own custom reports and memorize them for later use. Be sure to look at the special "Documenting Your Decisions" section to learn how to safeguard your time investment.

In Chapter 7, you had the opportunity to create several graphs to provide a look at your budget performance. These graphs are designed to give you a quick pictorial on your screen to help spot trends and make other analyses without all the detail of reports.

Creating a Custom Net Worth Report

You can create a Net Worth report by selecting the Net Worth option from the Personal Reports menu. If you choose the standard report item from the list of personal reports and don't make any changes, Quicken will prepare the report for assets and liabilities and show the balance of each of your asset and liability accounts. You used this standard option in Chapter 9, "Determining Your Net Worth," to assess your net worth.

Report Intervals

If you want to look at the effect of financial management activities on your net worth over time, the standard report will not provide what you need since it provides your balances at a specific time. The Create Account Balances Report window, which opens when you select F7 (Layout) for the Net Worth report, allows you to specify intervals for the report. Figure 10-1 shows the Create Account Balances Report window and the many interval options that can be chosen. You can select report intervals ranging from a week to a year. If you don't specify an interval, the default option is the specific time identified as

Documenting Your Decisions

As you work with Quicken's features, you will probably try a number of custom report options before you decide on the exact set of reports that meets your needs. If you had an accountant prepare these same reports, there might also be some trial and error the first time before the exact format to use would be determined. Once the decisions were made, the accountant would document them to ensure you received the exact reports you requested on a regular basis. You will benefit by following the same procedure and documenting the custom reports and options you select with Quicken. The following are steps to take in putting together your documentation:

✦   Place all your report documentation in one folder.

✦   Include a copy of each report you want to produce on a regular basis.

✦   If you are using a Quicken report to obtain information for another form, include a copy of the form and note on it which field in the Quicken report is used to obtain that number.

✦   Include the selections you used in the custom report windows. If you have a screen-capture utility, you can capture and print this screen when you create the report the first time.

✦   Include your entries on the Filter window. You can write them down or use a screen-capture utility.

✦   If you are creating multiple copies of some reports, write down the information on the extra copies and what must be done with the copies.

✦   Memorize each custom report to make it instantly available when you need it again.

the last date on the line "Report balances on dates through" (see Figure 10-1). In this example, if you request the report interval of Week, Quicken will prepare a Net Worth report at the end of each week for the month of August.

Changing the Accounts Used to Prepare the Report

The standard Net Worth report presents all accounts in the file when preparing the report. If you are concerned with only some of your balances, you can select those accounts you want to appear in the report. Entering **C** in the fifth field of the Create Account Balances Report window produces a report for the current account only. Entering **S** allows you to select from a list of all the accounts in the file.

Displaying Detailed Information on the Net Worth Report

When you created the Net Worth report in Chapter 9, "Determining Your Net Worth," all the detail available on your investments was not displayed. This occurred because Quicken's standard Net Worth report does not show all the detail. Including detailed information would

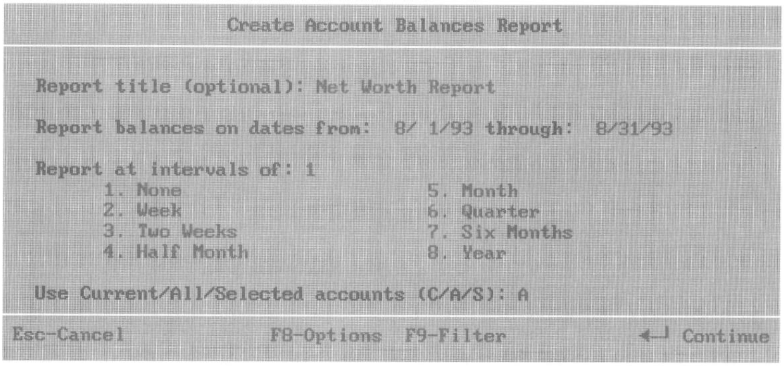

Custom Create
Account
Balances Report
window
Figure 10-1.

```
                  Create Account Balances Report


     Report title (optional): Net Worth Report

     Report balances on dates from:  8/ 1/93 through:  8/31/93

     Report at intervals of: 1
          1. None                    5. Month
          2. Week                    6. Quarter
          3. Two Weeks               7. Six Months
          4. Half Month              8. Year

     Use Current/All/Selected accounts (C/A/S): A

  Esc-Cancel              F8-Options  F9-Filter         ◄┘ Continue
```

10

provide a better picture of your investment holdings. To obtain this information, you need to customize the standard report.

To include detailed investment information on the Net Worth report, you need to enter **S** for Selected accounts in the last field of the Create Account Balances Report window (Figure 10-1). You will use the Investments account in the INVEST file created in Chapter 9. Since the last example used that file, you may already be there. If not, go to the "Changing Files" section of this chapter for instructions.

Follow these steps from the Main Menu to produce a Net Worth report with class detail.

1. Select **C**reate Reports.

Quicken will display the Reports menu shown earlier.

2. Select **P**ersonal Reports.
3. Select **N**et Worth.
4. Press F7 to change the layout of the report.

Quicken displays the Create Account Balances Report window shown in Figure 10-1.

5. Press Enter to use the default report title.
6. Type **8/1/93** and press Enter.
7. Type **8/31/93** and press Enter.
8. Press Enter to accept None for the Report at intervals of field.
9. Type **S** to use selected accounts in the report and press Enter. The Select Accounts To Include window, shown in Figure 10-2, appears on your screen.
10. Press ↓ until the arrow cursor moves to Investments.
11. Press Spacebar until the word "Detail" appears in the Include in Report column.

Pressing Spacebar changes the entry in the Include in Report column from "Include" to "Detail" to blank. "Detail" causes the detailed information to be shown in the report if any exists. A blank space means the account will be excluded from the report. "Include" shows

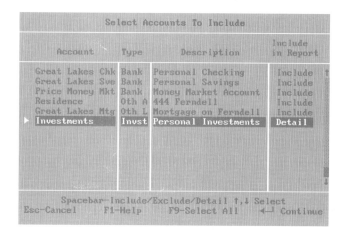

**Select Accounts
To Include
window
Figure 10-2.**

information from the account but does not use all the detail. Make sure your screen looks like that shown in Figure 10-2 before proceeding.

12. Press Enter, and the Net Worth report appears on your screen.
13. Select File/Print, and then select Print Report to display the Print Report window.
14. Select your printer and press Enter.

Quicken will produce the report shown in Figure 10-3. Notice that the report looks the same as the one generated in Chapter 9 except that the Investments section shows detailed stock information.

10

Creating a Custom Transaction Report

You can print all the transactions in any Quicken account register by opening the Print Register window from the Print/Acct menu. This procedure prints a listing of all the transactions in a given time frame. You can use this approach for printing a complete listing of register activity for backup purposes. However, it does not provide much information for decision making. The custom Transaction report item provides an alternative. By selecting this feature, you can choose to subtotal transaction activity in many different ways, use all or only selected accounts, or show split transaction detail. Thus, you are

```
                          Net Worth Report
                           As of 8/31/93
INVEST-Selected Accounts                                    Page 1
8/31/93
                                            8/31/93
                          Acct                Balance
-------------------------------  --------------------

ASSETS
  Cash and Bank Accounts
    Great Lakes Chk                            3,125.00
    Great Lakes Sve                            2,700.00
    Price Money Mkt                           14,750.00
                                           ------------
  Total Cash and Bank Accounts               20,575.00

  Other Assets
    Residence                                105,000.00
                                           ------------
  Total Other Assets                         105,000.00

  Investments
    Investments
      Douglas Marine          2,512.50
      Ganges Mutual Fund     13,500.92
      Glenn Packing           3,100.00
      Haven Publishing        9,400.00
      -Cash-                      0.00
                           ------------
    Total Investments                         28,513.42
                                           ------------
  Total Investments                           28,513.42


                                           ------------
  TOTAL ASSETS                               154,088.42

LIABILITIES
  Other Liabilities
    Great Lakes Mtg                           84,975.00
                                           ------------
  Total Other Liabilities                     84,975.00


                                           ------------
  TOTAL LIABILITIES                           84,975.00


                                           ------------
  TOTAL NET WORTH                             69,113.42
                                           ============
```

Net Worth report Figure 10-3.

allowed to select the specific transaction details you need for better decision making. Let's take a look at some examples.

Changing Files

All the remaining examples generated in this chapter are prepared in the PERSONAL file. The following sequence of steps demonstrates how to change from one file to another within Quicken:

1. While in Quicken, press (Esc) until you return to the Main Menu.
2. Select Set Preferences.
3. Select File Activities.
4. Choose Select/Set Up File.
5. Move the arrow cursor to the PERSONAL file and press (Enter). The Select Account to Use window appears.
6. Move the arrow cursor to the Cardinal Bank account, if necessary, and press (Enter). Quicken takes you to the account register for the Cardinal Bank account.
7. Press (Esc) to go to the Main Menu.

Showing Split Transaction Detail

If a transaction is split among several categories, the word "SPLIT" will appear in the Category field when the account register is printed. Suppose you want to prepare a customized report that captures all of the detail recorded in each split transaction within a selected time frame.

1. Select Create Reports.

Quicken will display the Reports menu showing both standard (Personal Reports, Business Reports, and Investment Reports) and custom report items.

2. Select Transaction from the Custom Reports section of the Reports menu.

Quicken displays the Create Transaction Report window.

10

3. Press (Enter) to use the default report title.

4. Type **8/1/93** and press (Enter).

5. Type **8/31/93** and press (Enter).

6. Press (Enter) to accept the default option, Don't Subtotal.

7. Type **C** to use the current account in the report.

At this point your screen should match the one in Figure 10-4.

8. Press (F8) (Options) and the Report Options window appears.

9. Press (Enter) to accept option 1, Income and expense, for the report organization.

10. Press (Enter) to accept option 1, Include all, in the Transfers field.

This will include in the report all transfers between the Investments account and others in the file.

11. Press (Enter) to accept N in the Show totals only field.

12. Type **Y** to indicate you want to show the split transaction detail and press (Enter).

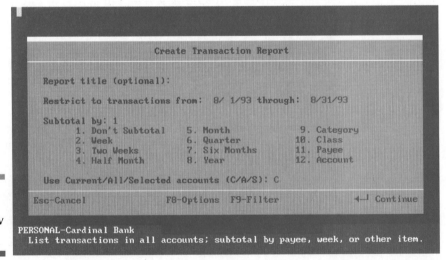

Create
Transaction
Report window
Figure 10-4.

Your screen now matches the window shown in Figure 10-5.

13. Press (Enter) to accept 3 in the next field, indicating that both memo and category data will be displayed.
14. Press (Ctrl)-(Enter) to accept the remaining defaults.

The Create Transaction Report window reappears on your screen.

15. Press (Enter), and the Transaction report appears on the screen.
16. Select File/Print and then select Print Report.
17. Select Report Printer and press (Enter) to create the report. Figure 10-6 shows the first few transactions in this report.

Notice that the report shows the details of the split transaction on 8/1, 8/2, and 8/3.

Adding Subtotals to the Transaction Report

When you produce a Transaction report without subtotals, the transactions are simply listed in order by date. If you change the

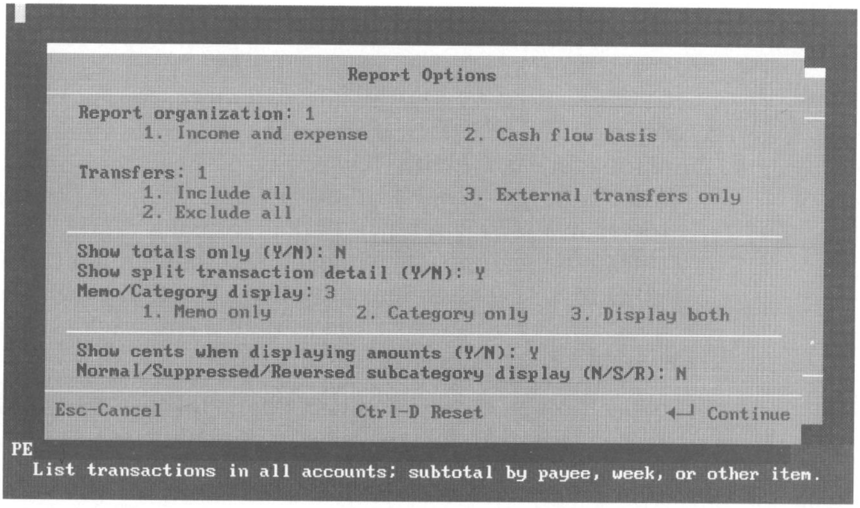

10

Report Options window for split transaction detail

Figure 10-5.

```
                        TRANSACTION REPORT
                     8/ 1/93 Through 8/31/93
     PERSONAL-Cardinal Bank                                    Page 1
     8/27/93


      Date    Num     Description        Memo          Category     Clr  Amount
     ------  ------  ----------------- -------------  ----------------- -  ---------


             BALANCE  7/31/93                                           2,260.70

     8/ 1    S Payroll deposit         Gross Wages Ea Salary           2,000.00
                                       FICA Withholdi Tax:FICA          -124.00
                                       Medicare Withh Tax:MCARE          -29.00
                                       Health Ins     Medical           -42.01
                                       Federal Income Tax:Fed          -130.00
                                       State Income T Tax:State         -80.00
                                       Local Income T Tax:Local          -9.00
     8/ 2 104 S Great Lakes Savings    Principal Paym Mort Prin         -49.33
                                       Interest Porti Mort Int         -300.67
     8/ 3 105  S Easy Credit Card      Blue Blouse    Clothing          -50.00
                                       Dinner at the  Dining            -60.00
                                       Gasoline - Jee Auto:Fuel         -23.00
                                       Green Rocker   Furniture        -217.00
                                       Play Tickets   Entertain         -50.00
                                                      Misc              -50.00
```

Transaction
report with split
transaction
detail
Figure 10-6.

subtotaling option, you can choose from the options Week, Two
Weeks, Half Month, Month, Quarter, Half Year, and Year. This still lists
the transactions by date but also provides a subtotal of the transactions
each time the selected interval occurs; selecting Month results in a
subtotal for each month. If you choose one of the options Category,
Class, Payee, or Account for the subtotal option, the transactions are
ordered by the field selected, and a subtotal is printed whenever the
value in the selected field changes. For example, a subtotal by category
for 8/1 to 8/31 transactions causes Quicken to list the transactions
alphabetically by category and by date within each category, with a
subtotal for each category.

Follow these steps from the Main Menu for the Cardinal Bank account
(in the PERSONAL file) to create a Transaction report subtotaled by
category:

1. Select **C**reate Reports.

Quicken will display the Reports menu showing both standard (Personal, Investment, and Business Reports) and custom report items.

2. Select **T**ransaction and the Create Transaction Report window appears.
3. Press Enter to use the default report title.
4. Type **8/1/93** and press Enter.
5. Type **8/31/93** and press Enter.
6. Type **9** and press Enter to subtotal by category.
7. Type **C** and press Enter to use the current account in the report.

The Transaction Report by Category will display on your screen.

8. Select **F**ile/Print and then select **P**rint Report to display the Print Report window.
9. Select Report Printer and press Enter.

The bottom of the first page of the report will show three transactions for the Groceries category, as shown in this partial report:

```
        Groceries
        _____

 8/ 4 106   Maureks      Groceries    Groceries     -60.00
 8/15 108   Meijer       Groceries    Groceries     -65.00
 8/27 112   Meijer       Food         Groceries     -93.20
                                                    _____
            Total Groceries                         -218.20
```

10

This report is essentially the same as the Itemized Categories report you saw in Chapter 7, "Quicken as a Budgeting Tool," unless you choose to make additional customization changes, such as selecting accounts or filtering the information presented.

Creating a Summary Report

Summary reports allow you to create reports based on categories, classes, payees, or accounts. You can use them to analyze spending patterns, prepare tax summaries, review major purchases, or look at the total charge card purchases for a given period.

With a Summary report you have more control over the layout of information than in other reports. You can select from a number of options to determine what information to place in rows and columns of the report. You can combine the summary features with the filtering features to further select the information presented.

Subtotaling a Summary Report by Month

Although you can choose any of the time intervals to control the subtotals for the report, a month is commonly chosen since many users budget expenses by month. This type of report allows you to look at a monthly summary of your financial transactions. Follow these steps from the Main Menu for the Cardinal Bank account (in the PERSONAL file) to create the Summary Report by Month:

1. Select the **C**reate Reports item.

Quicken displays the Reports menu showing both standard (Personal, Investment, and Business Reports) and custom report items.

2. Select **S**ummary, and the Create Summary Report window appears.
3. Press (Enter) to use the default report title.
4. Type **8/1/93** and press (Enter).
5. Type **10/31/93** and press (Enter).
6. Press (Enter) to accept the default Row headings item.
7. Type **5** and press (Enter) to select Month for the Column headings field.
8. Type **C**; then press (F8) (Options). The Report Options window appears.
9. Type **2** and press (Enter).

This step instructs Quicken to prepare the report on a cash flow basis. The report will be organized by cash inflows and outflows. This is the same basis as the monthly budget reports prepared in Chapter 7, "Quicken as a Budgeting Tool." It allows you to compare this report with those prepared earlier and provides additional information for assessing your budget results.

10. Type **1** and press Ctrl-Enter. You are returned to the Create Summary Report window.
11. Press Enter, and the Summary Report by Month appears on your screen. Figure 10-7 shows a printout of this report.

If you adjusted all of your salary and mortgage payment transactions to agree with the August entries discussed in Chapter 8, "Using Quicken to Organize Tax Information," some of your entries will look different. In that situation, your totals would show 6000 for salary, 390 for federal tax, 87 for Medicare, 372 for social security tax, and 240 for state tax.

12. Select **F**ile/Print and then select **P**rint Report to display the Print Report window.
13. Select Report Printer and press Enter.

The report presents a cash inflow and outflow summary by month for the period of August through October. It provides additional cash flow information about the budget reports prepared in Chapter 7. Thus, the Summary Report by Month supplements the previously prepared Monthly Budget reports.

10

Filtering to See Tax-Related Categories

Filters allow you to selectively present information in a report. In Chapter 3, "Quicken Reports," you used a filter to look for a payee name containing "Small." Other possible selection choices include memo, category, or class matches. You can also choose specific categories or classes for inclusion. Additional options allow you to specify tax-related items or transactions greater or less than a certain amount. You can also choose payments, deposits, unprinted checks, or all transactions.

```
                  Summary Report By Month
                   8/ 1/93 Through 10/31/93
PERSONAL-Cardinal Bank                              Page 1
8/27/93
                                                 OVERALL
 Category Description      8/93     9/93    10/93   TOTAL
------------------------ -------- -------- -------- -----------

INFLOWS
  Salary Income          2,000.00 1,585.99 1,585.99 5,171.98
                         --------- --------- --------- ---------
TOTAL INFLOWS            2,000.00 1,585.99 1,585.99 5,171.98

OUTFLOWS
  Automobile Expenses:
    Auto Fuel              23.00    23.00    37.00    83.00
                         -------- --------- --------- ---------
  Total Automobile Expenses 23.00   23.00    37.00    83.00
  Clothing                 50.00    50.00    75.00   175.00
  Dining Out               60.00    60.00    45.00   165.00
  Entertainment            50.00    50.00   100.00   200.00
  Entire Mortgage Payment   0.00   350.00   350.00    00.00
  Groceries               218.20   180.00   250.00   648.20
  Household Furniture      217.00     0.00   550.00   767.00
  Medical & Dental         142.01   170.00   100.00   412.01
  Miscellaneous             50.00    50.00   150.00   250.00
  Mortgage Interest Exp    300.67     0.00     0.00   300.67
  Mortgage Principal        49.33     0.00     0.00    49.33
  Taxes:
    Federal Tax            130.00     0.00     0.00   130.00
    Local Tax Withholding    9.00     0.00     0.00     9.00
    Medicare Withholding    29.00     0.00     0.00    29.00
    Social Security Tax    124.00     0.00     0.00   124.00
    State Tax               80.00     0.00     0.00    80.00
                         --------- --------- --------- ---------
  Total Taxes             372.00     0.00     0.00   372.00
    Telephone Expense       23.00    29.00    27.50    79.50
  Water, Gas, Electric:
    Electric Utilities      30.75    43.56    37.34   111.65
    Gas Utilities           19.25    19.29    16.55    55.09
                         --------- --------- --------- ---------
  Total Water, Gas, Electric 50.00   62.85    53.89   166.74
  TO Cardinal Saving       200.00   394.79   366.35   961.14
                         --------- --------- --------- --------
TOTAL OUTFLOWS           1,805.21 1,419.64 2,104.74 5,329.59
                         --------- --------- --------- --------
OVERALL TOTAL             194.79   166.35  -518.75  -157.61
                         ========= ========= ========= =========
```

**Summary
Report by
Month
Figure 10-7.**

Checking the cleared status is another option; that is, you may wish to prepare a report using only transactions that have cleared the bank as part of your reconciliation process.

In the example that follows, you will create a Summary report for tax-related items. Use the Cardinal Bank account in the PERSONAL file. Starting from the Main Menu, follow these steps:

1. Select C reate Reports.

Quicken displays the Reports menu showing both standard (Personal Reports, Business Reports, and Investment Reports) and custom reports.

2. Select S ummary. The Create Summary Report window appears on your screen.
3. Press (Enter) to use the default report title.
4. Type 8/1/93 and press (Enter).
5. Type 10/31/93 and press (Enter).
6. Press (Enter) to accept Category for the row headings.
7. Type 1 and press (Enter) to select the default Don't Subtotal option.
8. Type C to select the current account.
9. Press (F9) (Filter) to display the Filter Transactions window on your screen.
10. Press (Enter) six times to move to the Tax-related categories only field. Type Y and press (Enter). The Filter Transactions window will look like the one in Figure 10-8.
11. Press (Ctrl)-(Enter) to return to the Create Summary Report window.
12. Press (F8) (Options) to open the Report Options window.
13. Type 2 and press (Enter).
14. Press (Ctrl)-(Enter) to accept the default, option 1, which instructs Quicken to include in the report all transfers between this account and others. You are returned to the Create Summary Report window.
15. Press (Enter), and the Summary report appears on your screen.
16. Select F ile/Print and then select P rint Report to display the Print Report window.

10

```
                    Filter Transactions
       Restrict report to transactions matching these criteria
             Payee contains    :
             Memo contains     :
             Category contains:
             Class contains    :

       Select categories to include...(Y/N): N
       Select classes to include...    (Y/N): N

       Tax-related categories only     (Y/N): Y
       Below/Equal/Above (B/E/A):    the amount:
       Payments/Deposits/Unprinted checks/All (P/D/U/A) : A

       Cleared status is
       Blank ' ': Y  Newly cleared '*': Y  Cleared 'X': Y

     Esc-Cancel              Ctrl-D Reset            ◄┘ Continue
```

Filter
Transactions
window
Figure 10-8.

17. Select Report Printer and press (Enter).

Don't clear the report from your screen since you will want to use it in the next section.

Figure 10-9 shows the completed report with the information filtered for tax-related transactions only. (The report shown reflects the split salary and mortgage transaction for August only.) This type of report can be used to monitor your tax-related activities for any part of the tax year or for the year-to-date activity. You can use this information for tax planning as well as tax preparation.

Memorizing Reports

You have already seen the productivity that you can gain with Quicken's memorized transactions. Quicken also allows you to memorize reports. Memorized reports store your custom report definitions and allow you to produce a new report instantly by recalling the memorized report definition. This means you can enter a title or filter once and use it again if you memorize the report.

To memorize a report, you use the same (Ctrl)-(M) sequence used to memorize transactions. The only difference is that you must have a

```
                           SUMMARY REPORT
                      8/ 1/93 Through 10/31/93
PERSONAL-Cardinal Bank                                        Page 1
8/27/93

                                          8/ 1/93-
                 Category Description      10/31/93
                 -------------------------  -------------------
INFLOWS
   Salary Income                            5,171.98
                                          ----------
TOTAL INFLOWS                               5,171.98

OUTFLOWS
   Medical & Dental                           412.01
   Mortgage Interest Exp                      300.67
   Taxes:
      Federal Tax               130.00
      Local Tax                   9.00
      Medicare Withholding       29.00
      Social Security Tax       124.00
      State Tax                  80.00
                              ----------
      Total Taxes                             372.00
                                          ----------
TOTAL OUTFLOWS                              1,084.68
                                          ----------
OVERALL TOTAL                               4,087.30
                                          ==========
```

Filtered
Summary report
of tax-related
transactions
Figure 10-9.

report displayed on the screen. The following box will display to allow
you to enter a name for the report:

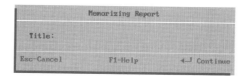

10

If you were memorizing the definition for the tax summary by month
shown in Figure 10-7, you might enter the title as Tax Related Summary
by Month. Although you can use the entire line for your name, you will
want to ensure that the first 27 characters of your entry uniquely define
your report since this is the entry that will display in the list of
memorized reports.

To create a report from a memorized report definition, select **M**emorized Reports from the Report menu. A list of memorized reports will display in a window like the one shown here,

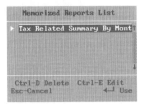

which shows a Tax Related Summary by Mont option. The *h* in Month is truncated from the display since it exceeds the 27-character display limit. After moving the arrow cursor to the desired report and pressing (Enter), the desired report is displayed on the screen. If you press (Esc), you can access the report definition and change it before displaying the report again.

Redo Last Report

The last report feature shows how you can always recover the previous report that was generated at any point during your current Quicken session. If you are not at the Main Menu, press (Esc) until you are.

1. Press (Ctrl)-(Z).

Quicken automatically recreates the last report you generated during this session (Figure 10-9). You can also select the Redo Last Report option from the Reports Menu or from the register **R**eports pull-down menu. The important point to recall is that Quicken can recapture your last report generated at any time during the current session.

Now that you've had a chance to look at both standard and custom report options, you should have some idea of the types of reports you will need. You will want to take full advantage of Quicken's ability to memorize reports in order to save time and produce a consistent set of reports for each time period.

Using Graphs for Additional Analyses

The graphs that you created in Chapter 7 related to your budget entries. Once you activate the View Graphs menu you will see that there are

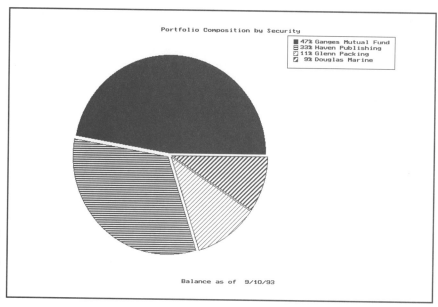

Pie graph
shows balances
Figure 10-10.

many additional options for analyzing your data with Quicken 6's new graphs. Follow these steps to create a graph showing the composition of your investment portfolio:

1. From the Main Menu select Set **P**references.
2. Select **F**ile Activities and then choose **S**elect/Setup Account.
3. Highlight Invest and press (Enter), and then highlight Investments and press (Enter) again.
4. Press (Esc) to display the Main Menu and then select View **G**raphs.
5. Select In**v**estment and then Portfolio **C**omposition.
6. Press (Ctrl)-(Enter) to accept the defaults of the current date and By Security.

The graph displays as shown in Figure 10-10.

7. Press (Esc) until the Main Menu displays again.

10

P A R T

3

BUSINESS
APPLICATIONS

C H A P T E R

11

SETTING UP QUICKEN FOR YOUR BUSINESS

Many small businesses will find that the Quicken system of record keeping can improve the quality of financial information used in making business decisions. Quicken can be used to record business transactions in your check register while maintaining cost and depreciation records for assets in other registers. Quicken can also be used to budget cash flow, track the cost of jobs in progress, monitor and record payroll, and generate summary tax information to assist in tax return preparation. If you are a contractor, you can track the cost incurred on various jobs as they progress through construction. If you provide landscaping services, you can track the cost incurred for each job and prepare summary reports to determine the profits generated by job. If you are an author, you can use Quicken to monitor royalties by publisher and record the costs incurred in your writing activities.

Even though Quicken improves your ability to record and monitor your business's financial transactions, it may not eliminate the need for accounting services. There are important tax issues that affect the business transactions you record. In addition, you may want your accountant to establish the hierarchy of categories you use to record transactions. This hierarchy, used to categorize all transactions, is called a *chart of accounts.* Your accountant should help establish the structure for your chart of accounts, which will ensure the information is organized to reduce the time required for other services, such as year-end tax preparation, that the accountant will continue to supply. This is particularly important if you will be recording business expenses in both your personal and business checking accounts.

The first section of this book introduced you to the basic features of Quicken. If you completed the exercises in Chapters 6 through 10, you built on the basic skills with split transactions, such as mortgage payments allocated between principal and interest, and with memorization of recurring transactions. In those chapters you also used Quicken to prepare and monitor budgets, collect tax-related transactions, and prepare customized reports. In the remaining chapters you will look at some of these concepts again, from a business perspective. If you plan to use Quicken for home and business use, you may find it beneficial to read through the earlier chapters, if you haven't done so, rather than moving directly to business transactions.

This chapter is longer than the others since there are many decisions you need to make as you begin. There are also a number of basic skills you need to develop to apply Quicken to all aspects of your business. The first step is to consider some alternatives. The next sections provide an overview of two important decisions that must precede all other activities with the package. If you need additional guidance, consult your accountant to be certain your information will be in the format you need for your entire business year.

Cash Versus Accrual Accounting

The first decision you need to make is the timing of recording financial transactions. You can record a transaction as soon as you know that it will occur, or you can wait until cash changes hands between the parties in the transaction. The former alternative is accrual basis accounting, and the latter is cash basis accounting. There is a third method, called modified cash basis, that is discussed shortly. If your business is organized as a corporation, the accrual method must be used.

Most small businesses use the cash basis because it corresponds to their tax-reporting needs and because the financial reports prepared provide information summarizing the cash-related activities of the business. With *cash basis* accounting, you report income when you receive cash from customers for services you provide. For example, if you are in the plumbing business, you would recognize income when a customer makes payment for services. You might provide the services in December and not receive the customer's check until January. In this case, you would record the income in January, when you received and deposited the customer's check. Similarly, you recognize your expenses when you write your checks for the costs you incurred. Thus, if you ordered supplies in December but didn't pay the bill until January, you would deduct the cost in January when you wrote a check to the supplier. Briefly, with a purely cash basis accounting system, you recognize the income when you receive cash and recognize expenses when you pay for expenses incurred for business purposes.

With the *accrual basis* approach, you record your revenues and expenses when you provide services to your customer, regardless of when the cash flow occurs. Using the plumbing example from the preceding paragraph, you would recognize the income from the plumbing services in December, when you provided the services to the customer, even though the cash would not be received until the next year. Likewise, if you purchased the supplies in December and paid for them in January, the cost of the supplies would be recorded in December, not in January when they were actually paid for. The same information is recorded under both methods.

The basic difference between the cash and accrual bases of accounting is what accountants call *timing differences*. When a cash basis is used, the receipt of cash determines when the transaction is recorded. When

11

the accrual basis is used, the time the services are provided determines when the revenue and expenses are recorded.

A third method of reporting business revenues and expenses is the *modified cash basis* approach. This method uses the cash basis as described but modifies it to report depreciation on certain assets over a number of years. In this case, you must spread the cost of trucks, computer equipment, office furniture, and similar assets over the estimated number of years they will be used to generate income for your business. The Internal Revenue Service has rules for determining the life of an asset. In addition, the tax laws also allow you to immediately deduct the first $10,000 of the acquisition cost of certain qualified assets each year without worrying about depreciation. Once again, these are areas where your accountant could be of assistance in setting up your Quicken accounts.

Whether you use the cash, accrual, or modified cash basis in recording your transactions is determined by a number of factors. Some of the considerations are listed for you in the special "Cash Versus Accrual Methods" section.

Since many small businesses use the modified cash basis of recording revenues and expenses, this method is illustrated in all the examples in Chapters 11 through 15.

Establishing Your Chart of Accounts

You can use the basic set of categories that Quicken provides to categorize your business transactions, or you can create a whole new set. Each of the existing categories will have a name similar to the category options used in earlier chapters. For example, there is a category name of Ads with the description Advertising. In Quicken, these organizational units are called categories despite the fact that you may have been referring to them as accounts in your manual system.

If you do not have an existing chart of accounts, making a few modifications to Quicken's standard category options is the best approach. The names in Quicken's categories are suitable for most businesses. Later in this chapter, you will learn to add a few accounts of your own.

If you already have an existing set of accounts, you will want to retain this structure for consistency. Many businesses assign a number to each category of income or expense, such as using 4001 as the account number for book sales. They may use the first two digits of the number to group asset, liability, income, and expense accounts together. If you have this structure, you will need to invest a little more time initially to establish your chart of accounts. You can delete the entries in the existing list of categories and then add new categories, or you can edit the existing categories one by one. The category names in your category list (chart of accounts) might be numbers, such as 4001 or 5010, and the corresponding descriptions 4001—Book Sales and 5010—Freight, respectively. When you are finished, each category will contain your account number and each description will contain both the account number and text describing the income or expense recorded in the category. You should work through all the examples in this chapter before setting up your own categories.

A Quick Look at the Business Used in the Examples

An overview of the business used for the examples in Chapters 11 through 15 will be helpful in understanding some of the selections made in the exercises. The business is run by an individual and is organized as a sole proprietorship. The individual running the business is married and must file a Form 1040 showing both business income and W2 income earned by the spouse. Income categories in addition to the standard ones provided with Quicken will be needed for the different types of income generated. Since the company in the example offers services rather than merchandise, the income categories will be appropriate for a service-type business. Quicken can also be used for retail or wholesale businesses that sell goods. You can use Quicken for any organization, including sole proprietorships, partnerships, and small corporate entities. Look at the special "Business Organization Options" section for a definition of these three types of businesses.

The business is home-based, which necessitates splitting some expenses, such as utilities and mortgage interest, between home and business categories. Other expenses, such as the purchase of office equipment, are business expenses. A number of expenses incurred by the business

11

do not have appropriate entries in the category list provided by Quicken; this will require adding categories.

The example selected is a little more complicated than a business run from outside the home that has no transactions split between business and personal expenses. When you have a clear separation, you can simply establish a file for all of your business accounts and another file for personal transactions. The example used here has separate checking accounts for business and personal records but places both accounts within one file. The use of separate accounts should be considered almost mandatory. All business income should be deposited into a separate account and all expenses that are completely business related should be paid from this account. Anyone who has experienced an IRS audit can testify to the necessity of having solid documentation for business transactions. One part of that documentation is the maintenance of a business checking account and supporting receipts for your expenses and revenues. If you maintain a separate business account, your bank statement provides the supporting detail for business transactions in a clear and concise manner that supports your documentation of business activities. If your business is so small that it is not feasible to establish and maintain two checking accounts, you will need to be particularly careful when recording entries in your Quicken register.

Quicken Files

When you first used Quicken, you created a file for your data. You named this file QDATA, and Quicken created four files on your disk to manage all the accounts and information within them. You could use this file to record all your transactions if you decide to handle your business and personal financial transactions through a single file.

In the first five chapters, you worked with only one account in QDATA. If you completed Chapters 6 through 10, you learned that it was possible to create additional accounts such as a separate savings account and an investment account. You can also have accounts for credit cards, cash, assets, and liabilities. A PERSONAL file was created in Chapter 6 to organize all the personal accounts.

You could continue to enter the transactions in this chapter in the QDATA file by setting up a new account. However, since you will want

Cash Versus Accrual Methods

Tax Requirements You must decide what your tax reporting obligations are and whether those requirements alone will dictate the method you select for financial reporting. For most small businesses, this is the overriding factor to consider. For instance, if inventories are part of your business, you must use the accrual method for revenues and purchases. If inventories are not a part of your business, you will probably find it best and easiest to use the cash basis of accounting.

Users of the Financial Reports The people who use your financial reports can have a significant influence on your reporting decisions. For example, do you have external users such as banks and other creditors? If so, you may find they require special reports and other financial information that will influence how you set up your accounting and reporting system.

Size and Type of Business Activity The kind of business you have will influence the type of financial reports you need to prepare and the method of accounting you will adopt. Are you in a service, retail, or manufacturing business? Manufacturing concerns will use the accrual method since they have sales that will be billed and collected over weeks or even months and they carry inventories of goods. Retail stores such as small groceries would also use the accrual method of accounting, at least for sales and purchases, since they have inventories that affect the financial reports they will prepare. On the other hand, a small landscaping business will probably use the cash basis since there are no inventories and the majority of the cost associated with the business is payroll and other costs that are generally paid close to the time the services are performed. In this case, the use of business equipment will call for the modified cash basis to record depreciation on the property.

11

to learn how to set up new transactions that are stored in separate files, you should create a new file. You also learn how to create a backup copy of a file to safeguard your data entry.

Adding a New File

If you completed Chapters 1 through 9, you already have files for QDATA, PERSONAL, and INVEST with all of the transactions entered in the first two sections of this book. If you skipped Chapters 6 through 10, you still have only the QDATA file. In this section, you learn how to create a new file and create accounts within it. You need to decide if you want to delete the other files to free the space on your disk. They can be deleted from the Select/Set Up File window when you are finished creating the new file.

You will use a file called BUSINESS and initially set up a business checking account, a personal checking account, and an asset account. The asset account will be used to record information on equipment. Later in this chapter, you will establish other accounts for this file. From the Main Menu, follow these steps to set up the new file and add the first three accounts to this file:

1. Select Set **P**references.
2. Select **F**ile Activities.
3. Select **S**elect/Set Up File.

Quicken displays the window for selecting or setting up a file. Notice the existing files. If you skipped Chapters 6 through 10, you will only have one file.

4. Select <Set Up New File> and press Enter.

Quicken opens the window for creating a new file.

5. Type **BUSINESS** as the name for the file and press Enter.

Quicken creates four DOS files from each filename and adds four different filename extensions to the name you provide. This means you must provide a valid filename of no more than eight characters. Do not include spaces or special symbols in your entries for account names.

6. Check the location for your data files and make changes to reference a valid file or directory if a change is required.

If you use the default directory, yours will display as C:\QUICKEN.

Business Organization Options

The following are the various options you choose when setting up your business.

Sole Proprietorship   A sole proprietorship provides no separation between the owner and the business. The debts of the business are the personal liabilities of the owner. The profits of the business are included on the owner's tax return since the business does not pay taxes on profits directly. This form of business organization is the simplest.

Partnership   A partnership is a business defined as a relationship between two or more parties. Each person in the partnership is taxed as an individual for his or her share of the profits. A partnership agreement defines the contributions of each member and the distribution of the profits.

Corporation   A corporation is an independent business entity. The owners of the corporation are separate from the corporation and do not personally assume the debt of the corporation. This is referred to as *limited liability*. The corporation is taxed on its profits and can distribute the remaining profits to owners as dividends. The owners are taxed on these dividends, resulting in the so-called "double tax" with the corporate structure. Unlike sole proprietorship and partnership businesses, corporations pay salaries to the owners.

S Corporation   An S corporation is a special form of corporation that avoids the double tax problem of a regular corporation. A number of strict rules govern when an S corporation can be set up. Some of the limitations are that only one class of stock is permitted and that there is an upper limit of 35 shareholders.

11

7. Press [Enter] to complete the creation of the new file.
8. Select the Both Home and Business category and press [Enter].

Note that you can see the size of all the files you have created here. You can delete some of them at this time if you need to clear disk space.

Quicken redisplays the window for selecting or creating files but shows the BUSINESS file this time.

9. Move the cursor to BUSINESS and press Enter.

Since this is a new file, Quicken does not have any accounts in the file. The window shown in Figure 11-1 appears to allow you to set up a new account. Leave your screen as it is for a few minutes while you explore some new account options.

Adding Accounts to the New File

Quicken makes it easy to create multiple accounts. All the accounts here will be created in the same file, so you will be able to create one report for all of them as well as print reports for individual accounts. There will be an account register for each account that you create.

Savings accounts, investment accounts, cash accounts, asset accounts, liability accounts, and credit card accounts are all possible additions. Savings accounts and investment accounts should definitely be kept separate from your checking account since you will be interested in monitoring both the growth and balance in these accounts separately.

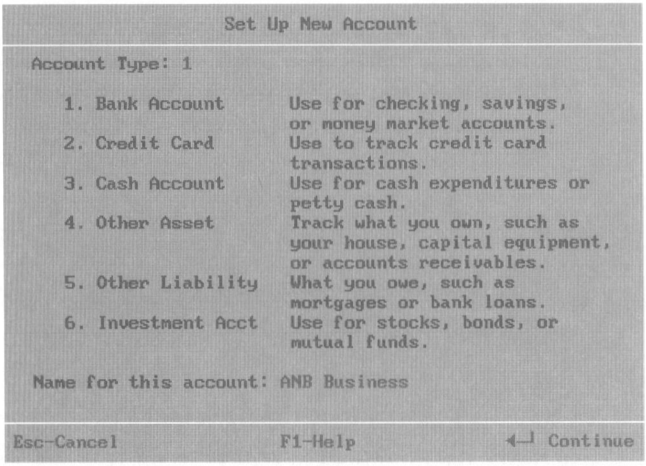

Entering
information for
the new account
Figure 11-1.

As mentioned earlier, separate business and personal checking accounts are another good idea.

Quicken accounts can be set up to conform to the needs of your business. In this section you will add the first few accounts. In later chapters, additional accounts will be established to monitor other business activities. From the Set Up New Account window, follow these steps to enter the new account:

1. Select Bank Account for the account type and press Enter.
2. Type **ANB Business** and press Enter.

ANB represents the bank name and Business indicates that it is the business checking account. Although you could use Cardinal Bank again in this new file, ANB (for American National Bank) will be used to eliminate confusion with the earlier examples.

3. Type **4000** for the balance and press Enter in the Starting Balance and Description window.
4. Type **1/1/93** and press Enter.
5. Type **Business Checking** and press Enter.
6. Select 1 and press Enter twice.
7. Move the arrow cursor to <New Account> and press Enter.
8. Select Bank Account and press Enter.
9. Type **ANB Personal** and press Enter.
10. Type **2500** and press Enter.
11. Type **1/1/93** and press Enter.
12. Type **Personal Checking** and press Enter.
13. Select 1 and press Enter twice.
14. Move the arrow cursor to <New Account> and press Enter.
15. Select Other Asset and press Enter.
16. Type **Equipment** and press Enter twice.

This account type selection is used to record financial transactions affecting the equipment you use in your business.

11

17. Type **0** and press Enter.

You enter the value of these assets later in this chapter.

18. Type **1/1/93** and press Enter.
19. Type **Capital Equipment** and press Enter.
20. Press Esc three times to return to the Main Menu.

You have now created a new file and three accounts for organizing personal and business transactions.

Changing the Active File

The result of the last exercise was to create another file. You can work in any file at any time and can work with any account within a file. To change from the BUSINESS file to QDATA from the Main Menu, follow these steps:

1. Select Set **P**references.
2. Select **F**ile Activities.
3. Select **S**elect/Set Up File.
4. Select QDATA and press Enter.

You are taken immediately to the first and only account in the QDATA file, 1st U.S. Bank.

5. Press Esc to return to the Main Menu.

The QDATA file is now active. If you went to the register or check writing screen, you would find that the 1st U.S. Bank account was active. Change the file back to BUSINESS and open the account for ANB Business by following the same procedure.

Backing Up a File

You should create backups on a regular basis of the data managed by the Quicken system. This will allow you to recover all your entries in the event of a disk failure since you will be able to use your copy to restore all the entries. You will need a blank formatted disk to record the backup information the first time. Subsequent backups can be made on this disk without reformatting it.

Creating Backup Files

Quicken provides a Backup and Restore feature that allows you to safeguard the investment of time you have made in entering your data. You can back up all your account files from the Print/Acct menu on the register screen. To back up specific files, select the backup option found in the File Activities screen, accessed from the Set Preferences menu. Follow these steps to back up the current file:

1. Press (Esc) to return to the Main Menu and select Set **P**references.
2. Select **F**ile Activities.
3. Select **B**ack Up File.
4. Place your blank, formatted disk in drive A and then press (Enter).
5. Select BUSINESS and press (Enter).
6. Press (Enter) to acknowledge the completion of the backup when Quicken displays the successful backup message.
7. Press (Esc) three times to return to the Main Menu.
8. Select Use **R**egister to open the register screen, as shown in Figure 11-2, and continue to work in the register.

NOTE: If you ever lose your hard disk, you can re-create your data directory from the Set Preferences, File Activities Options by selecting **R**estore File to copy your backup file to the directory. You should schedule backups on a regular basis to minimize the risk of data loss. You can also copy the Quicken data files from one floppy drive to another as a quick means of backup if you do not have a hard disk.

11

 **Customizing Categories**

When you set up the new BUSINESS file, you were instructed to select Both Home and Business as the categories option. This selection

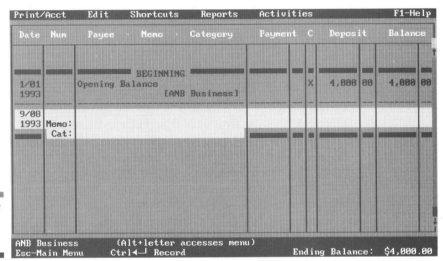

Register for the
new account
Figure 11-2.

provides access to the more than 60 category choices shown in Table
11-1. You can see from this table that some categories are listed as
expenses and others as income. Notice that some of the expense
categories have more detailed subcategories beneath an existing
category entry. You learn how to create additional subcategories in the
"Using Subcategories" section later in this chapter. Note the column in
the table that shows you which categories are tax related.

Editing the Existing Category List

You can change the name of any existing category, change its
classification as income, expense, or a subcategory, or change your
assessment of its being tax related. To make a change to a category
follow these steps.

1. Press Ctrl-C from the register to display the category list.
2. Move the arrow cursor to the category you want to change.
3. Press Ctrl-E to edit the information for the category.

Category	Description	Tax Rel	Type
Bonus	Bonus Income	*	Inc
Canada Pen	Canadian Pension	*	Inc
Div Income	Dividend Income	*	Inc
Gift Received	Gift Received	*	Inc
Gr Sales	Gross Sales	*	Inc
Int Inc	Interest Income	*	Inc
Invest Inc	Investment Income	*	Inc
Old Age Pen	Old Age Pension	*	Inc
Other Inc	Other Income	*	Inc
Rent Income	Rent Income	*	Inc
Salary	Salary Income	*	Inc
Ads	Advertising	*	Expns
Auto	Automobile Expenses		Expns
Fuel	Auto Fuel		Sub
Loan	Auto Loan Payment		Sub
Service	Auto Service		Sub
Bank Chrg	Bank Charge		Expns
Car	Car & Truck	*	Expns
Charity	Charitable Donations	*	Expns
Childcare	Childcare Expense		Expns
Christmas	Christmas Expense		Expns
Clothing	Clothing		Expns
Commission	Commissions	*	Expns
Dining	Dining Out		Expns
Dues	Dues		Expns
Education	Education		Expns
Entertain	Entertainment		Expns
Freight	Freight	*	Expns
Gifts	Gift Expenses		Expns
Groceries	Groceries		Expns
Home Rpair	Home Repair & Maint.		Expns
Household	Household Misc. Exp		Expns

Category List for a File in the Category Selection of Both
Table 11-1.

11

Category	Description	Tax Rel	Type
Housing	Housing		Expns
Insurance	Insurance		Expns
Int Exp	Interest Expense	*	Expns
Int Paid	Interest Paid	*	Expns
Invest Exp	Investment Expense	*	Expns
L&P Fees	Legal & Prof. Fees	*	Expns
Late Fees	Late Payment Fees	*	Expns
Medical	Medical & Dental	*	Expns
Misc	Miscellaneous		Expns
Mort Int	Mortgage Interst Exp.	*	Expns
Office	Office Expenses	*	Expns
Other Exp	Other Expense	*	Expns
Recreation	Recreation Expense		Expns
Rent Paid	Rent Paid	*	Expns
Repairs	Repairs	*	Expns
Returns	Returns & Allowances	*	Expns
RRSP	Reg. Retirement Sav. Plan		Expns
Subscriptions	Subscriptions		Expns
Supplies	Supplies	*	Expns
Tax	Taxes	*	Expns
Fed	Federal Tax	*	Sub
FICA	Social Security Tax	*	Sub
Other	Misc. Taxes	*	Sub
Prop	Property Tax	*	Sub
State	State Tax	*	Sub
Telephone	Telephone Expense		Expns
Travel	Travel Expense	*	Expns
UIC	Unemploy. Ins. Commission	*	Expns
Utilities	Water, Gas, Electric		Expns
Gas & Electric	Gas and Electricity		Sub
Water	Water		Sub
Wages	Wages & Job Credits	*	Expns

Category List for a File in the Category Selection of Both (*continued*)
Table 11-1.

4. Change the fields you wish to alter.

5. Press Ctrl-Enter to complete the changes.

If you change the name of the category, Quicken will automatically change it in any transactions that have already been assigned to the category.

If you need to totally restructure the categories, you may find it easier to delete the old categories and add new ones with the instructions in the next section. To delete a category, follow these steps:

1. Press Ctrl-C from the register to display the category list.

2. Move the arrow cursor to the category you want to delete.

3. Press Ctrl-D to delete the information in the category.

You should not delete categories already assigned to transactions. If you do, you delete that part of the transactions in your register. Make any changes in which you delete categories before you start recording transactions.

4. Press Ctrl-Enter to complete the changes.

Adding Categories

You can add categories to provide additional options specific to your needs. Each type of business will probably have some unique categories of income or expenses. For the example in this chapter, both income and expense category additions are needed.

The business in this example has three sources of business income: consulting fees, royalties, and income earned for writing articles. It would be inappropriate to use the salary category since this should be reserved for income earned from a regular employer (reported on Form W2 at year-end). You could use the Gross Sales category to record the various types of income for the business. Another solution would be to create new categories for each income source. The examples in this chapter use three new income categories.

Many of the existing expense categories are suitable for recording business expenses, but for this example additional expense categories are needed. Equipment maintenance, computer supplies, and overnight

11

mail service categories are needed. Although a category already exists for freight, a more specific postage category is also needed. New categories are not needed to record computer and office equipment and furniture purchases. These will be handled through an "other asset" type account, with the specific purchase listed in the Payee field to the transaction.

You can add a new category by entering it in the Category field when recording a transaction in a register or on a check writing screen. Pressing (Enter) to record the transaction will cause Quicken to indicate that the category does not exist in the current list. You are then given the choice of selecting another category already in the list or adding the new category to the list. You would choose to add it, just as you did with the category for auto loans in Chapter 4, "Reconciling Your Quicken Register."

If you have a number of categories to add, it is simpler to add them before starting data entry. To use this approach to add the new categories needed for the exercises in this chapter, follow these steps:

1. Press (Ctrl)-(C) (or select **S**hortcuts and then select **C**ategorize/Transfer).

Either one will open the Category and Transfer List window.

2. Press (Home) to move to the top of the category list. <New Category> is the top entry in the list.

3. Select <New Category>.

Quicken will allow you to enter a new category using the window shown here,

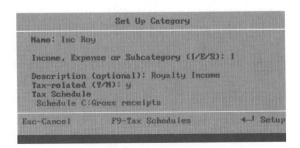

which contains entries for a new royalty income category called "Inc Roy." Note the use of Inc first in the category name. This allows you to later select all income categories by entering **Inc** in your report filter window (see Chapter 3, "Quicken Reports").

4. Type **Inc Roy** and press [Enter].
5. Type **I** and press [Enter].
6. Type **Royalty Income** and press [Enter].
7. Type **Y** and press [F9] (Tax Schedules).

Quicken presents a Tax Schedule window.

8. Select Schedule C, and a Tax Line window appears.
9. Select Gross Receipts.
10. Select Copy 1.

If you prepare multiple copies of a schedule, Quicken allows you to select different copies.

11. Press [Enter] to have Quicken return you to the Category and Transfer List window.
12. Repeat steps 3 through 11 for each of the categories that follow; then press [Esc] to return to the Register window.

Name:	Inc Cons
Income:	I
Description:	Consulting Income
Tax Related:	Y
Tax Schedule:	Schedule C: Gross receipts

Name:	Inc Art
Income:	I
Description:	Article Income
Tax Related:	Y
Tax Schedule:	Schedule C: Gross receipts

11

Name: Equip Mnt

Expense: E

Description: Equipment Maintenance

Tax Related: Y

Tax Schedule: Schedule C: Repairs and maintenance

Name: Supp Comp

Expense: E

Descritpion: Computer Supplies

Tax Related: Y

Tax Schedule: Schedule C: Supplies

Name: Postage

Expense: E

Description: Postage Expense

Tax Related: Y

Tax Schedule: Schedule C: Other business expense

Name: Del Overngt

Expense: E

Description: Overnight Delivery

Tax Related: Y

Tax Schedule: Schedule C: Other business expense

You should feel free to customize Quicken by adding any categories you need. However, be aware that available random-access memory limits the number of categories you can create in each category list. With a 512K system, approximately 1000 categories can be created.

Requiring Categories in All Transactions

Another customization option Quicken offers is a reminder that a category should be entered for each transaction before it is recorded. If you attempt to record a transaction without a category, Quicken will not complete the process until you confirm that you want the transaction added without a category.

To require categories in all transactions you choose Set **P**references from the Main Menu and then select **T**ransaction Settings. Select the fifth item in the Transaction Settings window and type **Y**. Press Ctrl-Enter to finalize the settings change. The next time you attempt to record a transaction without a category, Quicken will stop to confirm your choice before saving.

Using Classes

Classes are another way of organizing transactions. They allow you to define the who, when, or why of a transaction. It is important to understand that although they, too, allow you to group data, classes are distinct from categories. You will continue to use categories to provide specific information about the transactions to which they are assigned. Categories tell you what kind of income or expense a specific transaction represents. You can tell at a glance which costs are for utilities and which are for entertainment. In summary reports, you might show transactions totaled by category.

Classes allow you to slice the transaction pie in a different way. They provide a different view or perspective of your data. For example, you can continue to organize data in categories such as Utilities or Snow Removal yet also classify it by the property requiring the service. Classes were not needed in the earlier chapters of this book since categories provide all the organization you need for very basic transactions. But if you want to combine home and business transactions in one file, classes are essential for differentiating between the two types of transactions. Here, every transaction you enter will be classified as either personal or business. Business transactions will have a class entered after the category. By omitting the class entry from personal transactions, you classify them as personal. Class assignments can be used without category assignments, but in this chapter they are used in addition to categories.

11

Defining Classes

Quicken does not provide a standard list of classes. As with categories, you can set up what you need before you start making entries, or you can add the classes you need as you enter transactions. To assign a class while entering a transaction, you type the class name in the Category field after the category name (if one is used). A slash (/) must be typed before the class name.

To create a class before entering a transaction, follow these steps from the account register to add a class for business:

1. Press Ctrl-L to open the Class List window.

2. Press Enter with the arrow cursor on <New Class>. Quicken displays the Set Up Class window, shown here:

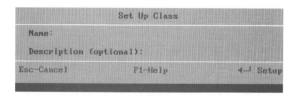

3. Type **B** and press Enter.

You can use a longer entry, such as Business, but you are limited in the number of characters used to display categories, classes, and other organizational groupings, so you should keep it as short as possible.

4. Type **Business** and press Enter.

Quicken completes the entry for the first class and adds it to the list in the Class List window. You could create a second class for personal transactions, but it is not really necessary. You can consider any transaction without a class of B to be personal.

5. Press Esc to return to the Register window.

Each new class is added to the Class List window.

REMEMBER: To create a class as you enter a transaction, simply type the category followed by a slash (/) and the class you want to use, and then press (Enter).

6. Move the highlight to the opening balance transaction.
7. Tab to the Category field; then press the (End) key.
8. Type **/B**
9. Press (Ctrl)-(Enter) to record the changed entry.

Entering Transactions with Classes

You record the business transaction in the same manner as earlier transactions. It is important that you remember to enter the class in the Category field. Follow these instructions:

1. Press (Home) twice to move the Date field.
2. Type **1/2/93** and press (Enter) twice.
3. Type **Arlo, Inc.** and press (Enter) three times.
4. Type **12500** in the Deposit field and press (Enter).
5. Type **Seminars conducted in Nov. 92** and press (Enter).
6. Type **Inc Cons/B**.

The first part of this entry categorizes the transaction as consulting income. The slash (/) and the B classify the transaction as business related.

When you start to record this category Quicken 6 uses its QuickFill feature to assist you in entering the transaction. In this case Quicken supplies the category Inc Art. You can easily move to the desired category by pressing the (Ctrl)-(+) or (Ctrl)-(−) keys to move through the list of categories that match the letter I that you entered since Quicken reveals all the expense and income categories that begin with I. If your category is not on the standard list you need to add it as you did earlier in this chapter. You can always continue to type the entire category

11

entry without using QuickFill's suggestions and complete the transactions.

7. Press Ctrl-Enter to record the transaction. Your screen looks like the one shown here:

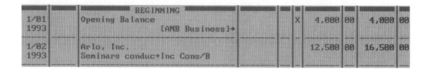

You can record an expense transaction in the ANB Business account in a similar fashion. Follow these instructions:

1. Type **1/2/93** and press Enter.
2. Type **101** and press Enter.
3. Type **Office All** and press Enter.
4. Type **65** and press Enter.
5. Type **Cartridge for copier** and press Enter.
6. Press Ctrl-C, move the arrow cursor to Supplies, and then press Enter.

This approach allows you to select the category from the list rather than typing it.

7. Type **/B** and press Ctrl-Enter.

The Register window matches the one in Figure 11-3.

The next transaction is for clothing. Since this is a personal expense paid with a personal check, it cannot be added to the current account. You must open the ANB Personal account for your entry. Follow these steps:

1. Press Esc to return to the Main Menu.
2. Choose Select Account.
3. Select ANB Personal.

When you enter the transaction for the clothing, the fact that you are not using a class will indicate that it is a personal expense. Although

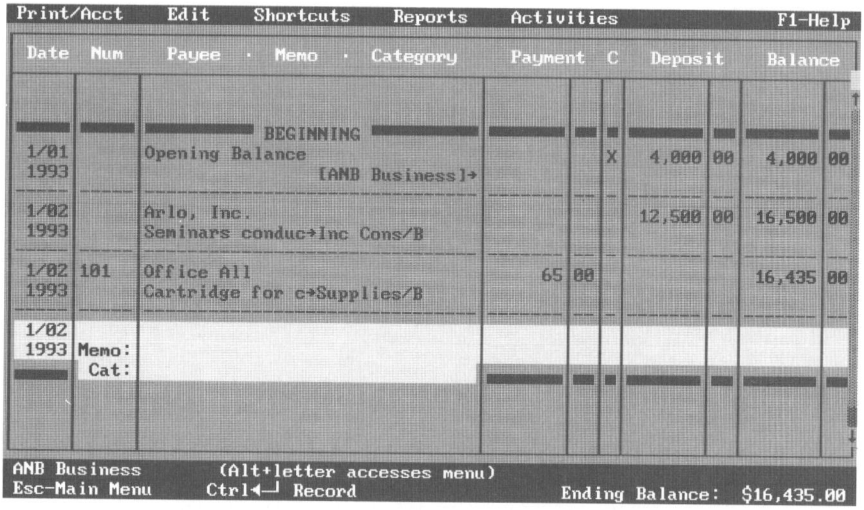

```
 Print/Acct    Edit    Shortcuts    Reports    Activities          F1-Help
  Date  Num    Payee  ·  Memo  ·  Category    Payment  C   Deposit    Balance

━━━━━━━━━━━━━━━━━━━━━ BEGINNING ━━━━━━━━━━━━━━━
 1/01         Opening Balance                          X   4,000 00   4,000 00
 1993                            [ANB Business]→
 1/02         Arlo, Inc.                                  12,500 00  16,500 00
 1993         Seminars conduc→Inc Cons/B
 1/02  101    Office All                        65 00               16,435 00
 1993         Cartridge for c→Supplies/B
 1/02
 1993  Memo:
       Cat :

 ANB Business        (Alt+letter accesses menu)
 Esc-Main Menu    Ctrl◄─┘ Record             Ending Balance:  $16,435.00
```

Recording business transactions in the Register window
Figure 11-3.

you could have created another class, called P, for personal entries, the approach used here minimizes typing; only business transactions require the extra entry. Follow these steps to add the transaction:

1. Type **1/3/93** and press (Enter).
2. Type **825** and press (Enter).

This check number is not sequential with the last business check used since it is in your personal account.

3. Type **Discount Coats** and press (Enter).
4. Type **120** and press (Enter).
5. Type **New winter coat** and press (Enter).
6. Type **Clothing**.

Notice that no slash (/) is used since a class is not being added for personal expenses.

11

7. Press `Ctrl`-`Enter` to record the transaction. Your entries should match the ones shown here:

1/01 1993		BEGINNING Opening Balance [ANB Personal]		X	2,500 00	2,500 00
1/03 1993	825	Discount Coats New winter coat Clothing	120 00			2,380 00

Splitting Transactions

Split transactions are transactions that affect more than one category or class. You decide how a transaction affects each of the categories or category-class combinations involved. If you split an expense transaction, you are saying that a portion of the transaction should be considered as an expense in two different categories or classes. For example, a purchase at an office products store might include school supplies for your children and products for the office. You need to know exactly how much was spent for personal versus business expenses in this transaction. Many expenses can be part business and part personal, especially if you operate a business from your home. Quicken allows you to allocate the amount of any transaction among different categories or classes with a special Split Transaction window. Before using the Split Transaction feature, you can define categories more precisely with the Subcategory feature, explained in the next section.

Quicken displays a Split Transaction window for entries in the Category field if you press `Ctrl`-`S`. You can enter different categories or classes for each part of the transaction with this method. Even though the largest portion of the following expense was for business, it was paid with a personal check and so must be recorded in the ANB Personal account. Follow these steps to complete an entry for the purchase at Campus Stationery, which includes both personal and office supply expenses:

1. Type **1/3/93** and press `Enter`.
2. Type **826** and press `Enter`.
3. Type **Campus Stationery** and press `Enter`.
4. Type **82** and press `Enter`.

5. Type **New calendar and computer paper** and press (Enter).
6. Press (Ctrl)-(S) to activate the Split Transaction window.
7. Type **Supp Comp/B** and press (Enter).
8. Type **Paper for laser printer** and press (Enter).

Quicken displays the entire amount of the transaction in the Amount field but adjusts it as you make a new entry.

9. Type **75.76** and press (Enter).

Quicken subtracts this amount from $82.00 and displays the amount remaining on the next line.

10. Type **Misc** and press (Enter).
11. Type **New calendar for kitchen**.

This completes the entries since $6.24 is the cost of the calendar. Your screen should look like the one in Figure 11-4.

12. Press (Ctrl)-(Enter) to close the Split Transaction window.
13. Press (Ctrl)-(Enter) to record the transaction.

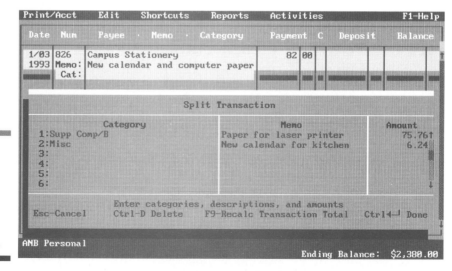

Split
Transaction
window for
Campus
Stationery
transaction
Figure 11-4.

The register entry looks like this:

```
1/03 826     Campus Stationery                        82 00            2,298 00
1993 SPLIT   New calendar and computer paper
        Cat: Supp Comp/B
```

Using Subcategories

Since you are quickly becoming proficient at basic transaction entry, you will want to see some other options for recording transactions. One new option is to create subcategories of an existing category. These subcategories further define a category. Unlike classes, which use a different perspective for organizing transactions, subcategories provide a more detailed breakdown of the existing category. For instance, you could continue to allocate all your utility bills to the Utilities category but create subcategories that allow you to allocate expenses to electricity, water, or gas. You will still be able to classify these transactions as either business or personal expenses using the classes you established.

You can add the subcategories by modifying the category list, as when you add new categories, or you can create them as you enter transactions and realize the existing category entries do not provide the breakdown you want.

Entering a New Subcategory

When you enter a subcategory for a transaction, you type the category name, followed by a colon (:), and then the subcategory name. It is important that the category be specified first and the subcategory second. If a transaction has a class assigned, the class name comes third in the sequence, with a slash (/) as the divider.

The business used in this example is run from the home of the owner, which necessitates the splitting of certain expenses between business and personal. Tax guidelines state that the percentage of the total square footage in the home that is used exclusively for business can be used to determine the portion of common expenses, such as utilities, allocated to the business. The business in these examples occupies 20 percent of the total square footage in the home. You can use Quicken's

Calculator to perform these computations and use both subcategories and split transactions to record the first transactions.

Enter the utility bills in the new account. Follow these steps to complete the entries for the gas and electric bills, creating a subcategory under Utilities for each, and allocating 20 percent of each utility bill to business by splitting the transactions between classes:

1. With the next blank transaction in the register highlighted, type **1/3/93** as the date for the transaction.
2. Type **827** and press Enter. You can also press ⊕ to have Quicken record the next check for you.
3. Type **Consumer Power** and press Enter.
4. Type **80.00** for the payment amount and press Enter.
5. Type **Electric Bill** and then press Enter.

The cursor is now in the Category field.

6. Press Ctrl-S to open the Split Transaction window.
7. Type **Utilities:Electric/B** and press Enter.

Quicken prompts you with the Category Not Found window. Notice that only Electric is highlighted in the Category field since Quicken already has Utilities in the category list and B in the class list.

8. Select Add to Category List. Quicken displays the Set Up Category window for you to define the category.
9. Type **S** to define the entry as a subcategory and then press Enter.

A note may be displayed by Quicken prompting you to be sure you understand what you are doing since subcategories are considered an advanced technique.

10. Type **Electric Utilities** and press Enter.

Although this description is optional, it is a good idea to enter one so that your reports will be informative.

11. Type **Y** and press F9 (Tax Schedules).

11

12. Select Schedule C, and a Tax Line window appears.

13. Select Utilities.

14. Select Copy:1.

15. Press ⌷Enter⌷.

The Set Up Category window shown here should match the one on your screen:

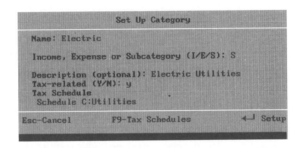

16. Press ⌷Enter⌷ twice to close the window and move to the Memo field in the Split Transaction window.

17. Type **Business portion of elect** and press ⌷Enter⌷.

18. Press ⌷Ctrl⌷-⌷O⌷ to open the Calculator and compute the portion of the expense allocable to business.

19. Type ***.20** and press ⌷Enter⌷ to multiply by .20.

Since the Amount field was highlighted, Quicken placed its value in the calculator. Quicken displays the result in the Calculator window.

20. Press ⌷F9⌷ (Paste) to place the result in the Amount field.

21. Press ⌷Enter⌷ to move to the next line.

22. Type **Utilities:Electric** and press ⌷Enter⌷.

Note that a class was not added to the entry so Quicken will consider the entry a personal expense.

23. Type **Home portion of electric** and press Enter.

The Split Transaction window looks like the one in Figure 11-5; Quicken has computed the difference between $80.00 and $16.00 and displayed it in the Amount field.

24. Press Ctrl-Enter to close the Split Transaction window.

25. Press Ctrl-Enter to record the transaction entry.

The transaction displays in the Register window, as shown here:

Completing the Utility Subcategories

You have one more utility bill to enter. The one for gas utilities also requires a new subcategory. Complete the following steps to create a subcategory for the gas bill and complete the transaction entry.

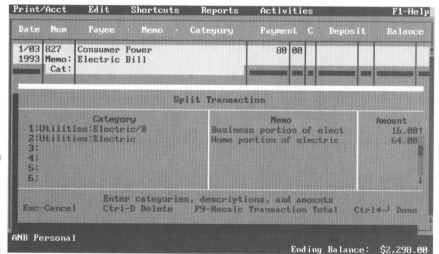

Split Transaction window for electric utilities
Figure 11-5.

11

1. Enter the following information in each of the fields shown:

    Date: 1/7/93
    Check: 828
    Payee: Western Michigan Gas
    Payment: 40.00
    Memo: Gas Bill

2. After completing the Memo field entry, press Ctrl-S to request the Split Transaction window.

Quicken's default categories include the subcategories Gas & Electric and Utilities:Water. Since you already have a subcategory established for electric, you will want to modify Gas & Electric for use with Gas Utilities.

3. Press Ctrl-C to display the Category Transfer List window.
4. Highlight Utilities: Gas & Elecric.
5. Press Ctrl-E to edit the current category.
6. Change the name on the Edit Category screen to Gas and press Enter.
7. Type **S** to define the entry as a subcategory and then press Enter.
8. Type **Gas Utilities** and press Enter.
9. Type **Y** and press F9 (Tax Schedules).
10. Select Schedule C.
11. Select Utilities.
12. Select Copy:1.
13. Press Enter.
14. Press Enter, type **/B** and press Enter.
15. Type **Business portion gas bill** and press Enter.
16. Press Ctrl-O to open the Calculator window.
17. Type ***.20** and press Enter. Quicken will display the result in the Calculator window.
18. Press F9 (Paste) to paste the result in the Amount field.

19. Press (Enter) to move to the next line.
20. Type **Utilities:Gas** and press (Enter).
21. Type **Home portion gas bill** and press (Enter).
22. Press (Ctrl)-(Enter) to close the Split Transaction window.
23. Press (Ctrl)-(Enter) to record the transaction entry.

If you press (Ctrl)-(Home) to move to the top of the register, your entries will look like the ones in Figure 11-6.

Entering the Remaining Business Transactions

You have now been introduced to all the skills needed to enter transactions that affect either a business or personal account. You should, however, complete the remaining transactions for January. Keystrokes for split transactions are shown in detail. The other transactions are shown in summary form; each field in which you need to enter data is shown with the entry for that field. Use these steps to complete the remaining entries:

1. Press (Esc) to return to the Main Menu.

Print/Acct	Edit	Shortcuts	Reports	Activities			F1-Help
Date	Num	Payee · Memo · Category		Payment	C	Deposit	Balance
		BEGINNING					
1/01		Opening Balance			X	2,500 00	2,500 00
1993	Memo:						
	Cat:	[ANB Personal]					
1/03	825	Discount Coats		120 00			2,380 00
1993		New winter coat Clothing					
1/03	826	Campus Stationery		82 00			2,298 00
1993	SPLIT	New calendar an→Supp Comp/B					
1/03	827	Consumer Power		88 00			2,210 00
1993	SPLIT	Electric Bill Utilities:Elec→					
1/07	828	Western Michigan Gas		40 00			2,178 00
1993	SPLIT	Gas Bill Utilities:Gas/B					
ANB Personal		(Alt+letter accesses menu)					
Esc-Main Menu		Ctrl↵ Record				Ending Balance:	$2,178.00

Register entries in ANB Personal account
Figure 11-6.

11

2. Choose Select Account.

3. Select ANB Business.

4. Type **1/8/93** and press Enter.

5. Type **102** and press Enter.

6. Type **Computer Outlet** and press Enter.

7. Type **300** and press Enter.

8. Type **Cartridges, ribbons, disks** and press Enter.

9. Press Ctrl-S to open the Split Transaction window.

The same category and class will be used for each transaction entered in this window. The transaction is split to provide additional documentation for purchases.

10. Complete the entries in the Split Transaction window as shown in Figure 11-7.

11. Press Ctrl-Enter twice.

The first time you press Ctrl-Enter, Quicken will close the Split Transaction window. The second time, Quicken will record the transaction.

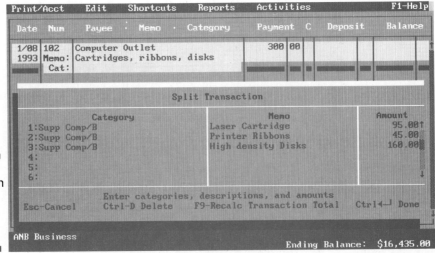

Splitting the cash transaction for office supplies
Figure 11-7.

12. Enter the following transactions by completing the entries in the fields shown and pressing `Ctrl`-`Enter` after each transaction:

Date:	1/15/93
Num:	103
Payee:	Quick Delivery
Payment:	215.00
Memo:	Manuscript Delivery
Category:	Del Overngt/B

Date:	1/15/93
Num:	104
Payee:	Safety Airlines
Payment:	905.00
Memo:	February Ticket
Category:	Travel/B

Date:	1/20/93
Num:	105
Payee:	Alltel
Payment:	305.00
Memo:	Telephone Bill
Category:	Telephone/B

13. Enter the beginning of this transaction as follows:

Date:	1/20/93
Num:	106
Payee:	Postmaster
Payment:	28.25
Memo:	Postage for Mailing

14. Press `Ctrl`-`S` with the cursor in the Category field.

11

15. Complete the entries shown on the Split Transaction window in Figure 11-8.

16. Press `Ctrl`-`Enter` twice.

If you press `↑` several times you will see that the entries in your register match the ones in Figure 11-9.

17. Complete this transaction to record a maintenance expense for existing equipment:

Date:	1/22/93
Num:	107
Payee:	Fix-It-All
Payment:	1100.00
Memo:	Equipment Contract
Category:	Equip Mnt/B

18. Press `Ctrl`-`Enter` to record the transaction.

The only remaining transactions relate to equipment. You will need to use the Equipment account you created earlier to handle these transactions.

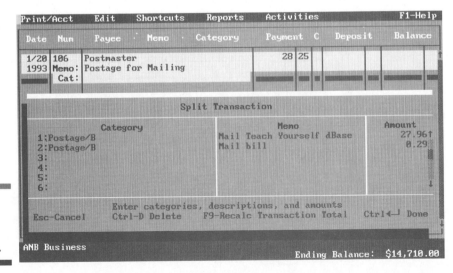

Splitting the postage transaction
Figure 11-8.

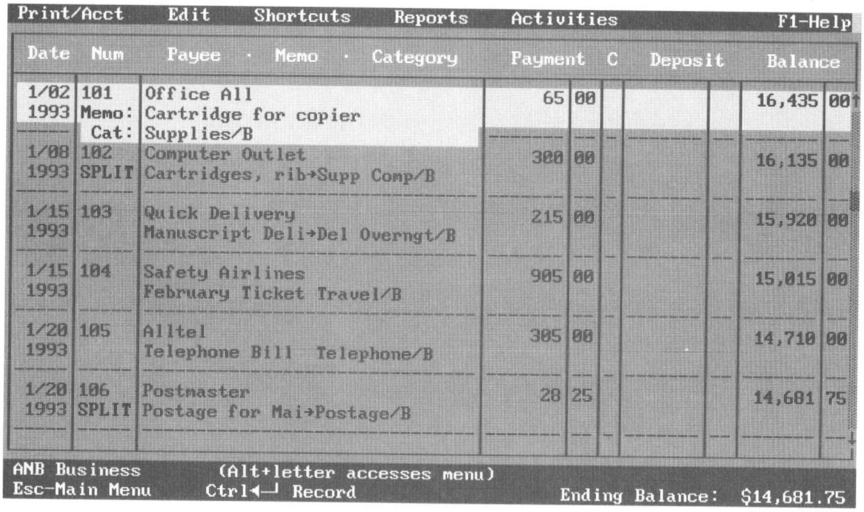

```
 Print/Acct     Edit     Shortcuts     Reports     Activities          F1-Help
┌──────┬─────┬─────────────┬──────────────────────┬─────────┬──┬─────────┬─────────┐
│ Date │ Num │  Payee  ·  Memo  ·  Category        │ Payment │ C│ Deposit │ Balance │
├──────┼─────┼─────────────────────────────────────┼─────────┼──┼─────────┼─────────┤
│ 1/02 │ 101 │ Office All                          │   65 00 │  │         │16,435 00│
│ 1993 │Memo:│ Cartridge for copier                │         │  │         │         │
│      │ Cat:│ Supplies/B                          │         │  │         │         │
│ 1/08 │ 102 │ Computer Outlet                     │  300 00 │  │         │16,135 00│
│ 1993 │SPLIT│ Cartridges, rib→Supp Comp/B         │         │  │         │         │
│ 1/15 │ 103 │ Quick Delivery                      │  215 00 │  │         │15,920 00│
│ 1993 │     │ Manuscript Deli→Del Overngt/B       │         │  │         │         │
│ 1/15 │ 104 │ Safety Airlines                     │  905 00 │  │         │15,015 00│
│ 1993 │     │ February Ticket Travel/B            │         │  │         │         │
│ 1/20 │ 105 │ Alltel                              │  305 00 │  │         │14,710 00│
│ 1993 │     │ Telephone Bill   Telephone/B        │         │  │         │         │
│ 1/20 │ 106 │ Postmaster                          │   28 25 │  │         │14,681 75│
│ 1993 │SPLIT│ Postage for Mai→Postage/B           │         │  │         │         │
└──────┴─────┴─────────────────────────────────────┴─────────┴──┴─────────┴─────────┘
 ANB Business          (Alt+letter accesses menu)
 Esc-Main Menu      Ctrl←┘  Record                      Ending Balance:  $14,681.75
```

Register entries in ANB Business account

Figure 11-9.

Using the Other Asset Account

Earlier in the chapter, you established an other asset type account called Equipment. You will be able to use this account to track total equipment holdings and depreciation expense. Purchase transactions for equipment will be recorded in your business checking account register as a transfer to the Equipment account. Other transactions, such as entering information on equipment purchased before you started using Quicken and a depreciation transaction, will be entered directly in this other asset register. In the next section, you look at recording transactions for existing equipment and a new purchase. In Chapter 14, "Organizing Tax Information and Other Year-End Needs," you learn how to record depreciation expense as the asset ages and declines in value.

Recording Transactions for Existing Equipment Holdings

The existing equipment cannot be recorded as a purchase since you do not want to affect the balance in the business checking account. You need to make the transaction entry directly in the Equipment account. Note that the fields are somewhat different in this type of account

11

compared to previous account registers, as shown in Figure 11-10.
Follow these steps to record the equipment:

1. Press Esc to return to the Main Menu.

2. Choose Select **A**ccount.

3. Select the Equipment account.

4. Type **1/1/93** in the Date field and press Enter twice.

5. Type **High Tech Computer** to enter the name of the asset in the
   Payee field.

   You can record an inventory number as part of this entry if one is
   assigned.

6. Press Enter three times.

7. Type **3000** and press Enter to record the original purchase price in
   the Increase field.

8. Type **Original cost of equipment** and press Enter.

9. Type **Equipment/B** and press Ctrl-Enter.

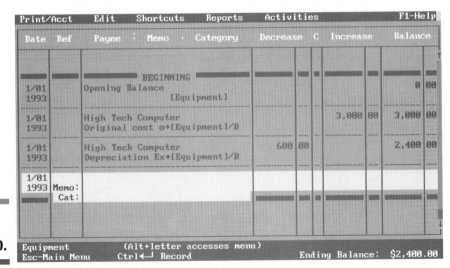

Equipment
transactions
Figure 11-10.

Quicken will display the category as [Equipment] since the category is an account name and will increase the balance of the account. (The brackets are always added when an account name is added in the Category field.)

To change the book value of the asset, another adjusting transaction is required. This transaction reduces the book value by the amount of the depreciation expense recognized last year. It must be recorded against the Equipment account rather than as a depreciation expense, or the amount of the depreciation for last year will appear in this year's expense reports. You do not want to record the depreciation expense in your checking account register because you are not writing a check for this expense. Follow these steps to complete the second transaction entry:

1. Type **1/1/93** and press (Enter) twice.
2. Type **High Tech Computer** and press (Enter).

NOTE: It is important to use the same name in all transactions relating to a given piece of equipment.

When you typed **H**, Quicken used its QuickFill feature to complete the payee field with "High Tech Computer." Quicken reviews all the payees for the past three months and all the payees in the memorized transaction list to make the suggestion for the payee name to use in the transaction. You can use (Ctrl)-(+) and (Ctrl)-(−) to review other options beyond QuickFill's first suggestion. When you find the correct payee, press (Enter). Quicken records the entire previous transaction for this payee. You must edit the copy of the original transaction if you want to make changes for the new entry. In this case, the following editing steps would be needed:

3. Press (Ctrl)-(Backspace) to remove the value in the field.
4. Press (Shift)-(Tab) twice.
5. Type **600** in the Decrease field and press (Enter).

11

6. Press Ctrl-Backspace.

7. Type **Depreciation Expense** and press Enter.

8. Press Ctrl-Enter to accept [Equipment]/B for the category.

The register entries should match the ones in Figure 11-10.

Adding a New Equipment Purchase

Purchasing an asset reduces the balance in a checking account. When the asset is equipment, there must also be an entry to the Equipment account. If you list the Equipment account as the Category field in the transaction, Quicken will handle the transfer. The other part of this transaction entry that differs is that you use the name of the asset in the Payee field in the check register. You will have to use the Memo field Equipment account to record the payee's name. Follow these steps to record the purchase of a laser printer:

1. Press Esc to return to the Main Menu.

2. Choose Select Account.

3. Select ANB Business.

4. Type **1/25/93** and press Enter.

5. Type **108** and press Enter.

6. Type **Laser 1** and press Enter.

7. Type **1500** and press Enter.

8. Type **Printer from Harry's Computers** and press Enter.

9. Type **Equipment/B**.

10. Press Ctrl-Enter to record the transaction.

Your transaction looks like this:

1/25	108	Laser 1	1,500	00			12,081	75
1993	Memo:	Printer from Harry's Computers						
	Cat:	[Equipment]/B						

11. Press Esc to return to the Main Menu.

12. Choose Select Account and then Equipment.

The screen in Figure 11-11 shows the transactions in the Equipment account after the transfer transaction is recorded.

Memorized Transactions

Many of your financial transactions are likely to repeat; you pay your utility bills each month, for instance. Likewise, overnight delivery charges, phone bills, payroll, and other bills are paid at about the same time each month. Cash inflows for some businesses are daily, weekly, or monthly. Other payments, such as supply purchases, also repeat, but perhaps not on the same dates each month.

As discussed in Chapter 6, "Expanding the Scope of Financial Entries," Quicken can memorize transactions entered in the register or check writing screen. Once memorized, these transactions can be used to generate identical transactions. Although amounts and dates may change, you can edit these fields and not have to reenter payee, memo, and category information.

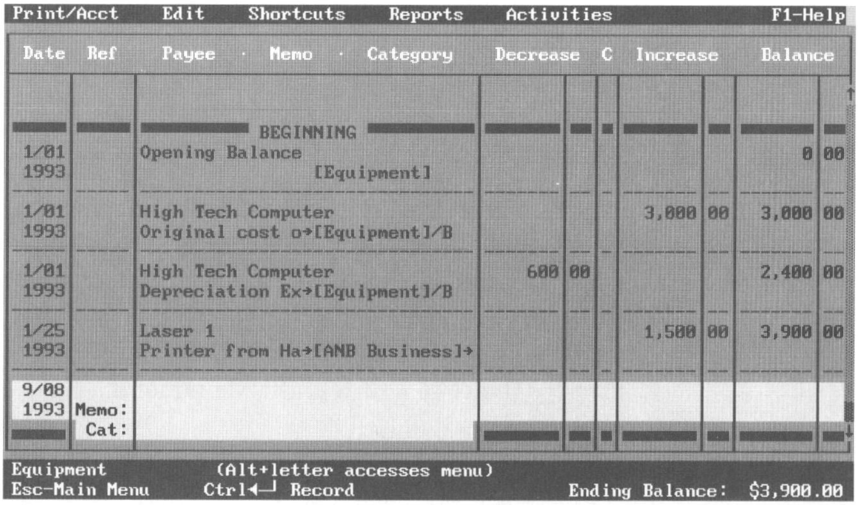

Print/Acct	Edit	Shortcuts	Reports	Activities		F1-Help
Date	Ref	Payee · Memo · Category	Decrease	C	Increase	Balance
		BEGINNING				
1/01 1993		Opening Balance [Equipment]				0 00
1/01 1993		High Tech Computer Original cost o→[Equipment]/B			3,000 00	3,000 00
1/01 1993		High Tech Computer Depreciation Ex→[Equipment]/B	600 00			2,400 00
1/25 1993		Laser 1 Printer from Ha→[ANB Business]→			1,500 00	3,900 00
9/08 1993		Memo: Cat:				

Equipment   (Alt+letter accesses menu)
Esc-Main Menu   Ctrl◄┘ Record   Ending Balance: $3,900.00

Register entries in Equipment account after printer purchase

Figure 11-11.

11

Memorizing a Register Entry

Any transaction in the account register can be memorized. **Memorized** transactions can be recalled for later use, printed, changed, and even deleted. You can elect to memorize as many transactions as you feel will repeat in the same relative time frame. To memorize the transaction for Consumer Power, follow these steps:

1. Press Esc to return to the Main Menu.
2. Choose Select **A**ccount.
3. Select ANB Personal.
4. Highlight the Consumer Power transaction in the register.
5. Press Alt - S to open the **S**hortcuts menu and select **M**emorize Transaction (or press Ctrl - M to select Memorize Transaction without opening the menu).

Quicken prompts you to memorize split amounts or percentages (A/P).

6. Press Enter to confirm the A prompt and memorize the transaction.

Using the same procedure, memorize the transaction for Western Michigan Gas. Quicken memorizes split transactions in the same way as any other transactions. You will want to carefully review the split transaction screen transactions for amounts that change each month to reduce errors.

7. Press Ctrl - T to display the memorized transactions; your list should match the one shown in Figure 11-12.

If you want to print the list once it is displayed, press Ctrl - P, type a number to select your printer, and press Enter to print.

Now you can open the ANB Business account and memorize some transactions from that account. Follow the steps listed here:

1. Press Esc twice to return to the Main Menu.
2. Choose Select **A**ccount.
3. Select ANB Business.
4. Highlight the Quick Delivery transaction in the register.

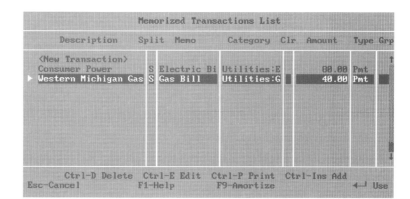

Memorized
transactions list
Figure 11-12.

5. Press [Alt]-[S] to open the Shortcuts menu and select **Memorize** Transaction (or press [Ctrl]-[M] to select Memorize Transaction without opening the menu).

Quicken will highlight the transaction and prompt you for a response.

6. Press [Enter] to confirm and memorize the transaction.
7. Press [Ctrl]-[T] to display the memorized transactions; your list should include Quick Delivery.

Quicken maintains only one list of memorized transactions for each file and does not show the filename in the list. Here, each of the memorized transactions has a type of Pmt since it was memorized from the register. Transactions memorized from the check writing window will have a type of Chk.

8. Press [Esc] to return to the account register.

Using Memorized Transactions   To recall a memorized transaction and place it in the register, move to the next blank transaction record. If you recall a memorized transaction while a previously recorded transaction is highlighted, the existing transaction will be replaced by the memorized transaction. Press [Ctrl]-[T] to recall the Memorized Transactions List window. The next step is to select the transaction you want to add to the register and then press [Enter]. If you type the first few letters of the payee name before pressing ⌃Ctrl-T, Quicken will take you to the correct area of the transaction list since it is in alphabetical order by payee. When it is added, the selected transaction appears with the date of the preceding transaction in the register, not the date on which it was last recorded. You can edit the transaction in the register and press ⌃Ctrl-Enter when you are ready to record the entry.

Follow these steps to record a payment to Quick Delivery for later in the month:

1. Press Ctrl-End to move to the end of the register entries.
2. Press Ctrl-T.
3. Select the Quick Delivery transaction.

Quicken adds the transaction to the register.

4. Press Shift-Tab three times, type **1/30/93** in the Date field, and press Enter.
5. Type **109** in the Num field and press Enter twice.
6. Type **55.00** and press Ctrl-Enter to record the transaction.

The transaction looks like this:

```
1/30 109    Quick Delivery                55 00            12,026 75
1993 Memo: Manuscript Delivery
     Cat: Del Overngt/B
```

Changing and Deleting Memorized Transactions

To change a memorized transaction, you must first recall it from the memorized transaction list to a blank transaction in the register. Then make your changes and memorize it again. When you press Ctrl-M to memorize it again, Quicken asks you if you want to replace the transaction memorized earlier or add a new transaction. If you confirm the replacement, Quicken makes the change.

To delete a memorized transaction, you must first open the transaction list by pressing Ctrl-T or by selecting the **S**hortcuts menu and then selecting **R**ecall Transaction. Select the transaction you want to delete and press Ctrl-D. A warning message will appear asking you to confirm the deletion. When you press ⌑Enter⌑, the transaction is no longer memorized.

Memorizing a Check

The procedure for memorizing transactions while writing checks is identical to the one used to memorize register transactions. You must be in the check writing window when you begin, but otherwise it is the same. Check and register transactions for the same file will appear in the same memorized transaction list and can be edited, deleted, or recalled from either the check writing or account register window.

Working with Transaction Groups

Although you can recall memorized transactions individually as a way to reenter similar transactions, a better method is to define several memorized transactions that occur at the same time as a transaction group. When you are ready to pay these transactions, you can have Quicken record the entire group for you automatically after you make any changes in amounts or other parts of the transaction entries. You can even have Quicken remind you when it is time to record these transactions again.

Defining a Transaction Group

Quicken allows you to set up as many as 12 transaction groups. Defining a group is easy, but it requires several steps after memorizing all the transactions that will be placed in the group. You will need to select the number of transactions in the group you want to define. Then you will need to describe the group. Finally, you will need to assign specific memorized transactions to the group. Although expense transactions are frequently used to create groups, you can also include an entry for a direct deposit payroll check that is deposited at the same time each month.

For your first transaction group, which you will title Utilities, you will group the gas and electric transactions that occur near the end of each month. Follow these steps to open the ANB Personal account and create the transaction group:

11

1. Press Esc to return to the Main Menu.
2. Select ANB Personal as the account to use.
3. Select the Shortcuts menu and select Transaction Groups.

Quicken displays the window shown in Figure 11-13.

4. Be sure the cursor is pointing at 1, since this is the first unused transaction group, and press Enter.

Quicken displays a window to allow you to define the group. Figure 11-14 shows this screen with the entries you will make in the next steps.

5. Type **Utilities** as the name for the group and press Enter twice.
6. Type **6** as the frequency for the reminder and press Enter.

When you don't want to be reminded weekly, every two weeks, twice a month, every four weeks, monthly, quarterly, twice a year, or annually, you can choose None.

7. Type **2/3/93** as the next scheduled date for the reminder and press Enter.

Quicken will remind you three days in advance of this date. In the section "Changing Other Settings" later in this chapter, you will learn

Select
Transaction
Group to
Execute window
Figure 11-13.

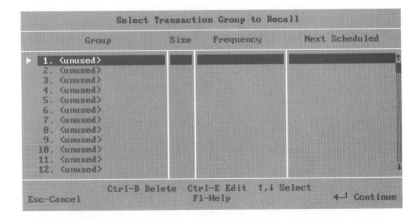

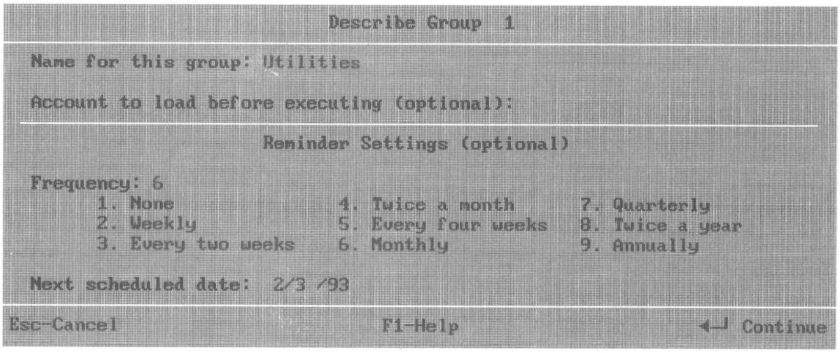

```
                    Describe Group  1

  Name for this group: Utilities

  Account to load before executing (optional):

                  Reminder Settings (optional)

  Frequency: 6
       1. None           4. Twice a month    7. Quarterly
       2. Weekly         5. Every four weeks 8. Twice a year
       3. Every two weeks 6. Monthly         9. Annually

  Next scheduled date:  2/3 /93

 Esc-Cancel                    F1-Help                   ← Continue
```

Setting up a
transaction
group
Figure 11-14.

how to adjust this setting. Quicken displays a window listing
transactions you can assign to Group 1. Only memorized transactions
are present in this list. They are listed in alphabetical order by payee to
make it easy to locate the desired transactions.

8. Select Consumer Power and press (Spacebar) to mark the transaction.

Note the 1 in the group column, which indicates that the transaction is
now a part of Group 1.

9. Select Western Michigan Gas and press (Spacebar).

Quicken also marks this transaction as part of Group 1, as shown in
Figure 11-15.

10. Press (Enter) to indicate you are finished selecting transactions.

You may want to define other transaction groups to include payroll,
loan payments, and anything else that you might pay at the beginning
of the month. You are not required to define additional groups in order
to complete the remaining exercises in this section.

You can also create transaction groups that generate checks for you.
These groups contain transactions that are memorized from the check
writing window. The procedure is the same as that just shown. You can

11

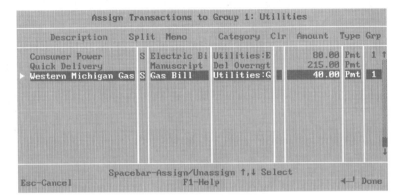

The transaction marked as part of Group 1

Figure 11-15.

identify these transactions in the Assign Transactions window by the Chk entry in the Type field. Remember that Pmt in the Type field indicates an account register transaction.

Changing a Transaction Group

You can add to a transaction group at any time by selecting Transaction **G**roups after pressing (Alt)-(S) to open the Shortcuts menu. As you proceed through the normal group definition procedure, you can select additional transactions for inclusion in the group.

To make a change to the description or frequency of the reminder, use the same procedure and make the necessary changes in the Describe Group window.

To delete a transaction group, open the Shortcuts menu (with (Alt)-(S)) and select Transaction **G**roups. Select the group you want to delete and press (Ctrl)-(D). Quicken eliminates the group but does not delete the memorized transactions that are part of it. It also does not affect any transactions recorded in the register by earlier executions of the transaction group.

If you want to alter a transaction that is part of the transaction group, you will need to alter the memorized transaction. This means you have to recall the transaction on the check writing screen or in the account register, depending on the type of transaction you have. Next, you need to make your changes and memorize the transaction again. Follow the procedures in the "Changing and Deleting Memorized Transactions" section earlier in this chapter.

Having Quicken Remind You to Record Transactions

Quicken will remind you to enter upcoming transaction groups. The reminder will either occur at the DOS prompt when you boot your system or at the Main Menu when you first load Quicken. Hard disk users who have the default setting for Billminder still set at Yes will see a message at the DOS prompt reminding them to pay postdated checks or to record transaction groups. If you do not have a hard disk or if you have turned Billminder off, the prompt will not appear until you start Quicken.

Recording a Transaction Group

Once you have defined a transaction group, you do not need to wait for the reminder to record the group in your register or check writing window. Since you can memorize entries for either the register or the check writing window, make sure you have the group correctly defined for your current needs. A group type of Chk is created in the check writing window and can be recorded in either the account register or the check writing window. Payment (Pmt) groups are recorded in the account register and can only be used to record account register entries.

To execute a transaction group from the account register, complete the following steps:

1. Press (Esc) to return to the register, select the **S**hortcuts menu, and then select Transaction **G**roups.

Quicken will display a list of transaction groups.

2. Select the Utilities group, as shown in Figure 11-16.
3. Press (Enter).

11

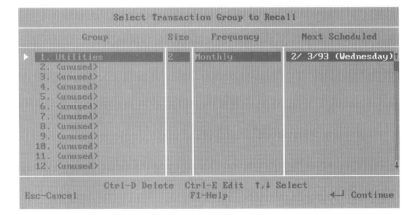

Quicken displays the date of the next scheduled entry of the Utilities group, as shown here:

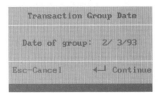

4. Press (Enter) to confirm that this date is valid and to enter the group of transactions in the account register.

Quicken will indicate when the transaction has been entered and recorded and allows you to make modifications if needed. The window displayed is shown here:

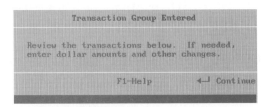

5. Press Enter to continue.

The new transactions are entered with a date of 2/3/93, as shown here:

2/03		Consumer Power	80	00			2,098	00
1993	SPLIT	Electric Bill						
	Cat:	Utilities:Electric/B						
2/03		Western Michigan Gas	40	00			2,058	00
1993	SPLIT	Gas Bill Utilities:Gas/B						

The check numbers and amounts will need to be altered for the new utility bills. Here, you will also need to use Ctrl-S to open the Split Transaction window for each transaction and distribute the new amounts.

6. Highlight the Consumer Power entry for 2/3/93, move the cursor to the Payment field, type **72.00**, and press Enter twice.

7. Press Ctrl-S and record **14.40** as the business portion of the expense and **57.60** as the home portion of the bill.

8. Press Ctrl-Enter twice.

9. Move the cursor to the Payment field in the Western Michigan Gas entry, type **45.00**, and press Enter twice.

10. Press Ctrl-S and record **9.00** as the business portion of the expense and **36.00** as the home portion of the bill.

11. Press Ctrl-Enter twice.

12. Highlight the Consumer Power transaction, move to the Num field, press +, and press Ctrl-Enter.

13. Press + and press Ctrl-Enter.

11

Important Customizing Options as You Set Up Your Files

Quicken provides a number of options for customizing the package to meet your needs. These include the addition of passwords for accessing files, options already discussed such as requiring category entries, and other options that affect the display of information on your screen and in reports. Once you know how to access these settings, you will find that most are self-explanatory. All of the changes are made by selecting Set **P**references from the Main Menu.

Adding Passwords

To add a password, select Pass**w**ord Settings from the Set **P**references menu. Quicken presents a menu that allows you to decide if you want to protect a file using **F**ile Password or protect existing transactions with **T**ransaction Password. Although you can add protection with a password at both levels, you will need to select each individually.

If you select File Password, Quicken will ask you to enter a password. Once you do so and press (Enter), the password will be added to the active file and anyone wishing to work with the file must supply it. Transaction Password is used to prevent changes to existing transactions entered before a specified date without the password. If you choose Transaction Password, you will be presented with a window that requires you to enter both a password and a date.

If you want to change or remove a password, you must be able to provide the existing password. Quicken will then provide a Change Password window for the entry of the old and new passwords. After completing the entries and pressing (Enter), the new password will be in effect.

Changing Other Settings

Figure 11-17 shows the window presented when **T**ransaction Settings is selected from the Set **P**references menu. It shows the default choice for each of the options. The first option allows you to turn off the beep you hear when recording and memorizing transactions. The second option controls whether Quicken prompts for confirmation when you make transaction changes.

The third option controls whether Quicken prompts for confirmation when deleting or voiding a transaction. The fourth option allows you to control the date format. Changing option 5 will require category entries on each transaction.

The information on the second line of a register entry can be changed with option 6. You can use it to display memo information if you

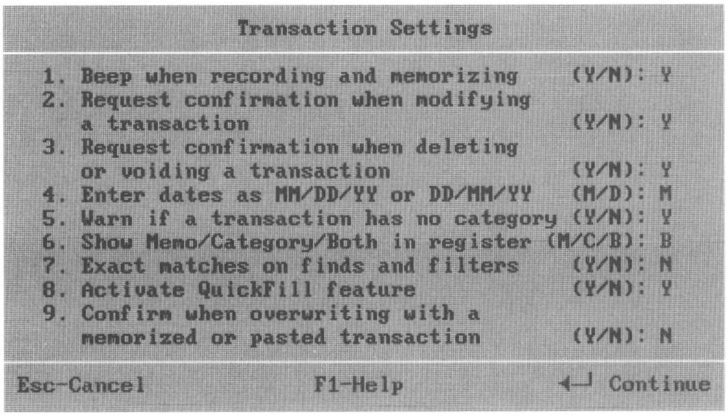

```
                    Transaction Settings

    1. Beep when recording and memorizing     (Y/N): Y
    2. Request confirmation when modifying
       a transaction                          (Y/N): Y
    3. Request confirmation when deleting
       or voiding a transaction               (Y/N): Y
    4. Enter dates as MM/DD/YY or DD/MM/YY     (M/D): M
    5. Warn if a transaction has no category   (Y/N): Y
    6. Show Memo/Category/Both in register   (M/C/B): B
    7. Exact matches on finds and filters      (Y/N): N
    8. Activate QuickFill feature              (Y/N): Y
    9. Confirm when overwriting with a
       memorized or pasted transaction         (Y/N): N

 Esc-Cancel              F1-Help           ◄┘ Continue
```

Transaction
Settings options
Figure 11-17.

change the setting to M. Changing this option to C displays category information only. The default setting of B displays both types of information.

Option 7 controls whether Quicken prompts for exact matches when performing "find" and "filter" commands. For example, if you want to find a payment for J. B. Smith, the default setting allows you to define the payee as J B Smith without the periods, and Quicken searches for a payee that contains your entry with or without the periods. If you change the default setting to Y, Quicken will search for an exact payee match.

Option 8 allows you to activate (the default option) or turn the QuickFill feature off. Option 9 tells Quicken whether you want a confirmation from Quicken if you overwrite an existing transaction with a memorized transaction.

11

CHAPTER

12

QUICKEN'S PAYROLL ASSISTANCE

For a small-business owner under the day-to-day pressure of running a business, preparing the payroll can be a time-consuming and frustrating task. Besides withholding forms and tables to complete, there are annual earnings limits that affect the amount you withhold in social security taxes from employees. In addition to these weekly considerations, there are monthly, quarterly, and year-end reports that may need to be filed for the federal, state, or local government.

In this chapter, you will see how Quicken can help to reduce the effort of preparing your payroll. Although you must still invest some time, you'll find that an early investment will substantially reduce your payroll activities once the system is running. With Quicken, you can easily prepare the payroll entry for each employee and maintain information for the Internal Revenue Service (IRS) about federal income tax withholding, Federal Insurance Contribution Act (FICA) withholding, and employer FICA payments. You can also maintain accounts for any state and local withholding taxes or insurance payments that must be periodically deposited. In addition to this information, you can accumulate data to be used in the preparation of W-2 forms for your employees at the end of the year. See the special "Payroll Forms" section in this chapter for a list of some of the standard payroll-related payment and tax forms that Quicken can assist you in preparing.

Intuit offers a separate package, QuickPay, that can provide additional payroll help with its built-in payroll tables.

The Quicken Payroll System

Payroll entries are processed along with your other business-related payments in your Quicken account register. To set up your system to do this, you will need to establish some new categories and subcategories specifically related to payroll.

Depending upon your state and local tax laws and the benefits you provide your employees, you can use Quicken's payroll support option to create some or all of the categories needed to record your payroll transactions.

✦ Payroll:Gross keeps track of the total wages earned by employees.

✦ Payroll:Comp FICA keeps track of matching FICA contributions.

The other payroll subcategories shown in Figure 12-1 will be used to record federal unemployment contributions, Medicare contributions, state unemployment contributions, and state disability insurance contributions.

In addition, you need to establish several *liability accounts* to maintain records of taxes withheld and other employee-authorized payroll

Payroll Forms

If you are thinking of hiring employees, you need to be prepared for your paperwork to increase. You must complete forms at the federal, state, and local level regarding payroll information.

Federal Payroll Forms

The following list provides an overview of the payroll-related tax forms that employers need to file with the Internal Revenue Service. You can obtain copies of the federal forms you need by calling the IRS toll-free number (800) 829-3676. If this number is not valid in your locale, check your telephone directory for the correct number. You will probably need to file these forms:

◆ *SS-4, Application for Federal Employer Identification Number* The federal employer identification number is used to identify your business on all business-related tax forms.

◆ *Form 46-190, Federal Tax Deposit Receipt* This is your record of deposits of withholding and payroll taxes made to a Federal Reserve bank or an authorized commercial bank.

◆ *Form 940, Employer's Annual Federal Unemployment (FUTA) Tax Return* This is a return filed annually with the IRS summarizing your federal unemployment tax liability and deposits.

◆ *Form 941, Employer's Quarterly Federal Tax Return* This return summarizes your quarterly FICA taxes and federal income tax withholding liability and the amount of deposits your business has made during the quarter.

◆ *Form 943, Employer's Annual Tax Return for Agricultural Employees* This is a special form completed annually for FICA taxes and federal income tax withholding liability for agricultural employees.

12

◆ *Form 1099-MISC, Statement for Recipients of Miscellaneous Income* This must be filed for all nonemployees paid $600.00 or more in income in the current tax year.

◆ *Form W-2, Wage and Tax Statement* This is a six-part form (an original and five duplicates) summarizing an employee's gross earnings and tax deductions for the year. The form must be prepared annually for each employee by January 31.

◆ *Form W-3, Transmittal of Income and Tax Statements* This form summarizes your business's annual payroll, related FICA taxes, and federal income tax withheld during the year. Sent with the Social Security Administration's copy of the W-2 by February 28th of the following year.

◆ *Form W-4, Employee's Withholding Allowance Certificate* This form is completed annually by employees and is used to declare the number of withholding exemptions they claim.

State and Local Government Payroll Information

These forms vary by state. The following list provides an indication of some of the forms you are likely to need to file.

◆ Unemployment insurance tax payments

◆ Workers' compensation tax payments

◆ State income tax withholding payments

◆ Local income tax withholding payments

◆ Form W-2, Wage and Tax Statement (one copy of federal form)

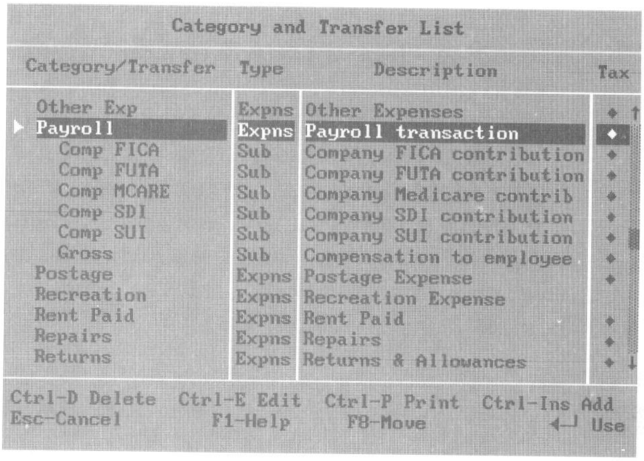

Partial category
list showing
payroll
subcategories
Figure 12-1.

deductions for medical insurance, charitable contributions, and so on.
These are liability accounts since you are holding the withheld funds
for payment to a third party. Some examples of these are as follows:

Payroll-FUTA	Federal unemployment taxes
Payroll-FICA	FICA liabilities owed by employer
Payroll-FWH	Federal income tax liabilities for employee withholdings
Payroll-MCARE	Medicare tax liabilities
Payroll-SWHOH	State income tax liabilities for employee withholdings (Ohio in this illustration)
Payroll-SUI	State unemployment tax liabilities
Payroll-SDI	State disability insurance liabilities

Notice that all of these account names begin with "Payroll." This allows
Quicken to prepare the payroll report by automatically finding all
transactions with a category title beginning with Payroll. All the
categories listed in this section start with Payroll and have subcategories
added, for example Payroll:Gross. When you prepare the Payroll report
in this chapter, you will see the relationship between the category
designation and the preparation of the report.

Another point to note is that although employees must pay federal,
state, and local taxes, the employer is responsible for the actual

12

withholding and payment of these funds to the appropriate agencies. In addition, there are certain payroll taxes that the employer must pay, such as unemployment, workers' compensation, and matching FICA. The amount of these taxes is not withheld from the employee's pay since the responsibility for these payments rests with the employer. With Quicken, you can monitor your liability for these payments. This is important since you will be assessed penalties and late fees for failing to file these payments on time. Quicken's ability to memorize payment formats and remind you of dates for periodic payments can be most helpful in this situation.

Recording Payroll Activity

You will be using the file BUSINESS, established in Chapter 11, "Setting Up Quicken for Your Business," to record your payroll entries in this chapter. As noted in the previous section, you need to expand your category list and accounts in order to accumulate the payroll information. Once you have completed the example for processing payroll, you will be able to customize your accounts to handle your own payroll needs. For example, you might withhold medical and life insurance premiums from your employees' checks. These amounts can be recorded in another liability account established just for that purpose.

The example used in this chapter assumes your work force consists of salaried workers paid monthly. This means their pay and deductions will be the same month after month. John Smith is paid $2000.00 a month and Mary McFaul is paid $3000.00 a month. If your employees are paid hourly, with a varying number of hours in each pay period, you will need to recompute the pay and deductions for each period. Otherwise, the same procedures shown in this chapter apply. In this example, you draw payroll checks on the last day of the month.

Establishing Payroll Liability Accounts and New Payroll Categories

The first step in recording payroll in the Quicken system is to establish the payroll liability accounts you will use throughout the year. The objective of establishing these accounts is to allow you to accumulate the amounts you withhold from employees so you can make periodic payments when they become due to the various governmental agencies, health insurance companies, and pension plans involved. When a payment is due, you can open the liability account to determine the balance in the account. This tells you the amount of the payment due. Quicken's Use Tutorials/Assistants Main Menu option will be used to establish the payroll liability accounts and new payroll categories used in this chapter's illustration.

Make sure you are in the ANB Business Account in the BUSINESS file. Then, from the Main Menu, follow these steps to establish the payroll liability accounts you will use in this chapter:

1. Select **T**utorials and Assistants.
2. Select Create **P**ayroll Support.
3. Press Enter, and your screen appears as follows:

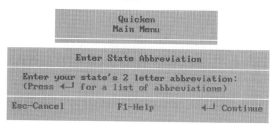

4. Enter your state's abbreviation and press Enter.

Ohio is used throughout this book. Quicken automatically creates all the required payroll accounts for your state.

5. Press Enter to acknowledge Quicken's message and return to the Main Menu.
6. Select Select **A**ccount.

The screen in Figure 12-2 shows that Quicken has established new payroll liability accounts for FICA, federal unemployment tax, federal income tax, medicare contributions, state unemployment tax, state income taxes, and state disability insurance.

7. Select the ANB Business account.

   Quicken displays the ANB register.
8. Press Ctrl-C and type **P**.

12

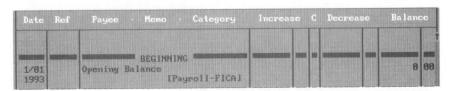

The Category and Transfer List window shown in Figure 12-1 appears.

Quicken's Payroll Assistant has created the basic categories as well as liability accounts you will use in this chapter. If you plan to complete the entries shown in chapter tutorials, there are several editing steps you must complete first.

When you use Quicken's Payroll Assistant feature, the opening balances for the liability accounts show the date in your machine at the time that you used the Assistant. The following steps demonstrate how to edit the account to make the opening balance date 1/1/93. From the Main Menu, follow these steps:

1. Select Select **A**ccount.
2. Select Payroll-FICA.
3. Highlight the Opening Balance transaction.
4. Type **1/1/93** in the Date field and press Ctrl-Enter.

Your screen now looks like this:

Using the steps just given, edit the Date field in all the other liability accounts established by Quicken's Payroll Assistant. These include FUTA, FWH, MCARE, SUI, SWHOH, and SDI.

Monthly Payroll Entries

In this section, you record paycheck entries for John Smith and Mary McFaul on January 31. Many steps are required to complete the entire entry for an individual. After you record basic information, such as check number and employee name, amounts must be determined. You establish each of the withholding amounts and subtract the total from the gross pay to compute net pay. For hourly workers, a computation is needed to determine the gross pay as well. Tax tables are used to determine the correct withholding for federal, state, and local taxes. For figures such as FICA and net pay, you can use Quicken's Calculator when computing the amount.

Once you have determined withholding amounts and net pay, you need to enter this information. Each of the withholding amounts, such as federal income tax, FICA, and state withholding, is entered on a Split Transaction window. Follow these steps to record the transactions:

1. From the Main Menu, select Select **A**ccount and then select ANB Business.
2. Press [Ctrl]-[End] to highlight the next blank transaction in the ANB Business account register.
3. Type **1/31/93** and press [Enter].
4. Type **110** and press [Enter].
5. Type **John Smith** and press [Enter].
6. Type **1560.13** and press [Enter].

This amount is equal to John's gross pay of $2000.00 less federal income tax, state income tax, FICA, and Medicare withholding.

7. Type **000-00-0001** and press [Enter].

This identifies the employee's social security number. You may find this field useful in filtering payroll reports.

12

8. Press Ctrl-S, and the Split Transaction window appears on your screen.

The screen in Figure 12-3 shows the top portion of the Split Transaction window you complete in the next series of steps. The final portion of the Split Transaction window is shown in Figure 12-4.

9. Type **Payroll:Gross/B** and press Enter.

You can use the QuickFill capability for the entries throughout this chapter even though they have subcategories and classes. When you type a **P**, Payroll will display. Type a **:** to accept Payroll and display the first subcategory. Use Ctrl-+ to advance through the categories to find the one that you want, type a **/**, and Quicken will add the B for you.

10. Type **Gross Earnings** and press Enter.
11. Type **2000.00** and press Enter.
12. Press Ctrl-C, and the Category and Transfer List window appears on your screen. Select [Payroll-FICA], press Enter, and type **/B.**

Quicken automatically records the brackets around the Payroll-FICA category, as shown in the Split Transaction window in Figure 12-3,

Print/Acct	Edit	Shortcuts	Reports	Activities			F1-Help
Date	Num	Payee · Memo · Category		Payment	C	Deposit	Balance
1/31	110	John Smith		1,560	13		10,466	62
1993	SPLIT	000-00-0001						
	Cat:	Payroll:Gross/B						
9/08								

Split Transaction

Category	Memo	Amount
1:Payroll:Gross/B	Gross Earnings	2,000.00↑
2:[Payroll-FICA]/B	FICA Withholding	-124.00
3:[Payroll-FWH]/B	Federal Withholding	-232.00
4:[Payroll-SWHOH]/B	State Withholding	-54.87
5:[Payroll-MCARE]/B	Medicare Withholding	-29.00
6:Payroll:Comp FICA/B	Payroll Taxes	124.00↓

Enter categories, descriptions, and amounts
Esc-Cancel   Ctrl-D Delete   F9-Recalc Transaction Total   Ctrl↵ Done

ANB Business

Ending Balance: $10,466.62

Partial Split Transaction window for Smith payroll entries
Figure 12-3.

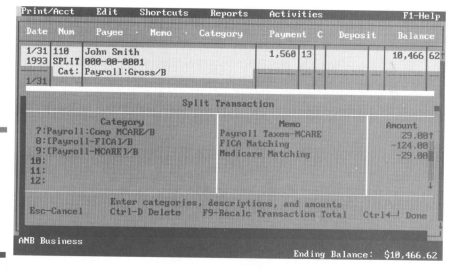

Partial Split
Transaction
window for
remainder of
Smith
payroll entries
Figure 12-4.

when the transaction involves a transfer between two Quicken
accounts. Here, Quicken records the other liability account name in the
Category field. This indicates that you are keeping track of the amount
of your employee withholding in this account until you make your
payment to the IRS.

13. Press Enter to move to the Memo field.

14. Type **FICA Withholding** and press Enter.

15. Type **–124.00** and press Enter.

This is the amount of FICA withheld from John's paycheck. The
negative amount indicates that this is a deduction from the $2000.00
gross earnings entered earlier. For 1992, the rate is .062 on the first
$55,500.00 of earnings per employee. You can calculate this amount
with the Quicken Calculator before starting the transaction. Although
the $55,500.00 earnings limit does not affect the employees in this
example, Quicken can be used to help monitor employees' gross
earnings to determine when the limit is reached.

16. Press Ctrl-C, select [Payroll-FWH], press Enter, and type **/B**.

17. Press Enter to move to the Memo field.

12

18. Type **Federal Withholding** and press [Enter].
19. Type **–232.00** and press [Enter].

This is the amount of federal income tax withheld from John's paycheck. Remember, you must manually determine the amounts from withholding tables before beginning the payroll transaction entry since you need it to compute net pay.

20. Press [Ctrl]-[C], select [Payroll-SWHOH], press [Enter], and type **/B**.
21. Press [Enter] to move the cursor to the Memo field.
22. Type **State Withholding** and press [Enter].
23. Type **–54.87** and press [Enter].

Once again, you would use the appropriate state withholding tables to determine the amount of the deduction from John's paycheck. If you live in an area where local taxes are also withheld, you need to add another liability account to accumulate your liability to that governmental agency. At this point, you have recorded John Smith's gross and net earnings and the related payroll withholding amounts.

24. Press [Ctrl]-[C], select [Payroll-MCARE], press [Enter], type **/B**, and press [Enter].
25. Type **Medicare Withholding** and press [Enter].
26. Type **–29.00** and press [Enter].

For 1992, the rate is .0145 on the first $130,200. The remaining steps record your employer payroll expenses.

27. Type **Payroll:Comp FICA /B** and press [Enter].

As an employer you have to match your employees' FICA contributions. This is an expense of doing business and must be recorded in your category list.

28. Type **Payroll Taxes-FICA** and press [Enter].
29. Type **124.00** and press [Enter].

This records the amount of your matching FICA payroll expense. Notice that this is a positive amount because this is a business expense that Quicken will record in the account register.

30. Type **Payroll:Comp MCARE/B** and press (Enter).
31. Type **Payroll Taxes-MCARE** and press (Enter).
32. Type **29.00** and press (Enter).
33. Press (Ctrl)-(C), select [Payroll-FICA], press (Enter), and type **/B**.
34. Press (Enter) to move the cursor to the Memo field.
35. Type **FICA Matching** and press (Enter).
36. Type **–124.00** and press (Enter).
37. Press (Ctrl)-(C), select [Payroll-MCARE], press (Enter), type **/B**, and press (Enter).
38. Type **Medicare Matching** and press (Enter).
39. Type **–29.00** and press (Ctrl)-(Enter).
40. Press (Ctrl)-(Enter) to record the transaction in the current register.

You have now completed the payroll entry for John Smith for the month of January. You must now complete the recording process for Mary McFaul. Follow these steps to record the transaction from the ANB Business account register:

1. Type **1/31/93** and press (Enter).
2. Type **111** and press (Enter).
3. Type **Mary McFaul** and press (Enter).
4. Type **2284.22** and press (Enter).
5. Type **000-00-0002** and press (Enter).
6. Press (Ctrl)-(S), and the Split Transaction window appears on your screen.
7. Type **Payroll:Gross/B** and press (Enter).
8. Type **Gross Earnings** and press (Enter).
9. Type **3000.00** and press (Enter).
10. Press (Ctrl)-(C), and the Category and Transfer List window appears on your screen. Select [Payroll-FICA], press (Enter), and type **/B**.

12

11. Press [Enter] to move to the Memo field.
12. Type **FICA Withholding** and press [Enter].
13. Type **–186.00** and press [Enter].
14. Press [Ctrl]-[C], select [Payroll-FWH], press [Enter], and type **/B**.
15. Press [Enter] to move to the Memo field.
16. Type **Federal Withholding** and press [Enter].
17. Type **–382.00** and press [Enter].
18. Press [Ctrl]-[C], select [Payroll-SWHOH], press [Enter], and type **/B**.
19. Press [Enter] to move the cursor to the Memo field.
20. Type **State Withholding** and press [Enter].
21. Type **–104.28** and press [Enter].
22. Press [Ctrl]-[C], select [Payroll-MCARE], press [Enter], type **/B**, and press [Enter].
23. Type **Medicare Withholding** and press [Enter].
24. Type **–43.50** and press [Enter].
25. Type **Payroll:Comp FICA/B** and press [Enter].
26. Type **Payroll Taxes-FICA** and press [Enter].
27. Type **186.00** and press [Enter].
28. Type **Payroll:Comp MCARE/B** and press [Enter].
29. Type **Payroll Taxes-MCARE** and press [Enter].
30. Type **43.50** and press [Enter].
31. Press [Ctrl]-[C], select [Payroll-FICA], press [Enter], and type **/B**.
32. Press [Enter].
33. Type **FICA Matching** and press [Enter].
34. Type **–186.00** and press [Enter].
35. Press [Ctrl]-[C], select [Payroll-MCARE], press [Enter], type **/B**, and press [Enter].
36. Type **Medicare Matching** and press [Enter].
37. Type **–43.50** and press [Ctrl]-[Enter].
38. Press [Ctrl]-[Enter] to record the transaction for Mary McFaul in the account register.

The paycheck transactions recorded in this section show the basic payroll expenses and liabilities associated with the payment of wages. Your payroll entries will be more complex if you withhold medical insurance, pension contributions, and other amounts such as contributions to charity or deposits to savings accounts from employee checks. The basic format of the split transaction remains the same; the number of categories in the split transaction would simply be expanded and additional liability accounts added to cover your obligation to make payment to the parties involved. Regardless of the number of withholding categories, the procedures you just performed can be used to expand your withholding categories and liabilities.

Recording Periodic Deposits for the Internal Revenue Service

You must periodically make deposits to the Internal Revenue Service for the amount of FICA and federal income tax withheld from employees' paychecks, as well as your matching FICA contribution. You make your deposits to authorized banks within the Federal Reserve System. You should check with your bank to be sure they can provide this service; otherwise you must take cash or a bank check, along with the appropriate forms, to an authorized bank and make your deposit. To record the withholding deposit, you will designate the Internal Revenue Service as the payee in your entry.

There are specific guidelines concerning the timing of the payments. At the time of this writing, the fictitious company used in this example would be required to make a withholding deposit for the January paychecks under the IRS's Rule #3. The rule states you must make a deposit for social security taxes and withheld federal income tax by the fifteenth of the following month if the total tax liability for any month is $500 or more but less than $3,000. (This can be more than one month's worth.) See the special "IRS Deposit Rules" section for other conditions that may apply to your situation. In this example, your total tax liability for the month is $1379.00. You should consult your accountant or read IRS Form 941 for a full explanation of the other deposit rules. Depending on the size of your payroll, you may have to make periodic payments throughout the month in order to comply with the regulations.

12

The following entry demonstrates how you would record a payment for your business's federal tax liabilities for social security taxes, Medicare, and federal withholding taxes. You would record the transaction in the ANB Business account register when you paid the federal government the amount of the liabilities for FICA, Medicare, and federal income tax withholding for the two paycheck entries recorded in the previous section.

From the ANB Business account register, record the following transaction for the required deposit:

1. Press Ctrl-End to highlight the blank new transaction form and move the cursor to the Date field.
2. Type **2/1/93** and press Enter.
3. Type **112** and press Enter.
4. Type **Internal Revenue Service** and press Enter.
5. Type **1379.00** and press Enter.
6. Type **Form 941 Withholding Payment** and press Enter.
7. Press Ctrl-S to open the Split Transaction window. The screen in Figure 12-5 shows the entries in the Split Transaction window.

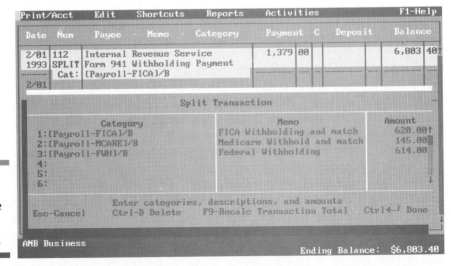

Split Transaction entries for the IRS deposit
Figure 12-5.

IRS Deposit Rules

The frequency with which you must make deposits of social security and federal income taxes is dependent on the amount of your liability. Currently there are five different rules that can affect when you must make these deposits. Also, the rule under which your company falls can change throughout the year as you add staff, pay overtime wages, or hire seasonal help. Since the penalties for non-compliance can be steep it is important to follow the rules exactly. IRS Circular E provides the details you will need to determine your filing requirements but a quick summary is provided here:

Rule 1	Tax liability for the quarter less than $500 -No deposit required
Rule 2	Tax liability for the month less than $500 -Carry forward to the next month
Rule 3	Tax liability for the month between $500 and $3,000 -Deposit within 15 days from the end of the month
Rule 4	Tax liability at the end of any of the 8 monthly periods greater than $3,000 and less than $100,000 -Deposit within 3 banking days
Rule 5	Tax liability at the end of any of the eight monthly periods greater than $100,000 -Deposit by the end of the next banking day

The IRS is proposing to change these rules for 1993 to simplify them for small businesses. Their proposal includes only two rules and is based on the companies withholding liability for the previous year and would remain in effect for the entire year once established. The two proposed rules at the time of printing are:

Rule 1	Tax liability for last year $50,000 or less -Monthly filing
Rule 2	Tax liability for last year greater than $50,000 -Semi weekly filings

12

8. Press `Ctrl`-`C`, select [Payroll-FICA], press `Enter`, and type **/B**. This account is now recorded in the Category field in the Split Transaction window.

9. Press `Enter` to move the cursor to the Memo field.

10. Type **FICA Withholding and match** and press `Enter`.

11. Type **620.00** and press `Enter`.

12. Press `Ctrl`-`C`, select [Payroll-MCARE], press `Enter`, and type **/B**.

13. Press `Enter` to move the cursor to the Memo field.

14. Type **Medicare Withhold and match** and press `Enter`.

15. Type **145.00** and press `Enter`.

16. Press `Ctrl`-`C`, move the arrow cursor to [Payroll-FWH], press `Enter`, and type **/B**.

17. Press `Enter` to move the cursor to the Memo field.

18. Type **Federal Withholding** and press `Enter`.

19. Press `Ctrl`-`Enter`. This records the split.

20. Press `Ctrl`-`Enter` to record the transaction in the account register.

You follow these same steps to record the payment of the state withholding tax liability when the required payment date arrives.

Notice that no expense category was charged in the Split Transaction window shown in Figure 12-5. This is because the deposit reduces the liability account balances that were established when payroll checks were written on 1/31/93. Looking at those transactions in your register, you can see that the gross earnings were charged to the Payroll:Gross category and your matching FICA contribution as an employer was charged to the Payroll:Comp FICA category. Both these categories are classified as expenses and will be shown on your business Profit and Loss statement. On the other hand, the amounts withheld for payroll taxes were charged to liability accounts that will be paid at a future date. Thus, when you pay these liabilities, as you just did, you are meeting your financial obligation to the government, not incurring additional expenses.

Other Liability Accounts

Let's look at the impact of recording the paychecks and the IRS payment on the other liability accounts. Specifically, you will see the effects of these transactions on the [Payroll-FWH] other liability account. Follow these steps to enter the [Payroll-FWH] account from the ANB Business account register:

1. Press Esc to return to the Main Menu.
2. Choose Select **A**ccount, and the Select Account to Use window appears.
3. Select the Payroll-FWH account and press Enter. The screen shown in Figure 12-6 appears.

Notice that the account had accumulated $614.00 as the FWH withholding liability for the January paychecks. Also note that the 2/1/93 entry reduced the balance to zero when you made your deposit. This will occur each month when you record your deposit to the IRS.

Print/Acct	Edit	Shortcuts	Reports	Activities			F1-Help
Date Ref	Payee · Memo ·	Category	Increase	C	Decrease	Balance	
		BEGINNING					
1/01 1993	Opening Balance	[Payroll-FWH]				0 00	
1/31 1993	John Smith 000-00-0001	[ANB Business]→	232 00			232 00	
1/31 1993	Mary McFaul 000-00-0002	[ANB Business]→	382 00			614 00	
2/01 1993	Internal Revenue Service Form 941 Withho→	[ANB Business]→			614 00	0 00	
9/08 1993	Memo: Cat:						

Payroll-FWH   (Alt+letter accesses menu)
Esc-Main Menu   Ctrl◄┘ Record   Ending Balance: $0.00

Activating the
Payroll-FWH
account
Figure 12-6.

12

4. Press Esc to return to the Main Menu.

5. Choose Select **A**ccount, select ANB Business, and press Enter. You are now back in the ANB Business account register.

Memorized Monthly Paycheck and Withholding Deposit Entries

Since you will be paying your employees on a regular basis and making monthly withholding deposits, you will want to memorize these entries to simplify future recording of the transactions. Since the employees in this example are all salaried, the only changes needed each month are new dates and check numbers on each transaction. All of the split transaction detail will be accurate. For hourly employees or employees making more than the FICA cap amount, some pay periods will require changes to the entries in the split transaction detail. While in the ANB Business account register, complete the following steps to memorize paycheck and withholding deposit transactions:

1. Highlight the John Smith paycheck transaction on January 31, 1993, and press Ctrl-M.

2. Press Enter to memorize the transaction amounts.

3. Highlight the Mary McFaul paycheck transaction on January 31, 1993, and press Ctrl-M.

4. Press Enter to memorize the transaction amounts.

5. Highlight the Internal Revenue Service transaction and press Ctrl-M.

6. Press Enter to memorize the transaction amounts.

7. Press Ctrl-T to display the Memorized Transactions List window. Your list should contain entries for Internal Revenue Service, John Smith, and Mary McFaul.

8. Press Esc to return to the account register.

Completing the Payroll Entries

In this section, you expand your payroll transactions by adding some entries to the ANB Business account register. These transactions are added so the examples will contain enough pay periods to generate realistic reports later in this chapter. Notice that you will not record check numbers for the remaining example transactions in this chapter. This will not affect the reports prepared in this chapter.

Establishing Transaction Groups

In Chapter 11, "Setting Up Quicken for Your Business," you established a transaction group for the utilities payments. The object of transaction grouping is to batch together similar transactions that occur around the same time each month so Quicken can automatically record them for you the next time they need to be made. Remember, only memorized transactions can be batched into transaction groups. From the ANB Business account register, perform the following steps to establish a transaction group for the payroll:

1. Press Ctrl-J, and the select Transaction Group to Execute window appears.
2. Select 2. <unused> and press Enter. The Describe Group 2 window appears.
3. Type **Payroll** and press Enter twice.
4. Type **6** and press Enter.
5. Type **2/28/93** and press Enter.
6. Select John Smith and press Spacebar to mark the transaction. Note the 2 in the group column, indicating that the transaction is now part of Group 2.
7. Select Mary McFaul and press Spacebar. This transaction also becomes a part of Group 2.
8. Press Enter to indicate that you are finished selecting transactions.
9. Press Esc.

You are returned to the account register to record further transactions.

12

Recording February Transactions

In this section, you add the remaining transactions to the account register to complete the payroll entries for the month of February. You should be in the ANB Business account register to record the following transactions:

1. Press Ctrl-End to highlight the next blank transaction form.
2. Press Ctrl-J.

Quicken displays a list of transaction groups.

3. Select the Payroll Group and press Enter.

Quicken displays the date of the next scheduled entry of the group, 2/28/93.

4. Press Enter to confirm that this date is valid and to enter and record the group of payroll transactions in the account register.

Quicken displays a message indicating that the transactions have been recorded. You can then make any required changes.

5. Press Enter to close the message box.

If the date was not the last date of the month for payroll purposes, you could have typed the correct date in the Transaction Group Date window and then pressed Enter. In this example, the payroll entries will not be modified since they are the same from month to month. If you have employees who work on an hourly basis, you would need to select each new transaction, open the Split Transaction window, and make the necessary modifications to the dollar amounts recorded.

The payroll entries are the only February transactions that are being added to the account register at this time. Figure 12-7 shows a printout of the account register including the two payroll entries recorded on 2/28/93, as well as the remaining transactions that will be entered in this chapter.

Recording March Transactions

The March entries can be divided into three groups. The first records a deposit for federal social security, Medicare, and income tax withholding in February. The second and third entries record income earned during the month from consulting and royalties. The last two entries record the payroll transactions for March.

```
                          Check Register
ANB Business                                                    Page 1
9/ 6/93


Date  Num           Transaction              Payment  C  Deposit    Balance
----- -----  ------------------------------  ---------- - ---------- ----------

2/28       John Smith                        1,560.13             5,243.27
1993  SPLIT 000-00-0001
                Payroll:Gross/B              2,000.00
                  Gross Earnings
                [Payroll-FICA]/B                            124.00
                  FICA Withholding
                [Payroll-FWH]/B                             232.00
                  Federal Withholding
                [Payroll-SWHOH]/B                            54.87
                  State Withholding
                [Payroll-MCARE]/B                            29.00
                  Medicare Withholding
                Payroll:Comp FICA/B           124.00
                  Payroll Taxes-FICA
                Payroll:Comp MCARE/B           29.00
                  Payroll Taxes-MCARE
                [Payroll-FICA]/B                            124.00
                  FICA Matching
                [Payroll-MCARE]/B                            29.00
                  Medicare Matching

2/28       Mary McFaul                       2,284.22             2,959.05
1993  SPLIT 000-00-0002
                Payroll:Gross/B              3,000.00
                  Gross Earnings
                [Payroll-FICA]/B                            186.00
                  FICA Withholding
                [Payroll-FWH]/B                             382.00
                  Federal Withholding
                [Payroll-SWHOH]/B                           104.28
                  State Withholding
                [Payroll-MCARE]/B                            43.50
                  Medicare Withholding
                Payroll:Comp FICA/B           186.00
                  Payroll Taxes-FICA
                Payroll:Comp MCARE/B           43.50
                  Payroll Taxes-MCARE
                [Payroll-FICA]/B                            186.00
                  FICA Matching
                [Payroll-MCARE]/B                            43.50
                  Medicare Matching
```

Account register showing additional transactions **Figure 12-7.**

12

```
                           Check Register
ANB Business                                              Page 2
9/ 6/93


Date  Num         Transaction          Payment  C  Deposit    Balance
----- -----  -------------------------- ---------- - ---------- ----------


3/ 1         Internal Revenue Service    1,379.00             1,580.05
1993 SPLIT Form 941 Withholding Payment
                  [Payroll-FICA]/B         620.00
                    FICA Withholding and match
                  [Payroll-MCARE]/B        145.00
                    Medicare Withhold and match
                  [Payroll-FWH]/B          614.00
                    Federal Withholding


3/ 1         Tyler Corp.                            25,000.00 26,580.05
1993 memo: Seminars conducted Jan. 92
       cat: Inc Cons/B


3/31         Big Books                              10,000.00 36,580.05
1993 memo: Royalties
       cat: Inc Roy/B


3/31         John Smith                  1,560.13             35,019.92
1993 SPLIT 000-00-0001
                  Payroll:Gross/B        2,000.00
                    Gross Earnings
                  [Payroll-FICA]/B                    124.00
                    FICA Withholding
                  [Payroll-FWH]/B                     232.00
                    Federal Withholding
                  [Payroll-SWHOH]/B                    54.87
                    State Withholding
                  [Payroll-MCARE]/B                    29.00
                    Medicare Withholding
                  Payroll:Comp FICA/B      124.00
                    Payroll Taxes-FICA
                  Payroll:Comp MCARE/B      29.00
                    Payroll Taxes-MCARE
                  [Payroll-FICA]/B                    124.00
                    FICA Matching
                  [Payroll-MCARE]/B                    29.00
                    Medicare Matching
```

Account register showing additional transactions *(continued)*
Figure 12-7.

```
                          Check Register
ANB Business                                              Page 3
9/6/93


Date   Num          Transaction         Payment  C  Deposit   Balance
-----  -----  ------------------------------  ---------- - ---------- ----------


3/31          Mary McFaul                  2,284.22              32,735.70
1993 SPLIT 000-00-0002
                    Payroll:Gross/B        3,000.00
                      Gross Earnings
                    [Payroll-FICA]/B                    186.00
                      FICA Withholding
                    [Payroll-FWH]/B                     382.00
                      Federal Withholding
                    [Payroll-SWHOH]/B                   104.28
                      State Withholding
                    [Payroll-MCARE]/B                    43.50
                      Medicare Withholding
                    Payroll:Comp FICA/B      186.00
                      Payroll Taxes-FICA
                    Payroll:Comp MCARE/B      43.50
                      Payroll Taxes-MCARE
                    [Payroll-FICA]/B                    186.00
                      FICA Matching
                    [Payroll-MCARE]/B                    43.50
                      Medicare Matching


4/ 1          Internal Revenue Service     1,379.00             31,356.70
1993 SPLIT Form 941 Withholding Payment
                    [Payroll-FICA]/B         620.00
                      FICA Withholding and match
                    [Payroll-MCARE]/B        145.00
                      Medicare Withhold and match
                    [Payroll-FWH]/B          614.00
                      Federal Withholding


4/15          Internal Revenue Service      104.00             31,252.70
1993 memo: FUTA
      cat: Payroll:Comp FUTA/B


4/15          Bureau of Employment Services 520.00             30,732.70
1993 memo: SUTA
      cat: Payroll:Comp SUI/B
```

Account
register
showing
additional
transactions
(continued)
Figure 12-7.

12

The Entry to Record February Withholding

The entry to record the deposit for taxes withheld during February involves the use of a memorized transaction. From the highlighted blank transaction form in the ANB Business account register, perform the following steps:

1. Press Ctrl-T in order to recall the Memorized Transaction List window.
2. Select the Internal Revenue Service transaction and press Enter.
3. Move the cursor to the Date field, type **3/1/93**, and press Ctrl-Enter.

Consulting and Royalty Income Entries

In the ANB Business account register, enter the following information for the two deposit entries shown in Figure 12-7:

1. Type **3/1/93** and press Enter twice.
2. Type **Tyler Corp.** and press Enter three times.
3. Type **25000** and press Enter.
4. Type **Seminars conducted Jan. 93** and press Enter.
5. Type **Inc Cons/B** and press Ctrl-Enter. This records the Tyler Corp. revenue transaction.
6. Type **3/31/93** and press Enter twice.
7. Type **Big Books** and press Enter three times.
8. Type **10000** and press Enter.
9. Type **Royalties** and press Enter.
10. Type **Inc Roy/B** and press Ctrl-Enter.

After completing these steps, you have recorded both income transactions for March.

March Payroll Entries

In this section, you add the remaining transactions to the account register to complete the payroll entries for the month of March:

1. Press Ctrl-J. Quicken displays a list of transaction groups.

2. Select the Payroll Group and press Enter. Quicken displays the date of the next scheduled entry of the group, **3/28/93**.
3. Type **3/31/93** and press Enter.

This changes the date to the end of March and enters the group of payroll transactions in the account register. Quicken will indicate that the transactions have been recorded.

4. Press Enter in response to the Transaction Group Entered window.

Recording April Transactions

The only transactions you will record for April are the Internal Revenue Service deposit for the March payroll and the Federal Unemployment Tax Act (FUTA) and State Unemployment Tax Act (SUTA) payments.

Complete the following steps to record the IRS transaction in the ANB Business account register. (This transaction will help you prepare several reports for the Internal Revenue Service later in this chapter.)

1. Press Ctrl-End to move to the end of the register.
2. Press Ctrl-T to recall the Memorized Transaction List window.
3. Select the Internal Revenue Service transaction and press Enter.
4. Move the cursor to the Date field, type **4/1/93**, and press Ctrl-Enter.

In addition to your withholding tax liabilities, employers must pay unemployment taxes. This program is mandated by the federal government but administered by the individual state governments. Because of this method of administration, you must make payments to both the state and federal government. At the time of this writing, you must contribute .008 percent to the federal government to cover their administrative costs and up to .054 percent to the state agency that administers the program. These percentages apply to the first $7000.00 of earnings for each employee. In some states, the salary cap on earnings may be higher; however, the example in this chapter uses a $7000.00 limit for both federal and state employer payroll tax contributions.

You must make deposits to the federal government whenever your contribution liability reaches $100.00. These deposits are made in the

12

same manner as the FICA, Medicare, and federal income tax withholding payments earlier in this chapter.

Your actual contributions to the state agency will be based on historical rates for your business and industry classification. You may qualify for a percentage rate lower than the maximum rate allowed by law. The contribution rate for the business in this example is assumed to be .04 percent.

Generally, payments to the state agency that administers the program are made quarterly. Each quarter, you are required to complete an Employer's Report of Wages form, summarizing your employees' total earnings during the quarter and the amount of your FUTA and SUTA liabilities.

From the ANB Business account register, make the following payments for federal and state unemployment payroll taxes during the month of April. Follow these steps to record the FUTA and SUTA payments:

1. Press [Ctrl]-[End] to make certain you are at the next available form for recording a transaction.

2. Type **4/15/93** and press [Enter] twice.

3. Type **Internal Revenue Service** and press [Enter].

4. Type **104** and press [Enter].

In the "Payroll Reports" section of this chapter, you will see that Smith received $6000.00 and McFaul received $9000.00 in gross pay. McFaul has reached the salary limit for employer unemployment contributions for the year. The amount entered here was determined by multiplying the first $7000.00 of McFaul's salary and all $6000.00 of Smith's by the FUTA rate of .008.

5. Type **FUTA** and press [Enter].

6. Type **Payroll:Comp FUTA/B** and press [Ctrl]-[Enter].

You have now completed the recording of the FUTA payroll tax deposit.

7. Press [Enter] twice.

This accepts the 4/15/93 date for the transaction entry and moves the cursor to the Payee field.

8. Type **Bureau of Employment Services** and press (Enter).
9. Type **520** and press (Enter).
10. Type **SUTA** and press (Enter).

The payment amount of 520 was determined by multiplying 13,000.00 ($7000.00+$6000.00) by .04.

11. Type **Payroll:Comp SUI/B** and press (Ctrl)-(Enter).

With the recording of these entries, you have completed all the transactions that will be added to the account register in this chapter. These new transactions are shown in Figure 12-7.

Workers' Compensation Payments

As an employer, you will make workers' compensation payments for your employees. The entries are recorded in the way just illustrated for unemployment insurance payments. To record this payroll expense, you need a new category, Payroll:Comp WCOMP.

Payroll Reports

Through the use of filters and customization features, you can obtain a substantial amount of the payroll-related information you need to prepare the various federal, state, and local payroll tax and withholding forms. However, as you will see in the following sections, there are some functions you must perform manually, such as totaling amounts from several Quicken reports to determine the numbers to place in some lines of tax forms.

The objective of this section is to prepare some of the reports you may find useful for your business filing requirements. Although it is impossible to provide illustrations of all the variations, preparing the reports that follow will help you become familiar with the possibilities. You can then begin to explore modifications that best suit your payroll and withholding reporting needs.

From the transactions you entered for January through April, you can gather information that will assist you in preparing your quarterly reports: the FUTA form, SUTA form, workers' compensation report, and federal, state, and local withholding tax reports. Although you have not

12

entered a full year's worth of transactions, you will see that Quicken can also help in the preparation of year-end W-2s, W-3s, 1099s, annual forms for federal, state, and local tax withholding, and other annual tax forms required for unemployment and workers' compensation purposes.

Payroll Report Overview

Quicken's Payroll report summarizes all your payroll activities in any period for which you need information—that is, you can prepare the report for weekly, monthly, quarterly, or yearly payroll summary information. You can gather information for all employees in one report, or you can limit the report to information concerning one employee at a time.

An important point to remember is that Quicken's Payroll report is preset to interface only with the Payroll category. If you recall, it was mentioned early in the chapter that all payroll-related charges would be charged against the main Payroll category. Quicken established subcategories for Payroll:Gross and Payroll:Comp FICA, and so on, to keep track of specific types of payroll charges. If you don't use this format, you need to select Summary Report from the Reports menu and customize your reports to gather the information necessary for tax-reporting purposes. All the reports prepared in this section are based on the Payroll Report option in the Business Reports menu.

Employer's Quarterly Federal Tax Return

In the previous sections of this chapter, you prepared entries that accumulated FICA and Medicare withholding, the matching employer's contribution, and the federal income tax withheld from each of the employees' paychecks. You also recorded the required payments to the IRS made to a local bank authorized to receive these funds.

Let's now examine how you can use Quicken to assist you in preparing Form 941 (shown in Figure 12-8) to meet your quarterly filing requirements. Consult the special "Dates for Filing Federal Payroll Tax Returns" section for the deadlines for filing quarterly Form 941 and

Dates for Filing Federal Payroll Tax Returns

Form 941, Employer's Quarterly Federal Tax Return	
First quarter (Jan - Mar)	
If deposit required with filing	April 30
If you deposited all taxes when due	May 10
Second quarter (Apr - June)	
If deposit required with filing	July 31
If you deposited all taxes when due	August 10
Third quarter (July - Sept)	
If deposit required with filing	October 31
If you deposited all taxes when due	November 10
Fourth quarter (Oct - Dec)	
If deposit required with filing	January 31
If you deposited all taxes when due	February 10
Form 943, Employer's Annual Tax Return for Agricultural Employees	
Calendar year filing	
If deposit required with filing	January 31
If you deposited all taxes when due	February 10

annual Form 943. Starting from the Main Menu of your ANB Business account register, complete the following steps:

1. Select **C**reate Reports.
2. Select the **B**usiness Reports item.
3. Select Pa**y**roll Report.
4. Press (Enter) to accept the default report title of Payroll Report.

12

Form 941
(Rev. January 1992)
Department of the Treasury
Internal Revenue Service

4141

Employer's Quarterly Federal Tax Return

▶ See Circular E for more information concerning employment tax returns.

Please type or print.

Your name, address, employer identification number, and calendar quarter of return. (If not correct, please change.)

If address is different from prior return, check here ▶ ☐

Name (as distinguished from trade name)	Date quarter ended
Trade name, if any	Employer identification number
Address (number and street)	City, state, and ZIP code

OMB No. 1545-0029
Expires 5-31-93

| T |
| FF |
| FD |
| FP |
| I |
| T |

IRS Use

1 1 1 1 1 1 1 1 1 1 1   2   3 3 3 3 3 3   4 4 4

5 5 5   6   7   8 8 8 8 8   9 9 9   10 10 10 10 10 10 10 10 10 10

If you do not have to file returns in the future, check here . ▶ ☐   Date final wages paid . . . ▶

If you are a seasonal employer, see **Seasonal employers** on page 2 and check here . ▶ ☐

1 Number of employees (except household) employed in the pay period that includes March 12th ▶ | **1** |

2	Total wages and tips subject to withholding, plus other compensation . . . . . ▶	**2**	
3	Total income tax withheld from wages, tips, pensions, annuities, sick pay, gambling, etc. ▶	**3**	
4	Adjustment of withheld income tax for preceding quarters of calendar year (see instructions) .	**4**	
5	Adjusted total of income tax withheld (line 3 as adjusted by line 4—see instructions) . .	**5**	
6a	Taxable social security wages **(Complete line 7)**	$	× 12.4% (.124) =	**6a**	
b	Taxable social security tips	$	× 12.4% (.124) =	**6b**	
7	Taxable Medicare wages and tips	$	× 2.9% (.029) =	**7**	
8	Total social security and Medicare taxes (add lines 6a, 6b, and 7)	**8**	
9	Adjustment of social security and Medicare taxes (see instructions for required explanation) .	**9**	
10	Adjusted total of social security and Medicare taxes (line 8 as adjusted by line 9—see instructions) . ▶	**10**	
11	Backup withholding (see instructions)	**11**	
12	Adjustment of backup withholding tax for preceding quarters of calendar year	**12**	
13	Adjusted total of backup withholding (line 11 as adjusted by line 12)	**13**	
14	**Total taxes** (add lines 5, 10, and 13)	**14**	
15	Advance earned income credit (EIC) payments made to employees, if any . . . . . ▶	**15**	
16	Net taxes (subtract line 15 from line 14). **This should equal line IV below** (plus line IV of Schedule A (Form 941) if you have treated backup withholding as a separate liability) . .	**16**	
17	**Total deposits for quarter,** including overpayment applied from a prior quarter, from your records . ▶	**17**	
18	**Balance due** (subtract line 17 from line 16). This should be less than $500. Pay to Internal Revenue Service . ▶	**18**	
19	**Overpayment,** if line 17 is more than line 16, enter excess here ▶ $		and check if to be:

☐ Applied to next return **OR** ☐ Refunded.

Record of Federal Tax Liability (You must complete if line 16 is $500 or more and Schedule B is not attached.) See instructions before checking these boxes.

If you made deposits using the 95% rule, check here ▶ ☐   If you are a first time 3-banking-day depositor, check here . ▶ ☐

Show tax liability here, **not deposits.** The IRS gets deposit data from FTD coupons.

DO NOT Show Federal Tax Deposits Here

Date wages paid		First month of quarter		Second month of quarter		Third month of quarter
1st through 3rd	A		I		Q	
4th through 7th	B		J		R	
8th through 11th	C		K		S	
12th through 15th	D		L		T	
16th through 19th	E		M		U	
20th through 22nd	F		N		V	
23rd through 25th	G		O		W	
26th through the last	H		P		X	
Total liability for month	I		II		III	

IV Total for quarter (add lines **I, II,** and **III**). **This should equal line 16 above** . . . . . ▶

Sign Here

Under penalties of perjury, I declare that I have examined this return, including accompanying schedules and statements, and to the best of my knowledge and belief, it is true, correct, and complete.

Signature ▶   Print Your Name and Title ▶   Date ▶

For Paperwork Reduction Act Notice, see page 2.   Cat. No. 17001Z

IRS Form 941
Figure 12-8.

5. Type **1/93** and press Enter.
6. Type **4/93** and press F7 (Layout). The Create Summary Report window appears.

Although the report is for the quarter ending 3/31/93, you need to include the March FICA, Medicare, and income tax withholding payment entered in the register on 4/1/93. Making April the last month of the report allows you to set the exact date in April to use as the cutoff date for the report.

7. Press Enter twice.
8. Type **4/1/93** and press Enter.

You have now set the final date of the reporting period to include the payment date of the last IRS deposit for withholding amounts.

9. Press Ctrl-Enter, and the Payroll report appears on your screen.

This is a wide-screen report; it will be printed on several pages.

10. Press Ctrl-P to print the report. The Print Report window appears.
11. Select the appropriate printer and press Enter to print the report.

This is a case where selection of the compressed print option or the landscape option will help you capture more of the report on each page.

Report Discussion

The report prepared is shown in Figure 12-9. (Note that unless you use a wide-carriage printer, the Payroll report will print on several pages instead of just one.) Let's take a look at the information gathered and discuss how you can use it to complete the appropriate lines of the Employer's Quarterly Federal Tax Return form, shown in Figure 12-8.

✦ *Line 2* This line shows the total wages subject to federal withholding. The Payroll report compensation to employee line shows that a total of $15,000.00 was earned by Smith and McFaul during the quarter.

12

```
                         Payroll Report
                    1/ 1/93 Through 4/ 1/93
BUSINESS-All Accounts                                          Page 1
9/ 6/93
                                  Internal Revenue
         Category Description     Service      John Smith
-----------------------------   --------------  --------------
INCOME/EXPENSE
  EXPENSES
    Payroll transaction:
      Company FICA contribution       0.00          372.00
      Company Medicare contrib        0.00           87.00
      Compensation to employee        0.00        6,000.00
                                  -----------   -----------
    Total Payroll transaction         0.00        6,459.00
                                  -----------   -----------
  TOTAL EXPENSES                      0.00        6,459.00


                                  -----------   -----------
  TOTAL INCOME/EXPENSE                0.00       -6,459.00


TRANSFERS
  TO Payroll-FICA               -1,860.00            0.00
  TO Payroll-FWH                -1,842.00            0.00
  TO Payroll-MCARE                -435.00            0.00
  FROM Payroll-FICA                   0.00          744.00
  FROM Payroll-FWH                    0.00          696.00
  FROM Payroll-MCARE                  0.00          174.00
  FROM Payroll-SWHOH                  0.00          164.61
                                  -----------   -----------
  TOTAL TRANSFERS               -4,137.00        1,778.61

BALANCE FORWARD
  Payroll-FICA                        0.00            0.00
  Payroll-FUTA                        0.00            0.00
  Payroll-FWH                         0.00            0.00
  Payroll-MCARE                       0.00            0.00
  Payroll-SDI                         0.00            0.00
  Payroll-SUI                         0.00            0.00
  Payroll-SWHOH                       0.00            0.00
                                  -----------   -----------
  TOTAL BALANCE FORWARD               0.00            0.00


                                  -----------   -----------
  OVERALL TOTAL                 -4,137.00       -4,680.39
                                  ===========   ===========
```

Payroll report
Figure 12-9.

```
                              Payroll Report
                         1/ 1/93 Through 4/ 1/93
        BUSINESS-All Accounts                                    Page 2
        9/ 6/93
                                                OVERALL
        Mary McFaul      Opening Balance         TOTAL
        ---------------  ---------------  ---------------


              558.00            0.00             930.00
              130.50            0.00             217.50
            9,000.00            0.00          15,000.00
           -----------      -----------      -----------
            9,688.50            0.00          16,147.50
           -----------      -----------      -----------
            9,688.50            0.00          16,147.50

           -----------      -----------      -----------
           -9,688.50            0.00         -16,147.50


                0.00            0.00          -1,860.00
                0.00            0.00          -1,842.00
                0.00            0.00            -435.00
            1,116.00            0.00           1,860.00
            1,146.00            0.00           1,842.00
              261.00            0.00             435.00
              312.84            0.00             477.45
           -----------      -----------      -----------
            2,835.84            0.00             477.45


                0.00            0.00               0.00
                0.00            0.00               0.00
                0.00            0.00               0.00
                0.00            0.00               0.00
                0.00            0.00               0.00
                0.00            0.00               0.00
                0.00            0.00               0.00
           -----------      -----------      -----------
                0.00            0.00               0.00

           -----------      -----------      -----------
           -6,852.66            0.00         -15,670.05
```

Payroll report
(continued)
Figure 12-9.

12

+ *Line 3* This line shows the amount of total income tax withheld from employee wages. The row titled Transfers from Payroll-FWH shows that the total federal income tax withheld from employees was $1842.00. Note that $696.00 was paid by Smith and $1146.00 was paid by McFaul.

+ *Line 6a* The amount of social security taxes accumulated during the quarter totals $1860.00. You obtain the FICA taxes owed from the Transfers from Payroll-FICA row.

To verify this, the gross earnings for the quarter are subject to FICA withholding and matching contributions. This means the total in the Compensation to employee row of the report, $15,000.00, is multiplied by .124 to get the amount on line 6. This should equal the total calculated in the preceding paragraph—$1860.00—which it does.

+ *Line 7* The amount of Medicare taxes accumulated during the quarter totals $435.00. You obtain this amount from the Transfers from Payroll-MCARE row of the report. To verify this, the gross earnings for the quarter are subject to Medicare withholding and matching contributions. This means the total in the Compensation to employee row of the report, $15,000, is multiplied by .029 to get the amount on line 7.

+ *Line 17* This line shows the total deposits made to the IRS during the quarter. This amount can be obtained from the Internal Revenue Service column in the Payroll report. The Overall Total column shows that $4137.00 was the amount deposited with the Internal Revenue Service during the quarter. Note that this amount includes the 4/1/93 payment. When you complete your IRS deposit slip, you designate the quarter for which the payment applies. In this case, the payment was made for the first quarter and would thus be included in this report.

Notice that the bottom portion of Form 941 requires the calculation of tax liabilities at specified time intervals during the deposit periods. Since you made your payments in a timely fashion during the quarter, you would not need to complete this portion. If you did need to complete this portion of the form for the example in this chapter, you would need to complete only Line H since you pay your employees monthly. Figure 12-10 shows the Federal Tax Liability report, which would capture the information for the first quarter to help you to complete lines H, P, and X. If you pay your employees weekly, you could produce this same report for weekly periods during the quarter. If you want to reproduce Figure 12-10 with your account register, you could complete the following steps from the ANB Business account register:

1. Press [Alt]-[R] to open the Reports window.
2. Select **B**usiness Reports.
3. Select **P**ayroll Report.
4. Type **Federal Tax Liability By Month** and press [Enter].
5. Type **1/93** and press [Enter].
6. Type **3/93** and press [F7] (Layout). The Create Summary Report window appears on the screen.
7. Move to Row headings, type **3**, and press [Enter].
8. Type **05** and press [F9] (Filter).

The Filter Transactions window appears. A tilde (~) is used in the Payee matches row to tell Quicken to exclude transactions with this payee from the report.

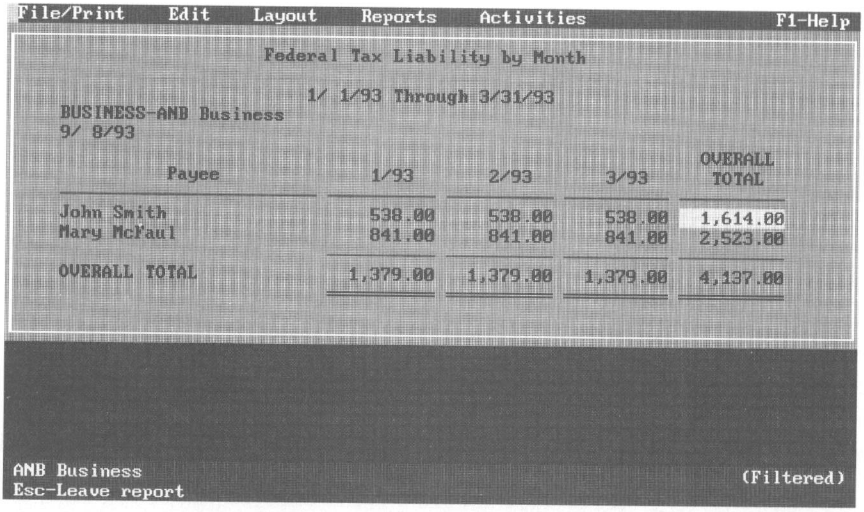

```
 File/Print     Edit     Layout     Reports     Activities              F1-Help
                       Federal Tax Liability by Month
                          1/ 1/93 Through 3/31/93
       BUSINESS-ANB Business
       9/ 8/93
                                                                 OVERALL
                Payee              1/93        2/93        3/93    TOTAL

       John Smith                538.00      538.00      538.00  1,614.00
       Mary McFaul               841.00      841.00      841.00  2,523.00

       OVERALL TOTAL           1,379.00    1,379.00    1,379.00  4,137.00


 ANB Business                                                     (Filtered)
 Esc-Leave report
```

Tax report for employee federal tax withholding
Figure 12-10.

12

9. Type ~**Internal Revenue Service** and press Enter twice.

10. Type [**Payroll . .** and press Enter twice.

This command tells Quicken to include only Payroll liability accounts.

11. Type **Y** and press Ctrl-Enter.

Quicken presents a Select Categories to Include window.

12. Press End and use Spacebar to exclude the following liabilities: [Payroll-SDI], [Payroll-SWHOH], [Payroll-SUI], and [Payroll-FUTA], as shown in Figure 12-11.

13. Press Enter.

14. Press Enter, type **C**, and press Enter.

15. Press Ctrl-P, and the Print Report window appears.

16. Select your printer and press Enter to print the Federal Tax Liability report shown in Figure 12-10. Press Esc until the Main Menu appears.

Before leaving this discussion, notice that there are several columns on your Payroll report (Figure 12-9) with zero balances—the Balance

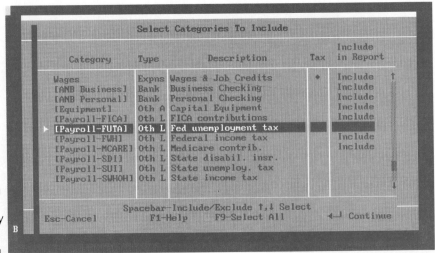

Selecting the correct category
Figure 12-11.

Forward (BAL FWD) columns. These columns represent any unpaid balances in these accounts at the end of the year. In this example, there were no balances in these accounts because the business just hired employees on January 1st. In future years, there would be balances carried forward and shown in this report. However, you still record your first deposit of the year the same way.

Other Quarterly Reports

In addition to the federal quarterly return, you will need to complete several other quarterly tax returns and reports, depending on the state where your business is located. These additional reports and tax forms may include state (SWHOH) and local (LWH) withholding tax reports, state unemployment tax reports (SUTA), and a report for workers' compensation (WCOMP) payments. Figure 12-9 provides the information needed to prepare some of these reports. For example, the row titled Transfers from Payroll-SWHOH shows that $477.45 was withheld from employee wages for state withholding. You have not recorded this entry in your register; however, it would be handled in the same manner as the payments to the IRS when the check is sent to the state taxing unit. You will also need to monitor individual employees' gross earnings when completing several of the other forms. Determining the total earnings for an employee for a given time period and determining your FUTA and SUTA contributions are discussed in the section "Other Annual Tax Forms and Reports" later in this chapter.

Preparing W-2 Forms

At the end of the year, you must give each employee who worked for you during the year a W-2 form. In the example developed here, assume that John Smith left your business at the end of March and received no further paychecks. The Payroll report prepared in this case is customized for John Smith and uses only the ANB Business account register. You will tell Quicken to limit the report preparation to the business account register since this is the account from which you write your payroll checks. Thus, all the information concerning John Smith's earnings are included in this account.

Starting from the Main Menu of the ANB Business account register, complete the following steps to gather information to complete John Smith's W-2 form:

12

1. Select **C**reate Reports.
2. Select **B**usiness Reports.
3. Select Pa**y**roll Report.
4. Type **Payroll Report-John Smith**. Press ⌨Spacebar to clear any remaining characters, and press ⌨Enter.
5. Type **1/93** and press ⌨Enter.
6. Type **12/93** and press ⌨F9 (Filter). The Filter Transactions window appears.

Notice that Quicken automatically limits all Payroll reports to Payroll category transactions, as shown by the line "Category contains: PAYROLL.." Earlier in the chapter, it was noted that this feature of Quicken requires you to record all payroll activity in the Payroll category. Otherwise, Quicken's Payroll report will not gather your payroll transactions in this report. In that case, you would need to prepare your reports from the Summary Report option.

7. Type **John Smith**, delete the remaining characters, and press ⌨Ctrl-⌨Enter until you are returned to the Payroll Report window. If Quicken returns you to the Select Account to Include Window, check to see that all are "included". If not, press ⌨Spacebar to include all the accounts.

You have filtered the Quicken report so that it will include only the payroll information for John Smith.

8. Press ⌨F7 (Layout) for the Create Summary Report window.
9. Press ⌨Enter five times, type **C**, and press ⌨Enter. The Payroll report appears on your screen.

This restricts the report preparation to the ANB Business account, on which all payroll checks were written.

10. Press ⌨Ctrl-⌨P, and the Print Report window appears.
11. Select the appropriate setting for your printer and press ⌨Enter.

The Payroll report shown in Figure 12-12 provides the payroll history for John Smith in 1993. Although you have not entered the entire

```
                        Payroll Report-John Smith
                         1/ 1/93 Through 12/31/93
        BUSINESS-ANB Business                                        Page 1
        9/ 6/93


                        Category Description        John Smith
        ----------------------------------- --------------------
             INCOME/EXPENSE
                EXPENSES
                   Payroll transaction:
                      Company FICA contribution       372.00
                      Company Medicare contrib          87.00
                      Compensation to employee       6,000.00
                                                    ----------
                   Total Payroll transaction                       6,459.00
                                                                  ----------
                TOTAL EXPENSES                                     6,459.00


                                                                  ----------
             TOTAL INCOME/EXPENSE                                 -6,459.00


             TRANSFERS
                FROM Payroll-FICA                                    744.00
                FROM Payroll-FWH                                     696.00
                FROM Payroll-MCARE                                   174.00
                FROM Payroll-SWHOH                                   164.61
                                                                  ----------
             TOTAL TRANSFERS                                       1,778.61


                                                                  ----------
             OVERALL TOTAL                                        -4,680.39
                                                                  ==========
```

Annual Payroll
report for John
Smith
Figure 12-12.

year's payroll transactions for Mary McFaul, the same steps would
generate her W-2 information as well.

Report Discussion

12

The payroll report can be used to complete John Smith's W-2 Wage and
Tax Statement:

✦ Gross Earnings is the amount ($6000) reported on the
   Compensation to employee line of the payroll report.

◆ Federal Withholding is the amount ($696.00) reported on the Transfers from Payroll-FWH line of the payroll report.

◆ FICA Withholding is one half the amount ($372.00) on the Transfers from Payroll-FICA line. Notice this is equal to the company FICA contribution since the company matches employee FICA contributions dollar for dollar up to $55,500 of gross earnings.

◆ Medicare Withholding is one half of the amount ($87.00) shown on the Transfers from Payroll-MCARE line. Notice that this is equal to the company Medicare contributions since the company matches the employee's Medicare contribution dollar for dollar up to the first $130,200 of gross earnings.

◆ State Withholding is the amount ($164.61) reported on the Transfer from Payroll-SWHOH line of the report.

◆ Local Withholding shows the local withholding taxes, although there were none in this example. If you do business in an area where local income taxes are withheld, you need to add the appropriate liability accounts to accumulate this information.

Other Annual Tax Forms and Reports

The information provided in the preceding reports can also be used to prepare other year-end tax reports. For example, Payroll reports for the full year, similar to those shown in Figures 12-9 and 12-12, can be used to complete sections of the following reports:

◆ Form W-3, Transmittal of Income and Tax Statements

◆ Form 940, Employer's Annual Federal Unemployment (FUTA) Tax Return

◆ Various state and local withholding and state unemployment tax (SUTA) reports

FUTA and SUTA Contributions

In the "Recording April Transactions" section you recorded entries on 4/15/93 for your FUTA and SUTA contributions. When completing your quarterly and annual reports, you can use Quicken's Filter option to prepare a report showing the total FUTA and SUTA contributions paid during the quarter or year. This would be accomplished by preparing a Summary report and using Quicken's Filter Transactions

```
                              FUTA Payments
                         1/ 1/93 Through 4/30/93
   BUSINESS-ANB Business                                          Page 1
   9/ 6/93
                                                      1/ 1/93-
                       Category Description           4/30/93
   ------------------------------------------ ----------------
   INCOME/EXPENSE
     EXPENSES
       Payroll transaction:
         Company FUTA contribution        104.00
                                        --------
       Total Payroll transaction                   104.00
                                                 --------
     TOTAL EXPENSES                                104.00

                                                 --------
   TOTAL INCOME/EXPENSE                          -104.00
                                                 ========
```

Report showing FUTA payments
Figure 12-13.

window to complete the category matches: Payroll:Comp FUTA. Then prepare a second report and complete the category matches: Payroll:Comp SUI. Figures 12-13 and 12-14 show filtered reports

```
                              SUTA Payments
                         1/ 1/93 Through 4/30/93
   BUSINESS-ANB Business                                          Page 1
   9/ 6/93
                                                      1/ 1/93-
                       Category Description           4/30/93
   ------------------------------------------ ----------------
   INCOME/EXPENSE
     EXPENSES
       Payroll transaction:
         Company SUI contribution         520.00
                                        --------
       Total Payroll transaction                   520.00
                                                 --------
     TOTAL EXPENSES                                520.00

                                                 --------
   TOTAL INCOME/EXPENSE                          -520.00
                                                 ========
```

Report showing SUTA payments
Figure 12-14.

12

prepared from your account register to show FUTA payments of $104.00 and SUTA payments of $520.00.

Reports filtered in this manner can be prepared to determine the total federal and state payments for unemployment withholding during the entire year. That information could then be used in completing Part II, line 4 of federal Form 940 and the corresponding line of your state's SUTA form.

Form 1099

The last payroll-related statement discussed here is Form 1099. You must provide a Form 1099 to all individuals who are not regular employees and to whom you have paid more than $600.00 during the tax year. The easiest way to record transactions for payments of this nature is to type **1099** in the Memo field when you record the transactions in your business account register during the year. You can then prepare a Transaction report for the year filtered by Payee and Memo field matches to gather the information needed to prepare 1099s for each payee. If you are not certain of all the payees to whom you have paid miscellaneous income, you may want to filter the Memo field for 1099 first and print all these transactions. You can then use that information to group your 1099 information by Payee matches. You could also assign all 1099 payments to a category (for example, Consult-1099) and screen a Summary or Transaction report by payee and category to accumulate the necessary 1099 information.

CHAPTER

13

PREPARING BUDGET REPORTS AND CASH FLOW STATEMENTS

Operating a successful business involves more than just having a good product or service to sell to customers or clients; you also need to develop a financial management program that will allow your business to grow and develop. Financial management is more than just being able to prepare the basic reports your banker or other creditors request; it includes a plan of action that will show your creditors you are prepared to manage your business in a changing environment. This means you need to start considering developing a program to manage the finances of your business. Your program would consist of the following:

◆ A business plan

◆ The development of strong business relations with your banker or other creditors

◆ The use of budgets and cash flow statements to help in managing your financial resources

In order to develop a financial management program, you need a sound accounting system that will provide the financial information you need to make better management decisions. Quicken can help you generate this type of information for your business.

Developing a Financial Management Program

If you look closely at the parts of the financial management program just listed, you will notice that two of the three parts do not directly involve the accounting system. Let's take a more in-depth look at the program components.

A business plan is a well-developed concept of where your business has been and where it is going. The special section entitled "Preparing a Business Plan" highlights the key points that should be covered in a business plan. You can see that nonfinancial considerations play a major role in your business plan—that is, you need to know your product and potential market before you can begin to budget sales and cost for your business. The budget process you follow in this chapter demonstrates how budgeting and cash flow statements are prepared. More important, you will see that the decisions you make in estimating budget income and expenses come from nonfinancial considerations. In short, developing a business plan forces you to think through your business, both financially and operationally, which, in the long run, will make it easier for you to estimate the expected sales and related costs.

The importance of developing strong relations with your banker and creditors cannot be underestimated. However, a word of caution is needed here. Don't expect a bank to finance a new business for you. A good banker is going to expect you to provide a significant part of the capital needed. You might think that you wouldn't need the banker if you had the money to finance your ideas. But from the banker's perspective, it isn't good business to risk the bank's money if you aren't willing to invest your own capital. The special section entitled "Sources of Funding" shows some alternative ways of obtaining financing for your business if a bank is not a realistic source of cash. An important point to remember is that you need to maintain a strong relationship with your banker over the long term. Although you may not need a loan now, you could in the future. One way of doing this is to obtain a modest bank loan when your business is prospering. This would help strengthen the relationship you have with your bank, and then when you really need a loan, your banker will already be familiar with you and your business activities. This might make the difference between loan approval or rejection.

Preparing a Business Plan

If you have never prepared a business plan before, it can be difficult to determine what to include. Your goal should be to create a concise document that presents a realistic picture of your company, including its needs, assets, and products. Outside lenders will be especially interested in the financial history and resources of the firm and your sales projections. Be sure to include the following as you prepare your plan:

◆ A brief overview of your firm, its products, and its financing requirements. It is important to keep this short and simple.

◆ A brief history of the firm, including product successes and copyrights or patents held. Include a résumé of the firm's owners or partners.

◆ A short description of your product(s). Include information on the competition, production plans, and prices.

◆ A description of the market for the product(s) and your distribution plans.

◆ Sales and cost projections showing current capital and financing requirements.

13

The final part of the financial management program is the use of budgets and the regular monitoring of your cash flow. A budget is a plan in which you estimate the income and expenses of your business for a period of time: week, month, quarter, year, or longer. Creating a budget report requires some advance work since you enter projected amounts for each category in the budget. Quicken guides you through the budget development process to minimize the work required. Then, you can enter your income and expenses and check the status of your actual and budgeted amounts whenever you wish. You can also use your budget figures to project your business's future cash flow. This type of information is valuable in forecasting loans you may need and demonstrates to your banker that you are anticipating your financial needs. This is a sign of sound business and financial planning.

Sources of Funding

It can be difficult to secure financing for a new business even if you have a good product. Banks are often wary of lending money for a new venture unless you are willing to take the high-risk position of offering your home or other assets as collateral. Some other financing options you might consider are

+ A commercial bank loan under the Small Business Administration Loan Guarantee Program.

+ Borrowing against your life insurance policy.

+ Short-term borrowing through supplier credit extensions.

+ Finance companies.

+ Venture capitalists; you must normally give up a part of the ownership of your business with this option.

+ Small business investment enterprises.

+ For economically disadvantaged groups and minority businesses, there may be other options for public or private funding.

A cash flow report is related to your budget and allows you to look at the inflow and outflow of cash for your business. This report is valuable since it can enable you to identify problems stemming from a lack of available cash, even though your business may be highly profitable at the current time.

In this chapter, you learn how to use Quicken in the preparation of a business budget. Remember the concepts discussed here as you go through the example; you are learning more than just the procedures involved. Budgeting and cash flow statement analysis can give you and your creditors important information. Quicken provides the necessary ingredients to help you prepare a financial management program that will make you a better business manager.

In the chapter example, you prepare budget entries for several months. Transaction groups from Chapters 11 and 12 are used to expedite the entry process while providing enough transactions to get a sense of what Quicken can do. After making your entries, you will see how Quicken's standard Budget and Cash Flow reports can help you keep expenses in line with your budget.

Quicken's Budgeting Process

Quicken allows you to enter projected income and expense levels for any category or subcategory. You can enter the same projection for each month of the year or choose to change the amount allocated by month. For the business in this example, it is essential to be able to enter different budget amounts each month, especially for the projected income figures. Royalties are received at the end of each quarter, which causes some months to show a zero income in this category. Also, some other income-generating activities are seasonal and vary widely between months.

Once you have entered the budget amounts, Quicken matches your planned expenses with the actual expense entries and displays the results in a Budget report. Although there is only one entry point for budget information, Quicken can collect the actual entries from all of your bank, cash, and credit card accounts in the current file. Therefore, if you have not paid any business expenses from your personal checking account, you may want to exclude this account from the Budget report. You can do this by selecting the accounts to use with the

13

report. However, since in this example you have paid both personal and business expenses from the ANB Personal account, you cannot exclude it here. Instead, you will use the class code of B to select all business transactions when preparing reports in this chapter. You can also choose whether or not transfers between accounts should be shown in the budget. This is a toggle option; you can change its status with the **E**dit Budget Transfers option in the Budget window.

Although Quicken can take much of the work out of entering and managing your budget, it cannot prepare a budget without your projections. Once you have put together a plan, it is time to record your decisions in Quicken. You can enter Quicken's budgeting process through the Activities menu of an account register. Quicken's budgeting process will be presented in the following stages: retrieving the Set Up Budgets screen, specifying revenue amounts, moving around the Set Up Budget screen, entering expense projections, and printing the report.

Setting Up the Budget

The Set Up Budget Screen is the starting place for Quicken's budget process. You can access this screen with the Activities menu in any account register. From the ANB Business account register, follow these steps to start the budget procedure:

1. Select **A**ctivities.

2. Select Set Up **B**udgets.

Figure 13-1 shows the top portion of the Set Up Budget screen. The category descriptions are listed down the left side of the screen and the months of the year across the top. The layout of the information is similar to a spreadsheet; if you have ever used a package such as 1-2-3 or Quattro Pro, you will feel instantly familiar with the format.

Only a few of the category descriptions are shown on the screen at any time. Quicken displays the total budget inflows and outflows at the bottom of the screen and updates these totals as you make changes. The instant updating allows you to make changes to a budget amount and immediately assess the effect on budget differences.

3. Select **L**ayout.

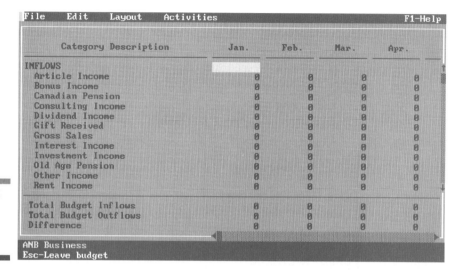

File	Edit	Layout	Activities				F1-Help

Category Description	Jan.	Feb.	Mar.	Apr.
INFLOWS				
Article Income	0	0	0	0
Bonus Income	0	0	0	0
Canadian Pension	0	0	0	0
Consulting Income	0	0	0	0
Dividend Income	0	0	0	0
Gift Received	0	0	0	0
Gross Sales	0	0	0	0
Interest Income	0	0	0	0
Investment Income	0	0	0	0
Old Age Pension	0	0	0	0
Other Income	0	0	0	0
Rent Income	0	0	0	0
Total Budget Inflows	0	0	0	0
Total Budget Outflows	0	0	0	0
Difference	0	0	0	0

ANB Business
Esc-Leave budget

Portion of Set Up Budget screen
Figure 13-1.

You can select budget periods of months, quarters, or years from the pull-down menu that appears.

4. Select **Q**uarter.
5. Select **L**ayout again, and then select **M**onth to change the time period back to the original display.

Other Budget Menu Options

You can select options from the menu at the top of your screen with either the mouse or the keyboard in the same way that you can make selections from the menu at the top of the Register window. Although you will look at many of the budget menu options in more detail in the exercises that follow, a quick overview will help you feel comfortable with this new Quicken screen.

You have already seen how you can change the time period for the budget with the **L**ayout selections of **M**onth and **Q**uarter. The other **L**ayout option allows you to look at the budget numbers on an annual basis.

The **F**ile options allow you to print a copy of the budget as well as to transfer copies of your budget layout to and from disk.

13

One **E**dit option allows you to create a budget from transactions; it is useful for creating a budget for next year from this year's transactions. Other **E**dit options allow you to enter numbers for two-week intervals, copy a number or a column across the budget layout, and control whether subcategories and transfers are shown on the budget layout.

From the **A**ctivities selection, you can return to the Register window, write checks, or use the Calculator.

Entering Revenue Projections

Entering budget projections is easy. If you want the same numbers in January through December, you will be able to enter a number for January and copy the number across to the other months. You can copy the last number entered across the row or you can copy an entire column across. After completing the copy, you can always customize entries for some of the months by typing a new number.

To set up the budget amounts for revenues, follow these steps:

1. Press ⊕ until the Jan column for Article Income contains the highlight.
2. Type **50** and then press Ctrl-→.

Quicken records 50 as the January amount and then waits for you to enter an amount for February.

3. Repeat step 2 twice more to record 50 for February and March, and then position the highlight for an April entry.
4. Type **3575** and press Ctrl-→.
5. Repeat step 4 to enter the same amount for May.
6. Type **2000** and then press Ctrl-→.
7. Type **3575** and press Ctrl-→.
8. Type **2000** and select **E**dit.

You will want to select the Edit menu before finalizing the 2000 entry, or the highlight will move to another row or column.

9. Select **F**ill Right.

Quicken automatically enters 2000 for the remaining months of the current category.

10. Move the highlight until it is on the Consulting Income for January.
11. Type **10000**, select **E**dit, and then select **F**ill Right.
12. Press ⌷End⌷ twice to move to the far right of the screen; you see the 120,000 total for Consulting Income.
13. Press ⌷Home⌷ to return to the January column.
14. Press ⌷Ctrl⌷-⌷→⌷ until you move to the July column for Consulting Income, type **12000**, and press ⌷Enter⌷.
15. Highlight the March column for Royalty Income, type **10000**, and press ⌷Ctrl⌷-⌷→⌷.
16. Repeat step 15 for the months of June, September, and December.

Moving Around the Budget Set Up Window

Before entering additional budget data, you will want to practice moving around within the budget window. After you complete the entries in the previous section, the highlight should be on the 40,000 in the Royalty Income total column. Follow these steps from that location:

1. Press ⌷Home⌷ three times.

The highlight appears at the top of your screen.

2. Press ⌷End⌷ to move to the top cell in the total column.
3. Press ⌷End⌷ again to move to the bottom of the total column.
4. Press ⌷Pg Up⌷ to move up one screen.
5. Repeat step 1 to move to the top left of the budget window.

Practice with moving on the budget window will facilitate quick entries for your data.

13

Entering Expense Projections

To complete your budget picture, you need to enter projections for
your expense categories. Using the information provided, complete the
Set Up Budgets screen for the categories. Follow these steps:

1. Enter the following amounts for the categories shown (use the Edit
   Fill Right option to enter the amounts for all budget periods):

Category	Budget Amount
Computer Supplies	210
Dues	25
Equipment Maintenance	100
Freight	20
Insurance	50
Miscellaneous	25
Office Expenses	80
Overnight Delivery	200
Payroll transaction:	
Company FICA contribution	310
Company Medicare contribution	73
Compensation to employees	5,000
Postage Expense	10
Supplies	50
Telephone Expense	120
Travel Expenses	300
Water, Gas, Electric:	
Electric Utilities	30
Gas Utilities	30

2. Press Ctrl-R after completing the last entry. You are returned to the
   ANB Business account register.

Printing the Budget Report

After entering your budget data, you can print your budget report by following these steps:

1. Return to the Register window.
2. Select **R**eports and then select B**u**dget.

The Create Budget Report window as you will complete it is shown in Figure 13-2.

3. Type **Johnson & Associates - Budget Report** and press (Enter).

You are limited to 39 characters for a customized title.

4. Type **1/1/93** and press (Enter).
5. Type **3/31/93** and press (Enter).
6. Type **6** and press (Enter).
7. Press (F9) (Filter).
8. Press (Enter) three times and then type **B**, as shown in Figure 13-3.
9. Press (Ctrl)-(Enter).
10. Press (Ctrl)-(Enter) to display the budget report on your screen.
11. Press (Ctrl)-(P), select the printer, and press (Ctrl)-(Enter). The report prints as shown in Figure 13-4. Remember you can press (Alt)-(L) and then type **E** so that cents will not be displayed on your reports.

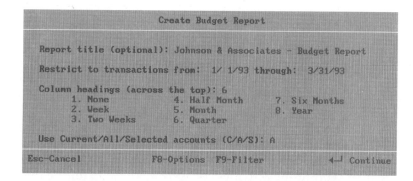

Create Budget
Report window
Figure 13-2.

13

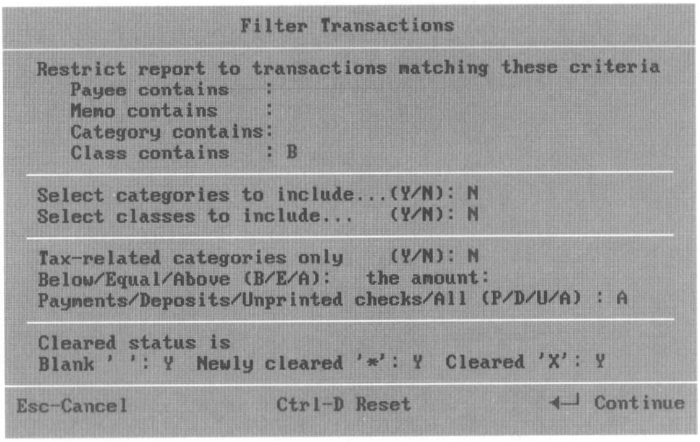

```
                          Filter Transactions

           Restrict report to transactions matching these criteria
                 Payee contains      :
                 Memo contains       :
                 Category contains:
                 Class contains      : B

           Select categories to include...(Y/N): N
           Select classes to include...    (Y/N): N

           Tax-related categories only     (Y/N): N
           Below/Equal/Above (B/E/A):    the amount:
           Payments/Deposits/Unprinted checks/All (P/D/U/A) : A

           Cleared status is
           Blank ' ': Y  Newly cleared '*': Y  Cleared 'X': Y

       Esc-Cancel              Ctrl-D Reset              ◄─┘ Continue
```

Use of a filter to
select only
business
transactions
Figure 13-3.

You can also use the "Report Options" window to tell Quicken which
categories you want displayed on your screen. If you designate "All
categories" Quicken will show the entire category list even if many of
the categories were not used for budgeting purposes (e.g., Canadian
Pension). You could also designate "Budgeted or non-zero" or "Budgeted
only" categories to be displayed. The default option is "Budgeted only"
where Quicken only displays the accounts for which budget
information was entered.

If you need to change printer settings, refer to Chapter 3, "Quicken
Reports." If your printer has compressed print capabilities, you may
want to use that setting when printing reports to capture more of your
report on each page. For example, your monthly report will be printed
across two pages unless you use the compressed print feature.

Report Discussion

Let's take a look at the report shown in Figure 13-4. The report
compares the actual expenditures made during the quarter with those
you budgeted. An analysis of the income section shows you received
more income than you budgeted during the period. This was due to
receiving more in consulting income than anticipated, although you
received no income from articles. You would want to examine whether
these differences were caused by your failing to project all the
consulting activities you were involved in during the quarter or perhaps
by a client paying you earlier than you had anticipated.

```
                    Johnson & Associates - Budget Report
                       1/ 1/93 Through 3/31/93
BUSINESS-All Accounts                                          Page 1
8/22/93
                                       1/ 1/93    -     3/31/93
              Category Description     Actual    Budget    Diff
         --------------------------------   ---------------------------
         INCOME/EXPENSE
           INCOME
               Article Income                0       150      -150
               Consulting Income        37,500    30,000     7,500
               Royalty Income           10,000    10,000       -0
                                        ---------  ---------  ---------
           TOTAL INCOME                 47,500    40,150     7,350


           EXPENSES
               Computer Supplies           376       630      -254
               Dues                          0        75       -75
               Equipment Maintenance      1,100       300       800
               Freight                       0        60       -60
               Insurance                     0       150      -150
               Miscellaneous                 0        75       -75
               Office Expenses               0       240      -240
               Overnight Delivery          270       600      -330
               Payroll transaction:
                 Company FICA contribution   930       930         0
                 Company Medicare contrib    218       219        -1
                 Compensation to employee 15,000    15,000         0
                                        ---------  ---------  ---------
               Total Payroll transaction 16,148    16,149        -1
               Postage Expense             28        30        -2
               Supplies                    65       150       -85
               Telephone Expense          305       360       -55
               Travel Expenses            905       900         5
               Water, Gas, Electric:
                 Electric Utilities         30        90       -60
                 Gas Utilities              17        90       -73
                                        ---------  ---------  ---------
               Total Water, Gas, Electric   47       180      -133
                                        ---------  ---------  ---------
           TOTAL EXPENSES              19,244    19,899      -655


                                        ---------  ---------  ---------
           TOTAL INCOME/EXPENSE        28,256    20,251     8,005
                                        =========  =========  =========
```

Budget report
for the first
quarter of 1993
Figure 13-4.

13

The expense portion of the report shows the actual and budgeted
expenses for the period. An analysis of individual categories is not

worthwhile since the data you entered did not include expense entries for all the months in the report. However, you can see that the report compares budgeted with actual expenses during the period and shows the differences in the Diff column. In general, you are concerned with all the differences shown in this report, but you will probably only want to spend your time investigating the large dollar differences between budgeted and actual amounts. For example, you might decide to investigate in detail only those budget differences that exceed $300.00. For these categories, you might want to examine the underlying transactions in more depth.

The essence of budgeting is to determine where potential problems exist in your business and detect them early. Quicken's budget reporting capabilities can help you in making these business decisions.

Modifying the Budget Report

In the early stages of budgeting, it will generally take several months to develop sound estimates for all your expense categories. You can change your projections at any time by selecting Set Up **B**udgets from the **A**ctivities menu. You can also modify the report you just created to show different time periods or a selected group of accounts. Follow these steps to look at a monthly budget report for the same time period:

1. From the ANB account register, select **R**eports and then select B**u**dget.

2. Press (Enter) three times to accept Johnson & Associates - Budget Report as the title (if the title is not shown, enter it) and 1/1/93 through 3/31/93 as the time period.

3. Type **5** and press (Enter) again. This tells Quicken you want a monthly report prepared.

4. Press (F9) (Filter).

5. Press (Enter) three times.

6. Type **B** in the Class matches field and press (Ctrl)-(Enter).

7. Type **A** to choose all accounts and press (Enter). The modified report appears on your screen.

8. Press (Ctrl)-(P) and the Print Report window opens. Select your printer and press (Ctrl)-(Enter), and the report is printed. Since this report is too wide for one page, Figure 13-5 is split across two pages.

```
                          BUDGET REPORT BY MONTH
                        1/ 1/93 Through 3/31/93
   BUSINESS-All Accounts                                          Page 1
   8/22/93
                                   1/ 1/93    -     1/31/93    2/ 1/93
            Category Description   Actual   Budget    Diff     Actual
   ----------------------------- ----------------------------- ---------
   INCOME/EXPENSE
    INCOME
       Article Income                  0        50      -50          0
       Consulting Income          12,500    10,000    2,500          0
       Royalty Income                  0         0       -0          0
                                 --------- --------- --------- ---------
    TOTAL INCOME                  12,500    10,050    2,450          0

    EXPENSES
       Computer Supplies             376       210      166          0
       Dues                            0        25      -25          0
       Equipment Maintenance       1,100       100    1,000          0
       Freight                         0        20      -20          0
       Insurance                       0        50      -50          0
       Miscellaneous                   0        25      -25          0
       Office Expenses                 0        80      -80          0
       Overnight Delivery            270       200       70          0
       Payroll transaction:
         Company FICA contribution   310       310        0        310
         Company Medicare contrib     73        73       -0         73
         Compensation to employee  5,000     5,000        0      5,000
                                 --------- --------- --------- ---------
       Total Payroll transaction   5,383     5,383       -0      5,383
       Postage Expense                28        10       18          0
       Supplies                       65        50       15          0
       Telephone Expense             305       120      185          0
       Travel Expenses               905       300      605          0
       Water, Gas, Electric:
         Electric Utilities           16        30      -14         14
         Gas Utilities                 8        30      -22          9
                                 --------- --------- --------- ---------
       Total Water, Gas, Electric     24        60      -36         23
                                 --------- --------- --------- ---------
    TOTAL EXPENSES               8,456     6,633    1,823      5,406

                                 --------- --------- --------- ---------
   TOTAL INCOME/EXPENSE           4,044     3,417      627     -5,406
                                 ========= ========= ========= =========
```

Budget Report
by Month for
the first quarter
of 1993
Figure 13-5.

13

```
                        BUDGET REPORT BY MONTH
                     1/ 1/93 Through 3/31/93
   BUSINESS-All Accounts                                        Page 2
   8/22/93
                               -      2/29/93   3/ 1/93     -
              Category Description  Budget   Diff    Actual   Budget
   ------------------------------------  -------------------  -------------------

   INCOME/EXPENSE
     INCOME
       Article Income              50      -50        0        50
       Consulting Income       10,000  -10,000   25,000    10,000
       Royalty Income               0        0   10,000    10,000
                                --------- ---------          ---------
     TOTAL INCOME              10,050  -10,050   35,000    20,050

     EXPENSES
       Computer Supplies          210     -210        0       210
       Dues                        25      -25        0        25
       Equipment Maintenance      100     -100        0       100
       Freight                     20      -20        0        20
       Insurance                   50      -50        0        50
       Miscellaneous               25      -25        0        25
       Office Expenses             80      -80        0        80
       Overnight Delivery         200     -200        0       200
       Payroll transaction:
         Company FICA contribution  310       0      310       310
         Company Medicare contrib    73      -1       73        73
         Compensation to employee 5,000       0    5,000     5,000
                                --------- --------- --------- ---------
       Total Payroll transaction 5,383      -1    5,383     5,383
       Postage Expense             10      -10        0        10
       Supplies                    50      -50        0        50
       Telephone Expense          120     -120        0       120
       Travel Expenses            300     -300        0       300
       Water, Gas, Electric:
         Electric Utilities        30      -16        0        30
         Gas Utilities             30      -21        0        30
                                --------- --------- --------- ---------
       Total Water, Gas, Electric  60      -37        0        60
                                --------- --------- --------- ---------
     TOTAL EXPENSES            6,633   -1,227    5,383     6,633

                                --------- --------- --------- ---------
   TOTAL INCOME/EXPENSE        3,417   -8,823   29,618    13,417
                                ========= ========= ========= =========
```

Budget Report by Month for the first quarter of 1993 (*continued*) Figure 13-5.

```
                          BUDGET REPORT BY MONTH
                        1/ 1/93 Through 3/31/93
    BUSINESS-All Accounts                                         Page 3
    8/22/93

                             3/31/93     1/ 1/93    -      3/31/93
         Category Description    Diff     Actual    Budget    Diff
    -----------------------------  ---------  -----------------------------
    INCOME/EXPENSE
     INCOME
         Article Income              -50         0       150      -150
         Consulting Income        15,000    37,500    30,000     7,500
         Royalty Income                0    10,000    10,000        -0
                                 ---------  ---------  ---------  ---------
     TOTAL INCOME                 14,950    47,500    40,150     7,350

     EXPENSES
         Computer Supplies          -210       376       630      -254
         Dues                        -25         0        75       -75
         Equipment Maintenance      -100     1,100       300       800
         Freight                     -20         0        60       -60
         Insurance                   -50         0       150      -150
         Miscellaneous               -25         0        75       -75
         Office Expenses             -80         0       240      -240
         Overnight Delivery         -200       270       600      -330
         Payroll transaction:
            Company FICA contribution   0       930       930         0
            Company Medicare contrib    -1       218       219        -1
            Compensation to employee     0    15,000    15,000         0
                                 ---------  ---------  ---------  ---------
         Total Payroll transaction    -1    16,148    16,149        -1
         Postage Expense             -10        28        30        -2
         Supplies                    -50        65       150       -85
         Telephone Expense          -120       305       360       -55
         Travel Expenses            -300       905       900         5
         Water, Gas, Electric:
            Electric Utilities        -30        30        90       -60
            Gas Utilities             -30        17        90       -73
                                 ---------  ---------  ---------  ---------
         Total Water, Gas, Electric  -60        47       180      -133
                                 ---------  ---------  ---------  ---------
     TOTAL EXPENSES              -1,251    19,244    19,898      -655

                                 ---------  ---------  ---------  ---------
    TOTAL INCOME/EXPENSE         16,201    28,256    20,251     8,005
                                 =========  =========  =========  =========
```

Budget Report
by Month for
the first quarter
of 1993
(*continued*)
Figure 13-5.

13

Budget Report Extension

The reports prepared so far in this chapter give you an overview of the budget report preparation process by comparing budget to actual expenditures for the first quarter of 1993. For your own situation, you need to extend the budget over a longer period. It is impractical to enter transactions for all of the included categories at this time, but you can still look at a report for a year, with budget and actual amounts shown monthly. To try working with a larger report, follow these steps from the Main Menu:

1. Select **C**reate Reports and then B**u**dget, and the Create Budget Report window opens.

2. Press [Enter] to accept the current report title.

3. Type **1/1/93** and press [Enter].

4. Type **12/31/93** and press [Enter].

5. Type **5** to select Month for column headings and press [Enter].

6. Press [F9] (Filter).

7. Press [Enter] three times.

8. Type **B** in the Class matches field and press [Ctrl]-[Enter] to have Quicken select only business transactions.

9. Type **A** and press [Enter].

The Budget Report by Month appears. Although there are no actual figures beyond the first few months, the instructions in the next section will show you how to look at a wide report like this on screen.

Wide-Screen Reports

The Monthly Budget report just generated spreads across more than one Quicken screen since it is wider than the screen width of 80 columns. It may be difficult to comprehend until you realize how it is structured. In this section, you explore the wide-screen report and become more familiar with Quicken results. The following discussion will help you become familiar with the Monthly Budget report generated from the additional data you entered.

Use Tab, Shift-Tab, Pg Up, Pg Dn, Home, and End to navigate through the report and become familiar with the appearance of the wide screen for the budget report. Notice how easy it is to move around the report. Pressing Home twice returns you to the upper-left side of the wide-screen report; Pressing End twice takes you to the lower-right side of the report. Tab moves you right one column, and Shift-Tab moves you left one column. Pg Up moves you up, and Pg Dn down, one screen. Note that to open the Print Report window, you only have to press Ctrl-P.

If you have the compressed print option, it is recommended you use that setting to print wide reports. This printer option significantly increases the amount of material you can print on a page. When you print wide-screen reports, Quicken numbers the pages of the report so you can more easily follow on hard copy.

Preparing a Cash Flow Report

Quicken's Cash Flow report organizes your account information by cash inflow and outflow. In this example, the results presented will be the same as the amounts in the budget. In Chapter 14, "Organizing Tax Information and Other Year-End Needs," you are introduced to depreciation expense, which would be shown on the budget report but not on the Cash Flow report. This is because this expense does not require a cash outlay in the current year. Prepare a Cash Flow report for the first quarter by following these steps:

1. From the Main Menu select Create Reports.
2. Select Business Reports.
3. Select Cash Flow.
4. Press Enter to accept the default report title.
5. Type 1/93 and press Enter.
6. Type 3/93.

13

7. Press F7 (Layout) to open the Create Summary Report window.

8. Press F8 (Options) to open the Report Options window.

Notice that the Report Organization, option 2, is selected for Cash Flow Basis and that Transfers, option 3, is selected to include only transfers to accounts outside this report. Quicken selected these options by default when you selected the Cash Flow report. Notice that you can also select whether you want to display cents or subcategories and subclasses in your report.

9. Press Ctrl-Enter to accept the current settings.

10. Press F9 (Filter) to open the Filter Report Transactions window.

11. Press Enter three times.

12. Type **B** in the Class matches field to restrict the report to business transactions.

This step is essential; you will need to include both ANB Personal and ANB Business in this report because business expenses were paid from both accounts. If you didn't restrict the class to business, all of the personal expenses included in ANB Personal would appear on the report as well.

13. Press Ctrl-Enter.

14. Press Enter five times to move to the Use Current/All/Selected Accounts field.

15. Type **S** and press Enter. The Select Accounts to Include window appears.

16. Move the arrow cursor to Payroll-FICA and press Spacebar until Include appears in the Include in Report field.

17. Repeat step 16 until your screen appears the same as the one in Figure 13-6.

Equipment is excluded because Quicken does not show transfers between accounts included in the Cash Flow report. However, since the purchase of equipment involved the use of cash funds, that amount

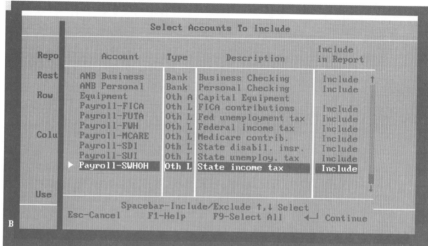

should be shown as a cash outflow. Quicken will show this as an outflow to the Equipment account on this report.

18. Press [Enter] to create the Cash Flow report. Quicken displays the report shown in Figure 13-7.

Remember, you can remove the cents shown on this report by pressing [Alt]-[L] and then **E** when the report is shown on your screen.

Notice that this report shows the entire amount of payroll ($15,000.00) as a cash outflow, even though you have not paid the entire amount of federal and state withholding to the governmental agencies at the end of the period. This is caused by Quicken's assumption that transfers between accounts included in the report are cash outflows. If you want to eliminate these amounts from the report you can re-create the report with only the ANB Personal and ANB Business accounts included. However, since the liability exists for the withheld amounts, the Cash Flow report shown in Figure 13-7 is a conservative approach to presenting the cash flow.

13

```
                         Cash Flow Report
                    1/ 1/93 Through 3/31/93
BUSINESS-Selected Accounts                              Page 1
8/22/93
                                            1/ 1/93-
             Category Description           3/31/93
--------------------------------- ----------------

INFLOWS
   Consulting Income                         37,500
   Royalty Income                            10,000
                                            -------
TOTAL INFLOWS                                47,500

OUTFLOWS
   Computer Supplies                            376
   Equipment Maintenance                      1,100
   Overnight Delivery                           270
   Payroll transaction:
     Company FICA contribution        930
     Company Medicare contrib         218
     Compensation to employee      15,000
                                   -------
   Total Payroll transaction                 16,148
   Postage Expense                              28
   Supplies                                     65
   Telephone Expense                           305
   Travel Expenses                             905
   Water, Gas, Electric:
     Electric Utilities               30
     Gas Utilities                    17
                                   -------
   Total Water, Gas, Electric                    47
   TO Equipment                               1,500
                                            -------
TOTAL OUTFLOWS                               20,744

                                            -------
OVERALL TOTAL                                26,756
                                            ========
```

Cash Flow
report for the
first quarter of
1993
Figure 13-7.

CHAPTER

14

ORGANIZING TAX INFORMATION AND OTHER YEAR-END NEEDS

For the small-business owner, it seems as though tax time is always just around the corner. If it is not time to file one of the payroll tax forms, it is time to file quarterly tax estimates or year-end tax returns. Just as Quicken lent assistance with payroll tax forms in Chapter 12, "Quicken's Payroll Assistance," it can save a significant amount of time and effort when you are preparing income tax returns.

In this chapter, you see how Quicken can be used to gather information to complete the tax forms for your business-related activities. You are introduced to the concept of depreciation and how it affects business profits. You learn how to use Quicken to prepare your Schedule C, Profit or Loss from Business statements (see Figure 14-1). You can also use Quicken features to help you prepare for recording the following year's transactions.

Depreciation

Depreciation is an expense recorded at the end of the tax year (or any accounting period). The concept of depreciation can be confusing since it does not follow the same rules as other expenses. Depreciation does not require a cash expenditure in the current year; you are recognizing a part of a cash outflow that occurred in a prior year when you record depreciation expense. Tax rules do not allow you to recognize the full cost as an expense in the earlier tax year because the resource is used in business for many tax years. For example, resources such as a truck or piece of machinery are not expensed in the year purchased since they benefit the business over a number of years. Purchases such as paper, on the other hand, would be consumed in the year purchased and their entire cost would be recognized in that tax year.

A basic definition of depreciation is that it is a portion of the original cost of an asset charged as an expense to a tax period. For the example developed in this section, suppose you purchased computer hardware that is used in your business. This is an asset of your business that will help generate revenues in the current and future tax years. You may think the cost of the equipment you purchased should be charged to your business in the year you paid for it, just as other cash expenses apply to the year paid. This seems fair since the purchase involved a significant cash outflow for the year. Unfortunately, from an accounting or tax perspective, the purchase of a piece of equipment is an acquisition that will affect your business operations over a number of years and thus cannot be expensed or deducted from revenues only in the year of purchase. The cost of the asset must be expensed over the years that it is expected to generate business revenues. For this reason, accountants and the Internal Revenue Service require that you apply the concept of depreciation when you prepare your Schedule C, Profit

SCHEDULE C (Form 1040)

Department of the Treasury
Internal Revenue Service (0)

Profit or Loss From Business

(Sole Proprietorship)

► Partnerships, joint ventures, etc., must file Form 1065.

► Attach to Form 1040 or Form 1041. ► See Instructions for Schedule C (Form 1040).

OMB No. 1545-0074

1991

Attachment Sequence No. 09

Name of proprietor | Social security number (SSN)

A Principal business or profession, including product or service (see instructions) | **B** Enter principal business code (from page 2) ►

C Business name | **D** Employer ID number (Not SSN)

E Business address (including suite or room no.) ►
City, town or post office, state, and ZIP code

F Accounting method: (1) ☐ Cash (2) ☐ Accrual (3) ☐ Other (specify) ►

G Method(s) used to value closing inventory: (1) ☐ Cost (2) ☐ Lower of cost or market (3) ☐ Other (attach explanation) (4) ☐ Does not apply (if checked, skip line H) | Yes | No

H Was there any change in determining quantities, costs, or valuations between opening and closing inventory? (If "Yes," attach explanation.)

I Did you "materially participate" in the operation of this business during 1991? (If "No," see instructions for limitations on losses.)

J If this is the first Schedule C filed for this business, check here ► ☐

Part I Income

1 Gross receipts or sales. **Caution:** If this income was reported to you on Form W-2 and the "Statutory employee" box on that form was checked, see the instructions and check here ► ☐	**1**	47,500 00
2 Returns and allowances	**2**	
3 Subtract line 2 from line 1	**3**	47,500 00
4 Cost of goods sold (from line 40 on page 2)	**4**	
5 Subtract line 4 from line 3 and enter the **gross profit** here	**5**	
6 Other income, including Federal and state gasoline or fuel tax credit or refund (see instructions)	**6**	
7 Add lines 5 and 6. This is your **gross income** ►	**7**	47,500 00

Part II Expenses (Caution: Enter expenses for business use of your home on line 30.)

8 Advertising	**8**		21 Repairs and maintenance	**21**	1,100 00
9 Bad debts from sales or services (see instructions)	**9**		22 Supplies (not included in Part III)	**22**	440 76
10 Car and truck expenses (see instructions—also attach **Form 4562**)	**10**		23 Taxes and licenses	**23**	1,147 00
11 Commissions and fees	**11**		24 Travel, meals, and entertainment:		
12 Depletion	**12**		a Travel	**24a**	905 00
13 Depreciation and section 179 expense deduction (not included in Part III) (see instructions)	**13**	275 00	b Meals and entertainment		
14 Employee benefit programs (other than on line 19)	**14**		c Enter 20% of line 24b subject to limitations (see instructions)		
15 Insurance (other than health)	**15**		d Subtract line 24c from line 24b	**24d**	
16 Interest:			25 Utilities	**25**	352 40
a Mortgage (paid to banks, etc.)	**16a**		26 Wages (less jobs credit)	**26**	15,000 00
b Other	**16b**		27a Other expenses (list type and amount):		
17 Legal and professional services	**17**		298.25		
18 Office expense	**18**				
19 Pension and profit-sharing plans	**19**				
20 Rent or lease (see instructions):					
a Vehicles, machinery, and equipment	**20a**				
b Other business property	**20b**		27b Total other expenses	**27b**	298 25
28 Add amounts in columns for lines 8 through 27b. These are your **total expenses** before expenses for business use of your home ►	**28**	19,518 91
29 Tentative profit (loss). Subtract line 28 from line 7	**29**	
30 Expenses for business use of your home (attach **Form 8829**)	**30**	
31 **Net profit or (loss).** Subtract line 30 from line 29. If a profit, enter here and on Form 1040, line 12. Also enter the net profit on Schedule SE, line 2 (statutory employees, see instructions). If a loss, you MUST go on to line 32 (fiduciaries, see instructions)	**31**	27,981 09

32 If you have a loss, you MUST check the box that describes your investment in this activity (see instructions)	**32a** ☐ All investment is at risk.
If you checked 32a, enter the loss on Form 1040, line 12, and Schedule SE, line 2 (statutory employees, see instructions). If you checked 32b, you MUST attach **Form 6198.**	**32b** ☐ Some investment is not at risk.

For Paperwork Reduction Act Notice, see Form 1040 instructions. | Cat. No. 11334P | Schedule C (Form 1040) 1991

Schedule C
Figure 14-1.

14

or Loss from Business statements. However, in the section "Section 179 Property" later in this chapter, you will see that there is one important exception to the requirement that you depreciate your long-lived assets.

You can depreciate only assets that lose their productivity as you use them in your business activity. For example, you cannot record depreciation on the land where your building stands. Even though you may feel your land has lost value in recent years, you cannot recognize this decline until you sell the land. Thus, equipment is an example of a *depreciable asset* while land is not. Throughout this chapter and on income tax forms, you will see the term "depreciable" assets used. This means assets that have a life longer than one year and that will benefit business operations in several accounting periods.

Depreciation Terminology

There are several terms pertaining to depreciation that need to be discussed in more depth. You must always depreciate the original cost of an asset. *Original cost* is the total cost of the asset. For example, if you purchased a piece of machinery and paid shipping charges and sales tax, these additional costs are considered to be associated with getting the asset into an income-producing condition and are therefore part of the original cost. The screen in Figure 14-2 shows the Equipment account register after recording the transactions in Chapter 11, "Setting

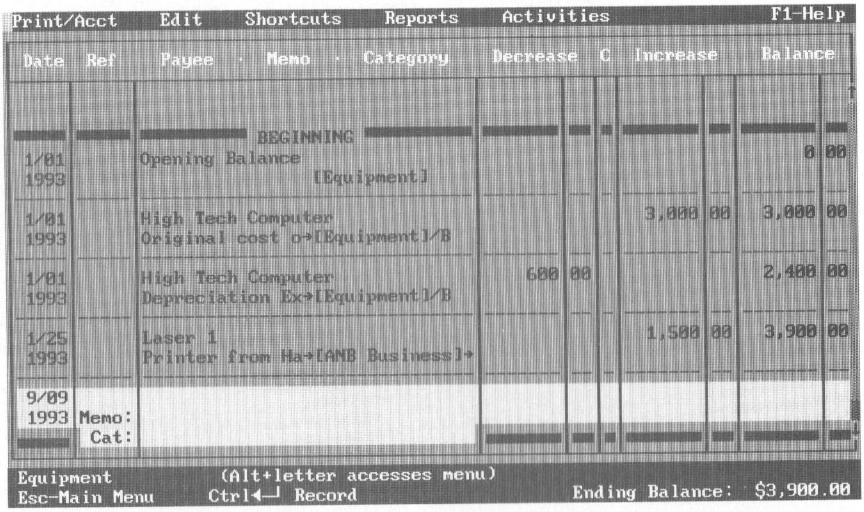

Equipment
Account
Register
window
Figure 14-2.

Up Quicken for Your Business." The first transaction recorded in the register shows the original cost of the High Tech Computer, $3000.00. The printer purchase on 1/25/93 is recorded at its original cost of $1500.00.

In Chapter 9, "Determining Your Net Worth," you learned to revalue personal assets to market value. You cannot do this with business assets. If your asset increases in value, you cannot recognize this increase in your Quicken system. You must always *carry* (show on your business accounting records) your business assets at their original cost.

Another important term is *accumulated depreciation*. This is the amount of depreciation you have recorded for an asset in all previous years. Your assets will always be shown on the balance sheet at original cost minus accumulated depreciation. For example, for the $3000.00 High Tech Computer asset, you recorded depreciation expense of $600.00 in the previous year. You have an accumulated depreciation of $600.00 from the previous year so your asset carrying value is $2400.00 before recording this year's depreciation.

Establishing Accounts for Assets

You probably will establish another asset account for each major type of depreciable asset used in your business. You would follow the same procedures used in Chapter 11, "Setting Up Quicken for Your Business," to set up the Equipment account. If you have equipment, office furniture, and buildings that you use in your business, including the portion of your home used exclusively for business purposes, you will depreciate the original cost of each of the assets. On the other hand, you may decide to establish a separate account for each asset if you have few depreciable assets. Quicken's default limit on the number of accounts in the system is 64, although you can increase this to up to 255 given sufficient memory and disk space. In the example, you learn how to depreciate more than one asset in an account.

NOTE: Quicken provides a shortcut for switching between accounts that you use frequently. Use the Select Account to Use window, and edit the account for which you want a shortcut. Select a number from 1 to 9. Activate the account when you need it by pressing Ctrl in combination with the number that you assigned it.

Depreciation Methods

The straight-line method of depreciation described in the next section is appropriate for income tax purposes. However, for the most part, you will probably use the modified accelerated cost recovery system (MACRS) and the accelerated cost recovery system (ACRS) methods of determining your depreciation amounts. Generally speaking, MACRS covers tangible assets put into business use after December 31, 1986, and ACRS covers tangible assets put into place after December 31, 1980. *Tangible assets* are property that can be felt and touched. All the assets mentioned in our discussion (equipment, office furniture, and buildings) would fit this description.

The reason most taxpayers use MACRS is that the method builds in a higher level of depreciation deductions in the early years of an asset's life than would be calculated using the straight-line method of depreciation. Consult IRS Publication 534 before computing your depreciation on tangible assets.

Straight-line Depreciation Method

In this example, you use the straight-line method to record depreciation on an asset. *Straight-line depreciation* expenses the cost of the asset evenly over the life of the asset. For example, the High Tech Computer has a useful life of five years, and you recorded depreciation expense at $600.00 in 1992. Since this method does not attempt to recognize more depreciation in the early years of an asset's life, it is always acceptable to the IRS. Many other depreciation methods can be used and may be more favorable since they recognize greater depreciation in the early years of the asset's life. IRS Publication 534 lists the many rules that apply to the selection of a depreciation method. One of the considerations that determines the depreciation method chosen is the year in which you placed the asset in service. A rule that applies to all types of depreciation is that once you select a method of depreciation for an asset, you cannot change to another depreciation method. Table 14-1 lists some of the other depreciation methods. You will need to check with your accountant or check IRS Publication 534 for specific rulings on which methods you can use.

When using the straight-line method of depreciating an asset, use the following formula:

$$\frac{\text{original cost} - \text{salvage value}}{\text{useful life of asset}}$$

The original cost of depreciable assets has already been discussed; however, "salvage value" is a new term. *Salvage value* is the amount of cash you expect to recover when you dispose of your depreciable asset. This is, obviously, always an estimate and in the case of a computer not easily estimated due to rapid changes in the computer field. For this reason, many accountants assign a salvage value of zero to this type of asset, stating in effect that it will have no value at the end of its estimated life. This is also the assumption made in the entries recorded here. When you record salvage values for your assets, you can use the history of similar assets when estimating depreciation. If equipment that is five years old typically sells for 20 percent of its original cost, that would be a good estimate for the salvage value of a piece of equipment with an estimated life of five years bought today.

Method	Description
ACRS	The Accelerated Cost Recovery System is an accelerated depreciation method that can be used for assets placed in service after December 31, 1980, and before December 31, 1986.
Declining-balance	This method allows the deduction of depreciation expense at a faster rate than straight-line. There are several different percentages used in computing this type of depreciation. One acceptable option is 150 percent of straight-line depreciation.
MACRS	The Modified Accelerated Cost Recovery System is an accelerated depreciation method used for assets placed in service after December 31, 1986.
Straight-line	This method is the easiest to compute since the cost of the asset is depreciated evenly over the life of the asset. It is also the least advantageous to the business owner since it does not accelerate depreciation expense in the early years of the asset's life.

Depreciation
Methods
Table 14-1.

14

Depreciation Calculation

The amounts used in the depreciation entries in this chapter were determined by the calculations shown here:

High Tech Computer:

$$\frac{\$3000.00 \text{ (original cost)} - 0 \text{ (salvage value)}}{5 \text{ years (useful life)}} = \$600.00 \text{ depreciation per year}$$

Laser printer:

$$\frac{\$1500.00 \text{ (original cost)} - 0 \text{ (salvage value)}}{3 \text{ years (useful life)}} = \$500.00 \text{ depreciation per year}$$

Depreciation is generally recorded only once, at the end of the year, unless you need financial statements prepared for a bank or other third party during the year. The amounts calculated in this example are the annual depreciation expenses for the computer and printer—the amounts you would use to record depreciation for the year ending 12/31/93. (Note that even though the printer was acquired at the end of January, it is acceptable to record a full year's depreciation on the asset since the difference between 11 and 12 months' worth of depreciation is so small that it would not be considered to have a material effect.)

In the examples developed in Chapters 11 and 13, the account register transactions have been limited to the first quarter of the year. (In Chapter 12, you completed several April 1993 entries in order to see the complete process of payroll accounting.) Since there is not a full year of expense entries, you can compute the depreciation on the computer and printer for just the first quarter of 1993. This is accomplished by dividing both annual amounts of depreciation by 4. Thus, the first quarter's depreciation charges that you will record are

High Tech Computer:

$$\frac{\$600.00 \text{ (annual depreciation)}}{4 \text{ (quarters)}} = \$150.00 \text{ depreciation for first quarter, 1993}$$

Laser printer:

$$\frac{\$500.00 \text{ (annual depreciation)}}{4 \text{ (quarters)}} = \$125.00 \text{ depreciation for first quarter, 1993}$$

Now that you are familiar with the method used to record depreciation in the example and how the amounts you will record were determined, you are ready to begin recording the depreciation entry in your account register.

Establishing Depreciation Categories

Before recording the depreciation entries in this chapter, you establish a Depreciation category with Computer and Printer subcategories in your category list. Select the Equipment account from the BUSINESS file, open the account register, and follow these steps:

1. Press Ctrl-C to open the Category and Transfer List window.
2. Press Home to move to <New Category>.
3. Press Enter to open the Set Up Category window.
4. Type **Depreciation** and press Enter.
5. Press Enter to accept E.
6. Type **Depreciation Expense** and press Enter.
7. Type **Y** and press F9 (Tax Schedules).
8. Select Schedule C.
9. Select Other Business expense.
10. Select Copy:1.
11. Press Enter.
12. Highlight the Depreciation category.
13. Press Ctrl-Ins.
14. Type **Computer** and press Enter.
15. Type **S** and press Enter.
16. Type **Depreciation-Computer** and press Enter.
17. Type **Y** and press F9 (Tax Schedules).
18. Select Schedule C.
19. Select Other Business expense.
20. Select Copy:1.
21. Press Enter.

22. Highlight the Depreciation category and press [Ctrl]-[Ins].

23. Type **Printer** and press [Enter].

24. Type **S** and press [Enter].

25. Type **Depreciation-Printer** and press [Enter].

26. Type **Y** and press [F9] (Tax Schedules).

27. Select Schedule C.

28. Select Other Business expense.

29. Select Copy:1.

30. Press [Enter].

31. Press [Esc] to return to the register.

You can now begin recording your depreciation expense transactions.

Depreciation Expense Transactions

Let's record the depreciation on the assets in your Quicken account. Starting from the next blank transaction form in the Equipment account register (Figure 14-2) in the BUSINESS file.

You may want to deactivate Quicken 6's QuickFill option (Set Preferences, Transaction Settings and type **N** for the QuickFill setting in option #8, press [Enter] twice, and then press [Esc] until the Main Menu appears) before entering transactions. Otherwise, Quicken will prompt you with proposed transactions for each payee and you will need to edit these entries. Although QuickFill may actually cause you some extra work if you do not deactivate it, you can still use the information in the steps provided to edit the transactions that QuickFill generates.

1. Type **3/31/93** and press [Enter] twice.

Notice that no check numbers are recorded in this register since all checks are written against the business checking account.

2. Type **High Tech Computer** and press [Enter].

3. Type **150** and press [Enter].

4. Type **Depreciation-1993** and press [Enter].

5. Type **Depreciation:Computer/B** and press [Ctrl]-[Enter].

You have just recorded the depreciation expense on the computer for the months January through March of 1993. The remaining steps record depreciation on the laser printer you acquired in January.

6. Type **3/31/93** in the Date field and press Enter twice.
7. Type **Laser 1** and press Enter.
8. Type **125** and press Enter.
9. Type **Depreciation-1993** and press Enter.
10. Type **Depreciation:Printer/B** and press Ctrl-Enter.

These register entries show how your depreciation transactions will appear after you record both of them:

3/31 1993	High Tech Computer Depreciation-19→Depreciation:C→	150 00		3,750 00
3/31 1993	Laser 1 Depreciation-19→Depreciation:P→	125 00		3,625 00

This completes the depreciation transaction entry for the first quarter of 1993. Remember, depreciation is normally recorded only at year end. However, for purposes of this example, we have prepared the entries at the end of the first quarter.

Customized Equipment Report

After recording the depreciation transactions in the Equipment account, you will want to look at a customized Equipment report. This report, which you will prepare shortly, summarizes all the activity in the account. Figure 14-3 shows the Equipment report for your business since 1/1/93. Notice that the report shows the depreciation expense taken during the first quarter for both the computer and the printer, as well as the total for the category. You can also see that there was a transfer of $1500.00 from business checking for the purchase of the printer in January.

Finally, you can see that the balance forward amount of $2400.00 is the $3000.00 original cost of the asset minus the $600.00 accumulated depreciation taken in the prior year. Thus, when you prepare a balance

14

sheet in Chapter 15, "Monitoring Financial Conditions," the equipment asset will total $3625.00.

If you want to produce the Equipment report, follow these steps starting from the Equipment account register:

1. Select the **R**eports pull-down menu item.
2. Select **S**ummary, and the Create Summary Report window appears.

```
                          Equipment Report
                      1/ 1/93 Through 3/31/93
   BUSINESS-Equipment                                        Page 1
   8/24/93
                                                  1/ 1/93-
                      Category Description        3/31/93
              ------------------------------   --------------------

              INCOME/EXPENSE
                 EXPENSES
                    Depreciation Expense:
                       Depreciation-Computer       150.00
                       Depreciation-Printer        125.00
                                                ----------
                    Total Depreciation Expense               275.00
                                                           ----------
                 TOTAL EXPENSES                              275.00


                                                           ----------
                 TOTAL INCOME/EXPENSE                       -275.00


                 TRANSFERS
                    FROM ANB Business                       1,500.00
                                                           ----------
                 TOTAL TRANSFERS                            1,500.00


                 BALANCE FORWARD
                    Equipment                               2,400.00
                                                           ----------
                 TOTAL BALANCE FORWARD                      2,400.00


                                                           ----------
                 OVERALL TOTAL                              3,625.00
                                                           ==========
```

Equipment
report
Figure 14-3.

3. Type **Equipment Report** and press [Enter].
4. Type **1/1/93** and press [Enter].
5. Type **3/31/93** and press [Enter].
6. Press [Enter] to accept option 1 for the Row Headings field.
7. Type **1** and press [Enter] to select Don't Subtotal for the column headings.
8. Type **C** and press [Enter].
9. Press [Ctrl]-[P], and the Print Report window appears.
10. Select the printer you are using and press [Enter].

Depreciation and the IRS

The transactions in this chapter record depreciation using the straight-line method to determine the amounts for the entries. This method was demonstrated to cover the recording process without going into too much detail about IRS rules for determining depreciation expense for tax purposes. However, we need to briefly discuss one additional aspect of deducting the cost of long-lived assets for IRS purposes, section 179 property. You should obtain IRS Publication 534 (free upon request) before making decisions concerning the amount of depreciation you will charge against income on your tax return.

Section 179 Property

Many small businesses will be interested in the type of property called *section 179 property*. Here, certain capital expenditures are treated as deductions in the current year rather than depreciating the cost of the asset over its life. Buildings, air conditioning units, and structural components of a building do not qualify as section 179 property. For a complete list of qualified property and the specific rules that apply, consult IRS Publication 534.

Under section 179 of the Internal Revenue Service code, you can deduct up to $10,000.00 of the cost of property in the current tax year. In this chapter, you would have been able to deduct the entire cost of the laser printer this year against your business income and not depreciate the asset in future years.

14

Schedule C, Profit or Loss from Business

Schedule C is the tax form sole proprietorships use when reporting
business income and expenses during the year. Quicken can be used to
provide the information you need to complete your form. If you
examine Schedule C (Figure 14-1), you see that it is a business profit
and loss statement. This statement can be prepared from the Quicken
Reports menu.

Starting from the Main Menu for the ANB Business account register in
the BUSINESS account group, complete the following steps:

1. Select **C**reate Reports.
2. Select **B**usiness Reports.
3. Select P & L **S**tatement.
4. Press `Enter` to accept the default title.
5. Type **1/93** and press `Enter`.
6. Type **3/93** and press `F9` (Filter).
7. Press `Tab` three times to move the cursor to the Class contains: row.
8. Type **B** and press `Ctrl`-`Enter`. You are returned to the Profit and Loss
   Statement window.
9. Press `Enter`, and the Profit and Loss statement appears on your
   screen.
10. Press `Ctrl`-`P` and the Print Report window appears.
11. Select the printer and press `Enter`.

The Profit and Loss statement is shown in Figure 14-4.

Completing Schedule C

With Quicken's Profit and Loss statement you can now complete the
appropriate lines of the federal tax form Schedule C. Because Schedule
C is basically just a profit and loss statement, many of the entries can
be obtained directly from your Quicken report. The following is a list of
line numbers and how you can complete them in Schedule C.

✦ *Line 1* This line shows gross sales. The total income ($47,500.00)
   shown on your report would be placed on this line.

```
                        PROFIT & LOSS STATEMENT
                        1/ 1/93 Through 3/31/93
    BUSINESS-All Accounts                                         Page 1
    8/24/93

                                                  1/ 1/93-
                  Category Description            3/31/93
    ------------------------------------    --------------------

    INCOME/EXPENSE
      INCOME
          Consulting Income                             37,500.00
          Royalty Income                                10,000.00
                                                      -----------
      TOTAL INCOME                                      47,500.00


      EXPENSES
        Computer Supplies                                  375.76
        Depreciation Expense:
          Depreciation-Computer            150.00
          Depreciation-Printer             125.00
                                         -----------
        Total Depreciation Expense                         275.00
        Equipment Maintenance                            1,100.00
        Overnight Delivery                                 270.00
        Payroll transaction:
          Company FICA contribution        930.00
          Company Medicare contrib         217.50
          Compensation to employee      15,000.00
                                         -----------
        Total Payroll transaction                       16,147.50
        Postage Expense                                     28.25
        Supplies                                            65.00
        Telephone Expense                                  305.00
        Travel Expenses                                    905.00
        Water, Gas, Electric:
            Electric Utilities            30.40
            Gas Utilities                 17.00
                                         -----------
          Total Water, Gas, Electric                        47.40
                                                       -----------
      TOTAL EXPENSES                                     19,518.91


                                                       -----------
      TOTAL INCOME/EXPENSE                               27,981.09
                                                       ===========
```

Profit and Loss
statement
Figure 14-4.

14

◆ *Line 13* This section shows depreciation and section 179 deduction from Form 4562, Depreciation and Amortization. The depreciation expense ($275.00) would be entered here.

◆ *Line 21* This line shows repairs. The amount you show for Equipment Maintenance ($1100.00) would be entered here.

◆ *Line 22* This line shows the total of all your business supplies. You would add the amounts shown for Computer Supplies ($375.76) and Supplies ($65.00) by using the Calculator and enter the total ($440.76) here.

◆ *Line 23* This line shows taxes. The amounts shown as Payroll Company FICA and Company Medicare Contributions ($1147.50) would be entered here.

◆ *Line 24a* This line shows the total amount of your business travel. The amount of Travel Expense ($905.00) would be entered here. This assumes that all these expenses are associated with travel and not meals or entertainment. You can establish separate categories for these items in your Quicken Category and Transfer list.

◆ *Line 25* The total for utilities and telephone is placed on this line. You would use the calculator to add the amounts shown for Telephone Expense ($305.00) and Water, Gas, and Electric ($47.40) and record the total expense as $352.40.

◆ *Line 26* This line shows the total wages paid. You would enter the amount shown as Gross Earnings ($15,000.00).

◆ *Line 27a* This line shows your other business expenses. You would add the amounts shown for Postage Expense ($28.25) and Overnight Delivery ($270.00) and show the total ($298.25) as Misc Exp in this section.

◆ *Line 28* This line shows your total deductions. This is the amount of Total Expense ($19,518.91).

◆ *Line 29* This line shows your net profit (or loss). This is the amount of net profit $27,981.09.

NOTE: You can round the cents to the nearest dollar when completing your tax forms.

After completing this exercise, you can see there are many alternatives for establishing classes to help in gathering your tax information. Remember, one of the constraints faced in this example was that you were recording business expenses in both personal and business checking accounts. However, this example could be modified to use subclasses to designate lines on the different tax forms when recording your entries. This would allow you to capture the information by form and line number.

Other Business-Related Tax Forms

When you completed line 13, Depreciation, you used the Total Depreciation Expense amount from your Profit and Loss statement. This information must be included on Form 4562, Depreciation and Amortization. After reading through Publication 534, you would have entered the appropriate amounts for section 179 property and ACRS or MACRS depreciation. This results in a total of $275.00, shown on line 20 of Form 4562 and transferred to line 13 on Schedule C.

As a sole proprietor, you also need to complete Schedule SE, Social Security Self-Employment Tax. The net profit from your Schedule C, $27,981.09, would be carried to line 2 of that form, and the rest of the form can be easily completed. See the special "Year-end Business Tax Forms" section for a list of important tax forms for the small-business owner.

Year-End Activities

You are not required to take any special actions at the end of the year to continue to use Quicken. The package allows you to select transactions by date if you want to purge some of the older transactions from your file. Unless you need the disk space or begin to notice sluggish response time from your system, you should plan on keeping at least three years of historical information in your file. You may find it convenient to be able to print historical reports for comparison with this year's results.

To copy accounts, categories, classes, and other information to a new file, you need to use the Set Preferences option from the Main Menu. You can then decide how far back to go in copying transactions to the new file. You can also remove uncleared transactions from an earlier date from this file.

The following steps explain how to copy the BUSINESS file you have been using since Chapter 11. Starting from the Main Menu in the ANB Business account register in the BUSINESS file, complete these steps:

1. From the Main Menu, select Set Preferences.

Year-End Business Tax Forms

Form	Title
Sole Proprietorship	
Schedule C (Form 1040)	Profit or Loss from Business
Form 4562	Depreciation and Amortization
Schedule SE (Form 1040)	Social Security Self-Employment Tax
Form 1040-ES	Estimated Tax for Individuals
Partnership	
Form 1065	U.S. Partnership Return of Income
Schedule D (Form 1065)	Capital Gains and Losses
Schedule K-1 (Form 1065)	Partner's Share of Income, Credits, Deduction, etc.
Corporations	
Form 1120-A	U.S. Corporation Short-Form Income Tax Return
Form 1120	U.S. Corporation Income Tax Return
Form 1120S	U.S. Income Tax Return for an S Corporation

2. Choose **F**ile Activities.

3. Select **C**opy File, and the Copy File window, shown in Figure 14-5, appears.

4. Press ⟨F9⟩ (Set Number of Accts), and the Set Maximum Accounts in File window appears.

Quicken will automatically copy up to 64 accounts from the selected file to a backup disk or another location on your hard disk. This number can be increased up to 255 accounts if needed. In this example, the predefined limit is more than enough to cover your needs. If you did need to increase the number of accounts to copy, you would type the desired number and press ⟨Enter⟩.

5. Press ⟨Esc⟩, and Quicken returns you to the Copy File window.

6. Type **Acct93** and press ⟨Enter⟩. This is the name of the new file.

7. Type a new directory location or press ⟨Enter⟩ to accept the existing location.

8. Type **1/1/93** and press ⟨Enter⟩.

9. Type **4/15/93** and press ⟨Enter⟩.

You have now defined all the transactions between 1/1/93 and 4/15/93 as those you want to transfer to the new file.

10. Type **Y** and press ⟨Enter⟩.

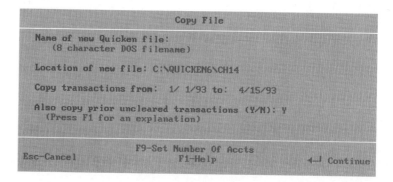

Copy File
window
Figure 14-5.

This command tells Quicken to copy all uncleared transactions from the period prior to 1/1/93. This means that any checks that clear your bank after the year-end will be included in your account register for reconciliation purposes.

11. Type **1** to tell Quicken to use the original file, and you are returned to the Main Menu.

If you were really ready to begin recording transactions in the next accounting period in the ACCT93 file, you would type **2** instead to use the new file.

CHAPTER

15

MONITORING FINANCIAL CONDITIONS

You have already seen that you can prepare financial statements with Quicken's report features. In previous chapters, you created a Profit and Loss statement, a Cash Flow report, and an Equipment report. You can use these reports to monitor the financial condition of your firm and to see how your business has performed over a period of time. These reports not only help you assess the success you've had in managing the business, but they can also be used by outsiders for the same purpose. Bankers and other creditors review your financial statements to determine whether to make loans to your business. Quicken can prove a valuable tool in preparing loan applications or, as you saw in earlier chapters, in providing information to other users of financial statements, such as the Internal Revenue Service.

In this chapter, a final major financial statement, the balance sheet, is presented. The balance sheet provides the reader with a snapshot of the financial resources and obligations of your business. Although the profit and loss statement, the Cash Flow report, and the balance sheet have been introduced separately, they are interrelated. Bankers and other readers will review these statements as a package when assessing the past and projecting the future success of your business.

The Balance Sheet

The balance sheet shows your business assets, liabilities, and equity or investment at a specific date. Remember, assets are things of value that are used in your business to generate revenue. Cash, for example, is an asset that is used to acquire other assets, such as supplies and labor, which are then used to generate revenue.

Liabilities are the obligations incurred as part of your business operations. If you borrow from the bank, this is a financial obligation. This obligation is shown as a liability on your balance sheet.

Owner's equity is the amount of personal resources you have invested in the business. In the example you've been working on in the preceding chapters, you opened your business checking with a $4000.00 deposit and put $2400.00 of equipment in the Equipment account ($3000.00 original cost – $600.00 of accumulated depreciation). This $6400.00 is the amount of your personal assets invested in the business and is your owner's equity at the beginning of the year. Bankers and other creditors are interested in your equity in the business. If you are asking for a loan, they will want to know how much of your own financial resources you are risking. This is measured by your equity in your business, as well as by any other personal assets you may be willing to offer as collateral.

Before you prepare a balance sheet, there are two concepts that need to be covered. First, the balance sheet is prepared at a specific date.

15

Quicken asks you to define the time period you want to use in preparing your balance sheet. For example, you will define the period 1/1/93 to 3/31/93 in this chapter's example; you are telling Quicken to prepare the balance sheet using transactions in that time period. The resulting printed balance sheet will show the balances in your business accounts on 3/31/93.

The second important concept is that the profit and loss statement and the balance sheet are related. While the balance sheet shows your assets, liabilities, and equity at a specific date, the profit and loss statement gives the detail of changes in your assets, liabilities, and equity between two balance sheets. Remember these two concepts as you prepare the balance sheets in this chapter: the balance sheet is prepared at a specific date and the profit and loss statement helps explain how assets, liabilities, and equity changed between two balance sheets. In the examples that follow, you see how the profit and loss statement demonstrates how changes in owner's equity occurred between 1/1/93 and 3/31/93.

Creating a Balance Sheet

In this section, you prepare a Balance Sheet as of 3/31/93 from the transactions you entered in the BUSINESS file in previous chapters. This report will show the assets, liabilities, and owner's equity of the business at the end of the quarter. Starting from the Main Menu of the ANB Business account register in the BUSINESS file, follow these steps:

1. Select **C**reate Reports.
2. Select **B**usiness Reports.
3. Select **B**alance Sheet.
4. Press F7 (Layout) to open the Create Account Balances Report window.
5. Press Enter to accept the default report title.
6. Type **1/1/93** and press Enter.
7. Type **3/31/93** and press Enter.
8. Press Enter to accept the default report interval, None.
9. Press F9 (Filter), and the Filter Transactions window appears.
10. Press Enter three times to move to the Class contains field.

11. Type **B** and press `Ctrl`-`Enter` to return to the Create Account Balances Report window.

12. Press `Enter` to accept A for all in the Current/All/Selected accounts field. The balance sheet appears on your screen.

13. Press `Ctrl`-`P`, and the Print Report window appears.

14. Select the desired printer and press `Enter`. Your balance sheet looks like the one in Figure 15-1.

Balance Sheet Discussion

The total of the Cash and Bank accounts is $32,612.54. This consists of the amount shown in your ANB Business checking account on 3/31/93 ($32,735.70) less $123.16. The deduction is the amount of cash used from your personal checking account to cover business expenses. (Remember that you wrote several personal checks and charged a portion of the cost to business by using the /B class entry.) These amounts were included in the Profit and Loss statement prepared in the previous chapter and the Cash Flow report in Chapter 13, "Preparing Budget Reports and Cash Flow Statements." Thus, Quicken is adjusting your business cash by the amount of expenses paid from your personal accounts. The importance of this is discussed shortly.

You can also see that the equipment is carried at a balance of $3625.00. The carrying value of depreciable assets was discussed in Chapter 14, "Organizing Tax Information and Other Year-End Needs." The Equipment report produced there shows the underlying transactions that explain the carrying value on this report.

The total assets are the resources available to your business on the date of the report. These resources are used to generate future income.

The liabilities shown are all related to the payroll prepared on 3/31/93. You owe the federal and state governments $1856.45 for withholding and social security tax payments. On 4/1/93, you made a deposit with your bank for all the federal government payroll liabilities. However, this did not affect the balance sheet prepared on 3/31/93. The payroll taxes were liabilities on the date the statement was prepared, even though the deposit on 4/1/93 will reduce your total liabilities by $1379. Likewise, the state withholding liability will remain on the balance sheet until you make a deposit to the state.

```
                          Balance Sheet
                          As of 3/31/93
BUSINESS-All Accounts                                       Page 1
8/24/93

                                                    3/31/93
                              Acct                  Balance
      ------------------------------------  -----------
      ASSETS

         Cash and Bank Accounts
            ANB Business                            32,735.70
            ANB Personal                              -123.16
                                                -----------
         Total Cash and Bank Accounts              32,612.54

         Other Assets
            Equipment                                3,625.00
                                                -----------
         Total Other Assets                          3,625.00


                                                -----------
      TOTAL ASSETS                                  36,237.54
                                                ===========
      LIABILITIES & EQUITY

         LIABILITIES
            Other Liabilities
               Payroll-FICA                            620.00
               Payroll-FWH                             614.00
               Payroll-MCARE                           145.00
               Payroll-SWHOH                           477.45
                                                -----------
            Total Other Liabilities                  1,856.45


                                                -----------
         TOTAL LIABILITIES                           1,856.45

         EQUITY                                     34,381.09
                                                -----------
      TOTAL LIABILITIES & EQUITY                    36,237.54
                                                ===========
```

Balance Sheet
as of 3/31/93
Figure 15-1.

The difference between the total assets of the business and the total liabilities is the owner's equity in the business. In this case you have $34,381.09 of your equity invested in the business. Thus, the balance sheet presented shows that most of the assets used in the business were contributed by you, with only $1856.45 outstanding to creditors.

Creating Comparative Balance Sheets

In this section, you will see how Quicken's profit and loss statement helps explain the changes that occur between two balance sheets. First, you will prepare a comparative Balance Sheet; then the relationship with the Profit and Loss statement will be discussed. Starting from the Main Menu of the ANB Business account register in the BUSINESS file, follow these steps:

1. Select **C**reate Reports.
2. Select **B**usiness Reports.
3. Select **B**alance Sheet.
4. Press F7 (Layout) to open the Create Account Balances Report window.
5. Press Enter to accept the default report title.
6. Type **1/1/93** and press Enter.
7. Type **3/31/93** and press Enter.
8. Type **6** to select Quarter for the report interval and press Enter. This entry will cause Quicken to create a comparative balance sheet, with account balances shown at the beginning and the end of the quarter.

NOTE: Quicken will only prepare quarterly reports for periods beginning on the first of January, April, July, and October—that is, you cannot prepare a quarterly report for the three months beginning February 1.

9. Press F9 (Filter); the Filter Transactions window appears.
10. Press Enter three times to move to the Class contains field.
11. Type **B** and press Ctrl-Enter to return to the Create Account Balances Report window.

12. Press Enter to accept A for All in the Current/All/Selected accounts field. The Balance Sheet appears on your screen.

13. Press Ctrl-P, and the Print Report window appears.

14. Select your printer and press Enter. Your report will look like that shown in Figure 15-2.

Comparative Balance Sheet Discussion

The comparative Balance Sheet prepared in this section shows the balances of the business on 1/1/93 and 3/31/93 side by side. You can see that the assets of the business on 1/1/93 consisted of the $4000.00 initial deposit made to the business checking account and the $2400.00 carrying value ($3,000.00 – $600.00) of the High Tech computer recorded in the Equipment account on 1/1/93. Thus, the total assets were $6400.00. There were no liabilities at that time so the owner's equity is the $6400.00 shown as the overall total.

The question you should be asking now is, "What is the cause of the changes in assets, liabilities, and equity between these two balance sheet dates?"

The change in assets is caused by the increase in cash, which is explained in the Cash Flow report. In Chapter 13, you prepared a Cash Flow report (see Figure 13-7) for which you selected all accounts except Equipment in the preparation of the report. Remember that this was a conservative approach to the preparation of the report since federal and state withholding was included as a cash transfer, even though the deposit for these liabilities was not made until 4/1/93. In order for your Cash Flow report to accurately reflect cash transactions for the period 1/1/93 through 3/31/93 you would need to re-create the report using only the ANB Personal and ANB Business accounts. Figure 15-3 shows how the recreated report would appear. This is important since it shows the connection between the amounts in the Cash and Bank Accounts sections of the comparative Balance Sheet, as shown in Figure 15-2. There is a change of $28,612.54 in the total cash balance between 1/1/93 and 3/31/93, which equals the overall total or the amount of the net cash flow shown in Figure 15-3. If you were presenting financial reports to a banker, you would want to use the Cash Flow report prepared in this chapter. If you were using the report for internal purposes, the one prepared in Chapter 13 would be satisfactory and the more conservative of the two.

```
                          Balance Sheet
                          As of 3/31/93
BUSINESS-All Accounts                                          Page 1
8/24/93
                                            1/ 1/93    3/31/93
                              Acct          Balance    Balance
-------------------------------------- ----------- -----------

ASSETS

   Cash and Bank Accounts
      ANB Business                         4,000.00  32,735.70
      ANB Personal                             0.00    -123.16
                                       ----------- -----------
   Total Cash and Bank Accounts            4,000.00  32,612.54

   Other Assets
      Equipment                            2,400.00   3,625.00
                                       ----------- -----------
   Total Other Assets                      2,400.00   3,625.00


                                       ----------- -----------
   TOTAL ASSETS                            6,400.00  36,237.54
                                       =========== ===========

LIABILITIES & EQUITY

   LIABILITIES
      Other Liabilities
         Payroll-FICA                          0.00     620.00
         Payroll-FWH                           0.00     614.00
         Payroll-MCARE                         0.00     145.00
         Payroll-SWHOH                         0.00     477.45
                                       ----------- -----------
      Total Other Liabilities                  0.00   1,856.45


                                       ----------- -----------
   TOTAL LIABILITIES                           0.00   1,856.45

   EQUITY                                  6,400.00  34,381.09
                                       ----------- -----------
   TOTAL LIABILITIES & EQUITY            6,400.00  36,237.54
                                       =========== ===========
```

Comparative
Balance Sheet
as of 3/31/93
Figure 15-2.

The increase in the Equipment account is explained by examining
the Equipment report prepared in Chapter 14, and the changes in the

```
                          Cash Flow Report
                    1/ 1/93 Through 3/31/93
BUSINESS-Selected Accounts                                  Page 1
8/24/93

                                            1/ 1/93-
              Category Description           3/31/93
    ----------------------------------- -----------------------
    INFLOWS
       Consulting Income                         37,500.00
       Royalty Income                            10,000.00
       FROM Payroll-FICA                          1,860.00
       FROM Payroll-FWH                           1,842.00
       FROM Payroll-MCARE                           435.00
       FROM Payroll-SWHOH                           477.45
                                               -----------
    TOTAL INFLOWS                                52,114.45

    OUTFLOWS
       Computer Supplies                            375.76
       Equipment Maintenance                      1,100.00
       Overnight Delivery                           270.00
       Payroll transaction:
          Company FICA contribution     930.00
          Company Medicare contrib      217.50
          Compensation to employee   15,000.00
                                      -----------
       Total Payroll transaction                 16,147.50
       Postage Expense                               28.25
       Supplies                                      65.00
       Telephone Expense                            305.00
       Travel Expenses                              905.00
       Water, Gas, Electric:
          Electric Utilities            30.40
          Gas Utilities                 17.00
                                      -----------
       Total Water, Gas, Electric                    47.40
       TO Equipment                               1,500.00
       TO Payroll-FICA                             1,240.00
       TO Payroll-FWH                              1,228.00
       TO Payroll-MCARE                              290.00
                                               -----------
    TOTAL OUTFLOWS                                23,501.91


                                               -----------
    OVERALL TOTAL                                28,612.54
                                               ===========
```

Cash Flow
report
Figure 15-3.

liabilities are clearly related to the payroll withholdings you owe on 3/31/93.

The owner's equity (investment) in the business is the difference between the total assets and total liabilities of the business. As just noted, the owner's equity on 1/1/93 was $6400.00, while the owner's equity on 3/31/93 is $34,381.09. Let's look at the $27,981.09 change in the owner's equity. This change can be explained by examining the Profit and Loss statement prepared in Chapter 14, shown in Figure 15-4.

The Profit and Loss statement covers a period of time, in this example the first quarter of 1993. You can see that the net profit (total income–total expenses) is $27,981.09. This is equal to the change in the owner's equity between the two balance sheet dates. Thus, the net profit or loss of a business helps explain changes that occur between balance sheets from the beginning and end of the profit and loss period.

One final point to note is that the number –123.16 shown on the 3/31/93 Balance Sheet appears because you entered business expense transactions in your personal checking account. Although this is not recommended, it is not uncommon for small-business owners to encounter this situation. You must remember that the $123.16 is included in the Profit and Loss statement as a business expense; thus, the reported net profit was reduced by that amount. Since cash was used for the payment, Quicken is telling you that the use of personal funds has reduced the total assets associated with your business activities.

NOTE: Although Quicken can handle the payment of business expenses out of both business and personal checking accounts, it is better to limit business expense payments to your business checking account. If the nature of your business necessitates the payment of expenses in cash rather than from a checking account, you would probably find it useful to establish a Quicken cash account for your business and use it in combination with your business checking account to record payment of business expenses with personal cash.

15

```
                         Profit & Loss Statement
                         1/ 1/93 Through 3/31/93
BUSINESS-All Accounts                                          Page 1
8/24/93

                                              1/ 1/93-
              Category Description            3/31/93
------------------------------------- ----------------------
INCOME/EXPENSE
  INCOME
    Consulting Income                        37,500.00
    Royalty Income                           10,000.00
                                             -----------
  TOTAL INCOME                               47,500.00

  EXPENSES
    Computer Supplies                           375.76
    Depreciation Expense:
      Depreciation-Computer          150.00
      Depreciation-Printer           125.00
                                     -----------
    Total Depreciation Expense                  275.00
    Equipment Maintenance                     1,100.00
    Overnight Delivery                          270.00
    Payroll transaction:
      Company FICA contribution      930.00
      Company Medicare contrib       217.50
      Compensation to employee    15,000.00
                                     -----------
    Total Payroll transaction               16,147.50
    Postage Expense                             28.25
    Supplies                                    65.00
    Telephone Expense                          305.00
    Travel Expenses                            905.00
    Water, Gas, Electric:
      Electric Utilities              30.40
      Gas Utilities                   17.00
                                     -----------
    Total Water, Gas, Electric                  47.40
                                             -----------
  TOTAL EXPENSES                             19,518.91

                                             -----------
  TOTAL INCOME/EXPENSE                       27,981.09
                                             ===========
```

Profit and Loss statement for the period ending 3/31/93 **Figure 15-4.**

Sole Proprietor Withdrawals from the Business

So far in the example, you have not spent any of the cash generated from your business for personal use. In accounting, it is called a *withdrawal,* or simply *draw,* when sole proprietors take cash or other assets out of the business for personal use. Obviously, these are not business expenses, so the profit and loss statement is not affected. On the other hand, you are reducing the assets of the business when you transfer cash from your business to your personal checking account.

In this section you will see how owner withdrawals affect the balance sheet of the business. Starting from the Main Menu in the ANB Business account register, follow these steps to record your withdrawal of cash from the business checking account:

1. Select Use **R**egister and press Ctrl-End to move to the end of the account register.

2. Press Shift-Tab if you are not in the Date field.

3. Type **3/31/93** and press Enter twice.

The cash withdrawal is being handled as a transfer between your business and personal checking accounts. Just as it is not good practice to pay business expenses from a personal checking account, neither should you use business checks to pay for personal expenditures.

4. Type **Mr. Johnson** and press Enter.

The payee name matches the name of the business owner since it is a withdrawal.

5. Type **5000** and press Enter.

6. Type **Transfer - Withdraw** and press Enter.

7. Press Ctrl-C to open the Category and Transfer List window.

8. Press End to move to the end of the list.

9. Move the arrow cursor up to [ANB Personal] and press Enter.

10. Type **/B** after [ANB Personal] in the Category field and press Ctrl-Enter.

15

The class designation indicates to Quicken that this transaction will affect the business checking account balance. This transaction appears in your ANB Business account register after recording the transaction as shown here:

```
3/31         Mr. Johnson                    5,000 00              27,735 70
1993 Memo: Transfer - Withdraw
      Cat: [ANB Personal]/B
```

11. Press `Ctrl`-`X` to view the transaction in the ANB Personal register after highlighting the transaction you just entered.

12. Press `Tab` to move to the Memo field.

13. Type **Withdraw from business** and press `Ctrl`-`Enter`.

    This is an important step in the recording of the transaction. This memo is used to describe all withdrawals from the business, so it can later be used as a filter in preparing the Balance Sheet. Here is how this transaction appears in your ANB Personal account register after it is recorded:

```
3/31         Mr. Johnson                              5,000 00   7,061 00
1993 Memo: Withdraw from business
      Cat: [ANB Business]/B
```

14. With the withdrawal transaction highlighted, press `Ctrl`-`X` to return to the ANB Business register.

15. Press `Esc` to return to the Main Menu.

Balance Sheet After an Owner's Withdrawal of Capital

Now that you have recorded your owner's withdrawal, let's take a look at the balance sheet of the business. Follow these steps from the Main Menu of the ANB Business account:

1. Select **C**reate Reports.

2. Select **B**usiness Reports.

3. Select **B**alance Sheet.

4. Press [F7] (Layout) to open the Create Account Balances Report window.

5. Press [Enter] to accept the default report title.

6. Type **1/1/93** and press [Enter].

7. Type **3/31/93** and press [Enter].

8. Type **6** to select Quarter for the report interval and press [Enter]. This entry will cause Quicken to create a comparative Balance Sheet with balances shown for the beginning and the end of the quarter.

9. Press [F9] (Filter), and the Filter Transactions window appears. Figure 15-5 shows how the window appears when completed.

10. Press [Enter] to move to the Memo contains field.

11. Type **~Withdraw** and press [Enter] twice.

12. Type **B** in the Class contains field and press [Ctrl]-[Enter] to return to the Create Account Balances Report window.

13. Press [Enter] to accept A for all in the Current/All/Selected accounts field. The Balance Sheet appears on your screen.

14. Press [Ctrl]-[P], and the Print Report window appears.

15. Select the printer you will be using and press [Enter]. Your Balance Sheet looks like the one in Figure 15-6.

Effects of Owner's Withdrawal

As you can see, the Balance Sheet after recording the withdrawal shows your total equity to be $29,381.09. This illustrates how the owner's

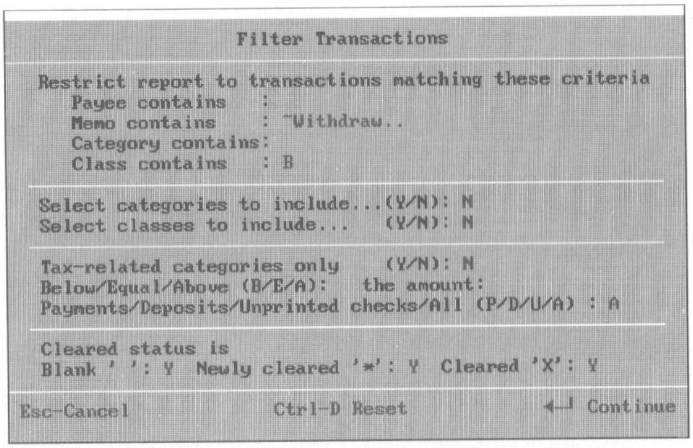

Filter Transactions window for owner withdrawals

Figure 15-5.

```
                              Balance Sheet
                              As of 3/31/93
BUSINESS-All Accounts                                            Page 1
8/24/93

                                              1/ 1/93      3/31/93
                               Acct           Balance      Balance
          -------------------------------- ----------- -----------
          ASSETS

             Cash and Bank Accounts
               ANB Business                    4,000.00    27,735.70
               ANB Personal                        0.00      -123.16
                                            ----------- -----------
             Total Cash and Bank Accounts      4,000.00    27,612.54

             Other Assets
               Equipment                       2,400.00     3,625.00
                                            ----------- -----------
             Total Other Assets                2,400.00     3,625.00

                                            ----------- -----------
          TOTAL ASSETS                         6,400.00    31,237.54
                                            =========== ===========
          LIABILITIES & EQUITY

             LIABILITIES
               Other Liabilities
                 Payroll-FICA                      0.00       620.00
                 Payroll-FWH                       0.00       614.00
                 Payroll-MCARE                     0.00       145.00
                 Payroll-SWHOH                     0.00       477.45
                                            ----------- -----------
               Total Other Liabilities            0.00     1,856.45

                                            ----------- -----------
             TOTAL LIABILITIES                    0.00     1,856.45

             EQUITY                            6,400.00    29,381.09
                                            ----------- -----------
          TOTAL LIABILITIES & EQUITY           6,400.00    31,237.54
                                            =========== ===========
```

Comparative
Balance Sheet
after recording
owner's
withdrawal
Figure 15-6.

equity in the business is affected not only by net profits and losses, but
also by owner withdrawals of equity. You also know that an investment
of additional cash or assets in the business increases the owner's equity.

This occurred on 1/1/93 when you invested cash and equipment in setting up the business. Thus, the owner's equity change between the two balance sheets is accounted for by adding the net profits for the period to the beginning owner's equity and then reducing it by withdrawals ($6,400.00 + $27,981.09 - $5,000.00 = $29,381.09).

Quicken Graphs

Now that you have prepared reports for your business data, you will want to learn how to graph this data. Quicken will display graphs of income and expenses, net worth, budget and actual figures, and investments. In this section you will prepare an asset composition pie graph. From the Main Menu follow these steps:

1. Select View **G**raphs.

2. Select **N**et Worth.

Quicken provides six different net worth graph options: **M**onthly Assets and Liabilities, Mo**n**thly Assets less Liabilities, **A**sset Composition, Asset **T**rend, **L**iability Composition, and L**i**ability Trend.

3. Select **A**sset Composition, type **3/31/93**, press Enter, and type **Y**.

Notice there is an option for F9 (Filter) to allow you to filter the data used in the graph. Although you will not use it in this example, it works just like the filter option you have used for reports in earlier chapters.

4. Press Enter, and Quicken displays the Asset Composition graph shown in Figure 15-7.

If you have not used the graph feature before, Quicken prompts you with a Select Graphics Driver window and a Graphics Driver Options window. Both have been preset during installation of Quicken for your machine. Unless you need to make changes, just press Enter until the graph appears.

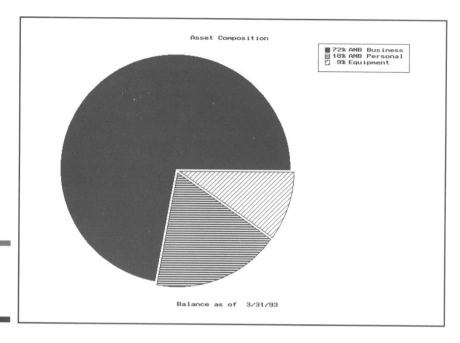

The Asset
Composition
graph
Figure 15-7.

This graph shows that your business bank account constitutes 72
percent of your total assets, your personal bank account 18 percent, and
business equipment constitutes 9 percent of your combined business
and personal assets.

PART

4

APPENDIXES

APPENDIX

A

SPECIAL QUICKEN TASKS

Quicken is easy to install with the right equipment. The package handles most of the installation work for you.

Since the package runs on so many different systems, it is likely you have at least the minimum configuration. For the MS-DOS version of the software discussed in this book, you need an IBM PC, XT, AT, PS/2, or a compatible machine. You must have at least 512K of RAM in the machine and an 80-column monitor. You must have a hard disk with 2.6MB of available disk space. You need MS-DOS version 2.0 or later as your operating system.

Installing Quicken

Quicken is so easy to install that almost all you need to do is put the correct disks in drive A and type **A:INSTALL**. Quicken displays a few prompts during installation and expects you to respond with answers to questions such as whether or not your monitor is color. Quicken's installation program copies all the files to the hard disk.

The exact procedure will depend on whether or not you have a prior release installed on your hard disk. Quicken will assist you with the process. You should accept Quicken's suggestions, including the default location of C:\QUICKEN for your data, or if you prefer, specify a new directory such as QUICKEN6.

Starting Quicken

To start the Quicken program, make the drive containing your Quicken program active. If you are using drive C, you will expect to see the DOS prompt C>. If the wrong drive is active, type the drive letter followed by a colon and press (Enter). You also need to make the correct directory active. You can change directories by typing **CD** followed by the directory name. To activate the QUICKEN directory, you type **CD\QUICKEN** and press (Enter).

Once you have activated the Quicken drive and directory, type **Q** to start Quicken. Quicken will help you set up your first file and account as descibed in Chapter 2, "Making Register Entries."

Upgrading from an Earlier Release

If you have been using Quicken 5.0, Quicken will copy your files to work with Quicken 6. You can use all the new features with your existing data immediately.

If you are upgrading from Quicken 1, 2, or 3, you will need to contact Intuit, the developers of Quicken, for a conversion program. You will find a toll-free number at the back of your Quicken manual.

APPENDIX

B

GLOSSARY

There are various financial terms that are important to understand how Quicken supports your financial activities. A brief definition of terms used throughout this book is included here for your convenience.

Accelerated Depreciation   A method of depreciation in which more expense is recognized in the early years of an asset's life.

Account   Quicken document where personal and/or business transactions are recorded that increase or decrease the amount of money in the account. Examples include bank, cash, credit card, other assets, and other liabilities accounts.

Account Balance   The amount of money in an account.

Accounts Payable   Money owed to suppliers for goods or services.

Accounts Receivable   Money owed to you by customers or clients.

Accrual Basis   An accounting method in which income is recorded when services are provided rather than when cash is received. Expenses are treated similarly.

Accumulated Depreciation   The total amount of depreciation expense taken on an asset since the time it was placed in service.

ASCII (American Standard Code for Information Interchange)   This is a standard set of codes used for storing information. When you write information to disk with Quicken, the data is stored in ASCII format. This makes it easy to transfer the data to a word processing package or any other package that reads ASCII data.

Asset   Any item of value that a business or individual owns.

Average Annual Total Return   The average annual percent return on your investment. Interest, dividends, capital gains distributions, and unrealized gains/losses are used in computing this return on your investment.

Average Cost   The total cost of all shares divided by the total number of shares.

Balance Sheet   A financial statement that summarizes a business's assets, liabilities, and owner's equity at a specific time.

Book Value   The cost of an asset less the amount of depreciation expensed to date.

Brokerage Account   An account with a firm that buys and sells shares of stocks and other investments on your behalf.

Budget   A plan indicating projected income and expenses. Budget also refers to a comparison between the projections and actual amounts for each income or expense category.

Cash   Money or currency.

Cash Basis   A method of accounting used for business or tax purposes. Income is recorded when cash is received, and expenses are charged when cash is paid.

Cash Flows   The inflow and outflow of cash during a specific time period.

Category   Identifies the exact nature of income and expenses, such as salary income, dividend income, interest income, or wage expense. Categories are distinct from classes.

Chart of Accounts   A list of the categories used to charge income and expenses for a given account.

Class   Allows you to define the time period, location, or type of activity for a transaction. Classes are distinct from categories.

Cleared Item   An item that has been processed by the bank.

Control Codes   Special codes that can request a specific feature or function from your printer, such as compressed printing. Each manufacturer has its own unique set of codes for each printer model manufactured.

Corporation   A form of business organization that limits the liability of the shareholders.

Cost Basis   Total cost of stock bought or sold plus commission.

Current Balance   The present balance in an account. This does not include postdated items.

Deductions   Amounts that reduce the gross pay to cover taxes and other commitments, such as health insurance premiums.

Deposit   An amount of funds added to an account. A deposit is sometimes referred to as a "credit" to the account.

Depreciable Base   The cost of an asset that will be expensed over its useful life.

Depreciation   The portion of the cost of an asset that is expensed each year on a profit and loss statement.

Dividends   Cash payments made to the shareholders of a corporation from current or past earnings.

Double Entry System   An accounting method that requires two accounts to be used when recording a transaction. For example, when supplies are purchased, both the cash and supplies accounts are affected.

Equity   The amount of the owner's investment in the business. For individuals, this is the money invested in a property or other asset.

Expense   The cost of an item or service purchased or consumed.

FICA   Social security tax paid by employers and employees.

File   A group of related accounts, such as a personal checking account, a savings account, and an asset account for your home.

Financial Obligations   Commitments to pay cash or other assets in return for receiving something of value—for example, a bank loan for equipment or an automobile.

Financial Resources   Objects or property of value owned by a person or business that are expected to increase future earnings.

Financial Statements   Periodic reports prepared by businesses to show the financial condition of the firm. Major financial statements include balance sheets, profit and loss statements (income statements), and cash flow reports.

FUTA   Federal unemployment tax.

Future value   An expected value at some future point, given that today's investments appreciate at the expected rate.

FWH   Federal income tax withheld from employees' earnings.

Gross Earnings   Total earnings of an employee before deductions are subtracted.

Income   The money earned by an individual or business. On a cash basis, it is the amount of cash received for goods or services provided. On an accrual basis, it is the amount of income recognized and recorded during the year for services provided.

Income Statement   A summary of the income and expenses of a business.

IRA   Individual Retirement Account. Depending upon your income level, you may experience tax benefits from setting up an IRA.

Job/Project Report   A method of reporting revenues and expenses on a job or project basis.

Liability   The money you owe to a vendor, creditor, or any other party.

Life of an Asset   The number of years that the asset is expected to last.

Liquidity   A measure of how easy it is to convert an asset to cash.

Memorized Transaction   A transaction that you have asked Quicken to remember and recall at a later time.

Menu   A related list of commands, called "items," presented for selection. A menu is frequently used in software packages as a means of offering features to choose from.

Money Market Account   An account held with a bank or other institution used to preserve capital. Most provide limited checking account privileges.

Mutual Fund   An investment vehicle that allows you to purchase shares in the fund; the proceeds are used by the fund to buy shares in a variety of stocks or bonds.

Net Pay   The amount of pay received after deductions.

Net Worth   An amount determined by subtracting the value of financial obligations from financial resources.

P & L Statement   An abbreviation for profit and loss statement; it shows the profit or loss generated during a period.

Partnership   A form of business organization where two or more individuals share in the profits and losses of the business.

Payment   The amount paid to a vendor, creditor, or other party.

Payroll SDI   State disability insurance payments often referred to as Workman's Compensation.

Payroll Taxes   The taxes a business pays on employee earnings—for example, matching FICA contributions, federal and state unemployment taxes, and workers' compensation payments.

Point in Time   A specific time where some activity is occurring.

Postdated Transaction   A check dated after the current date.

Present value   A value in today's dollars for a sum that will not be received until a later time.

Reconciliation   The process of comparing a copy of the bank's records for your account with your own records. Any differences should be explained in this process.

Revenue   The money or income generated.

Salvage   The worth of an asset at the end of its useful life.

Security   An investment such as a stock, bond, or mutual fund.

Service Charge   A fee the bank adds for maintaining your account. This fee can be part of the difference in reconciling a bank statement.

Single Entry System   For any transaction to which only one entry is made, either to an income or expense category or to an account. An accounting method in which one account is used to record a transaction. When supplies are purchased, only the cash (or checking) account is affected.

Sole Proprietorship   The simplest form of small-business organization. There is no separation between the owner and the company.

Straight-line Depreciation   A method of expensing the cost of an asset evenly over its life.

SUTA   State unemployment tax.

SWH   State income taxes withheld from employee gross earnings.

Transaction Group   A group of memorized transactions that can be recalled together whenever you need them.

Transfer   A transaction that affects the balance in two accounts at the same time by moving funds between them.

Unrealized Gain/Loss   A gain or loss estimated on the basis of current market value.

Valuation   The current value of an asset.

B

APPENDIX

ADVANCED OPTIONS

You have had enough practice with the examples in this book to feel comfortable with basic transaction entry and report creation. You might want to think about using Quicken for some more sophisticated tasks such as managing your accounts payable and receivable or setting up job order costing. Although these sophisticated tasks can be handled with the same basic Quicken transactions that you have already mastered, the tips in this section will provide the secrets to getting them set up quickly.

Accounts Receivable

You can use Quicken to track invoicing and to record the collection of cash. To set up this accounts receivable monitoring, you will need to create a new account. Name this account to indicate that it contains accounts receivable information and set it up as an other asset account with a zero balance. When you open the account, mark the opening balance as cleared with an asterisk in the Cleared column to prevent its inclusion in reports. You will also want to set up a new category named Sales as an Income category.

As you invoice customers, you will create a transaction for each invoice in the Accounts Receivable account. The Ref field can be used for the invoice number and can be incremented with a + for each new invoice. The amount of the invoice is entered in the Increase field, since it is a credit invoice. The invoice date can be placed in the Memo field.

As customer payments are received, you will want to match them with the invoices that they cover. Highlight the matching invoice transaction and press Ctrl-S. Next, enter your business checking account for the second category, type a – and the amount of the payment in the amount field and recalculate the split transaction so it shows a zero total.

You can use the A/R by Customer Business Report to prepare an accounts receivable aging. This report will allow you to track unpaid invoices and attempt collection.

Accounts Payable

Quicken can help you manage your accounts payable by tracking amounts owed and dates due. If you buy from vendors who give a discount for timely payment, you can ensure that you pay within this time period.

You will not need a separate account for accounts payable and can enter the transaction directly into your checking account. You will record these payable when you receive the supplier's invoice but use the due date in the Date field. The other secret is using an * in the Num field and the invoice number in the Memo filed.

Since you are recording the payable transaction before the check is written, Quicken handles it as a postdated check. The current balance will not show the effect of the entry although the ending balance will.

Use Quicken Transaction report with headings by week to see which invoices will come due each week. When you make the payment, record the check number in the Num field and finalize the transaction.

Job Order Costing

The objective of a job order costing system is to record the income and costs of jobs over the time services are performed. The secret to getting it set up correctly is to create a class for each job that you must track. When you incur expenses that must be allocated to several jobs, use the split transaction to allocate the costs among the jobs and use the classes that you created within the split transaction. Likewise, income is recorded with the classes you created for each job.

You can use Quicken's Job/Project Business report to summarize income and expense by job. The date range for the report should begin with the current date and encompass the due date range that you want to review. You will want to use a filter with ~Opening.. in the Payee field to exclude the opening balance from the report.

INDEX

D

G

H

I

S

Expand Your Skills Even More

with help from our expert authors. Now that you've gained greater skills with **Quicken 6 Made Easy,** *let us suggest the following related titles that will help you use your computer to full advantage.*

Timeslips III Made Easy
by Bryan Pfaffenberger

If you're a lawyer, consultant, or anyone whose services are billed by the clock, then Timeslips III can help you track and invoice your clients easily and efficiently. With *Timeslips III Made Easy*, you'll quickly learn how to set up the expense billing strategy that best works for your business.

$19.95 ISBN: 0-07-881739-0 304 pages 7 3/8 x 9 1/4

1-2-3 Release 2.4: The Complete Reference
by Mary Campbell

Mary Campbell's ever popular reference is updated and revised to cover the newest version of Lotus 1-2-3. Every 1-2-3 feature, command, and function is fully described and accompanied by a short example of its use so you can quickly find the information you need.

$29.95, ISBN: 0-07-881853-2, 912 pages, 7 3/8 x 9 1/4

1-2-3 Release 2.4 Made Easy
by Mary Campbell

Whether you're a first-time 1-2-3 user or experienced in 1-2-3 but new to release 2.4, Lotus expert Mary Campbell takes you step-by-step from the basics to more advanced techniques so you'll build the skills you need to master the latest release of Lotus 1-2-3.

$19.95 ISBN: 0-07-881839-7, 512 pages 7 3/8 x 9 1/4

1-2-3: The Pocket Reference, Fourth Edition
by Mary Campbell
Mary Campbell's classic Pocket Reference is back and revised to cover the new Lotus 1-2-3 Release 2.4. Every important 1-2-3 command, feature, and function is listed alphabetically and briefly described with a short example to demonstrate its use.
$9.95 ISBN: 0-07-881854-0, 224 pages, 4 3/4 x 8

1-2-3 for Windows Made Easy
by Mary Campbell
Learn all about using this popular spreadsheet in the Windows graphical environment. Whether you're a first time 1-2-3 user or experienced in 1-2-3 but new to Windows, Campbell takes you through the basics one step at a time.
$19.95, ISBN: 0-07-881731-5, 385 pages, 7 3/8 x 9 1/4

1-2-3 for the Macintosh Made Easy
by Mary Campbell
Internationally recognized Lotus expert Mary Campbell, author of five best-selling editions of *1-2-3 Made Easy*, has now written another classic to cover the newest version of the Lotus 1-2-3 spreadsheet that runs on the Macintosh.
$19.95, ISBN: 0-07-881774-9, 408 pages, 7 3/8 x 9 1/4

Simply 1-2-3
by Mary Campbell
Lotus 1-2-3 beginners will welcome this quick guide to the basics of the world's most widely used spreadsheet. Filled with illustrations and computer screen displays, you'll quickly learn the basics of creating worksheets and performing calculations.
$14.95, ISBN: 0-07-881751-X 208 pages, 5 3/4 x 8 3/4
Covers All Releases of Lotus 1-2-3

Agenda 2 Made Easy
by Mary Campbell
This Made Easy book puts all the new features of Agenda Release 2.0 at your command. Lotus expert Mary Campbell, author of the acclaimed *Using Agenda*, skillfully guides you from fundamentals to more advanced features like macros and data import capabilities.
$19.95, ISBN: 0-07-881675-0, 458 pages, 7 3/8 x 9 1/4

Excel 4 for the Macintosh: Spreadsheet Strategies & Data Design
by Edward Jones
Get up and running fast with Microsoft's bestselling spreadsheet program for the Apple Macintosh. Even if you've never used a computer before, you can learn to create spreadsheets with this clearly written book. Jones also helps you create charts and work with databases.
$24.95, ISBN: 0-07-881808-7, 450 pages, 7 3/8 x 9 1/4

Excel 4 for Windows Made Easy
by Martin S. Matthews
Excel expert Matthews offers you instruction, examples, and a handy reference for all your Excel questions. It's the very best way to get a quick start with the new release 4 of Microsoft's super-spreadsheet for Windows.
$19.95, ISBN: 0-07-881807-9, 512 pages, 7 3/8 x 9 1/4

Quattro Pro 4 Made Easy
by Lisa Biow
You'll get productive results with Borland's popular spreadsheet in just a few short chapters. This step-by-step guide is packed with examples and hands-on exercises to help you master Quattro Pro 4 with minimum effort.
$19.95, ISBN: 0-07-881788-9, 722 pages, 7 3/8 x 9 1/4

Quattro Pro 4 Inside & Out
by Stephen Cobb
Here's the fast-paced guide that leads you quickly from fundamentals to advanced concepts and provides a thorough understanding of Borland's newest spreadsheet version. All the new version 4 features are discussed including the Optimizer and the Audit analysis tools.
$27.95, ISBN: 0-07-8818797-8, 912 pages, 7 3/8 x 9 1/4

Quattro Pro 4: The Pocket Reference
by James Keogh
This handy memory-jogger covers Borland International's popular spreadsheet for versions 2.0, 3.0, and the new 4.0. The book includes an alphabetical command and task reference, alphabetical @function reference, and a reference to Quattro Pro macros.
$9.95, ISBN: 0-07-881795-1, 200 pages, 4 3/4 x 8

Ami Pro Made Easy
by Daniel J. Fingerman
Get a quick start with Ami Professional, the windows-based word processing software from Lotus. After covering all the basics, Fingerman helps you master Ami Pro's exciting features including page layouts, style sheets, tables, and drawings; using the charting tool and customizing macros.
$19.95 ISBN: 0-07-881019-1 400 pages, 7 3/8 x 9 1/4

Microsoft Word 5 for the Macintosh Made Easy
by Paul Hoffman
With Paul Hoffman's outstanding Made Easy guide, you'll learn all the basics as Hoffman leads you through short hands-on exercises. All the newest features and capabilities are explained, including features for handling the new Macintosh System 7 operating system.
$19.95, ISBN: 0-07-881769-2 450 pages, 7 3/8 x 9 1/4

Microsoft Word for Windows 2 Made Easy
by Paul Hoffman
Best-selling author Paul Hoffman will quickly teach you the newest version of Microsoft Word for Windows. Plenty of hands-on examples and helpful illustrations are included to build your skills fast. You'll also explore all of the powerful features including menus, linking documents, macros, and graphics.
$19.95p ISBN: 0-07-881770-6, 303 pp., 7 3/8 X 9 1/4

Simply WordPerfect
by Kris Jamsa
If you're new to computers and WordPerfect, this book is for you. *Simply WordPerfect* is a short guide that gives you the basics of this popular word processing program in a user-friendly format, accompanied by practical illustrations.
$14.95, ISBN: 0-07-881752-8, 200 pp., 5 3/4 x 8 3/4
Covers All Releases of WordPerfect

Teach Yourself WordPerfect 5.1
by Mary Campbell
Mary Campbell is back with another timely update to the "Teach Yourself" series. Using 15-minute hands-on lessons, Campbell shows you all the basics of WordPerfect 5.1 so you can get to work fast.
$24.95, ISBN: 0-07-881666-1, 1041 pages, 7 3/8 x 9 1/4

WordStar for DOS Made Easy
by Walter A. Ettlin
Osborne's all-time bestselling Made Easy guide now appears in an edition covering the newest release of one of the most popular word processing software packages. Ettlin provides users with step-by-step instructions spanning basic concepts to intermediate level usage.
$19.95, 0-07-881772-2, 450 pages, 7 3/8 x 9 1/4

CorelDRAW! 2 Made Easy
by Ihrig & Matthews
This Made Easy guide offers both step-by-step instruction to this popular graphics program for IBM PCs and an easy reference to menus, keyboard shortcuts, available fonts, and clip art. A wealth of illustrations guarantee quick understanding of everything from basic drawing tools to advanced features.
$24.95,   ISBN: 0-07-881726-9,   7 3/8 x 9 1/4
Covers Versions 1.1, 1.2, 2.0, 2.01

Harvard Graphics 3.0 Made Easy
by Mary Campbell
Campbell covers the basics of the latest version of Harvard Graphics before showing you how to create a variety of charts and demonstrates new drawing features. You'll also learn the latest presentation techniques for producing professional slide shows.
$24.95,   ISBN: 0-07-881746-3,   358 pages,   7 3/8 x 9 1/4

Harvard Graphics 3: The Complete Reference
by Cary Jensen & Loy Anderson
Bestselling authors Jensen and Anderson have written this comprehensive reference covering Harvard Graphics' powerful Release 3 providing detailed explanations of every Harvard Graphics feature, including its enhanced drawing tools and expanded interactive presentation capabilities.
$29.95,   ISBN: 0-07-881749-8,   672 pages,   7 3/8 x 9 1/4

Harvard Graphics for Windows Made Easy
by Mary Campbell
Now one of the most popular graphics packages for the IBM PC and compatibles runs under the Windows operating environment to provide you with even better visuals. Find out how to make the best graphics presentations possible with this excellent introduction.
$19.95, ISBN: 0-07-881790-0, 464 pages, 7 3/8 x 9 1/4

Microsoft Publisher Made Easy
(Includes One 3.5 Inch Disk)
by James Nadler
Nadler takes you through this program step-by-step, and includes numerous practical examples and exercises for easy learning. The book includes a design library of ready-to-use layouts, along with a 3.5-inch disk containing fabulous clip art graphics from the Dover Pictorial Archive Series.
$29.95, ISBN: 0-07-881811-7, 457 pages, 7 3/8 x 9 1/4

Publish It! 2 Made Easy
by Paul Garrison
This book is as user-friendly as the Publish It! program, virtually guaranteeing you the fastest possible start with the newest version of this widely used desktop publishing program for the IBM and PC compatibles. You'll find plenty of real-world desktop publishing exercises and help with design, layout, and publishing techniques.
$19.95, ISBN: 0-07-881722-6, 496 pages, 7 3/8 x 9 1/4

Using PageMaker 4 for the PC, Third Edition
by Martin S. Matthews and Carole Boggs Matthews
The Matthews lead the way as you learn PageMaker Release 4.0, the latest version of Aldus Corporation's full-featured desktop publishing software for your IBM PC or compatible. You'll discover this guide is the easiest route to creating your own newsletters, ads, catalogs, and more.
$26.95, ISBN: 0-07-881629-7, 650 pages, 7 3/8 x 9 1/4

DOS: The Complete Reference, Third Edition
by Kris Jamsa
The first two editions of Jamsa's book have been run-away bestsellers with hundreds of thousands of copies sold. Now Kris Jamsa returns with the revised third edition covering all DOS versions through DOS 5 for both MS-DOS and PC-DOS users.
$29.95, ISBN: 0-07-881700-5, 1124 pages, 7 3/8 x 9 1/4

DOS 5 Made Easy
by Herbert Schildt

DOS 5 Made Easy delivers the ideal one-volume tutorial on the operating system's newest features and functions. Written by best-selling author Herb Schildt, *DOS 5 Made Easy*, starts with the file system basics, works through I/O and configuration options, the editor, and concludes with a discussion of hard disk management.

$19.95p ISBN: 0-07-881690-4, 412 pp., 7 3/8 x 9 1/4

Simply DOS
by Kris Jamsa

Simply DOS is the ideal book for everyone who needs to learn the basics of DOS, the ever popular Disk Operating System. Clear, step-by-step instructions introduce the most essential DOS commands that you need for everyday tasks.

$14.95, ISBN: 0-07-881715-3, 200 pages, 5 3/4 x 8 3/4

Windows 3.1: The Complete Reference, Second Edition
by Tom Sheldon

You'll find every Windows feature, command, and function thoroughly described along with in-depth coverage of multitasking under Windows, Windows utilities, and much more. All the details that every Windows user wants to know are clearly explained in this handy reference.

$29.95 ISBN: 0-07-881889-3 800 pages, 7 3/8 x 9 1/4

Available: Winter, 1992

Windows 3.1 Made Easy
by Tom Sheldon

Find out how to install the program and get a quick start with the newest version of Microsoft Windows. You'll learn all the newest features and how to apply them to customize your applications. *Windows 3.1 Made Easy* is loaded with short examples, follow-along projects, screen illustrations, and plenty of insights for everyday use.

$19.95p ISBN: 0-07-881725-0, 496 pp., 7 3/8 X 9 1/4

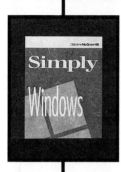

Simply Windows
by Mary Campbell
What is Windows and how can you use it? *Simply Windows* tells you all you need to know to get started with Microsoft's graphical user interface for IBM and compatible PCs.
$14.95, ISBN: 0-07-881743-9, 212 pages, 5 3/4 x 8 3/4

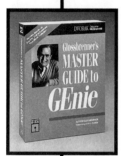

Glossbrenner's Master Guide To GEnie
(Includes Aladdin on One 5.25-Inch Disk)
by Alfred Glossbrenner
Here's the first book about General Electric's increasingly popular on-line service. Drawing on his technical expertise and time-tested teaching skills, Glossbrenner makes it easy for everyone to install GEnie and enjoy its many information and entertainment services.
$39.95, ISBN: 0-07-881659-9, 600 pp., 7 3/8 x 9 1/4

The Mac Made Easy
by Martin S. Matthews
Using the step-by-step Made Easy format, you'll learn all about the Macintosh, its concepts, features, the System 7 operating system and more. It's packed with illustations, hands-on exercises, and confidence-building instructions that will have you operating your Mac like a pro.
$19.95, 0-07-881773-0, 545 pages, 7 3/8 x 9 1/4

Simply PCs
by Bob Albrecht
First-time computer users won't want to miss this short, beautifully illustrated guide that thoroughly explains what a computer system is and how to use it. *Simply PCs* provides a clear overview of software, hardware, peripherals, and systems.
$14.95, ISBN: 0-07-881741-2 208 pages, 5 3/4 x 8 3/4
Covers All IBM PCs and Compatible Computers

The King's Quest Companion, Second Edition
by Peter Spear

Master the world of King Graham, Gwydion, and Rosella. This revised edition of Spear's book on Sierra On-Line's million-selling entertainment software series provides plenty of answers to help you solve the first four King's Quest games as well as the new and exciting King's Quest V.

$19.95, ISBN: 0-07-881671-8, 450 pp., 7 3/8 X 9 1/4
Available Now

Railroad Tycoon Master Strategies for Empire Builders
by Shay Addams

Here's a strategy guide to Sid Meier's Railroad Tycoon, a railroad-building simulation game of great complexity. Addams provides winning strategies that are presented with clarity, precision, and the twisted sense of humor that is most appreciated by stymied players.

$19.95, ISBN: 0-07-881728-5, 208 pages, 7 3/8 x 9 1/4

The SimCity Planning Commission Handbook
by Johnny L. Wilson

The SimCity planning simulator may be the most thought-provoking computer game of all, and *The SimCity Planning Commission Handbook* ensures that you'll enjoy all of the game's many dimensions. Author Johnny Wilson, the respected editor of Computer Gaming World, also presents prevailing theories of urban design, and challenges you to design a city that works for individuals and industry alike.

$19.95, ISBN: 0-07-881660-2, 193 pages 7 3/8 X 9 1/4

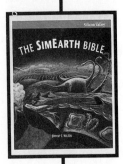

The SimEarth Bible
by Johnny L. Wilson

With the new game from Maxis, SimEarth, you can design the ecosystem for an entire planet -- determine geological, biological, and climatic development while contemplating interplanetary travel and intelligent life forms. This colossal game can pose colossal problems, but renowned gamer Johnny Wilson sheds new light on creation. Every SimEarthling who is searching for enlightenment will need *The SimEarth Bible*.

$19.95, ISBN: 0-07-881843-5, 224 pp., 7 3/8 X 9 1/4

▶——— Osborne **McGraw-Hill** ■ **Available at local book and computer stores**

Register and Check Writing Screens

Key Presses	Action Taken
Ctrl-A	Select/Set Up account
Ctrl-B	Repeat Find (backwards)
Ctrl-C	Categorize/Transfer
Ctrl-D	Delete transaction
Ctrl-Enter	Record current transaction
Ctrl-F	Find
Ctrl-G	Go to date
Ctrl-I	Insert transaction
Ctrl-Ins	Copy transaction
Ctrl-J	Transaction groups
Ctrl-K	Popup calendar
Ctrl-L	Select/Set Up class or security action
Ctrl-M	Memorize transaction
Ctrl-N	Repeat Find (next)
Ctrl-O	Calculator
Ctrl-P	Print register
Ctrl-Q	Register View
Ctrl-S	Split transaction
Ctrl-T	Recall transaction
Ctrl-U	Update security prices
Ctrl-V	Void transaction
Ctrl-W	Write checks
Ctrl-X	Go to transfer
Ctrl-Y	Electronic payee list or security list
Ctrl-Z	Redo last report
Shift-Ins	Paste transaction

Report Screen

Key Presses	Action Taken
Ctrl-M	Memorize report
Ctrl-O	Calculator
Ctrl-P	Print report
Ctrl-R	Register
Ctrl-W	Write checks
Ctrl-Z	Quick zoom

Special Date Field Entries

+	Increase the date by 1
−	Decrease the date by 1
H	Set date to the end of month
M	Set date to the beginning of the month
R	Set date to last day of the year
T	Set date to the current system date
Y	Set date to the first of the year

Other Quicken Keys

" (Quotes)	Copy payee and address to check or other special copy
Ctrl-End	Move to the end of the register
Ctrl-F1	Display help index
Ctrl-Home	Move to beginning of register
Ctrl-Pg Dn	Move to next month
Ctrl-Pg Up	Move to previous month
End	Move to end of field
End, End	Move to last field
Enter	Move to next field
F1	Display help
Home	Move to beginning of field
Home, Home	Move to first field
Pg Dn	Move down one register screen or check
Pg Up	Move up one register screen or check
Shift-Tab	Move to previous field
Tab	Move to next field